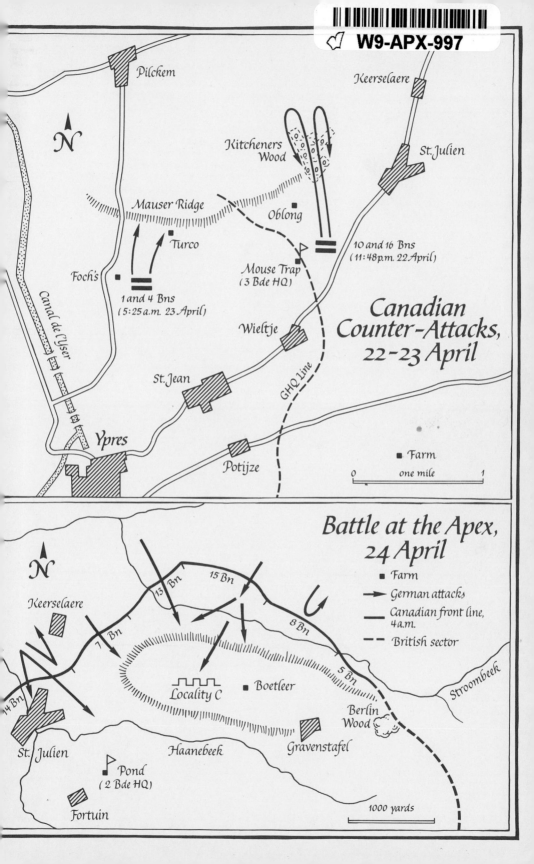

Pilckem

Keerselaere

Kitcheners
Wood

St. Julien

Mauser Ridge

Oblong

Turco

Foch's

10 and 16 Bns
(11:48 p.m. 22 April)

Mouse Trap
(3 Bde HQ)

1 and 4 Bns
(5:25 a.m. 23 April)

Wieltje

Canadian
Counter-Attacks,
22–23 April

Canal de l'Yser

St. Jean

GHQ line

Ypres

■ Farm

0   one mile   1

Potijze

Battle at the Apex,
24 April

■ Farm
→ German attacks
── Canadian front line,
        4 a.m.
- - - British sector

Keerselaere

13 Bn

15 Bn

7 Bn

8 Bn

5 Bn

Stroombeek

14 Bn

Locality C

Boetleer

Berlin
Wood

St. Julien

Haanebeek

Gravenstafel

Pond
(2 Bde HQ)

Fortuin

1000 yards

Welcome to Flanders Fields

Welcome to Flanders Fields

*The First Canadian Battle
of the Great War:
Ypres, 1915*

Daniel G. Dancocks

Canadian Cataloguing in Publication Data

Dancocks, Daniel G. (Daniel George), 1950-
    Welcome to Flanders Fields

Includes bibliographical references and index.
ISBN 0-7710-2545-9

1. Ypres, 2d Battle of, 1915.   2. Canada. Canadian
Army — History — World War, 1914-1918.   3. World
War, 1914-1918 — Canada.   I. Title.

D542.Y7D36 1988   940.4'24   C88-094302-5

Printed and bound in Canada by Friesen Printers
Design / Bookends East (David Shaw)
Composition / Pickwick Typesetting
Cartography / Jack McMaster

A Douglas Gibson Book

McClelland and Stewart
The Canadian Publishers
481 University Avenue
Toronto   M5G 2E9

For Derek Howat

Contents

"The Most Perfect Military Rifle"

It began, like so much of Canadian history, on a windswept plain outside Quebec City. This time, though, there were no opposing armies, no flags and drums, only a handful of officers and some civilians standing around quietly in the humid heat watching two men carefully load their rifles. It was August 1901, and what the sharpshooters did with these weapons in the next few minutes would decide the fate of hundreds of Canadians fourteen years later and three thousand miles away.

One of the civilians was understandably nervous. Sir Charles Ross, a corpulent, twenty-nine-year-old Scottish aristocrat, knew all too well that his own future would be determined in the next few hours. A blue-ribbon committee appointed by the Canadian government had prepared a rigorous competition between his new Ross rifle and the traditional Lee-Enfield, which was used by the British army and throughout the Empire, including Canada. Sir Charles knew that if the Ross rifle did well in this test, it might be adopted by Canada.

The Canadian search for a substitute for the Lee-Enfield had begun in the late 1890s. As the young nation grew, so did the feeling that Canada's military should not be so dependent on British stores for its weaponry; although small-arms ammunition had been manufactured at the Dominion Arsenal in Quebec since 1882, there were no arms factories in this country. Shortly after Canada adopted the English-made Lee-Enfield in 1896, the Liberal minister of militia and defence, Sir Frederick Borden, tried to arrange to have the rifles produced on this side of the Atlantic. The British manufacturer, the Birmingham Small Arms Company, rejected the proposal. The situation became intolerable in 1900 when, at the height of the South African War, a Canadian order for 15,000 Lee-Enfields went unfilled because the British army was given priority. At that point, the Canadian government embarked on a policy of making its own weapons, "assuming of course that the rifle to be manufactured is a satisfactory rifle and is worth the money paid."[1]

Enter Sir Charles Ross. A noted sportsman – he bagged his first stag when he was only twelve, and one glorious morning in 1910 he shot twenty-five – Ross had invented a rifle-breech mechanism, which he patented in 1894. His self-named sporting rifle was manufactured in limited quantities in the United States by an agent in Hartford, Connecticut. With its straight bolt action the Ross rifle was virtually a copy of the 1890-model Austria Mannlicher and shared many of that weapon's defects. Sir Charles had hoped to interest the military in his rifle, but there were no takers, despite the claim of a British magazine, in August 1900, that it was "the rifle of the future."[2]

When he learned of the Canadian situation, the enterprising Sir Charles saw the chance of a huge sale and travelled to Ottawa in early 1901, taking several samples of his .303-calibre rifle to show Militia Minister Borden. Sir Frederick was impressed – so impressed that he drafted an agreement on 28 June calling for the manufacture of 12,000 Ross rifles in Canada during 1902 and 50,000 more during the next five years. The same day, Borden appointed a five-man committee, headed by Col. William Otter – whose main claim to fame was that his bungling at the Battle of Cut Knife Hill during the Riel Rebellion almost made him a Canadian Custer – to "enquire into and report upon the merits of a rifle invented and submitted by Sir Charles Ross."[3] After meeting Colonel Otter's committee, Sir Charles agreed to make a number of design changes, then submit the new weapon for a series of twelve comprehensive tests to be conducted simultaneously with the Lee-Enfield.

The officers present at the testing were astounded by the inventor's curious behaviour. His rifle performed similarly to the Lee-Enfield in ten of the tests. But in one of them – the dust test, in which both rifles were "heavily sanded" to simulate combat conditions – Sir Charles stooped to sabotage. Just prior to the trial, he was discovered oiling the Lee-Enfield's bolt to encourage the sand to stick. "This was objected to by the Committee," reads its report, "and both rifles were fired dry."[4]

In the other two tests, however, the Lee-Enfield outperformed the Ross by a wide margin. Indeed, Sir Charles withdrew his rifle from both when problems became apparent. In the test for excessive charges – where extra powder was packed in the cartridge to test the stress on the chamber, bolt, and barrel of the weapon – the Ross rifle jammed; its breech had to be hammered open by the marksman's heel. After only two rounds had been fired, Sir Charles refused to permit further testing along these lines. The Lee-Enfield, in the meantime, continued to fire faultlessly at pressures well above its design specifications. In the endurance test, the Lee-Enfield fired 1000 rounds and "worked easily and satisfactorily throughout." The Ross "misfed and jammed repeatedly"; after 300 rounds, "the heat of firing melted away [the] foresight, which was fastened with common solder." Sir Charles explained that there had been no difficulties firing bullets of Austrian or American make, and that "the standard called for in the manufacture of British .303 cartridges is not of the same precision and quality of material hence greater limits have to be allowed."[5]

The committee not only accepted Ross's explanation but it concluded, "after discussion with expert machinists and experienced marksmen, that on the whole the Ross had features which afford advantages over the Lee-Enfield."[6] In its final report, issued in September, the committee unanimously recommended the Ross rifle as a suitable alternative to the Lee-Enfield – which was precisely what Sir Frederick Borden wanted to hear. (The committee's unanimity was somewhat affected a short time later by the resignation of one of its members, Maj. F.M. Gaudet, the superintendent of the ammunition factory whose bullets had been slighted by Sir Charles.) Several months of negotiations followed, and on 27 March 1902 the Canadian government signed a contract with Ross, enabling the Scot to establish a factory at Quebec City and begin manufacturing his rifle especially, and uniquely, for the Canadian army.

The controversy that would dog the Ross rifle for years to come had only just begun. It was not until a month after the signing of the Ross rifle contract that the commander of the Canadian militia, a British major-general named Richard O'Grady Haly, received a copy of the committee's report of the previous September. While hesitating to criticize the Ross rifle, General O'Grady Haly argued that "the superiority of the untried Ross should be conclusively demonstrated before discarding the Lee-Enfield, a proved weapon." He also pointed out that two of the five committee members had been absent during the trials. His appeal fell on deaf ears.[7]

The British government was none too pleased, either. The Colonial Office informed Ottawa that in its own tests "the inferiority of the Ross was most marked" in comparison with the Lee-Enfield. (When told of this, Sir Charles haughtily responded that the British, in their attempts to deliberately discredit his rifle, had conducted the testing under the "worst conditions.")[8] Joseph Chamberlain, the colonial secretary, issued his own protest two months after Canada concluded its deal with Ross. Stressing "the very great importance of adhering to absolute uniformity of pattern in the weapons with which the forces of the Empire are armed," Chamberlain urged the Canadians to "arrange that whatever arms are made for them in Canada shall be identical with the arms with which the Imperial troops are equipped." Similar concerns were raised at a colonial conference later that year, yet while Canada accepted in principle the need for uniformity of arms, no formal agreement was reached.[9]

The Ross Rifle Factory, a modest brick building on the edge of the Plains of Abraham, opened in 1903, and in the summer of 1904 made its first delivery of 1000 Mark I Ross rifles to the Royal North West Mounted Police; the militia received its first shipments in August 1905.

Complaints about the rifle were quick to follow. The earliest recorded grievance was filed in February 1906 by the commissioner of the RNWMP, and many more were registered in subsequent weeks and months. After a marksman was injured in the eye by a bolt flying back, the mounted police, citing "many weak points . . . in both design and manufacture," withdrew the Ross rifle from service in the fall of 1906.[10]

Militia complaints began pouring in during the summer. Unable to ignore the many criticisms, and deluged by bad publicity – one parliamentary critic claimed that "it kills as much behind as in front"[11] – the militia department finally scrapped the Mark I, of which 10,500 had been produced, in favour of a revamped model, the Mark II. But the Ross rifle controversy was far from over. The Mark II was destined to undergo more than eighty design changes, "which altered the weapon almost beyond recognition." While the factory continued to produce a thousand rifles a month, Militia Minister Sir Frederick Borden stubbornly continued to defend the weapon in the House of Commons. His public pronouncements notwithstanding, Borden was in possession of expert advice that suggested that "the rifle is not yet entirely suitable as a perfect military arm."[12]

By now, Sir Charles Ross was most unhappy. The seemingly endless changes to his rifle were in his view unnecessary, but there was nothing he could do about them, as he later complained:

> I made for the Canadian Government, as I was bound to under my 1902 contract, rifles according to a standard set and frequently changed by the Militia Department. Whatever changes were ordered, I was compelled to carry out. The true "Ross Rifle" was my sporting rifle, which I designed myself; the military rifles turned out at my factory were an official arm over whose structure I had no control.[13]

The Mark II lasted until 1911, when the Mark III went into production. The Ross rifle now bore little resemblance to the original: intended to be shorter, lighter, and cheaper than the Lee-Enfield, it was now longer, heavier, and more expensive. Not even the outstanding efforts of Canadian marksmen, who distinguished themselves using the Ross rifle in international shooting matches between 1910 and 1913, could defuse the controversy. Its value as a target weapon went unquestioned, but the military had grave doubts about its suitability as a service weapon: committees and subcommittees continued to analyze its performance and recommend countless alterations.

When the Liberals lost the 1911 general election, the Conservatives installed an Ontario militiaman, Sam Hughes, as minister of militia and defence. Hughes had been on the 1901 committee that had endorsed the Ross rifle in the first place, and the years of often-acrimonious debate had in no way diminished his enthusiasm for it. In 1907 he had called the Ross "the most perfect military rifle in every sense in the World today," and a year later had described it as "unequalled in the world." Hughes was only too happy to introduce the Mark III Ross to the Canadian militia in February 1913, and in the same month he made his friend, Sir Charles Ross, an honorary colonel and gave him the grandiose title of Consulting Officer, Small Arms, Ammunition and Ballistics.[14]

In another year Canada, and the rest of the British Empire, stood on the brink of war. To the end of July 1914, the Ross Rifle Factory had delivered 112,000 rifles, but it was having difficulty keeping up with orders, especially for the new Mark III. Of the initial order for 10,000, placed in November 1911, only 3863 had been delivered; since then, two more orders had been placed, in April 1913 and May 1914, for 10,000 each.

The Ross rifle was still undergoing changes on the eve of war, but Sam Hughes had complete confidence in it. On 30 July 1914 the militia department had instructed the Ross Rifle Factory: "Increase immediately to your utmost capacity manufacture and delivery of Mark three rifles and bayonets already ordered." On 10 August, less than a week after the war broke out, the militia department ordered 30,000 Mark IIIs, to equip the first Canadian contingent being sent overseas.[15]

Canadian soldiers, armed with a combat weapon of dubious value, would pay the ultimate price for Sam Hughes's blind faith in the Ross rifle.

CHAPTER ONE

"Some Damned Foolish Thing"

In 1897 Germany's Otto von Bismark predicted that the next great European war would "come out of some damned foolish thing in the Balkans."[1] Seventeen years later, his prediction was realized, at a place called Sarajevo. There, on 28 June 1914, Serbian nationalists assassinated Archduke Franz Ferdinand, the heir to the throne of Austria-Hungary. The incident sparked the conflagration known to history as the Great War of 1914-1918, but the real cause was a complex combination of international treaties and bungled diplomacy, nationalism and jingoism, xenophobia and paranoia.

By the end of July, Austria-Hungary and Serbia were at war. Russia mobilized at Serbia's side, and Germany came to the aid of Austria-Hungary. But Russia was allied with France, the factor that turned a localized conflict into a world war.

As Europe continued its inexorable slide towards general war, only one major power remained unaccounted for – Great Britain. Almost until the last moment, British participation was doubtful. Britain was loosely allied to France and Russia, in the so-called Entente Cordiale, but with no direct threat to British interests in the current crisis, there was considerable reluctance to go to war merely to assist the French and Russians. In fact, on 1 August two-thirds of the British cabinet voted against sending France a pledge of support. The foreign secretary, handsome, humourless Sir Edward Grey, favoured such a move for diplomatic reasons, but he was not concerned at the setback in cabinet. Grey warned his colleagues that "Belgian neutrality might become a factor."[2]

This proved to be precisely the case. Germany had predicated its mobilization plans on a two-front war, against France in the west and Russia in the east. While fighting a delaying action against the Russians, the Germans planned to knock out the French with a decisive blow delivered through Belgium. It was an excellent strategic plan, but for the minor problem that Belgian neutrality had been guaranteed by an 1839 treaty signed by, among others, Germany and Britain. On 2 August Berlin presented Brussels with an ultimatum calling for the free and unopposed passage of German troops across Belgium. The Belgian government defiantly rejected the demand the next day, declaring itself "firmly resolved to repel by all means in its powers every attack upon its rights."[3]

The threat to Belgium cast the coming conflict in much different light in London. On 3 August, the day Germany declared war on France, Foreign Secretary Grey told the House of Commons, to thunderous applause, that if they were to ignore their obligations to Belgium, the British people "should, I believe, sacrifice our respect and good name and reputation before the world."[4]

At 8:02 A.M. on Tuesday, 4 August, German troops crossed the border into Belgium. The British government responded with a demand that Germany withdraw immediately from Belgian soil. The ultimatum expired at 11 P.M. London time. Twenty minutes later, a telegram was dispatched to all British ministries: "War, Germany, act."[5]

British honour would be defended, but Sir Edward Grey was far from happy. The consequences of a major war in Europe would, he feared, be terrible, perhaps catastrophic. At the height of the crisis, Sir Edward stood at the window of his Whitehall office watching the street lamps below being lit. He muttered to a companion the chillingly prophetic words: "The lamps are going out all over Europe; we shall not see them lit again in our lifetime."[6]

CHAPTER TWO

"Who in the World Are We Going to Fight?"

"When Britain is at war, Canada is at war. There is no distinction."[1] So said Prime Minister Sir Wilfrid Laurier in 1910, and by the summer of 1914 it was still true, although Laurier was no longer in power.

Canada's status was strange, as baffling to modern eyes as it was to contemporaries. As a self-governing dominion, Canada was only semi-autonomous; Confederation in 1867 had given it control over domestic affairs, but London still spoke for the entire Empire in external matters. Yet, while automatically at war at Britain's behest, Canada was allowed to determine the extent of its participation. And the young country plunged into it wholeheartedly.

This cannot have been surprising. After all, in 1914 Canada was a British nation. The British flag, the Union Jack, was Canada's flag. The British monarch, King George V, was the King of Canada. British heroes and traditions and values were cherished by Canadians. Canada did not even have a national anthem. Patriots contented themselves with rousing renditions of "God Save the King" or "Rule Britannia," although a song originally penned by a pair of French-Canadians was gaining popularity in an English translation based on R. Stanley Weir's 1909 poem:

> With glowing hearts we see thee rise,
> The true north strong and free.

The song, of course, was "O Canada."

At the same time, there was a growing awareness that Canada occupied a special place within the Empire, and not just because it had been the first colony to be granted self-government. There was a belief in some quarters that Canada had a more important part to play in Imperial affairs than merely, and meekly, following Britain's lead. These Canadians called themselves Imperialists, and though they were fiercely proud of the Empire, they were no longer content with second-class status. As Stephen Leacock had declared in 1907: "I am an Imperialist, because I will not be a Colonial."[2] Indeed, Imperialism in this period was an early form of nationalism.

If nationalism was in its infancy, this is not to say that Canadians had nothing of their own in which to take pride. Culturally, this was an exciting era. Lucy Maud Montgomery published *Anne of Green Gables* in 1908, and Leacock had followed in 1912 with *Sunshine Sketches of a Little Town*. Canada, in fact, boasted an impressive array of writers, poets, and artists: Ralph Connor, Emile Nelligan, Emily Carr, Tom Thomson, Bliss Carman, Albert Nozeau, William Henry Drummond, Sir Charles G.D. Roberts, Pauline Johnson. Canadians could even take pleasure in their own genuine star of the silver screen, Toronto's Gladys Smith, somewhat better known by her Hollywood name, Mary Pickford.

On the surface, at least, it appeared to be a happy time. Canadians danced to the fox trot, the turkey trot, the tango, and the ever-popular waltz, and sang songs like "I Wonder Who's Kissing Her Now," "I'm Always Chasing Rainbows," "When You Were Sweet Sixteen," and even "I Picked a Lemon in the Garden of Love, Where I Thought Only Peaches Grew." The lucky few who could afford a gramophone could listen to this music in the comfort of their sitting rooms at home, springing up to rewind the machine whenever the tempo began to slow. They attended movies (silent, of course) and the theatre, which was enriched in the larger centres by touring stage companies from New York and, best of all, London. There were public band concerts in the park, and public libraries were being built from coast to coast. Sports were popular pastimes, too: lacrosse (drawing huge crowds), football (amateur clubs were fighting it out for the trophy donated by the governor-general, Lord Grey, in 1909), hockey, rugby, soccer, cricket, baseball, basketball (invented by a Canadian, James Naismith, in 1892), tennis, horse-racing, golf (for the wealthy only), and curling (the rage on the prairies). Sports figures were revered, then as now: hockey players Fred "Cyclone" Taylor and Edouard "Newsy" Lalonde, who also excelled at lacrosse; Toronto's Johnny Coulon, the world bantamweight boxing champion from 1910 until 1914; and Tom Longboat, the legendary long-distance runner.

In 1914 Canada had just come through a period of spectacular growth and considerable prosperity. Between the census years of 1901 and 1911, the nation's population increased by 34 per cent – unmatched before or since – thanks to an aggressive immigration policy implemented by Laurier's Liberals just before the turn of the century. By 1911 there were 7,206,643 people in Canada; one in five was a recent immigrant. One-third of the newcomers came from Britain or elsewhere in the Empire, another third from the United States, and most of the rest from continental Europe – Scandinavians and Slavs, in particular.

Most of these new Canadians had one thing in common. They were white. This was an important consideration, because Canadian society was white, not to mention racist. Blacks were unwelcome, as the small and isolated black communities in Nova Scotia, Montreal, and southern Ontario were well aware. Asians and East Indians were barely tolerated, as shown by anti-Asian rioting in Vancouver in 1907 and the infamous *Komagata Maru* episode in May 1914, also on the West Coast.* Native Indians – who, if only because they were already here, could not be denied entry – were shunted off to reserves where they could be conveniently forgotten.

Canada was white, but far from united. Tension between English-speaking and French-speaking Canadians was never lacking, arising out of the inability, or unwillingness, of the former to understand the desire of the latter to preserve their language and culture. The most recent row had occurred in Ontario in 1912 and 1913 over Regulation 17, which restricted French-language instruction in that province's elementary schools. Franco-Ontarians, with support from Quebec, opposed the policy, without success. Regulation 17's constitutionality was eventually upheld in the courts, but not before it had become a bitter national issue.

Regulation 17 was only one of several burning issues of the day. Free trade with the United States, which had played a major part in Prime Minister Laurier's defeat in the 1911 election, was still being hotly debated, as it is today. The temperance movement was gaining momentum, promoting prohibition of alcohol in an age when fathers drank away their pay in bars designed for the purpose. Then there were those insufferable suffragettes and their persistent demands for women's rights, including the right to vote. Notable among these early feminists were Marie Gérin-Lajoie in Montreal, Toronto's Flora MacDonald Denison, Nellie McClung and Emily Murphy on the prairies, and Dorothy Davis in Vancouver.

Agriculture was the mainstay of Canada's economy; the prosperity of the years between 1900 and 1912 was fuelled by the success of wheat sales in overseas markets. There is a certain irony in that. The flourishing economy attracted foreign investment, which in turn led to industrial growth. It would be many years before agriculture's predominance would be seriously challenged, but an unmistakable trend had begun. According to the 1901 census, 60 per cent of Canadians lived in rural settings; twenty

---

Komagata Maru was a Japanese charter vessel that pulled into Vancouver harbour with 376 East Indians on board. Local immigration officials flatly refused to let them disembark, and after an impasse that lasted two months, the federal government finally ordered the dilapidated cruiser *Rainbow* – one half of Canada's navy – to escort it out of Canadian waters.

years later, half of them were urban dwellers. Coupled with immigration, most cities were growing at remarkable rates. The dominion's largest municipality, Montreal, nearly doubled in size, to half a million, while second-place Toronto saw its population climb by 80 per cent during the century's first decade. It was a similar story in western Canada, where half of the immigrants were locating. Winnipeg, the country's transportation hub, was a bustling city of 136,035 by 1911, and Vancouver had broken the hundred-thousand barrier. In the newest provinces, Alberta and Saskatchewan, the growth was little short of astounding. Regina, a mere village in 1901 with a population of 2249, grew to 30,213 by 1911, and boasted a beautiful new legislative building, its dome 188 feet above ground-level, appropriate to its stature as Saskatchewan's capital. The Calgary–Edmonton rivalry was well under way. Edmonton, the capital, could proudly point to a new Legislature and a growth rate of 750 per cent, but Calgary was nearly twice as big, its population of 43,704 ten times its 1901 total.

For all but their richest inhabitants, however, Canadian cities were not pleasant places to live. True, they were taking on the trappings of sophistication, with streetcar systems and electric lights, paved roads for the growing number of automobiles – no longer a novelty, with an estimated fifty thousand in Canada by 1913 – and ever-bigger and better buildings. But they had a long way to go. Urban planning was virtually nonexistent, and adequate sewage facilities were rare. Housing shortages were chronic across the country, and crowded, filthy slums sprang up in Halifax, Montreal, Toronto, Winnipeg, Regina, Calgary, and Vancouver. Infant mortality rates were appallingly high, prompting a prominent physician, Helen McMurchy, to declare that "the Canadian city is still essentially uncivilized – it is neither properly paved nor drained, nor supplied with water fit to drink, nor equipped with any adequate public health organization."[3]

Poverty was endemic. While the prosperous prewar years gave rise to an increasingly large middle class, much of the wealth was concentrated in the hands and pockets of a relative few. The flourishing economy meant more jobs, but these did not always pay well. At a time when trade unions were viewed with suspicion and struggled for credibility, hours were long – six-day work weeks were the norm – amid conditions that were often abominable and downright unsafe, and benefits such as medicare were, naturally, unknown. A 1913 survey indicated that a family of five required at least $1,200 a year just to make ends meet – and that was a sum far above the income of the average unskilled worker. There were child-labour laws, but reality still forced children to drop out of school and seek menial jobs to help support their families.

To make matters worse, Canada's economy was in dire trouble in the summer of 1914. A worldwide depression the previous year, coming as it did on the heels of an economic slowdown in 1912, hit Canada very hard, producing what *The Times History of the War* called a "period of great financial and industrial difficulty." Foreign investors fled, and wheat prices plummeted. Crop failures hit parts of Alberta and Saskatchewan. The boom years had seen land prices in western Canada reach ridiculous proportions (a square foot fronting on Edmonton's main street, Jasper Avenue, sold for as much as $10,000); now, suddenly, land could not be given away. Bankruptcies, especially among real estate speculators, became everyday occurrences. The stock exchanges were closed, as even such blue-chip stocks as Canadian Pacific, $254 the previous year, plunged to $157 1/2. By August unemployment everywhere had soared. According to official reports, the situation had "entered upon a more serious phase than at any previous time in the history of Toronto," while in Sault Ste. Marie, the existing crisis "threatened many hardships during the coming winter." In Winnipeg "the Provincial Government ordered the stoppage of work on the law courts and Parliament buildings, owing to financial stringency." In Regina, stated the experts, "a general depression prevails in all lines of business, and many establishments have found it necessary to reduce their staffs." The Rocky Mountains could not shield British Columbia from the grim effects. Prince Rupert's situation was described as "very grave," and Victoria was facing the fact "that labour of all classes has been very irregularly employed."[4]

And now this vast, unsophisticated country, which so much resembled a gangly adolescent, blessed with tremendous potential but unsure of what it wanted or where it was headed, found itself at war. It was an undertaking that would soon eclipse every other endeavour in Canada's short history.

Not that much was expected of Canada. In a 1911 book, *Germany and the Next War*, a Prussian general named Friedrich von Bernhardi dismissed the Canadians contemptuously: "They can be completely ignored so far as concerns any European theatre of war."[5] The Germans considered the Canadians, and all other colonial forces, nothing more than "trash, feeble adversaries."[6]

British opinion was hardly better. In 1910, at Ottawa's invitation, Sir John French, the British army's inspector-general, spent six weeks touring Canada's military establishment. He rated the small regular army, or permanent force, "satisfactory," but the militia worried him. Although admitting that the men were "excellent material," with "fine spirit," he noted a number of serious problems. The organization was in his view "defective because the proportion between the various arms of the Service was not correctly adjusted." He observed that the annual summer training-camps were merely "large collections of troops without any organization in formations of all arms." If the militia's standard of training left something to be desired, even more alarming was the shortage of all types of equipment. "At present," Sir John stated in his report, "it would not be possible to put the militia into the field in a fit condition to undertake active operations until after the elapse of a considerable period."[7]

French's concerns were valid. The Canadian militia was as much a social institution as a military organization. In that post-Victorian era, it was still a matter of considerable prestige to wear a uniform, a major attraction for these part-time soldiers. Moreover, the militia adopted and promoted the traditions of the British army, and many Canadian units were affiliated with famous British regiments – for example, the Victoria-based 50th Regiment, Gordon Highlanders of Canada. The officers, who took staff courses that familiarized them with the basics of leadership and tactics, were usually businessmen and community leaders. The wealthier they were the better, because government funding was limited and officers were not only expected to contribute their pay to regimental funds but had to buy their own uniforms as well. The training given the other ranks was rudimentary. During the winter, there would be drill one night each week, plus Saturday at the musketry range with an antiquated rifle; in the summer, a two-week camp was highlighted by manoeuvres and by sports events in the sun.

By 1913 things had improved to a certain extent. Sir Ian Hamilton, the one-armed inspector-general of overseas forces (later to command the assault on a remote piece of Turkish coastline called Gallipoli), travelled across Canada that summer and "considered that a remarkable advance had been made since the inspection of Sir John French." Hamilton was particularly impressed with the militia's artillery, commenting that "these batteries . . . are, in my opinion, effective units as they stand, for active service." Other arms were less impressive, however. The infantry, he pointed out, was still chronically short of equipment and plagued with a variety of training problems, not to mention low enlistments.[8]

Canada's preparedness for war was still uncertain in 1914. As late as 8 May the nation's foremost soldier, Maj.-Gen. Sir William Otter, alarmed many when he declared: "I can tell you as an old campaigner, and as one who has been intimately connected with the Militia, that as we stand at present we are totally unprepared, not only in numbers, but in *Materiel*."[9] It was hard to argue with General Otter's claim. The permanent force numbered only 3110, all ranks, on the eve of the war; the militia, with an authorized strength of 77,323, was actually several thousand short of that mark. The Royal Canadian Navy was in even worse shape. It consisted of 393 officers and enlisted men and two old cruisers, *Niobe* and *Rainbow*, purchased from the British for training purposes.[10]

More money – much more – was an obvious answer, but not a popular one. Indeed, one of the causes of Laurier's fall in 1911 had been his government's expensive proposal to create a real navy for Canada. Ironically, under the Conservatives, led by Prime Minister Robert Borden and Col. Sam Hughes, his minister of militia and defence, militia expenditures had risen from $7.5 million in the fiscal year 1911/12 to $11 million in 1913/14, and Hughes was planning to raise that sum to $14 million in the coming year.

Such an increase was bitterly opposed. C.B. Keenlyside, a temperance leader from Regina, declared that funds "for the spreading of the Gospel will be a greater national protection" than the spending of millions on the armed forces. Parliamentary critics were even more outspoken in their condemnation of Hughes's $14-million militia bill. Labelling it "a disgrace," a Liberal member of Parliament, New Brunswick's Frank Carvell, called Hughes "militia mad" and asked, "Who in the world are we going to fight with?" That was on 7 May 1914. Three weeks later, an equally prescient Conservative backbencher, Hugh Guthrie from Guelph, told the House of Commons that such spending "will never . . . be justified. There is no reason for it; there is no emergency in sight and there will be none in our day and generation."[11]

Yet in the first week of August 1914 such pacific sentiments were noticeably lacking. "If ever a country wanted war," commented G.R. Stevens, a participant and historian, "it was Canada in that week."[12] War fever gripped the whole nation.

Early in the summer of 1914, most Canadians, it seems, were oblivious to the alarming events taking place in Europe. This is not surprising, for the newspapers on which they relied for their information were no better informed. "The relations between Great Britain and Germany are most satisfactory," the Toronto *Globe* assured its readers on 16 July, "and . . . all their immediate interests are bound up with the maintenance of peace."

Certainly, the government of Canada detected no urgency. Parliament had been prorogued for the summer on 12 June. Prime Minister Borden – now *Sir* Robert, having reluctantly accepted on 19 June the prestigious Knight Grand Cross of the Order of St. Michael and St. George – had left Ottawa on 29 June, the day after the assassination of Archduke Franz Ferdinand in far-off Sarajevo. After a long rail trip – in those days everyone travelled by train – Borden visited his hometown of Halifax, where he "received various delegations, chiefly respecting patronage" and spent time with his eighty-nine-year-old mother.[13] He returned to the national capital to attend to paperwork, and then headed for Ontario's Lake Muskoka on 23 July for a long-overdue holiday. "I was greatly fatigued and still suffered from the disorder of carbuncles," he later wrote, and he looked forward to four weeks of golfing, bathing, and fresh air.[14]

By 30 July, however, the crisis on the Continent could no longer be ignored. Cabinet ministers were being recalled to Ottawa, but Borden's private secretary, A.E. Blount, informed the prime minister that his presence was not immediately required. Ignoring his advice, Borden chose to forgo the remainder of his holiday and left Ontario's cottage country for the capital on the thirty-first, arriving on the morning of 1 August. On the same day the governor-general, the elderly Duke of Connaught, returned to Ottawa's grand downtown train station from a holiday in Banff. After attending a cabinet meeting later that day, the prime minister authorized the duke to offer Britain "the firm assurance that if unhappily war should ensue the Canadian people will be united in a common resolve to put forth every effort to make every sacrifice necessary to ensure the integrity and maintain the honour of the Empire."[15]

Cabinet met again on Sunday and Monday, 2 and 3 August. Although Borden still believed that "there was a faint hope of peace," his cabinet took decisive, if less than legal, steps to place Canada on a war footing, as he later related:

> We established censorship, declared bank notes legal tender, authorized excess issue of Dominion notes, empowered the proper officers to detain enemy ships, prohibited the export of articles necessary or useful for war purposes, and generally took upon ourselves responsibilities far exceeding our legal powers. All these measures, which were wholly without legal validity until they were afterwards ratified by Parliament, were accepted through the country as if [Privy] Council had possessed the necessary authority.[16]

In most of Canada Monday was a civic holiday. It was a melancholy long weekend, in retrospect, the last weekend not only of peace but of an entire way of life. Canadians marked it in idyllic fashion, with picnics and parades and sporting events, but even the holiday atmosphere was tempered by talk of war. "There was but one topic of conversation on the lips of all," reported the Toronto *Globe*, and "huge crowds" gathered around newspaper offices to await the latest bulletins from overseas. Toronto, like most communities across Canada, was in the grip of an "all-engrossing war-spirit," which soared on the holiday Monday. "The people jammed every available inch of space," said the *Globe*, "vibrating with unrestrained enthusiasm and a display of what might be termed 'Britishism'." Each bulletin was cheered, hats were thrown in the air, and flags were waved, followed by impromptu parades – all of it, according to the *Globe*, "an undeniable testimony of Canada's unswerving loyalty."[17]

No one was more enthusiastic than Sam Hughes, the formidable minister of militia and defence. The sixty-one-year-old, rock-jawed Hughes had been expecting war for a long time. As far back as August 1912, he had warned a Vancouver audience that "war is closer than you dream; the great peril is from Germany."[18] Although it earned him the enmity of many, Hughes had devoted all of his impressive energy to building up Canada's modest military machine. "I don't find in the history of nations," he explained, "that war is averted by being unprepared."[19] If Canada's preparations at this time were incomplete, it was no fault of the militia minister.

Canada has produced few characters to equal Sam Hughes. A teetotalling, nonsmoking Methodist and Orangeman, he was, in the words of one historian, "a man destined to live and die without a single doubt," especially about himself.[20] A former schoolteacher and newspaper proprietor, he had represented his adopted hometown of Lindsay in the eastern Ontario riding of Victoria North since 1892. As a militia colonel, Hughes had seen service in the South African War, where he had befriended a young British officer named Sir Charles Ross at the turn of the century; for his own gallantry in action Sam claimed that he should have won not one but two Victoria Crosses. Fellow officers considered him "a little bit mad,"[21] and he wore out his welcome when he publicly criticized his British superiors in South Africa for what he regarded as their inept conduct of the conflict. By nature he was a blustering bully, but he was the quintessential Imperialist. Although intensely proud of the British Empire and everything it stood for, Hughes was also a nationalist who felt that Canada deserved full equality with Britain.

His abrasive manner won him few friends in the corridors of power in Ottawa. A fellow minister, Sir George Foster, privately called Hughes "crazy . . . in part unbalanced and absolutely untruthful,"[22] and Arthur, the Duke of Connaught, variously described him as "an impossible fellow," "mentally off his base," and a "conceited lunatic."[23] Prime Minister Borden was a bit more tolerant of the militia minister's peculiarities. "His moods might be divided into three categories," Sir Robert wrote, "during about half the time he was an able, reasonable, and useful colleague, working with excellent judgement and indefatigable energy; for a certain other portion of the time he was extremely excitable, impatient of control and impossible to work with; and during the remainder his conduct and speech were so eccentric as to justify the conclusion that his mind was unbalanced."[24]

Hughes assumed personal charge of Canada's war preparations, convening meetings of the Militia Council even before the prime minister's return to Ottawa. The militia minister revelled in the limelight and, shirtsleeves rolled up, held daily news conferences in his office on Parliament Hill, prompting Borden to complain that he "gives too many interviews."[25] Borden later admitted, however, that Hughes "displayed astonishing energy" and was "a great asset to Canada at that time. No other man could have accomplished during a similar period what he did achieve."[26]

There were, to be sure, embarrassing moments. One of these occurred on 3 August when Hughes, reading his morning paper, was enraged by Britain's apparent unwillingness to go to war. "England is going to skunk it," he fumed to his secretary. "Oh! What a shameful state of things! By God, I don't want to be a Britisher under such conditions; to think that they would want to go back on France!" In his displeasure, Hughes ordered the Union Jack hauled down from the masthead above his headquarters, but was later persuaded to rehoist it.[27]

Tuesday, 4 August, was a day of high anxiety. The Borden cabinet met twice, late in the morning and again that afternoon, awaiting word from London. Finally, at 8:55 P.M., news arrived via the governor-general's office that "war has broken out with Germany."[28] Although expected, it still came as a shock. Sir Thomas White, one of Borden's senior ministers, lamented that the war signalled "the suicide of civilization."[29]

Before adjourning, the cabinet authorized Canada's first official response to the outbreak of hostilities, instructing that the so-called war book be implemented. The war book, drawn up on Prime Minister Borden's orders in January 1914 and completed only in July, contained detailed emergency steps to be taken by various government departments in the event of war. This resulted in the first visible evidence that the country was at war, as parties of militiamen took up positions near key installations such as wireless stations, harbour facilities, bridges, and public buildings, guarding them against German saboteurs who might operate from the neutral United States.

The declaration of war was greeted with unbridled enthusiasm across Canada. Few Canadians, it seems, shared Sir Thomas White's glum view. "Impromptu parades, waving flags, decorated automobiles, cheering crowds, patriotic songs"[30] – the scene was repeated in every city and town from coast to coast. The news had an electrifying effect on the people gathered that night on Yonge Street in Toronto, according to the *Globe*'s account:

> For a minute the thousands stood silent. Then a cheer broke. It was not for the war, but for the King, Britain, and – please God – victory. . . . Toronto is British and its reception of the most sensational news in the history of the city was British. . . . Heads were bowed and the crowd began to sing "God Save the King."[31]

Western Canadians were equally boisterous. "Winnipeg is in throes of war fever," reads one newspaper report. "Scenes of greatest enthusiasm were witnessed in the streets" of Edmonton that night, while in the southern Alberta city of Lethbridge "the streets were alive with crowds parading with bands playing and flags unfurled up to an early hour of the morning." The Calgary *Daily Herald* urged its readers "to treat with caution and moderation residents in our midst who happen to belong to the nationalities with whom our country is at war," but such appeals fell on deaf ears in other centres. In Regina crowds set fire to nine buildings believed to be owned by Germans, while a mob in Vancouver stormed the German Consulate, inflicting minor damage before retreating. In Edmonton a German who criticized the British Empire was attacked by an angry crowd and "badly beaten."[32]

Anti-German hysteria was by no means restricted to western Canada. It was evident even in Berlin, Ontario, where two-thirds of the eighteen thousand citizens were either German immigrants or descended from German stock. Vandals uprooted a statue of Germany's Kaiser Wilhelm II and tossed it into the lake in Victoria Park. Fished out of the water, it was subjected to the final indignity of being "melted down to make souvenir napkin holders."[33] In a telegram to Lord Kitchener, the British secretary of state for war, Berlin civic officials proposed to raise £15,000 for the war effort.[34] Not content with that show of patriotism, Berlin went a step further in May 1916 by renaming itself Kitchener, after the war secretary.

French Canada's response to the war was fervent, too. In Montreal people paraded through the streets singing "La Marseillaise" and "Rule Britannia," fuelled by patriotic rhetoric in the French-language press. "The fate of the British Empire being at stake," commented *La Patrie*, "we will not hear – at least, we hope so – one discordant voice," while *La Presse* declared that "all Canadians, regardless of race, have but one heart and one soul in this hour of danger."[35] Even a nationalist firebrand like Henri Bourassa grudgingly admitted that it was Canada's duty "to contribute within the bounds of her strength, and by means which are proper to herself, to the triumph, and especially to the endurance, of the combined efforts of France and England."[36] Sadly, Sam Hughes neglected to take advantage of the early ardour of French Canadians, sowing the seeds of discontent that would flower into political strife in late 1917 and early 1918.

Recruiting offices did a booming business. In fact, they had already been busy for several days. As early as 31 July, Hughes had confidently stated that "every Canadian would respond to the old flag," and he was not far off the mark.[37] By 2 August an estimated eleven thousand men had volunteered to go overseas;[38] no fewer than forty-eight militia units had signed up en masse prior to the fateful fourth.[39] Now that the war was a reality, recruiters were nearly overwhelmed by the flood of volunteers. The armoury on University Avenue in Toronto, recalled one participant, "was besieged by a milling mob, all there to enlist for overseas service," and a guard with fixed bayonets had to be posted at the main door to maintain some semblance of order.[40] The scene at Ottawa's main recruiting centre, bedecked with Union Jacks and posters, resembled the rush at a land office at the height of the boom in western Canada, with men pushing and shoving each other in their haste to get inside and enlist.

Small wonder, then, that Hughes was able to dismiss concerns about conscription. With so many volunteers flocking to the colours, it was evident that there would be no need to conscript anyone into the army – at least, not for the foreseeable future – and Hughes assured Parliament later in August: "I am absolutely opposed to anything that is not voluntary in every sense, and I do not read in the law that I have any authority to ask Parliament to allow troops other than volunteers to leave the country."[41]

From today's perspective, it is difficult to comprehend the mood of that era or the enthusiasm with which these young men signed up to die. In 1914 war was still considered a "glorious" undertaking. Canadians had been weaned on the stories, fictional or true, of late-Victorian campaigns against the "fuzzy-wuzzies," "wogs," and Boers, small-scale skirmishes that solidified the Empire from Rorke's Drift to Khartoum, and from Auckland to the Khyber Pass. Lord Tennyson and Rudyard Kipling, G.A. Henty and the *Boy's Own Paper* had done their work well. In schoolrooms dominated by maps plastered in pink denoting the extent of the Empire, where was the lad whose heart was not stirred by images of cavalrymen charging into battle, swords and lances glittering in the sunshine, bugles blaring, flags waving? "All we of that generation who were on the younger side had the spirit of adventure in us," Vancouver's Victor Odlum, a thirty-four-year-old newspaperman who ended the war as a brigadier-general, later rationalized, "and I think that a spirit of adventure took us there." Some, like twenty-year-old Georges Bernier of Montreal, enlisted simply because, as he put it, "I had always been liking to be a soldier."[42]

For a few, at least, economic considerations were a factor. These men saw the war as an opportunity to escape an impoverished lifestyle; in the summer of 1914, when slaving from dawn to dusk at the harvest might get you a dollar, the army's pay rate – $1.10 a day for privates – did not look too bad.

Patriotism was another powerful motive. "I am not doing it," one lad explained in a letter to his mother, "for want of a fight or the love of adventure; it is to fight for our country."[43] Such sentiments were particularly true of the immigrants from Britain, who accounted for one-third of the more than two million who had come to Canada since the start of the century. "I had only been in Canada two years," recalled O. Bright, a Regina policeman, "but I felt I had to go back to England. I was an Englishman, and I thought they might need me."[44]

Joseph Sproston would have understood. The twenty-five-year-old expatriate Englishman was in the leather-chaired comfort of Montreal's University Club when word of the declaration of war arrived. Immediately, a patriotic member announced his intention to recruit a battery of field artillery to go overseas, and Sproston was one of the first to sign up. It was an easy decision, he later said. "I felt as, being an Englishman, it was my duty to join, and I had had previous experience in the field artillery in England before I came to Canada."[45]

For some of these expatriates, the call to go home was irresistible. Such was the case of Alfred Hornby, a twenty-nine-year-old Yorkshireman living in Winnipeg. A reservist in the Coldstream Guards, Hornby chose to return to England and serve with that regiment rather than join the Canadian army. Quitting his job at the Canadian Bank of Commerce, Hornby was on his way back to Britain by mid-August, and a month later he was in the firing line in France with the Coldstream Guards. His war was short-lived, however. He was invalided in December with a new malady known as trench foot, and within a year he was back at the bank in Winnipeg.[46]

Duty was a strong tonic, indeed. In Moose Jaw, Saskatchewan, two hundred veterans of the South African War were rebuffed in their attempt to enlist locally as cavalrymen, so they paid their own way to Ottawa, purchased uniforms, and presented themselves as the militia department. "If not accepted for service by the Government," went the sympathetic news story, "they threaten to hire a cattle ship and sail for Europe."[47] That extreme measure proved to be unnecessary; the men from Moose Jaw joined the growing Canadian army.

Duty. Grace Morris of Pembroke, Ontario, witnessed its influence.

She had had a wonderful summer, with her brothers Ramsey and Basil home for vacation from the University of Toronto. They had been joined by one of Ramsey's friends and classmates, handsome, athletic Alf Bastedo, a member of the U. of T. tennis team. They had played tennis – Grace won the first time, but never again – and laughed, and gone on picnics in the beauty of the Upper Ottawa Valley. And Grace Morris had fallen in love.

Then came the fourth of August. That warm Tuesday evening found Grace sitting on the veranda with Alf, Ramsey, and a cousin waiting for Basil to return from the telegraph office on Main Street, where he had joined the crowd seeking news of the impending war in Europe. Their pleasant chatter was interrupted by Basil's breathless voice as he ran up the sidewalk. "War is declared," he cried. "Canada is at war!"

They began to talk about it, and during the discussion, someone asked, "How do you get into a war?"

Alf Bastedo had the answer. "I know how I get into it," he said, taking the pipe out of his mouth. "I leave on an early morning train for home. I am a captain in the militia in Milton."

When Captain Bastedo departed the next day, waving through the steam at the Pembroke station, it was the last that Grace Morris ever saw of him.[48]

Senior militia officers offered their services almost as a matter of course. Many were no longer young, such as fifty-five-year-old Malcolm Mercer, a noted Toronto lawyer who was a long-time militiaman, a former commanding officer of the 2nd Queen's Own Rifles of Canada. That regiment's current commander, fifty-two-year-old businessman Robert Rennie, also stepped forward, as did the head of a rival militia unit, Lt.-Col. John Currie of the 48th Highlanders of Canada. Colonel Currie, at age forty-six, was also the member of Parliament for North Simcoe and a close friend of Sam Hughes. From Niagara Falls came Frederic Hill, forty-eight, a former mayor and currently a major in the 44th Lincoln and Welland Regiment. Lt.-Col. Edward "Dinky" Morrison, the forty-nine-year-old editor of the Ottawa *Citizen*, was a long-time artilleryman and made haste to join his unit.

English-speaking Quebeckers were equally prepared to do their part. Foremost was forty-three-year-old Col. Richard Turner. A scholarly-looking Quebec City wholesale merchant, Turner had served in the South African War, where he had won both the Victoria Cross* and the Distin-

---

*At Lillefontein on 7 November 1900, Lieutenant Turner, a member of the Royal Canadian Dragoons, rescued two artillery pieces that had been cut off by the enemy. In the successful rescue Turner was wounded twice.

guished Service Order. Joining him was Lt.-Col. David Watson, forty-six, the officer commanding the 8th Royal Rifles and the managing director of the Quebec City *Chronicle*, which served the city's flourishing English-speaking minority. Three lieutenant-colonels from Montreal were determined not to be left out. McGill-educated Frank Meighen was, at forty-four, president of a milling company and the commander of the 1st Regiment, Canadian Grenadier Guards. Frederick Loomis was the same age as Meighen; a private contractor, he led the 5th Royal Highlanders of Canada. Completing the Montreal trio was John Creelman, a thirty-three-year-old gunner who was a noted lawyer and businessman in Canada's biggest city.

From the prairies came two especially rugged gentlemen. Lt.-Col. George Tuxford commanded the 27th Light Horse in Moose Jaw, Saskatchewan. Tuxford, who farmed nearby, had organized and led the longest cattle drive in history. In an epic journey across the mountains, he had taken a herd from Moose Jaw to the Yukon's Dawson City in 1898, bringing meat on the hoof to the boom town at the height of the Klondike gold rush. Russell Lambert Boyle, nearly thirty-four years old, was an Ontario-born South African War veteran who had moved to Alberta in 1902, taking up ranching near Crossfield, just north of Calgary. Boyle – a big, strong man, well able to deal with a troublesome steer or ranch-hand – was a major in the 15th Light Horse and prominent in local politics.

Vancouver offered up three notable officers, all veterans of South Africa. William Hart-McHarg and R.G. Edwards Leckie were both forty-five and active in the militia. A lawyer, the Irish-born Hart-McHarg was a crack shot, having represented Canada in several international shooting competitions. Leckie, a lieutenant-colonel, commanded the 72nd Seaforth Highlanders of Canada; by profession, he was a mining engineer. Thirty-four-year-old Victor Odlum also went to war, leaving behind the Vancouver *Daily Star*, which he had just purchased.

One man who very nearly did not go was Victoria's Arthur Currie. A lieutenant-colonel commanding the 50th Gordon Highlanders of Canada, the big, amiable Currie – no relation to Toronto's Colonel Currie – was having grave financial problems. He was a real estate speculator who recently had held an impressive-looking list of properties on Vancouver Island. But thanks to falling land prices, most of them were now virtually worthless, and Currie faced the prospect of bankruptcy, having borrowed heavily to purchase these properties at inflated figures. His first impulse was to accept the post proferred by Sam Hughes, the command of Military District 11, which would have enabled him to remain in Victoria and possibly salvage his failing business. His regimental officers would not hear of it, however, and one of them had considerable influence with Sam

Hughes – Maj. Garnet Hughes was the militia minister's son. Badgered by his officers to hold out for something better, Currie finally agreed, and, according to Maj. Lorne Ross, "it was decided that Garnet would get in touch with his father to suggest that it would be much preferable if Colonel Currie got a command in the field." Minister Hughes responded by offering him the command of an infantry brigade. That was too tempting to resist, and thirty-eight-year-old Arthur Currie joined the thousands of Canadian men flocking to the colours in August 1914.[49]

The scions of some of Canada's most prominent families were quick to respond to the call. In that era, Montreal was clearly the leading city in the land, not only in terms of population, but culturally and financially. The wealthy young men who enjoyed their socially-admired role as officers in the militia were quick to offer their services, displaying the leadership that was expected of the English-speaking, moneyed class who resided in the mansions in "the Square Mile." One of the most notable among them was twenty-six-year-old Guy Melfort Drummond, son of the late president of the Bank of Montreal, Sir George Drummond. Young Drummond, an officer in the 5th Royal Highlanders, seemed to have a glittering future. Handsome and very tall (six foot four), fluently bilingual and a millionaire, Drummond was being groomed for a career high in Conservative party politics, and there were those who whispered that the post of prime minister was not unlikely for Drummond some day.

Toronto's leading families, including the Ryersons, the Jarvises, and the Gordons, also sent their sons to war. Col. George Ryerson, who had helped found the Canadian Red Cross, proudly watched his two officer sons volunteer their services, Arthur in the artillery, George in the infantry. W.D.P. Jarvis, son of the noted financier Aemilius Jarvis, was the darling of the Royal Canadian Yacht Club, after skippering *Nirwana* to victory in the international George Cup in July. Now he marched off to war, along with his crewman Leslie Gordon.

Most of the ordinary volunteers who swarmed to the recruiting centres in the early days of the Great War often had no specific reason for doing so. "Curiosity as much as anything. You see your friends going and say, 'Gee, it's up to me to go, too'." Or: "I don't think there was any particular reasons. . . . I figured, well, it will be a change – I would get overseas to see the world."[50]

Wally Bennett fell into that category. At nineteen, the English-born Bennett was being trained as an accountant in Calgary when he enlisted with a group of his friends. "We just went into it – might have been in a hurry, thinking the war might be over before we got there."[51]

That kind of spontaneity is a recurring theme. F.G. Layton, a farmer in south-central Manitoba, rode into nearby Gladstone with a friend on the night of 4 August. Unaware that war had been declared, they ran into a group of men on the main street. "Have you fellows come in to join?" they asked Layton and his companion.

"Join what?"

"The army."

Both of them enlisted immediately.[52]

In Yorkton, Saskatchewan, twenty-one-year-old R.L. Christopherson, a bank clerk, was watching a movie at the local theatre that evening. When the war news was flashed on the screen, Christopherson walked out of the theatre and down the street to the office of the 16th Light Horse, where he signed up for overseas service. The bank could get along without him.[53]

Harold Peat was sitting in his Edmonton kitchen discussing the war with two acquaintances, Bill Ravenscroft and Ken Mitchell. Peat was small and slender and only twenty-one, and he listened respectfully while Ravenscroft, a veteran of the South African War, told how he wanted no part of the latest conflict. "I know what war is . . . and here's one chicken they'll not catch to go through this one."

Young Mitchell interjected: "If I was old enough to go, boys, I'd go."

After they had talked about it for a while, Peat found himself saying to Ravenscroft, "Well, Bill, I'm game to go, if you will."

Ravenscroft, the man who knew war, changed his mind, and he and Peat went out and joined the 101st Edmonton Fusiliers.[54]

Naturally, not everyone in Canada was so moved. Large numbers of native-born Canadians stayed away from the recruiting offices. In *The Scotch* John Kenneth Galbraith recalled that among his compatriots in his area of south-western Ontario "passion for the Allied cause burned very low." When some lad did join up "it was invariably said that he went because he was tired of doing chores." Unlike the British, few other recent immigrants displayed much interest in this war, as Pierre Berton has pointed out. "The Slavs and Scandinavians stayed on their new farms. The Germans found it difficult to fight their countrymen. The Doukhobours, Mennonites, and Hutterites would not fight for religious reasons. And many of the Americans who had swarmed into Saskatchewan and Alberta a few years before went back across the border."[55]

Yet support came from surprising sources. Canada's hundred thousand Native Indians offered their endorsement in declarations from coast to coast. None was more eloquent than the statement issued by Alberta's Blood Indians:

The first citizens of Canada, the old allies of warring French and British, the redskins, the devoted wards of Victoria the Good and of her grandson, King George, are no whit behind the Sikhs of India, the men from South Africa, or the British Regulars, in testifying to their loyalty to the Crown or to the unity of the British Empire.[56]

But Natives who wished to fight for their King and country found that they were not wanted. A handful, including three descendants of Ontario's famed Mohawk leader, Joseph Brant, managed to enlist before the militia department decided not to accept Native volunteers, a ruling that remained in effect until December 1915. Similarly, blacks were flatly rejected at first, although an all-black construction company was later formed, and a few blacks were taken into combat by two Ontario battalions during the last year of the war.

The recruiting rush was unprecedented in Canada's short history. The outburst far exceeded the enthusiasm for the South African War, which, from Canada's point of view, had been an impressive undertaking. Of 8300 Canadians who enlisted in the British army to fight the Boers, eighty-nine had been killed, and 135 others had died of disease or accidents. More men volunteered in the first few days of August 1914 than had served during the three years of the war in South Africa.

For a while, it appeared as though the volunteers were jumping the gun. The British, preoccupied with organizing their own military forces, needed time to consider the potential contributions from all parts of the Empire, including Canada. Responding to the Canadian offer of assistance, Lewis Harcourt, the colonial secretary in London, cabled Ottawa on 4 August – mere hours before Britain and her Empire went to war – to say that there was "no immediate necessity for any request on our part for an expeditionary force from Canada."[57]

London's request came two days later. Harcourt wired Ottawa on the sixth, accepting the offer of a Canadian contingent, adding that he "would be glad if it could be despatched as soon as possible."[58] The same day, the Borden cabinet authorized the "raising and equipment of such units," which would "be composed of officers and men who are willing to volunteer for Overseas service under the British Crown."[59] On 7 August the Army Council in Britain advised Canada that "one division would be suitable composition of expeditionary force."[60] Taking this into account, the cabinet issued an order-in-council on the tenth setting the strength of the contingent at 25,000.

Sam Hughes was in his glory. He viewed Canada's war effort as his personal responsibility, believing – with some justification – that his military expertise was unrivalled in the cabinet. He also expected that his methods and measures would go unchallenged, particularly by the prime minister, who freely admitted his ignorance of martial matters. Hughes, who fully intended to exploit the situation, had a less than flattering opinion of Borden, saying that he was "a lovely fellow, very capable, but not a very good judge of men or tactics and is gentle-hearted as a girl."[61]

Hughes's first act was to scrap the existing mobilization plans. These were embodied in Memorandum C.1209, drawn up in 1911 by Col. Willoughby Gwatkin, a British career soldier who now served as the chief of Canada's General Staff. On 31 July Hughes informed commanders of divisional districts and areas across the country that Memorandum C.1209 should be regarded "as purely tentative" and asked them to "consider what procedure you would adopt on receiving orders that troops were to be raised in your command for service overseas."[62] When the war broke out, Hughes side-stepped these senior officers by dispatching on 6 August a night telegram direct to 226 militia commanders authorizing each unit to raise an unspecified number of recruits. The telegram stated age limits (eighteen to forty-five), physical qualifications (for the infantry, the minimum height was five-foot-three), with preference given to men with military experience or training. Single men were preferred, followed by married men with no children. (On 14 August a regulation was issued requiring married men to obtain their wives' permission to enlist. This rule remained in effect until August 1915.) Hughes also stated that the contingent would assemble at Valcartier, Quebec.[63]

The minister's action was neither surprising nor out of character. By circumventing the established mobilization procedure, Hughes was expressing his contempt for professional soldiers. He believed that "the best soldiers are such men as engineers, barristers, contractors, large businessmen with military training. . . . They far surpass the professional soldier."[64] It was a prejudice that would become more apparent in the days and weeks ahead. In any case, Hughes later justified his decision by explaining that he preferred his own method, which he described as "a call to arms, like the fiery cross passing through the highlands of Scotland or the mountains of Ireland in former days." He also argued that "it would have taken several weeks to have got the word around through the ordinary channels."[65]

His explanation is not without merit. Although historians often condemn Hughes for his amateurish interference, they overlook the imperfections in Colonel Gwatkin's scheme. For example, it specified Petawawa, Ontario, as the assembly site for the contingent, and Petawawa was nowhere near a port. By contrast, Hughes's choice, Valcartier, lay within easy marching distance of the harbour at Quebec City.

There was one problem with Camp Valcartier. It did not exist. The site on the east bank of the gentle Jacques Cartier River, sixteen miles northwest of Quebec City, had been selected for a military camp in 1912. But no work had been done, and as a result a camp had to be created virtually overnight. On 7 August Hughes handed the task to William Price. He was a namesake and grandson of the legendary lumber pioneer who was known as "the father of the Saguenay." Still heavily involved in the pulp and paper business, the Price family was very powerful in Quebec, and commanded a huge labour force. Even better, as a former Tory MP, Price was a friend of Sam Hughes. The militia minister made Price an honorary colonel and gave him twenty days to perform a minor miracle.

Framed to the north and east by rocky, wooded hills and standing on a sandy, terraced plateau, Camp Valcartier at that time was mainly farmland, interspersed with patches of scrub, swamp, and timber. One of the early arrivals at the Camp was Dan Ormond, a twenty-nine-year-old lawyer from Portage-la-Prairie, Manitoba. "It was absolutely breaking new ground," marvelled Major Ormond. "There was nothing there at all. The brush had to be cut down. There was no latrine, there was nothing."[66]

Somehow, Price pulled it off. The transformation of the farmland and bush into a major military camp was truly remarkable, and not even the most vocal of Sam Hughes's many critics, contemporary or modern, can deny the success of the undertaking. The militia minister pictured it in a glowing speech to the House of Commons:

> On Saturday, the 8th, Valcartier was taken over, and on Monday the 10th, [rifle] ranges and waterworks were begun. By the 20th, [two] and a half miles of ranges were completed, and 1,500 targets were put in position up to the same date, 12 miles of water mains had been laid in, and 15 miles of drains, open and covered, had been located. Army Service Corps and Ordnance buildings were constructed, railway sidings laid in, fences removed, crops harvested, ground cleared, streets made, upwards of 200 baths for the men put in, water chlorinated, electric light and telephones installed . . . and 35,000 men got under canvas in less than three weeks from the acceptance of the call.[67]

There can be little doubt, however, that Hughes's success in raising, assembling, and accommodating Canada's first contingent had more to do with good luck than with good management. He was notably unwilling to delegate authority. Everything had to cross his desk, and he attended to every detail. That was his style, in peacetime as in wartime. "I am boss while I am here," he once declared. "So long as I am Minister of Militia . . . I am going to supervise the department and every branch of it."[68] Hughes got away with this seat-of-the-pants approach only because Canada was new at this business of war, and there were no precedents on which ministers and their deputies could base their actions. The improvisation in Hughes's department was more noticeable than in most, not only because of its high profile but also because of the militia minister's flamboyance.

He was not always successful, especially in his soon-notorious arrangements to procure war materiel. Standard practices such as tendering went out the window as Hughes concluded a series of deals with personal and political cronies. It was unorthodox, the spending was unauthorized, and Hughes soon clashed with his fellow cabinet members over the controversial contracts. Sir George Foster, the grandfatherly trade and commerce minister, was appalled at the blatant patronage. "The current of seekers is ceaseless," he complained in his diary. "This system is all wrong; and we should really have it put on a business basis."[69]

The potential for abuse was staggering. Sir Thomas White, the finance minister, repeatedly took exception to Hughes's habit of letting war contracts without cabinet approval. Hughes refused to listen; whatever he felt was needed for Canada's war effort, he obtained. In late September the auditor-general, J. Fraser, pointed out that the militia department had spent "over $1,000,000" that had not been authorized by orders-in-council; this was, he noted, "a clear violation" of the law.[70] Eventually, in December, the auditor-general temporarily cut off the department's credit. By then the evidence of mismanagement had become, in Sir George Foster's eyes, overwhelming. "The waste of money had, I am convinced, been very great," the trade minister wrote Prime Minister Borden. "My impression is that reorganization alone can save the situation already compromised, and . . . that a thorough and businesslike investigation should be instituted into the methods and transactions of the Dept. since the War commenced."[71]

But Hughes did get things done. He and the prime minister shared a determination that Canada should benefit economically from the war. Hughes noted that some people were "going without bread in Canada while those across the line [in the U.S.] are receiving good wages for work that could be done as efficiently and as cheaply in this country."[72] Prime Minister Borden saw the war as an opportunity to revive the nation's struggling economy; but it was not easy to do, he confessed:

British officials seemed disposed in some instances, to obtain supplies from the United States which could have been procured in Canada and the provision of which would have given employment to some of our people. I made sharp protests against this practice; and on one occasion I learned that a British official had sent a considerable order to a city in the United States under the impression that he had placed it in Canada.[73]

Where Borden fussed and fretted, Hughes acted. It was on his personal initiative that Canada became a major munitions manufacturer. On 24 August the British secretary of state for war, Lord Kitchener, had cabled Hughes to inquire whether he could "provide or obtain from American trade" a considerable quantity of 18-pounder artillery shells.[74] Hughes promptly set up the Shell Committee to encourage Canadian companies' production of this ammunition. By the end of 1915, 422 Canadian plants were taking part in a $30-million industry. Largely as a result of this, steel production in Canada trebled between 1914 and 1918, and by war's end the British army had been supplied with 66 million Canadian-made shells.[75]

(This impressive achievement notwithstanding, Hughes still managed to get into trouble. His embarrassing persistence in patronizing his friends prompted Opposition allegations of political partisanship, and Hughes's Shell Committee was replaced by the Imperial Munitions Board in November 1915. This in turn led to a royal commission in 1916 to investigate the abuses in the militia department. The commission absolved Hughes of wrongdoing, but condemned his questionable methods of management.)

And so Canada lurched off to war. By fits and starts, by trial and error, the young dominion applied its human and material resources to the task at hand. Never before, and rarely since, had Canadians been so united in a common cause, regardless of race or religion, region or politics.

Support for the war manifested itself in several ways. Provincial governments climbed on the bandwagon. Taking their cue from Ottawa's offer of nearly fifty thousand tons of flour for the mother country, Ontario – whose seventy-year-old premier, Sir James Whitney, urged Canadians to "exert our whole strength and power at once on behalf of the Empire" – and Manitoba both pledged smaller quantities of flour. Alberta and Prince Edward Island offered oats, cheese was promised by Quebec, and British Columbia* shipped 25,000 cases of canned salmon. Saskatchewan offered 1500 horses, while Nova Scotia sent a cheque for $100,000 for war relief.[76]

---

*British Columbia acquired its own navy, if only briefly. On the eve of the war, alarmed at the reported presence in the Pacific of the German cruiser *Leipzig* and doubtful of the creaky Canadian cruiser *Rainbow*'s ability to defend the province's coastline, Premier Sir Richard McBride secretly arranged the purchase of a pair of submarines from a firm in Seattle, Washington. They arrived at the Canadian naval base at Esquimalt on 5 August, the day after the war started. The provincial government duly handed the submarines over to the Royal Canadian Navy, which blessed them with the rather unromantic names *CC-1* and *CC-2* (Goodspeed, *Armed Forces*, 69-71).

Fund-raising was a popular method of enlisting public support. In ten weeks, the Patriotic Relief Fund, organized in eighteen cities, raised over $5 million, more than half of it in Montreal and Toronto. Donations were spurred by the story of the Toronto newsboy who, having nothing else to contribute, gave his streetcar ticket to the cause. It was later auctioned for $1,000.[77]

The country's sense of purpose was exemplified by the four-day special session of Parliament that began on 18 August. In seven sittings totalling less than sixteen hours, eight major pieces of legislation were passed, including a war appropriation of $50 million and the War Measures Act, which gave the government sweeping powers to ensure "the security, defence, peace, order and welfare of Canada."[78]

Political differences had been set aside, if only temporarily. For the aging Liberal leader, Sir Wilfrid Laurier, it was one of the finest moments in a distinguished career. The white-haired seventy-two-year-old had served as prime minister from 1896 until 1911, and he was still a brilliant orator. "It is our duty," he told a hushed House of Commons, "to let Great Britain know, and to let the friends and foes of Great Britain know, that there is in Canada but one mind and one heart, and that all Canadians stand behind the mother-country."[79]

Prime Minister Borden was no less eloquent. Carbuncles and all, the former Halifax lawyer addressed his fellow members of Parliament:

> In the awful dawn of the greatest war the world has ever known, in the hour when peril confronts us such as this Empire has not faced for a hundred years, every vain or unnecessary word seems a discord. As to our duty, we are all agreed; we stand shoulder to shoulder with Britain and the other British Dominions in this quarrel, and that duty we shall not fail to fulfil as the honour of Canada demands. Not for love of battle, not for the lust of conquest, not for greed of possessions, but for the cause of honour, to maintain solemn pledges, to uphold principles of liberty, to withstand forces that would convert the world into an armed camp; yes, in the very name of the peace that we sought at any cost save that of dishonour, we have entered into this war; and while gravely conscious of the tremendous issues involved and of all the sacrifices that they may entail, we do not shrink from them but with firm hearts we abide the event.[80]

"A Dark Shadow"

The speed with which the first contingent assembled further validates Sam Hughes's impetuous mobilization policy. The first troops began arriving at Valcartier, which was still under construction, on 18 August, via the Canadian Northern Railway line from Quebec City. By 8 September, 32,665 men were in camp.*[1]

Before entraining for Valcartier, most of the volunteers flocking to the colours were funnelled through their local militia units, and the competition among these regiments for recruits was often fierce. Nowhere was the rivalry stronger than in Victoria, where the 50th Gordon Highlanders of Canada and the 88th Victoria Fusiliers tried to outdo each other. Both regiments had downtown recruiting offices, but the Gordons' commander, Lt.-Col. Arthur Currie – who, for business reasons, was still debating whether or not to volunteer – outmanoeuvred the opposition by posting his recruiters outside the Victoria *Daily Colonist*, where large crowds gathered daily to read the latest war bulletins. It was, commented the *Colonist* on 8 August, "a smart thing," because "the strength of the [Gordons] has been increased by over 100 men since the campaign started."

Few recruits were rejected. All were subjected to medical examinations, but these were superficial at best. In Brampton, Ontario, W.C. Sterling, a veteran of the 36th Peel Regiment, found himself being examined by a familiar face, his regimental medical officer, who blandly asked, "What's wrong with you?"

"Nothing," Sterling shrugged.

"What the hell do you want to get examined for?"[2]

Poor eyesight nearly cost Winnipeg's Norman Fraser his chance to enlist in a local cavalry unit, the Fort Garry Horse. The eye test was

---

*Hughes's haphazard recruiting scheme remained in place well into the third year of the war and, indeed, outlasted the minister, who was sacked late in 1916. If nothing else, it was cheap: up to 1 April 1917, the federal government spent a paltry $26,571.72 on recruiting advertising (Wilson, xxxi).

simple: each man had to identify a beer advertisement in the corner of a newspaper page hanging on the far wall. The near-sighted Fraser could only vaguely make it out. In desperation he took a guess: Budweiser. "I was right." Another Winnipegger, George Boyd, of the 90th Rifles, actually failed his eye test, but he bribed his way into the army. Approaching the orderly-room sergeant, a personal friend, Boyd said, "Now, you destroy that paper, mark me fit, and I'll buy you a bottle." With that, Private Boyd went to war.[3]

Manpower was the only excess commodity enjoyed by the Canadian army in the summer of 1914. Everything else was in short supply. Some units were fortunate enough to parade in the appropriately military surroundings of an armoury; most had to make do with a barn on the county fairground, or an arena. Uniforms were scarce: the newcomers could not even dress like soldiers. Some only received parts of their uniform; Pte. Georges Bernier, a twenty-year-old member of Montreal's 65th Carabiniers who had enlisted because he had always wanted to be a soldier, recalled that it "was funny how I was dressed. I was in civvies with the web equipment and a big bowler hat on. Gee, what a funny army!" The lucky few who did get complete uniforms at this time were not invariably impressive. An eighteen-year-old gunner, Sgt. Fred Fish, remembered that "my uniform was not too well fitting. The britches, the fork, came down to my knees. I had puttees like funnels, the wrong way around, and spurs, and when my father saw me he almost cried."[4]

Their training, too, left much to be desired. With shortages of all kinds of equipment, including rifles, there was a strict limit to what could be achieved. Carrying broomsticks instead of rifles, the rank and file learned foot drill and the manual of arms, but somehow the broomsticks hampered their military zeal. In some instances, the training was useless anyway. Officers of the 48th Highlanders of Canada, a Toronto regiment, were forced to endure sword practice each morning before breakfast, "and we'd go through all the motions of attack and defence with a sword," recalled Lieut. Ian Sinclair, "which was the only time we ever used a sword in the course of the war."[5]

The naïveté of some of these men could be amusing, and a little touching. Canadian privates were paid $1.10 a day to serve in the Great War, and many were surprised when they were summoned to their first pay parade. "It never occurred to us that we were going to be paid," said Pte. R.L. Christopherson, the Yorkton banker who had joined the 16th Light Horse. "I knew they fed them and clothed them, but I had no idea that they paid the army."[6]

Their exuberance was matched only by their impatience, fuelled by the widespread belief that the war would end by Christmas. Many volunteers felt the way this member of the Prince of Wales's Canadian Dragoons did when he wrote his fiancée in Peterborough, Ontario: "It'll probably all be over before I can get in on the fun."[7]

One hundred trains took the men to Valcartier. They arrived steadily during the second half of August and early September. As each unit departed from its hometown, bands played, dogs and small boys raced alongside and everyone cheered the march down the main street to the station. There, amid the hissing steam and a forest of waving handkerchiefs, the men received a rousing send-off from fathers and mothers, wives and sweethearts, children and friends. At Toronto's Union Station, where the 10th Royal Grenadiers departed on 22 August, a famous photograph shows a harried conductor, hands on hips, realizing with disgust that he is fighting a losing battle to maintain order on the platform. Hundreds of people, along with a brass band, have gathered to wish the Grenadiers farewell, and several women can be seen clasping hands with soldiers hanging precariously from the windows of their Canadian Northern Railway coach.

Among those who turned out to watch the Grenadiers depart was fourteen-year-old Mary Mallon. "I guess to me it was rather thrilling," she later said. "We didn't realize what was going to happen." Perhaps a few Torontonians would watch the troops marching off to war and note with irony that 1914 was supposed to be "Peace Year" at the Canadian National Exhibition.[8]

An equally impressionable Montrealer hurried out to watch the troop trains pass through Canada's biggest city. Twelve-year-old Helen Drummond, whose Uncle Guy had volunteered to go overseas, was thrilled by the sight. At the time, she later admitted, she thought the whole thing was "terrific."[9]

The departure of the 101st Edmonton Fusiliers was typical. Thousands of cheering, flag-waving Edmontonians lined the streets to Union Station as the 350 members of the regiment marched past. One soldier was loudly cheered when he shouted: "God help the Kaiser if we get hold of him!"[10]

To some, the carnival atmosphere that prevailed seemed inappropriate, even absurd. "Strangely enough, no one was crying," wrote young Harold Peat, one of the newest privates in the 101st Fusiliers. "Men were cheering; women were waving. Weeping was yet to come."[11]

The scene was repeated countless times all across Canada. Everywhere, weeping was yet to come.

Sam Hughes was on hand to greet many of the troops at Valcartier. The militia minister had become a regular visitor, arriving in his private railcar and living in a specially constructed brick bungalow. For most of the troops, this was their first opportunity to see the man about whom they had heard so much. The 48th Highlanders of Canada arrived from Toronto on 1 September, and Hughes strolled among the ranks repeatedly declaring in a loud voice, "The boys are looking fine." Lieut. Ian Sinclair noted that the minister's remarks were "meant to cheer the men up but only resulted in the lads waxing highly sarcastic" about Hughes.[12] They would see a lot more of him, and have much more to say about him, in the next few weeks.

If their initial impression of Hughes was subdued, the soldiers were even less enamoured of the camp itself. They did not appreciate, of course, that it had not existed before mid-August, and that one of Price's initial tasks (as reported by Hughes in the Commons) had been to harvest crops from it. But even by the first week in September, when the Highlanders from Toronto arrived, it was still in ramshackle shape, as Lieutenant Sinclair recalled:

> There were stumps all over the place. There were no roads, there were just sand tracks, and when a wind blew your food filled with sand, and your eyes and ears and everything else, and there were masses of horses and therefore masses of flies and things like that. [We] were all so green that everything seemed to be quite natural to us.[13]

There was, however, "continued daily improvement," and by the end of September many considered Valcartier to be "an excellently planned camp."[14] Somehow, by heroic efforts, the sandy plateau had been turned into a camp that could accommodate and feed the thousands of men who had descended on it. Now they had to turn these eager young civilians into soldiers.

The first task facing the authorities was daunting. The more than thirty thousand men at Valcartier, representing dozens of militia units of all services, somehow had to be organized into something resembling a military formation. The infantry, who made up the majority of the volunteers, posed the biggest problem; the solution involved a compromise that, like all compromises, satisfied few. Because it was clearly impossible to send every militia regiment overseas as an individual unit, Sam Hughes opted to incorporate them into numbered battalions. This was begun on 22 August, when twelve provisional infantry battalions were formed. When too many troops arrived to be comfortably accommodated in this manner, the number was increased to sixteen on 2 September. A seventeenth battalion was added later, to look after the surplus.

In 1914 the battalion was the basic combat unit in the British army and, therefore, in the Canadian army. Commanded by a lieutenant-colonel, it consisted, in round numbers, of 1000 officers and other ranks. Each battalion was subdivided into companies – there were eight at Valcartier, but this was later reduced to four, each 250 strong – commanded by a major or captain. A company – designated by number (1, 2, 3, or 4) or letter (A, B, C, or D), depending on the battalion's preference – consisted of four platoons, each under a lieutenant, and there were four sections in a platoon. A section was led by a senior non-commissioned officer, or NCO, such as a sergeant.

Regional origins were reflected in the organization of the battalions at Valcartier. This is how they were formed:

1st Battalion – considered a western Ontario unit, it drew its strength from centres such as Windsor, London, Parry Sound, Sarnia, Stratford, and Galt

2nd Battalion – mainly from eastern Ontario, its members were from Ottawa, Toronto, and such places Whitby, Perth, and Peterborough

3rd Battalion – entirely from Toronto, it was a union of three local militia regiments: the Governor-General's Body Guard, 2nd Queen's Own Rifles of Canada, and 10th Royal Grenadiers

4th Battalion – called a central Ontario unit, its troops were recruited from Aurora, Barrie, Brampton, Brantford, Hamilton, Milton, and Niagara Falls

5th Battalion – dubbed Western Cavalry, it was an assortment of dismounted cavalry regiments from the four western provinces

6th Battalion – also dismounted cavalry, though only temporarily, it was built around the Fort Garry Horse from Winnipeg

7th Battalion – entirely from British Columbia, its members came from Vancouver, Victoria, New Westminster, and Kamloops, along with a large Kootenay contingent

8th Battalion – primarily the 90th Winnipeg Rifles, famed as the "Little Black Devils," from their service in the Riel Rebellion

9th Battalion – the 101st Edmonton Fusiliers

10th Battalion – an amalgamation of the 103rd Calgary Rifles, drawing from southern Alberta and the foothills, and the 106th Winnipeg Light Infantry

11th Battalion – an assortment of regiments from Saskatchewan and Manitoba

12th Battalion – representing twenty-three militia units from Quebec and the Maritimes, it included five "regiments" with fewer than five men

13th Battalion – based on Montreal's 5th Royal Highlanders of Canada

14th Battalion – its main strength came from three of Montreal's militia units, 1st Canadian Grenadier Guards, 3rd Victoria Rifles of Canada, and 65th Carabiniers de Mont-Royal

15th Battalion – built around Toronto's 48th Highlanders of Canada

16th Battalion – later called the Canadian Scottish, it was a blend of four Highland regiments from across Canada: the 50th Gordon Highlanders from Victoria, Vancouver's 72nd Seaforth Highlanders of Canada, the Winnipeg-based 79th Cameron Highlanders of Canada, and the 91st Canadian Highlanders from Hamilton.*[15]

Noticeably lacking was a French-Canadian unit. There were 1245 French Canadians at Valcartier, more than enough for a French-speaking battalion. But the idea was flatly rejected by Hughes, who, according to a recent biographer, "had always been remarkably insensitive to French-Canadians."[16] The French Canadians of the first contingent were integrated primarily in two English-speaking battalions, the 12th and 14th. Although Hughes authorized a French-speaking Battalion, the famous 22nd, or "Van Doos," to be raised later that year, the minister's short-sighted reaction dampened French Canada's early enthusiasm for the war, with tragic consequences.

The sixteen battalions were melded into four provisional brigades on 2 September. The First Brigade was composed of the 1st, 2nd, 3rd, and 4th battalions, all from Ontario, while the Second – the 5th, 6th, 7th, and 8th battalions – was primarily from western Canada. The Third, made up of the 9th, 10th, 11th, and 12th battalions, represented the prairies, Quebec, and the Maritimes. The Fourth was considered a Highland formation, although only three of its battalions – the 13th, 15th, and 16th – wore the kilt.

Some of Canada's most distinguished officers were appointed to command these brigades. The First went to Toronto's Lt.-Col. Malcolm Mercer, the fifty-five-year-old lawyer who, in peacetime, had commanded the 2nd Queen's Own Rifles of Canada. Command of the Second Brigade

---

*Unable to agree on a tartan, the 16th wore khaki kilts overseas until, in 1917, the battalion adopted the Mackenzie tartan kilt. Since the khaki did not arrive until mid-1915, until then the men continued to wear the tartans of the four founding units.

was what convinced Lt.-Col. Arthur Currie to leave the world of real estate speculation in Victoria. The Fourth Brigade went to the scholarly-looking former regular-army officer and v.c. winner, Col. Richard Turner, now a bespectacled forty-three-year-old businessman from Quebec City. The Third Brigade went leaderless until 25 September, when a slight adjustment was made in the brigade organization: the Fourth Brigade was redesignated the Third, with Colonel Turner in command, and the Third was renamed the Fourth, under a long-time militiaman from Ontario's Niagara district, Lt.-Col. John Cohoe. In the British army, a brigade was commanded by a brigadier-general, but several months passed before the Canadian ranks would conform.

The contingent would eventually be transformed into a division, which was the smallest self-contained formation in the British army. Under the command of a major-general, a 1914-era division numbered around eighteen thousand men. Its primary combat element was the infantry, three brigades of four battalions each. The balance was comprised of artillery, engineers, signallers, transport, and medical services, all well represented at Valcartier. There were three brigades of field artillery, under Lt.-Col. Harry Burstall, a member of Canada's tiny prewar army. Three field companies of engineers supervised and co-operated with the infantrymen relegated to the drudgery of digging trenches, building roads, stringing barbed-wire entanglements, and laying telephone cable. These field telephones were manned by a signal company, which handled all messages at divisional headquarters; signal lamps and messengers were used as well as the telephone for transmitting information, orders, and reports. Army Service Corps troops ensured, in theory, that all units were supplied with all their needs. The Canadians had also assembled generous medical facilities, far in excess of their divisional requirements. In addition to three field ambulances and a casualty clearing station, there were two stationary hospitals and two general hospitals, staffed by well-trained doctors, among them a man named John McCrae.

Valcartier bore the unmistakable and indelible imprint of the dictatorial Sam Hughes. Although Col. Victor Williams, a personal friend of the militia minister, had been named camp commandant, there was no doubt in anyone's mind who was really in charge. Fifty-three-year-old Canon Frederick Scott of Montreal, who hoped to go overseas as a chaplain (and whose son Francis Reginald would win fame in his own right), considered Hughes "the dominating spirit" at Valcartier, observing that the minister "rode about with aides-de-camp in great splendour like Napoleon. To me it seemed that his personality and his despotic rule hung like a dark shadow over the camp."[17] Maj. Victor Odlum, the newspaper publisher now serving with British Columbia's 7th Battalion, believed that Hughes "was a good actor. You saw him all the time. He was a picturesque creature and he played his part. Always on a horse, always picturesque, always in complete command of the whole thing."[18]

Needless to say, Hughes ran a one-man show. "I have to do things in a summary way," he admitted. "I have done so all my life and I will go on doing so until the end."[19]

Hughes brought with him "unutterable confusion."[20] He had a quaint habit of promoting officers on the spot with a hearty slap on the back. This left some units with too many officers. A subaltern from the 16th (Canadian Scottish) Battalion, named Hugh Urquhart, remembered that one battalion "had three lieut.-colonels at the same time; another battalion . . . had four majors waiting around for the appointment of Second in Command, and, incidentally, for the one horse which had to do service for the four of them."[21]

Pte. Frank Yates, a member of the 3rd (Toronto) Battalion, never forgot his first meeting with the militia minister. Hughes, accompanied by a cavalry escort, rode up to the battalion as it drilled on the parade ground and shouted, "Form square!" The men, many of whom were having difficulties as it was, were dumbfounded by the order, which had been dropped from the training manual years before. Fortunately, one grizzled corporal remembered the formation and eventually shuffled Yates and the others into the proper position, kneeling in a square with bayonets fixed.

But the ordeal had just begun. Now Hughes was looking right at young Yates, who was sweating profusely. "What do you do after that?" the minister demanded.

Yates, of course, had no idea. Luckily, his corporal again came to the rescue, gruffly whispering, "Unload."

"Unload, sir," Yates repeated to Hughes. Satisfied, the minister rode off, but he left a lasting impression on the troops from Toronto. That night, as Yates and some of his friends discussed the episode, one man's comment seemed to sum up everything that was happening at Valcartier. "Good God," he muttered. "What sort of army are we in?"[22]

Hughes also abused his officers at every opportunity. Even battalion commanders could not escape his sharp tongue, often in front of their assembled units, a breach of military tradition, not to mention common sense. "The undisciplined tommy liked seeing his senior getting told off," recalled Capt. Paul Villiers, a long-time militiaman from Victoria, "and this was just the cheap sort of publicity that Hughes cared for."[23] One battalion went through five commanders in a single day, thanks to Hughes and his explosive temper.

Complaints about his conduct soon reached the prime minister's office. In mid-September Borden was told by the governor-general, the Duke of Connaught, "that Hughes' language to his officers has been violent and insulting." Although he considered the reports "disturbing," the prime minister did nothing about them.[24]

Hughes's slapdash methods had more serious consequences in other areas. No task was more important, or demanding, than that of equipping the Canadian contingent. Hughes later complained that he had to deal with "thousands upon thousands of cranks, contractors, grafters, self-seekers and interlopers,"[25] but that was his own fault. Not only did he persist in attending to all details personally but his predilection towards political patronage carried a hefty price tag, as a lengthening line of personal and party friends waited at his door. The demands on the minister's time did not go unnoticed. The Second Brigade's Colonel Currie sympathetically remarked that "the Minister's life must have been a misery for days on end every squirt of a politician in the country and especially those in camp were trying to arrange things to suit their own selfish ends."[26]

Supply shortages remained a problem, and as August gave way to September, factories in Montreal and Toronto worked overtime to fill the militia department's rush orders. Here, too, the Sam Hughes touch was strongly evident. The contingent was equipped with 133 motor vehicles of five different makes and 853 wagons from no fewer than eight manufacturers. Quality control was nonexistent. The wagons proved to be unsatisfactory: poorly built, they could never withstand the rigours of a military campaign, and poorly designed, they "might do very well on the illimitable prairie [but] there was not a road in Europe wide enough to allow them to turn."[27]

Uniforms and boots were no better. The tight-fitting, stiff-collared tunics had a tendency to fall apart at the seams, and the boots, though lighter and more comfortable than those worn by the British army, could not take much wear and tear. Featuring paper soles – cheap and easy to make – "after twelve parades these boots were reduced to a sodden mass," according to Sir Andrew Macphail, serving at that time as a captain in the Canadian Army Medical Service.[28]

Then there was the Oliver leather harness. A total of 13,920 sets were purchased, at a cost of $6.75 each, from manufacturers in Toronto and Montreal.[29] The harness was designed to carry a soldier's ammunition and personal equipment, but it was uncomfortable – the troops called it the "Oliver torture"[30] – poorly made, and held only half as much small-arms ammunition as British webbing. Lt.-Col. John Currie, the officer commanding the 15th (48th Highlanders) Battalion, bluntly labelled the Oliver harness "a joke."[31] Currie's criticism carries considerable weight, because he was both a Conservative member of Parliament from Toronto and a personal friend of Sam Hughes. In any case, there was not enough Oliver equipment to be distributed to the entire contingent, and nearly half of the infantry went overseas with comfortable British webbing.

One especially peculiar acquisition was the MacAdam shield-shovel. Intended to serve as a combination bullet-proof shield and entrenching tool, it had been patented by Ena MacAdam, Hughes's private secretary, after she had seen Swiss troops using a similar invention during manoeuvres in 1913. The militia department bought 25,000, at $1.35 each, from a surprised and delighted manufacturer. While Hughes thought it "perfect,"[32] few soldiers agreed with him. One observer sarcastically pointed out that it was good only for "opening tins" or "cleaning a pipe."[33] The MacAdam shield-shovel was later discarded and sold as scrap metal for $1,400 to an American firm.[34] It was perhaps fortunate that Miss MacAdam never caught sight of a Swiss army knife.

Small arms were another sore point. The Ross rifle was issued to the contingent – the infantry, cavalry, and artillery all used it – but there were problems, both in quantity and quality. In spite of countless design changes, the Ross still showed a disturbing tendency to jam during rapid fire, particularly when fed British .303-calibre bullets, which were not made to the same exacting standards as Canadian ammunition. There also were not enough Ross rifles to go around: 22,128 Mark IIIs, the latest model, were shipped to Valcartier, but one infantry battalion, the 48th Highlanders of the 15th, had to go overseas with the outdated Mark II.

The contingent's machine-guns were also of doubtful value. Unable to obtain the British-made Vickers heavy machine-gun, the Canadians eventually obtained a similar weapon, the Colt, from the United States. Each infantry battalion was allotted four of the air-cooled, belt-fed Colts, but unfortunately, like the Ross rifle, they tended to jam when British ammunition was used. Colonel Currie, the Second Brigade's commander, later commented, "I do not consider the Colt a very serviceable machine gun,"[35] and few machine-gunners would have disagreed with him. Lt.-Col. W.K. Walker complained that after dismantling the Colt for cleaning "even the experienced machine gunner occasionally had a part left over when the assembly process was thought to be complete."[36] Lieut. Walter Critchley of the 10th (Calgary-Winnipeg) Battalion laughingly recalled that the Colt "had a pistol grip on it. I can remember one thing they said: 'If you ever have to leave your gun, all you do is hit it like that, and the grip'll fall off and it'll immobilize the gun.' Well, you didn't have to do that to immobilize it. All you had to do was get a little dirt in it, and you could throw it away."[37]

The artillery, meanwhile, was having its own problems. The authorities were able to procure enough 18-pounders – the standard field gun used by the British army, which could fire an 18.5-pound shrapnel shell 6200 yards – to form three field brigades. But there were no modern 4.5-inch howitzers in Canada, so the howitzer brigade that was usually attached to a division was not formed until well after the Canadians had arrived on the Continent. Even so, equipping the first contingent in September 1914 all but stripped Canada's artillery arsenal. Col. Willoughby Gwatkin, the chief of the General Staff, warned later that month: "Canada cannot supply another Division properly organized and self-contained; for she will soon have parted with the whole of her field artillery, with the exception of a few guns and howitzers of an antiquated type."[38]

Horses were also required. Even with the increasing use and availability of motor transport, horses were still important to all armies in 1914 and would remain so throughout the war. The contingent needed more than seven thousand horses, for the officers and the cavalry and for the artillery, as well as the draught animals for hauling supply wagons and the like. Since only the artillery brought their own horses to Valcartier, fifty-five government purchasing-agents rounded up the rest, and more. Altogether, 8150 were bought, at an average price of $172.45. Accommodated in temporary corrals at Valcartier, they twice broke out and stampeded through the camp, although knowledgeable observers would have been surprised that some of the horses were capable of such strenuous activity. Before the contingent left Canada, 480 horses, deemed more suitable for the glue factory than for the fighting front, were auctioned at Quebec, bringing less than a third of their original price.[39]

Little meaningful training was given at Camp Valcartier. No one could fault the weather: September was, for the most part, warm and dry, and the maples that covered the nearby hills were resplendent in the golds, oranges, and reds of early autumn. Training was supposed to follow the guidelines contained in the "Memorandum for Camps of Instruction, 1914," issued by the militia department, but most of the available time was devoted to organizing and outfitting the contingent – considerable achievements in themselves. Had serious training been a major goal at this time, it would have been defeated by Militia Minister Hughes. For reasons that baffle the modern observer, he deprived the contingent of a prime source of instructors when he dispatched Canada's only regular-army unit, the Royal Canadian Regiment, to Bermuda – that well-known front-line position – where it relieved a British battalion on garrison duty. This left the training of more than thirty thousand citizen-soldiers in the hands of an instructional force of eighty Canadian and British veterans at Valcartier.

The troops were kept busy with a variety of tasks, including sports, physical exercise, parade-ground drill, and route marches, and in mid-September brigade-size manoeuvres were staged. The men also spent considerable time on Valcartier's rifle ranges. "I want, first of all, men who can pink the enemy every time," Hughes had declared.[40] Beginning on 25 August, the troops were put through their "pinking" paces, each man firing fifty rounds at up to 300 yards. "When our boys marched away from Valcartier," Hughes later boasted, "they were an army of free men, trained to handle a rifle as no men had ever handled it before."[41]

That was typical Hughes bravado. In fact, the work on the rifle ranges did little more than generate grumbling about the performance of the Ross rifle. This particularly upset the inventor when he paid his first visit to Valcartier in September. "I found the rifle situation astounding and disheartening," Sir Charles later wrote, claiming that poor-quality ammunition was being issued – all of it either "of obsolete pattern" or "condemned as defective by War Office inspectors" – which caused his rifle to jam on the firing ranges. "Is it any wonder that [the] men blamed the rifle?" asked Ross in exasperation.[42]

There was also the inevitable military bureaucracy to be satisfied. Each man had to swear an oath of allegiance to King George and fill out attestation papers, a bewildering array of documents that secured personal information about everything from birthplace and date to next-of-kin. Everyone was subjected to a medical examination, which resulted in the rejection of 6 per cent of the soldiers at Valcartier. And all were vaccinated, or were supposed to be. Theoretically, the triple shots for typhoid and smallpox were voluntary because of Hughes's refusal to make anything mandatory about overseas service. But the reality was much different, as the medical officer of Montreal's 13th (Royal Highlanders of Canada) Battalion frankly told the assembled troops: "You can't be forced into this, it's purely voluntary, but you damned well can't go to war without it. Take your choice!"[43] Still, some men managed to slip through untreated, or only partially so, including Pte. Harold Peat of the 9th Battalion. After suffering through the first inoculation, the little guy from Edmonton "resolved that one was more than enough for me. German bullets could not be worse, I thought."[44] Not until March 1916 were vaccinations made mandatory for Canadians headed overseas.

Private Peat's independent thinking was common among these Canadians. They proved it the night they burned down the tent that served as a theatre. Enraged by the "exorbitant" prices charged for "ancient and poor" movies,[45] angry soldiers cut the ropes, and the tent collapsed. As the canvas slowly settled to the ground, it somehow caught fire, and Valcartier's only theatre went up in flames.[46] The incident illustrates, perhaps better than anything, the spirit of the men. "There was a tremendous keenness in the quality about the old first crowd," recalled the young gunner, Sgt. Fred Fish. "Morale, or whatever you'd like to call it, was very high." Victor Trowles of the 4th (Central Ontario) Battalion agreed: "I never met that kind of spirit in any conglomeration of men, never."[47]

That spirit, of course, had to be controlled. Discipline is essential in an army; it is the only quality that separates it from an armed mob. While there were considerable numbers of South African War veterans at Valcartier, as well as many long-time members of the militia, to whom military traditions and formalities were second nature, discipline was unknown to most of these citizen-soldiers. Men used to the easy camaraderie of the logging camp or the threshing gang did not take as easily to discipline – and the ranks, the endless saluting, and the bellowed orders that went with it – as did the products of a more hierarchical society like Britain itself. Canadian soldiers – like Australians – were to be a sore trial, in this respect, to the more old-fashioned style of British officer.

"When we joined up," recalled the 7th (British Columbia) Battalion's Pte. James Chambers, "we'd go to the colonel and say, 'say, Bub, when do we eat?' something of that kind, you see. We always got into difficulty through not knowing what we were supposed to be doing." But the contingent eventually acquired a reasonably high standard of discipline, according to Company Sgt.-Maj. Charles Price of the 14th Battalion:

> Considering the heterogeneous state of the units in the Division and the fact that so many men had no training, the surprising thing wasn't that there was a lack of discipline, but that there wasn't far more. Of course, what you've got to remember was that the worst threat you could make to a man was that he'd be sent home, and I think that was the best maintainer of discipline there was.[48]

The Canadians could never hope to measure up to British professional-army standards of spit and polish. One of the first senior officers to realize this, if reluctantly, was the Second Brigade's Colonel Currie, a stickler for proper saluting. Currie noted that the concept of discipline "in European armies, where all classes were brought up with the respect for rank amounting almost to veneration," was "totally foreign" to Canadians who, he said, "were unaccustomed to showing respect or deference to anyone who could not stand firmly on his own two feet without the artificial support of wealth or titles."[49] Currie's own view was that "discipline is simply the self-control which makes you do the right thing at all times."[50] Unfortunately, the Canadians at Valcartier were sometimes unable to meet even Currie's relaxed definition of discipline.

No one had a bigger adjustment to make than the handful of Native Indians with the contingent. Because warriors had "prestige and status in traditional Indian society," many had enlisted to "assert their manhood." Now they were undergoing culture shock. Not only was the regimentation of army life totally foreign to them, but they were expected to adopt the white man's ways of doing everything. Many Natives had brought with them lucky charms – crucifixes, rosary beads, complete sets of buckskin clothes, and, in the case of a Blood Indian from Alberta, a complete head-dress. The army was able to make few concessions to what it saw as bizarre eccentricities of this sort.[51]

One Native they should not have laughed at was Francis Pegahma-gabow. The twenty-three-year-old from the Parry Island Band amused his white colleagues by spending his spare time decorating his tent with painted emblems such as the deer, his clan's symbol. He also had in his possession a medicine bag, given him by an elder before he departed, to bring him good luck. Private Pegahmagabow undoubtedly believed that with the help of the medicine bag he would survive this war – as, indeed, he did – but he could not have known that he would emerge as the war's most-decorated Native soldier, winning the Military Medal and two bars at Mount Sorrel, Passchendaele, and Amiens. And his exploits as a sniper would be legendary. His comrades in the 1st (Western Ontario) Battalion called him Peg, but none could have imagined that this soft-spoken Native was probably the most dangerous man in the entire Canadian army.[52]

The officers, too, had a lot of learning to do, and Victoria's Arthur Currie was no exception. Although a long-time militiaman who had held every rank save that of sergeant, Currie had no combat experience and had never before commanded more than the few hundred men in the 50th Gordon Highlanders; now, he was in charge of a brigade of more than four thousand. Aware that his "every move was scrutinized and reported on," Currie claimed that he "never left the camp once after having reached it. My hours were always from 5.30 A.M. to 11.30 or 12 midnight." He prided himself on being "the hardest working brigadier in camp," believing that only through total devotion to duty could he compensate for his inexperience.[53] He later admitted:

> I doubted myself. I knew that the routine would prove simple enough. One knew it already or could learn it from books. But I knew that was not all – that the rest, which was the greater part, was not to be learned from any book or at second hand from the experience of any other man. I had to find it out for myself and master it if I could.[54]

Currie's dedication paid impressive dividends. "He had good administration; he had *order*," commented the contingent's artillery commander, Colonel Burstall, and Lt.-Col. Herbert Kemmis-Betty, a British officer who served as Currie's brigade-major, noted that he "was always on the training ground" and "studied closely, not only his officers but the NCOs of the brigade. He knew he had to trust them to lead and he wanted to make certain as to their makeup."[55] Prime Minister Borden met Currie for the first time when he addressed the Second Brigade at Valcartier in mid-September, and later wrote: "I was impressed by Currie's reply. He spoke with evident emotion, with apt expression and in thorough appreciation of the duty that lay before him and his men. From the first he was an outstanding commander among the Canadians."[56] Similarly, the Duke of Connaught, a field-marshal in the British army, commented of Currie: "I felt convinced he would be a very suitable man to command a brigade and I was delighted when I heard he was to be given one."[57]

The governor-general, who in those days enjoyed a much more active role, was having plenty of his own problems by this point. He and Hughes were barely on speaking terms, which doubtless suited the militia minister. Contending that Hughes was "mentally off his base," the duke fumed to the Colonial Office that his advice was "seldom taken."[58] Prime Minister Borden was unsympathetic, later pointing out in his memoirs that the governor-general "failed to realize that his status and powers as Commander-in-Chief in Canada, under the British North America Act, were purely nominal."[59] Privately, he admitted that Hughes was a perplexing individual. "On matters which touch his insane egotism he is quite unbalanced," the prime minister told his diary. "On all other matters able and sometimes brilliant."[60] Publicly, Borden praised Hughes's achievements to date: "I venture to say that the organization and arrangement of Valcartier Camp has not been excelled in any part of our Empire since the commencement of this war," he declared after his first visit in early September.[61]

Hughes liked nothing better than to show off his contingent, and he staged three reviews in September. The first, on Sunday the sixth, took place in a downpour that drenched troops and spectators alike, but perfect weather graced the other two, on Monday the fourteenth and Sunday the twentieth. The reviews were not welcomed by officers more concerned with the fighting condition of their units. A twenty-six-year-old artillery captain from Hamilton, Harry Crerar, believed that the spectacles were purely "for Sam Hughes' benefit and for moving picture operators. A damn nuisance and a waste of time."[62] The final review attracted the governor-general – in full military uniform – and the prime minister, along with several thousand excited civilians from Toronto, Ottawa, and Montreal, mothers and fathers and brothers and sisters – not to mention sweethearts – of the volunteers, brought in by special trains. Borden, dressed for the occasion in a three-piece tweed suit topped by a black bowler hat, considered this martial display "very good,"[63] and in his stirring speech Montreal's Canon Scott declared that "we are fighting not only for Canada, England, and the Empire, but for the greater, loftier cause of liberty."[64]

A young gunner got into trouble at one of these reviews. Twenty-seven-year-old Andrew McNaughton, a McGill-educated electrical engineer who had spent several years in the militia in Montreal, was engaged to Mabel Weir of that city. Eager to see her handsome and athletic fiancé, Mabel was in the crowd that attended the 6 September review, and Major McNaughton was reprimanded "for grinning and dipping my sword at you," he wrote her the following day. "It was worth the breaking of discipline to catch your wave and smile." Mabel's mother opposed their marriage on the grounds that Andy might be killed or maimed overseas, so the love-struck couple eloped on the seventeenth. They were married by a rural priest, and McNaughton, unable to obtain leave for a honeymoon, installed his bride at the luxurious Chateau Frontenac in Quebec City, while he returned to Valcartier.[65]

It was left to Prime Minister Borden to make the most important decision about the contingent. At the War Office's request, the Canadians were to be sent to England as soon as possible, in order to complete their training under the watchful eyes of British professionals. The problem was, however, that Valcartier now held 35,800 troops, almost twice the number needed for a front-line division.[66] On 21 September, at a conference in Hughes's brick bungalow in the heart of the camp, the prime minister announced that everyone who was medically fit would be dispatched overseas. The reasons were "obvious," he explained.

> These men have come forward with great earnestness and enthusiasm and have spent some weeks at Valcartier in training and in preparation. The numbers assembled, while greatly exceeding the strength of the force at first proposed . . . will to a considerable extent be necessary for the purpose of reinforcements which from time to time will be required.[67]

Borden certainly made Sam Hughes a happy man. The prime minister recalled that his militia minister "suddenly broke down and sobbed audibly. He presently explained his emotions as joy and relief; he had been, he told me, agonized by the thought of a selection for which he would be responsible and which he must determine." Borden dismissed the display

as another example of the minister's "extremely emotional temperament."[68]

Borden's decision, although well meant, upset the embarkation plan
that had been implemented only four days earlier. Twenty-five vessels had
already been chartered, based on a contingent of 25,000 men; the change
meant that approximately 31,200 troops and 7500 horses would be
shipped to England.

Hughes stepped into the breach. Assuming responsibility for the
embarkation, he looked to his good friend, William Price, the man who
had worked a near-miracle in creating Camp Valcartier. Hughes named
Price director-general of embarkation and gave him a deadline of 28
September. Colonel Price accepted the challenge, but then discovered that
he had been given no staff to help him meet it; he fumed that "apparently
the embarkation of his force was considered a matter of little importance
and much ease."[69] To his relief, Price soon acquired a small staff and a
civilian assistant, A.J. Gorrie.

"Chaos reigned supreme." That is how Gorrie described the embarkation of the first contingent from Quebec City. "In the first place, no one
had any idea of what was to be loaded on the vessels, and we had to
exercise our own judgment in a great measure, taking into consideration
the space in the holds of the vessels in port, and the advice we had of the
available space . . . in nearly every instance was incorrect."[70]

Equipment and supplies were loaded first, and Price and Gorrie were
somewhat surprised to learn that, although an embarkation plan was in
place, nothing had been done. For example, the Red Star liner *Lapland* –
at 18,694 tons, the biggest ship to accompany the contingent – had arrived
in Quebec on the morning of 16 September but, according to Gorrie, "not
a pound of freight was put into her hold" until the twenty-third: a whole
week was thus wasted. Even when loading commenced, it was often done
in what Gorrie called "a most incompetent manner."[71] Few vessels ended
up with their allotted cargoes. The holds of many were smaller than
expected, and the hatchways of most were too narrow to accommodate
the contingent's motor vehicles. Room also had to be found for a considerable quantity of nonmilitary supplies, notably a large shipment of flour, a
gift from Canada to the mother country. What happened to artillery
exemplified the confusion. The militia department had sensibly decreed
that each of the contingent's 18-pounder field guns had to be accompanied
by its own stock of 1500 shells, but these orders did not arrive until the
guns had already been loaded and half the ships had sailed. The ammunition had to be ferried to those vessels by tugboat.

The infantry, too, played a game of musical ships. Marching through the streets of Quebec City singing "O Canada," "Tipperary," and "Auld Lang Syne," the troops began boarding their assigned vessels on Friday, 25 September. The 8th (90th Winnipeg Rifles) Battalion's troubles were typical. The battalion, 1161 strong, boarded the Canada Steamship Line's *Bermudian*. The ship's documents indicated that it could handle that number of troops with ease. In truth, it could accommodate only half, and the 8th Battalion had to disembark wearily and transfer to the larger *Lapland*. *Bermudian* later sailed with 562 men, most of them members of Lord Strathcona's Horse.[72]

Despite such inefficiency, the embarkation was almost complete by Thursday, 1 October, when thirty transports had been loaded. A miscellaneous assortment of supplies was placed on the late-arriving *Manhattan*, which sailed independently of the convoy on the fifth. "Not a single package of any kind belonging to the Expeditionary Force," Price's assistant A.J. Gorrie wrote with pride, "was left on hand when the *Manhattan* sailed."[*][73] There were slightly more horses than anticipated – 7679 – and slightly fewer men – 30,617. Less than a third of the troops in that first force were Canadian-born; nearly two-thirds had been born in Britain or elsewhere in the Empire. The total included 762 Americans.[74]

While the ships of the convoy drifted at anchor, one man was making a startling confession. On board *Lapland*, Colonel Currie of the Second Brigade was writing to a friend and colleague in Victoria, Sam Matson, admitting to a white-collar crime that would haunt him for the rest of his life. In the course of his unsuccessful real estate speculations in the British Columbia capital, Currie had dipped into regimental funds to avert personal bankruptcy. He had defrauded his militia regiment out of $10,883.34, government money that was supposed to be spent on the purchase of new uniforms. Currie, holding a lot of near-worthless property, could not repay the debt immediately, and realized that if this scandal came to light, "the truth is I would have to go back to Victoria." Asking Matson to keep the matter "confidential," the colonel begged his friend to arrange for time to allow him to replace the missing money.[75]

Currie would have been appalled to learn what Matson did next. He sent the letter to, of all people, the prime minister. "I do not wish to encourage crime," Matson wrote in a covering letter, "but I believe that Currie's is a case for generous treatment and I ask you as a special favour to do your best to prevent an investigation until this poor unfortunate fellow has been given the chance he asks for."[76] Others were soon writing

---

*The cost of chartering the thirty-one transports came to $3,363,240.42 (Duguid, Appendix 182).

the prime minister, too. One anonymous letter, demanding to know when Currie would "be brought to the bar of justice," charged that he "is crooked as very many people in Victoria know, and this latest crime, now known to all Victoria, comes as a natural sequence to a career of intrigue, underhand dealing, and actual crime."[77] None of that was true, but it was clear that Currie left himself vulnerable to influential enemies, if not potential prosecution.

For the time being, nothing happened. Prime Minister Borden took no action, and neither did the militia department. Sam Matson tried to raise the money as a favour to Currie, but failed in Victoria's straitened economic circumstances. So, with that skeleton stashed somewhat carelessly in his closet, Currie prepared to leave Canada, along with the rest of the contingent.

It was an unforgettable moment when, one by one, the transports weighed anchor and set off down the St. Lawrence. Toronto's Lieut. Ian Sinclair, now a member of the 13th (Royal Highlanders of Canada) Battalion, later wrote:

> It was a memorable sight . . . when we finally got away, the great ships slipping their moorings one-by-one and drifting downstream through the dusk, bands playing on most of the ships and the pipes playing on ours in a manner that sent thrills of excitement through every man on board. Cheer after cheer kept coming from the crowded shores and we on the ships answered with one long continuous cheer and songs innumerable. If they live to be a thousand years, there wasn't a man on board that night that will ever forget the impression it made on him.[78]

The first destination of the thirty grey-painted ships was Gaspé Bay. It was an appropriately ironic choice of locations, for it was here, in 1534, that Jacques Cartier landed, erected a cross, and took possession of this new land in the name of the King of France. Now the Canadians were on their way to France, to help Cartier's descendants drive out the invaders of their homeland.

No one should have been surprised to see Sam Hughes here. Renting a launch in Quebec City, the minister had followed the convoy in order to wish his beloved contingent a proper farewell. As his boat weaved its way among the transports, Hughes smiled and waved. His appearance caused some anxious moments for the officers on one ship, *Athenia* (Canada's first U-boat casualty in the next world war), which a Quebec benefactor had supplied with beer, in direct contravention of Hughes's orders that the convoy must be "dry." The ministerial launch veered away from *Athenia*, to the immense relief of the troops lined up to receive their ration of the illicit beverage.[79]

Hughes had a more important mission. Intending to inspire the troops, he delivered to each ship copies of his pamphlet, *Where Duty Leads*. The purple prose was vintage Hughes:

> Soldiers! The world regards you as a marvel. Within six weeks you were at your homes, peaceful Canadian citizens. Since then your training camp has been secured. . . . You have been perfected in rifle shooting and today are as fine a body – Officers and Men – as ever faced a foe. The same spirit as accomplished that great work is what you will display on the war fields of Europe. There will be no faltering, no temporizing – the work must be done. The task before us six weeks ago seemed Herculean – but it has been successfully accomplished. So following the same indomitable spirit, you will triumph over the common enemy of humanity.[80]

The effect of these windy words fell somewhat short of Hughes's intended mark. They "fairly made our ears burn!" noted Lieutenant Sinclair,[81] and Prime Minister Borden just shook his head at his militia minister's oratory. "It did not enhance his reputation," Sir Robert wrote, "and indeed excited no little mirth in various quarters."[82]

Yet Hughes can perhaps be forgiven. His pamphlet expressed his justifiable pride in raising and equipping the largest armed force Canada had ever assembled, with no precedents on which to proceed – although he undoubtedly exaggerated his role when he told the prime minister's wife of his "perfect arrangements" for the contingent. The drawback was that this success, as historian Ronald Haycock notes, "reinforced Hughes' tendency to think himself infallible and indispensable to the war effort."[83] For an egomaniac like Hughes, such a dose of self-importance could, and would, prove fatal to his career.

Although Hughes was happy with the convoy carrying the contingent, he was most upset with the British warships assigned to guard it. The escort comprised four light cruisers belonging to the Royal Navy's 12th Cruiser Squadron, under Rear-Admiral Sir Rosslyn Wemyss. Hughes took one look and wired his prime minister: "Escort altogether inadequate," he complained, "should increase strength." His views were relayed via the governor-general to the Admiralty in London. There, naval authorities hastily assured the Canadian government that two battleships, *Glory* and *Majestic*, would join the escort en route, as would one of Britain's newest and fastest ships, the battlecruiser *Princess Royal*. But such was the navy's concern about lax Canadian security that word of *Princess Royal* was withheld. Not even Admiral Wemyss was told.[84]

Wemyss was himself displeased with the convoy's escort arrangements. Like most senior British naval officers at this stage of the war, he opposed the convoy concept, believing that it offered a tempting target for German surface raiders and "that the Admiralty were taking too great risks in transporting these troops in such a manner." He contended that a fast enemy cruiser, attacking at night, could have inflicted devastating damage with impunity. "None of my old tubs had sufficient speed to chase off such an enemy. . . . I consider that under the circumstances the risks were not justifiable." Wemyss argued that it would have been better for each transport to sail separately and at top speed, and rendezvous with guard ships at various points along the way.[85]

These concerns notwithstanding, the convoy sailed at 3 P.M. on Saturday, 3 October. It took three hours to clear Gaspé Bay. Once in the Gulf of St. Lawrence, the transports formed into three columns, each headed by a British cruiser, with the fourth cruiser stationed at the rear. Steaming at ten knots, the speed of the slowest ship, the convoy quickly disappeared into the gathering gloom. Ahead lay the 2504-mile journey to England.

Tragically few of these thirty thousand Canadians would make the return trip. And within just seven months, 20 per cent of them would be wounded, missing, or dead.

"What Terrible Weather"

It was the largest armed force that had ever crossed the Atlantic. When joined on 6 October by the little *Florizel*,* carrying the battalion-sized Newfoundland contingent, the convoy totalled thirty-two transports. Besides the thirty carrying Canadians, one ship was transporting the 2nd Lincolnshire Regiment, which had been relieved of its garrison duties in Bermuda by the Royal Canadian Regiment. Altogether, there were 32,330 soldiers and 7011 sailors in the convoy.[1]

The escort was strengthened en route, as planned. The same day that *Florizel* arrived, HMS *Glory*, a battleship, and the cruiser *Lancaster*, took up their positions, although *Lancaster* departed two days later. On 10 October another battleship, *Majestic*, appeared, along with one of the Royal Navy's best battlecruisers, *Princess Royal*.

Two days later *Princess Royal* provided one of the trip's most memorable moments. At twenty-two knots, the 27,000-ton warship steamed past the convoy with flags flying and its band playing "O Canada" and "The Maple Leaf Forever." It was "a thrilling sight," according to Wally Bennett, on board the transport *Scandinavian*, which carried his prairie battalion, the 10th. Private Bennett, the Calgary accountant who could not recall precisely why he had enlisted, had another reason for celebrating. He turned twenty that day.[2]

The powerful escort went untested. The journey to England was uneventful, aside from scattered sightings of unidentified ships on the horizon and the rescues of a couple of men who fell, or jumped, over-

---

*The 3081-ton *Florizel* had six months earlier been deeply involved in calamity as one of the ships in the great Newfoundland sealing tragedy that saw seventy-eight men left to freeze on the ice floes. Making several trips across the Atlantic to deliver young Newfoundlanders to their deaths in places with strange-sounding names like Gallipoli and the Somme, *Florizel*, too, failed to survive the war. In February 1918 the ship ran aground during a storm on the Newfoundland coast, with the loss of ninety-four lives.

board. The weather co-operated, too. "The sea treated us very nicely throughout the trip," remarked the 13th Battalion's Lieutenant Sinclair, on board the Cunard liner *Alaunia*, "and to my surprise and delight, I wasn't an atom sea-sick."[3] Indeed, very few Canadians suffered from the landlubbbers' ailment, and "20,000 boxes of a secret remedy for sea-sickness" were not needed.[4]

The twelve days at sea passed pleasantly. "We had a beautiful voyage," commented the 1st (Western Ontario) Battalion's Lieut. Donald Douglas.[5] There were isolated complaints about the quality of the food on some ships, and the supply of cigarettes ran dangerously low, resulting in a thriving black-market trade. Fatigues such as hosing down the decks, lectures, and physical exercise kept the troops busy during the day, and at night they were entertained by sports and concert parties; the primary purpose of these activities was to keep the men out of trouble. "The daily parades, sports and amusements were not real exercise," Lieutenant Sinclair noted in his diary, "but contrived to give us huge appetites, with the result that we all took on no end of weight."[6]

Senior officers took their tasks more seriously. The commander of the 2nd (Eastern Ontario) Battalion, Lt.-Col. David Watson – in peacetime, the saturnine managing director of the Quebec City *Chronicle* – commented: "Still studying hard, with view of getting in every way proficient for the big responsibilities ahead."[7]

One of the more successful in this regard was Maj. Andy Mc-Naughton, the Montrealer who had eloped at Valcartier. A brilliant scientist, he had obtained his master's degree in electrical engineering at McGill, where he had been exposed to such eminent instructors as economist-humorist Stephen Leacock and Ernest Rutherford, a physicist who later won the Nobel Prize for his theory of radioactivity. "If war had not broken out in 1914," surmised one of his colleagues at school, "Andy McNaughton, instead of becoming a general, would have become the most eminent engineer in Canada."[8] Now, as a gunner who was "ahead of his time," he composed and delivered a series of lectures on the use of 18-pounders in close support of the infantry in combat. Serious, slender, moustachioed, McNaughton held views that reflected his prewar interest "in trying to improve gunnery in every way I could." So sound were McNaughton's shipboard lectures that they formed the basis of Canadian gunnery tactics throughout the war.[9]

For many Canadians, the worst part of the trip was something none of them had any control over. Exaggerated reports of British and French victories seemed to make the days agonizingly long, as Pte. James Chambers of the 7th (British Columbia) Battalion recalled:

The thing that bothered us mostly going over was that every day we'd get messages that there was another half-million Germans taken prisoners and we pleaded with the captain to please speed up a bit before they were all used up. We were sure the war would be finished before we got there.[10]

The weather finally broke just off the English coast. Late on 13 October, a northerly gale combined with heavy seas and rain to make the final few hours terribly uncomfortable. "Roughest day of passage, wind blowing 60 miles an hour," observed Colonel Currie of the Second Brigade, who as a Victorian must have been used to judging winds over water.[11] The 2nd Battalion's Colonel Watson added: "A good thing we are so near England, as this would be a snorter a bit farther out."[12]

While the transports rolled and pitched off the coast, the Admiralty was making a last-minute change in plan. The convoy's destination had already been switched several times: Liverpool, the original choice, was ruled out because of congestion in the Mersey; Southampton was then selected, but a submarine scare in the English Channel provoked another substitution, this time Devonport. The War Office protested, and as late as 10 October, Southampton was restored as the port of disembarkation for the Canadians. But by the evening of the thirteenth, reports of German U-boats in the area again deterred the naval authorities, who ordered Admiral Wemyss to bring the convoy into Plymouth.

The first ships pulled into Plymouth Sound at 7 A.M. on Wednesday, 14 October. The honour of being the first to enter went to the transports *Alaunia* and *Montreal*, escorted by the cruiser *Diana*. Thirty-six hours later, the Admiralty was informed that the entire convoy had been safely secured in the Sound.

The Canadians received a rousing welcome. Colonel Currie, aboard the liner *Lapland*, which arrived on the afternoon of the fourteenth, remarked on the "people lining the Hoe and cheering lustily" as the ship passed by that piece of land associated with Naval heroes from Sir Francis Drake onward. There was no let-up in subsequent days, noted Currie, as "crowds of people sailed around [the] harbor in small steamers – mostly side-wheelers, cheering and waving handkerchiefs."[13]

Unprecedented publicity greeted the newcomers. The Plymouth *Western Morning News* editorialized on the twelfth:

To Canada belongs the immortal distinction of sending the first contingent of Dominion troops to war. Canada has always been foremost in great imperial movements, and in advance of the empire's honour. . . . The Canadian contingent will in battle prove themselves worthy of the traditions of their race and the Dominion. May the Maple Leaf distinguish itself in many battles.

"Nothing like the Canadian contingent," commented *The Times* of London, "has been landed in this country since the time of William the Conqueror." It was a comment to give pause to every Canadian soldier. First Lord of the Admiralty Winston Churchill cabled his own Churchillian greetings: "Canada sends her aid at a timely moment. The conflict moves forward and fiercer struggles lie before us than any which have yet been fought."[14]

One man who was not impressed was Germany's Kaiser Wilhelm II. When informed of the arrival of the thirty Canadian troopships, he reportedly sneered: "They will go back in thirty rowboats!"[15]

Standing on the quay to meet the contingent was its commanding officer, Lt.-Gen. Edwin Alderson, a thirty-six-year veteran of the British army. At fifty-five, General Alderson was "a kind, gentle, little man" with piercing dark eyes, smooth hair brushed straight back and a fashionably enormous moustache.[16] A fox-hunting enthusiast, Alderson had commanded Canadians in the South African War, a factor that was not unimportant in his selection to command the Canadian Division.

Selecting a commander had proved to be a lengthy and involved process. Alderson had not been Sam Hughes's first choice. That distinction belonged, not surprisingly, to Sam Hughes. Prime Minister Borden had long believed that the militia minister would go overseas "if convinced that he would command [the] Canadian division . . . and be in [the] fighting line."[17] And Hughes publicly admitted, in mid-August, that he might "lead the boys – I may do that yet, I am not sure. If I can possibly manage it I shall cast politics to the winds and go to the front."[18] Fortunately for all concerned, Lord Kitchener put an end to the discussion when he declared that it would be a "mistake" to let Hughes leave his political post.[19]

The search for a suitable commander ensued. The War Office proffered the names of three Canadian officers serving in the British army, but none was deemed sufficiently experienced. Three British officers were then proposed: Lt.-Gen. the Earl of Dundonald, who had served in Canada in the early 1900s, Maj.-Gen. Sir Reginald Carew, and Maj.-Gen. Edwin Alderson. Hughes considered Alderson the "best qualified by far," and on 5 September Kitchener decided that "as the Canadian Government show a preference for General Alderson to command the Canadian Division, I am glad to be able to designate him for that command."[20] The announcement was made on the twenty-fifth, the appointment to take effect on the day the contingent arrived in England. Alderson was also promoted to lieutenant-general.

Alderson was a popular choice. Soon afterward, former newspaper editor Colonel Watson of the 2nd Battalion wrote approvingly in his diary:

> Our General is a great soldier & his remarks of the other day – "A cheery word & a happy smile" – to brush away any feelings of complaint, is the right feeling to have, & he shows by his example, the right spirit throughout. He doesn't ask anyone to do anything that he won't do himself. I think he has won them all over already.[21]

Although Alderson would prove to be a mediocre combat commander – "His best friends will not claim that he was a genius," one Canadian officer later commented[22] – he was the ideal choice for the chore of whipping the Canadian contingent into a coherent and effective fighting force.

Also awaiting the contingent in England was none other than Militia Minister Hughes. "Sam is reported to be here!" remarked Lt.-Col. John Creelman, the Montreal lawyer who commanded the 2nd Field Artillery Brigade. "Surely," he added with detectable sarcasm, "Canada is not safe without him!"[23]

Such a comment was typical of the prevailing feelings about Hughes. Few authorities, on either side of the Atlantic, were excited about his first wartime visit to Britain, which he had suggested to Prime Minister Borden as soon as the Canadian convoy had departed. "This proposal did not arouse our enthusiasm," Borden later wrote of his cabinet's response. "Finally we consented, but not before I had given him grave warning that he must control his temperament and have no friction with the authorities on the other side."[24] Hughes readily agreed to go overseas in an "unofficial capacity for a holiday."[25] In Hughes's absence, John Douglas Hazen, the fisheries minister, looked after the militia department, which he discovered was being run in what he called a "most unbusiness-like and irregular" fashion.[26]

Meanwhile, Hughes had hurried to New York to catch a fast ship. Before departing on 7 October, he unabashedly told the American press that Canada would soon have 50,000 men, "good men, the best in the world," at the front, and that he could easily supply another "500,000 picked men." He went on: "This number will not be required from us, however, nor anything like this number, but they are available. Why, we have been turning men away from the recruiting offices – good men, too."[27]

His arrival in England was no less brash. Stepping ashore at Liverpool on the seventeenth, he told the assembled reporters that the Canadian contingent now disembarking at Plymouth contained the best soldiers the dominion had to offer, adding that "nothing finer ever left the shores of Canada."[28]

The British, for the most part, went out of their way to treat Hughes with kid-gloves. The colonial secretary, Lewis Harcourt, wrote: "I am keeping on the best possible terms with him and hope that he will return to Canada shortly in a fairly good temper." Prime Minister Borden did his bit by granting Hughes something he had long sought, – promotion to the rank of major-general. During his brief stay in Britain, General Hughes revelled in the spotlight by giving a series of speeches, in which he promised that Canada could supply anywhere from 70,000 to 300,000 more men for the cause.[29]

According to legend, in the course of this visit Hughes clashed with Lord Kitchener. At six foot two, with a moustache to match, the war secretary cut a formidable figure. After conducting countless campaigns in the far-flung corners of the Empire in the late nineteenth century, the sixty-four-year-old Kitchener was a legend in his own time. His fierce face adorned recruiting posters – "Your country needs YOU" – all over the United Kingdom. ("He is not a great man," British prime minister Herbert Asquith said of Kitchener. "He is a great poster.")[30]

Hughes, of course, was not the type to be intimidated by anyone, and a confrontation might have been expected when these two powerful personalities met. While visiting the War Office, Hughes supposedly learned from Kitchener that the Canadian contingent would be broken up. Their conversation reportedly went something like this:

KITCHENER: Hughes, I see you have brought over a number of men from Canada; they are of course without training and this would apply to their officers; I have decided to divide them up among the British regiments; they will be of very little use to us as they are.

HUGHES: Sir, do I understand you to say that you are going to break up these Canadian regiments that come over? Why, it will kill recruiting in Canada.

KITCHENER: You have your orders, carry them out.

HUGHES: I'll be damned if I will.[31]

Hughes stormed out of Kitchener's office and into mythology as the man who kept the Canadians together, now and for the rest of the war.

However, the story is rooted in a misunderstanding. As early as 26 August, the War Office had assured Ottawa that "the Canadians will most probably be used as organized and be sent in a complete division."[32] The British intention to keep the Canadian Division intact was underlined by Alderson's promotion to lieutenant-general, which made him the highest-ranking divisional commander in the British Expeditionary Force. (A division was normally commanded by a major-general.) It is true that the British planned to break up the Canadians on their arrival in France, but for training purposes only, which is what transpired in February and March 1915.

While Hughes was fighting imaginary battles with the British, the Canadian contingent began disembarking at Plymouth. The Admiralty had expected it to take six days. It took nine, and then several additional weeks to reunite the various units with their equipment because, in most cases, they had sailed separately: the contingent was now paying the price for the chaos and confusion in Quebec City. It was easiest to stockpile the miscellaneous material on the docks in Plymouth and the nearby facilities of Devonport and Amesbury and then ship it all to Salisbury Plain, where the Canadians were in training and where everything could be sorted out.

Trouble dogged the Canadians in other ways. Watching the disorganized disembarkation was a British colonel, J.F.C. Fuller, later famous as a tank-warfare theorist and military historian. Shaking his head in disbelief, Colonel Fuller felt that the men in the ranks would be good enough after six months of training, but only "if the officers could be all shot."[33] The sentiment soon gained wide acceptance "that the Canadian troops carried their officers as mascots."[34]

Then, too, expectations of the Canadians were exceedingly high. As Maj. Arthur Kirkpatrick of Toronto's 3rd Battalion noted on his arrival, "the papers say so many kind things of Canada and of us that we will have difficulty in living up to the high standards they are setting for us."[35] It was difficult, true, and the first Canadians ashore did not even come close to attaining these "high standards." They had, after all, been cooped up on ships for more than two weeks, and now, with plenty of money burning holes in their pockets and Plymouth's public houses enticing them to spend it, and with so many British-born men making "their return to their own country in heroic role,"[36] the potential for drunken, disorderly conduct was very real, and soon realized. The Second Brigade's hard-working Colonel Currie wrote with alarm in his diary just two days after reaching England: "Crude accounts appear in English papers re Canadians." A staff officer was sent ashore to investigate, and when he returned with reports of "a great many drunken officers and men in Plymouth," Currie forbade any of his troops to leave their ships until their turn came to entrain for Salisbury.[37]

But it was too late. The damage had been done, and for the rest of the war Canadians would be generally and popularly considered ill-disciplined, even when their performance on the battlefield contradicted the allegation.

Salisbury Plain is more than a hundred miles northeast of Plymouth, which meant a seven-hour train ride for the men. A tract six miles by fifteen had been acquired years before by the War Office and had been used by the British army for manoeuvres and summer camps. The area reminded one Canadian observer of "the foot-hills of the Rockies near Calgary."[38] Gently rolling, with few trees, the countryside was dotted by isolated farms and quaint, thatched-roof villages, and featured the prehistoric remains at Stonehenge. "A thin turf cropped by grazing sheep grew in the few inches of poor soil overlying impervious chalk";[39] the Canadians were about to become well acquainted with the impervious nature of the chalk.

They were destined to spend sixteen memorable weeks here, from October 1914 to February 1915. It was memorable not for the useful training they undertook – of that, there was precious little – but for the appalling conditions of rain and mud, stemming from one of the worst winters the region had ever experienced. The weather broke on 21 October, while the contingent was still arriving on the plain, and it rained on 89 of the next 123 days; the precipitation doubled the thirty-two-year average. To make matters worse, numerous storms – raw, cold, violent windstorms – flattened the sodden tents occupied by the shivering Canadians. The occasional frost merely compounded the men's misery.

The diary of the 2nd (Eastern Ontario) Battalion's Colonel Watson reveals the former journalist's urge to write, and details the disruption and discomfort of those first few weeks:

30 October: Such rain & mud, I never saw the like.

2 November: What terrible weather. I never saw such rain and mud. . . . The rain at night was worse than I have ever experienced & in my tent, I could not keep dry.

5 November: This is another rotten day. Rain. Rain all the time, & such mud. . . . Cannot do any drill today.

11 November: On Ranges in the afternoon – got soaking wet, & then attended lecture in big mess tent. While there the storm got so bad that

this big marquee was blown down, & our large orderly tent with Regimental papers &c. was also blown down, & in pitch dark, & rain. . . . Fearful night.

13 November: Still raining & most disagreeable. It is a wonder that more of our men are not sick. It is simply heartbreaking. We cannot get a chance to do any good work.

19 November: It was so cold last night that the large tin of water beside me was frozen solid & Harry had to hammer it to break it up, & I washed in the ice. It was fearfully cold drilling all morning. The ground was white all morning. . . . In the afternoon, to add to our miseries, the rain has started again. I never dreamed of such weather.

25 November: Raining again. I never saw such weather & the mud is so bad, sucks your rubbers off.

28 November: Pouring rain again. This is about the limit. The Doctor is complaining about the health of the men. It is really getting serious.

4 December: What a terrible day this is, such rain & such a wind. It is simply awful. All our musketry & other parades are cancelled.

Watson's mood was not improved when, a few days later, he fell off his horse and landed on his sword-handle, injuring his side.[40]

During one particularly violent storm, the wind flattened the 14th (Montreal) Battalion's pay-master's tent just prior to pay parade. "Five shilling notes flew over the plain like white birds over the sea," wrote the chaplain, Frederick Scott, now an honorary major, who had been granted his wish to go overseas. "The men quickly chased them and gathered them up, and on finding them stained with mud thought it unnecessary to return them."[41]

Some had to endure multiple miseries. One such was the artillery's Col. John Creelman, the Montreal lawyer, who described his difficulties in his diary:

It poured last night and this morning Brown (my servant) was drunk and took my feather bed out for airing, leaving it in the rain long enough to get well soaked. He is now under arrest and tomorrow I shall get rid of him for good. This is his third offence and my comfort is suffering.[42]

There seemed to be no end to the rain and the resultant discomfort. According to R.D. Haig of the 6th Battalion from Winnipeg, the Canadians "soon learned that there was only one way to be reasonably comfortable. That was never take your clothes off, because it was much easier to get up in the morning damp-wet than get up in the morning and try to put on cold, damp clothes. So we kept our clothes on."[43] Colonel Creelman agreed:

> No one tries any longer to keep clean and we look like barbarians. Everyone wears rubber coats and caps and we all resemble fishermen. . . . The mud here absolutely beggars description. The main roads . . . are about four inches deep in flowing mud, which is very liquid, while everything else is covered with sticky mud from four to ten inches thick. There are frequent holes, the depth of which is only ascertained after one has stepped into them. . . . However, everybody is cheerful and our English visitors remark that an English regiment would mutiny if it were kept here.[44]

The mud was so bad that it inspired at least one poem:

> In the morn when we arise
> There are but the rainy skies –
>   And the mud.
> Nine inches deep it lies.
> We are mud up to our eyes,
> In our cakes and in our pies
>   There is mud.[45]

Morale remained remarkably high. Capt. D.H.C. Mason of the 3rd (Toronto) Battalion was pleased to recall that his men "never lost their sense of humour. They always understood war was hell and this was hell." Pte. Cuthbert Johnson of the 14th (Montreal) Battalion added: "We were a pretty lively bunch, and we made the best of everything and didn't do too much growling about it."[46]

Still, the situation was causing concern. In December, General Hughes received a warning from his personal representative in England, Col. John Carson, a thirty-year-old insurance executive from Montreal, that Canadian camp conditions were "simply appalling, and in my judgment are bound to have a serious effect on the health and morale of our troops." Appealing to the militia minister's nationalism, Carson cunningly added: "They would have been a thousand times better off in Canada than they are at Salisbury Plains [sic]."[47] Hughes passed this report to the prime minister, who demanded an explanation from the War Office. "I am sorry that Salisbury Plain has got such a bad name in Canada," Lord Kitchener replied soothingly, "but I am glad to be able to inform [you] that not a single complaint was received from either officers or men of the Canadian Contingent."[48]

In spite of Kitchener's bland assurance, action was being taken to deal with what was in fact a very real problem. One possible solution, briefly but seriously considered – and favoured by Colonel Carson – was to ship the Canadians to Egypt, where the contingents from Australia and New Zealand had arrived at the beginning of December. Because of the miseries encountered by the Canadians, the Australians and New Zealanders had been kept in Egypt for the winter, and were thus available for the ill-fated Gallipoli expedition in early 1915. The Canadians were spared a part in that fiasco when the War Office decided to leave them on Salisbury Plain and provide them with ostensibly better living quarters.

Huts had been under construction on the plain since early October. Each of the one-storey, wood-frame buildings could accommodate forty men, but work had lagged due to a labour shortage in England. To speed things up, Canadian working parties were employed on the project. Skilled, experienced carpenters were sought, but few were found. The 5th Battalion's R.L. Christopherson, the former Yorkton bank clerk, volunteered in order to have a change of pace and found himself in colourful company. "Talk about rag-tag and bobtail," Christopherson recollected. "Every unit, when they saw a chance to get rid of their troublesome soldiers, they shipped them off there."[49] Still, steady progress was made, and by 18 December all but one infantry brigade, the First, had been moved into the huts.

Huts seemed a great improvement on rain-sodden, wind-blown tents, but they were no panacea. Capt. Thomas Morrisey of the 13th (Royal Highlanders of Canada) Battalion remembered that "the funny thing was that we got into the huts and the sick rate went up by three and four times. In other words, if we were in a constant state of being wet and cold it didn't affect our health, but when we got into these huts and you sat in front of a hot stove and then went out on parade, you chilled."[50] Indeed, the huts soon resembled sick wards, in the opinion of a 16th (Canadian Scottish) Battalion diarist: "A fearful lot of sickness here in these huts. Flu reigns supreme in the shape of sore heads, sore throats and racking coughs. At night it sounds like hell with all those graveyard coughs around."[51]

Worst of all was an outbreak of meningitis. This highly contagious disease, which affects the brain and spinal column to deadly effect, had first appeared at Valcartier, where four cases had been reported, and three more were discovered en route to England. It was widely rumoured that the epidemic was caused by the typhoid inoculations that had been administered before the contingent left Canada.[52] By the time the Canadians left Salisbury Plain in February 1915, despite frantic treatment by serum, meningitis had claimed twenty-eight lives out of thirty-nine it afflicted.[53] One victim was the 3rd (Toronto) Battalion's chaplain, Capt. G.L. Ingles, who contracted it on New Year's Day while visiting those ill with the disease. Captain Ingles was dead and buried within three days.[54]

The weather was not the sole source of health problems: out of 4000 Canadians hospitalized during this period, 1249 were treated for venereal disease.[55]

To survive at Salisbury required toughness and stamina. "Only native hardihood," notes the official history of the Canadian medical service, "carried the soldiers through that long and desolate winter."[56]

If the conditions took their toll on humans, they were even harder on horses. "A small percentage of animals died of exposure," wrote Lt.-Col. Edward Morrison, the former editor of the Ottawa *Citizen* who now commanded the 1st Field Artillery Brigade, "and by the end of the year they were all very much reduced in condition." Many were "little better than scarecrows," said Morrison, and some were "so weak . . . that they could scarcely pull the guns."[57]

An attempt to reduce their suffering nearly cost one Canadian officer his career. Maj. Andy McNaughton, saddened by the sight of his battery's horses standing hock-deep in slime, ordered his men to cut down some small trees and to spread the branches on the ground around the animals to give them a footing. This contravened strict instructions against chopping down trees on Salisbury Plain, for this was fox-hunting country, and destroying the cover for the foxes was considered damned unsporting, if not sacrilegious. McNaughton was arrested, and a fellow officer warned the major's new wife – just arrived in England, via the ill-fated ocean-liner *Lusitania* – that he "might be sent home." For three days his fate hung in the balance. In the end, common sense prevailed, and McNaughton was allowed to return to his battery with merely a reprimand – a close call for a young man who was one of the best gunners in the Canadian contingent.[58]

It took a royal visit to give the Canadians a brief break in the weather. On 4 November, King George and Queen Mary arrived to inspect the contingent, accompanied by Field-Marshal Lord Roberts,* Lord Kitch-

---

*This proved to be the last public appearance by the eighty-two-year-old Roberts. A legend in his own time, he had previously inspected the Canadians in a driving rainstorm on 24 October, telling them: "I need not urge you to do your best, for I know you will" (Tucker, 11). Ten days after his second visit to the Canadians, he was dead. A holder of the Victoria Cross, Roberts was among the "best generals of the late Victorian era," according to historian Byron Farwell (Farwell *Mr. Kipling's Army*, 50). The short, one-eyed soldier was one of the few British army successes in the South African War, where his exploits earned him an earldom. The entire Empire mourned his passing, and the Canadians provided a small detachment for his funeral at St. Paul's Cathedral in London on 19 November.

ener, George Perley, Canada's acting high commissioner in London, and British Columbia premier Sir Richard McBride. A steady downpour deposited two inches of rain in the three days before the inspection, but it let up just before the arrival of the King and Queen. His Majesty warmly greeted the contingent; its presence, he said, "is of inestimable value both to the fighting strength of my Army and in the evidence which it gives of the solidarity of the Empire."[59]

The Canadians responded with equal warmth. According to the artillery's Captain Crerar, "We cheered with much gusto and received graceful bows from the two of them." This is the same Crerar who had grumbled in his diary the day before that these inspections were "a blasted nuisance . . . and a waste of time."[60]

Queen Mary made a particularly good impression. "What a fine lot of men," she complimented Lt.-Col. John Currie, the Toronto politician who commanded the 15th (48th Highlanders of Canada) Battalion. "And they all look like professional men and students."[61] Walking past the 7th (British Columbia) Battalion, she stopped before Pte. Henry McArthur. "Young man, how old are you?"

"Nineteen, Your Majesty."

"You naughty boy," she replied with a shake of her head and moved on down the line.[62]

Disciplinary problems resurfaced at Salisbury. One battalion commander came up with a novel but effective method of dealing with recalcitrants in his unit. Lt.-Col. Russell Boyle was over six feet tall, broad-shouldered and athletic, a wounded and decorated veteran of the South African War. Now, at thirty-four, the Alberta rancher commanded the 10th (Calgary-Winnipeg) Battalion, which he summoned to the parade ground soon after arriving at Salisbury. Throwing his officer's coat on the ground and rolling up his sleeves, he delivered a tough speech to the assembled ranks:

> Now, I'm the same as you fellows. I'm just an ordinary private, as far as you're concerned. There were four men on that boat [from Canada] who said they'd like to punch the hell out of me. Now, I invite you four men, if you have the guts enough, to come up, and we'll have it out right here.

Not surprisingly, no one accepted the colonel's challenge. If anything, the incident endeared Boyle to his troops. One of them, Pte. Victor Lewis, a twenty-two-year-old former night watchman for the Canadian Pacific Railway, later called Boyle "a wonderful man."[63]

Nevertheless, the Canadians' reputation for indiscipline grew by leaps and bounds. It was clear to all by now that they were falling well short of the spit-and-polish standards of their more respectful British counterparts. This shortcoming, however, did not concern the Canadians. "We didn't come here to salute," they would say defiantly, "we came here to fight."[64] The stories of their lack of respect for authority acquired legendary status, including the following exchange between a British sentry and an approaching figure.

"Who goes there?" challenged the sentry.

"Who the ——— wants to know?"

"Pass, Canadian," sighed the sentry, shrugging his shoulders, "all's well."[65]

But there was more to being a good soldier than throwing snappy salutes. A noncommissioned officer in the 13th (Royal Highlanders of Canada) Battalion addressed the issue in a letter home to Montreal:

> The Canadians as a whole have a frightful name all over the country for bad discipline, but that is earned by not saluting when on leave. But after all these things are not the important part of discipline. What is important is to get orders obeyed and that is done very well indeed.[66]

One problem did demand action. The Canadian camps at Salisbury were "dry"; no liquor was allowed, according to an 1893 militia regulation religiously enforced by the teetotalling Sam Hughes. Within days of the contingent's arrival on the plain, General Alderson was receiving "serious complaints from local authorities" about his men, who would "go to the neighbouring villages, get bad liquor, become quarrelsome and then create disturbances."[67]

Alderson acted quickly: on 19 October he authorized the sale of beer in Canadian canteens in camp. Hughes, who was in England at the time, said nothing publicly, but temperance groups in Canada were not so reticent. Protesting Alderson's "lamentable attitude" towards alcohol, the powerful Women's Christian Temperance Union declared: "Unless our Government can validate its tacit pledge of immunity from drink, can it be expected that Canadian mothers and wives will consent to the enlistment of their sons and husbands even in defence of the Empire's honour and life?"[68]

It took time for the new rules to have a noticeable effect. All Canadian soldiers were, at different times, granted six days' leave, with a free ticket to anywhere in the United Kingdom, and most headed for the larger cities like London, where they fell victim to unaccustomed temptations. Readily available women and alcohol proved irresistible to the farm boys, and the clerks and students and labourers from unsophisticated Canadian cities were no less vulnerable. When Alderson continued to receive "numerous reports . . . of considerable numbers of men being drunk and disorderly in public places of entertainment in London and other towns," he severely curtailed the generous leave arrangements on 6 November.[69] After that, the situation steadily improved; the artillery colonel from Montreal, John Creelman, whose mattress had suffered from the neglect of a drunken batman, observed in December:

> The wet canteen is a Godsend and drinking has been reduced to a minimum. A man who is free to buy a mug of beer a couple of times a day does not try to keep a bottle of whiskey in his tent. Drunkenness has been practically stamped out and offences of all sorts have tended to steadily decrease.[70]

So improved was their behaviour that half of the contingent was allowed six days' leave at Christmas; the other half received the same at New Year's.

The holidays were a difficult period. Many of these young Canadians shared the sentiments of the 13th Battalion's Lieutenant Sinclair, who wrote that it was "the first time that I have ever been away from home" at Christmas.[71] The prevailing homesickness was eased by the restored leave privileges, the hospitality shown by British civilians, and the arrival of sixty thousand parcels from family and friends in Canada. The Duchess of Connaught, the governor-general's wife, at her own expense shipped twelve thousand pounds of maple sugar for distribution among the Canadian troops.[72]

And more Canadians would soon be on their way. The initial outburst of enthusiasm had died down somewhat, but recruiting was continuing at a steady pace across Canada – except in Quebec, where French Canadians, enraged at Sam Hughes's insensitivity, were already refusing to join an English-speaking army. On 6 October, just three days after the first contingent sailed, Hughes offered a second to the War Office in London. Without waiting for a reply, the militia minister dispatched orders to each of the military districts across the country: "A Second Overseas Contingent will be mobilized."[73]

But the British were surprisingly cool to the idea. "As soon as the first contingent arrives and has been examined," the War Office answered on 9 October, "the details of the organization of the new contingent will be carefully considered and communicated to your Government."[74] Not until the end of October did London finally accept the proffered second division, which was formally authorized by Ottawa on 7 November and sent to England in April 1915. In the meantime, Hughes was proclaiming that Canada could easily send many more divisions: "a fifth, a sixth, a tenth or a twentieth."[75]

If Sam Hughes was unhappy, as he must have been, about the disappearance of "dry" camps, he was almost apoplectic with rage over another development. Canadian equipment was being replaced by its British equivalent; by the time the Canadian Division departed for the Continent in February 1915, just about everything they took with them was British-made. British-pattern webbing was replacing the uncomfortable Canadian-made Oliver belt – in spite of Hughes's decision in early 1915 to redesign it – though Canadian troops continued to take it overseas until 1917; all of the first contingent wore webbing into action on the Western Front.[76] Canadian-made boots were also chucked. They literally disintegrated in the mud at Salisbury, and General Alderson flatly refused to use them. Before his division departed for the front, he gave the order that "every man must be in possession of a pair of perfectly serviceable Imperial pattern Army Regulation boots. . . . No Canadian pattern boots are to be taken overseas."[77] The tight-fitting Canadian tunics with stand-up collars gave way to the looser, more comfortable – and better-made – British jackets. Similarly, the MacAdam shield-shovel, brain-child of Hughes's secretary, was abandoned in favour of the British army's entrenching tool. Hughes exploded when he heard that news. Calling the British tool "absolutely useless for any purpose," he declared: "I will not permit this improper interference."[78] His complaints were ignored by the War Office.

The British also replaced all the trucks and wagons the Canadians had brought with them. As Hughes's London representative, Col. John Carson, pointed out, the War Office considered that having five makes of motor vehicles was unacceptable. But Carson was none too pleased with the solution:

> I am more than astonished to find that six English makes of motor lorries were supplied to us. . . . These people beat me! They impressed on me in no uncertain terms that we must positively get down our makes of motor lorries to if possible two, as the question of taking spare parts to the Continent and keeping them in stock was a very serious one indeed, and here they are doing the very thing that we were instructed not to do and doing it to a much greater extent than we had ever dreamt of doing.[79]

Carson's argument overlooked the fact that it was easier to obtain spare parts from England for British-made trucks, than from Canada for North American makes.

Canadian-made wagons suffered the same fate. The switch to British wagons – "real ones," according to one artillery officer[80] – was welcomed by the contingent, but Hughes was irate, insisting for years afterwards "that the Canadian wagons were in every sense better than the English wagons."[81]

It became a familiar refrain. Hughes never forgot or forgave what he considered a slight against Canada and against himself. The only piece of equipment to escape the housecleaning was the Ross rifle, and even its days were numbered. Hughes was still bitter when, more than two years later, he publicly declared: "Our transport, our rifles, our trucks, our shovels, our boots, our clothing, our wagons; those were all set aside and in many cases . . . they were supplanted by inferior articles."[82]

Hughes was hardly in a position to be critical. Not only had he saddled the contingent with shoddy, Canadian-made merchandise – and the infantry would be carrying the unreliable Ross rifle into combat in early 1915 – he had established the beginnings of a bloated, inefficient bureaucracy to oversee Canada's military interests in Britain. The first step was the appointment of the Montreal insurance executive, Colonel Carson, as his "special representative" in London. Carson's vague responsibilities included "certain financial and other questions in connection with the Canadian Contingent."[83] This arrangement confused the British. Normally they would have dealt with George Perley, who, as Canada's acting high commissioner, was the accredited representative of the Canadian government. While Carson worked tirelessly to carve out a niche for himself, Hughes further complicated matters by making other appointments in which responsibilities overlapped and personalities conflicted. The resulting organization – if, indeed, it can be called that – was so chaotic, confusing, and embarrassing that it became a major issue in Hughes's downfall.

The militia minister even managed to leave General Alderson in an administrative limbo. Never before had Canada fielded a formation of this size, and it is remarkable that no one, either in London or in Ottawa, had given much thought to its status within the British army. The War Office simply assumed that the Canadian Division was no different than any other division, and treated it as such. Alderson, on the other hand, quickly realized that it was unique, as was his own position, when he found himself dealing with inquiries and requests from the Canadian government. When he replied to these cables, he was reprimanded by the War Office, which bluntly told him "that direct communication between the General Officer Commanding 1st Canadian Division and the Canadian Civil or Military Authorities in Canada is not permissible." However, a compromise eventually evolved: Alderson was allowed to deal directly with the Canadian government in matters of special concern, while routine business was channelled through the War Office. It was not ideal.[84]

As trivial as it might appear, this development is significant for what it held for future British-Canadian relations. For the time being, difficulties were minimized by the attitude of the Canadians, who proudly considered themselves British and nothing more. However, this feeling would change as the war went on, and Canada would demand, and receive, special consideration in return for its ever-increasing contributions to the Empire's war effort. A Canadian identity, albeit hazy, would be forged on the battlefields of Europe, and its reluctant recognition by the British is what gives the Great War its unusual importance in Canada's growth as a nation.

While the Canadians continued to train, the war proceeded without them. The German juggernaut had by now been halted, and the two sides had settled into static warfare for the winter along the four-hundred-mile-long Western Front, which stretched from neutral Switzerland, across northern France and through the extreme western end of Belgium to the North Sea. The Canadians on Salisbury Plain were aware only of the general situation; as Victoria's Colonel Currie later pointed out, no one in the contingent had detailed knowledge "of actual fighting conditions in France, which could only be guessed at from short press cables of doubtful accuracy."[85]

By the end of 1914, training of the Canadian Division was still far from satisfactory, for rainy, cold conditions continually interrupted manoeuvres and practice schedules. New Year's Day 1915 brought no promise of improvement. The first day of January was, according to Colonel Currie, the "stormiest rainy day I ever saw."[86] The Montreal gunner Colonel Creelman, his mattress presumably now dried out, was still being plagued both by the weather and by incompetent and inebriated help, as he complained in his diary:

> Happy New Years! I mean it although I don't feel like it. It is now 4.15 P.M. and rain has poured down since I got up this morning. My servant got drunk last night, raised a disturbance, allowed the stove in my tent to smoke for four hours until everything in the tent was covered with a layer of lamp-black. My khaki British warm now resembles a black Persian lamb coat. It was simply horrible and I had to send the servant to jail at Devizes for 21 days.[87]

Despite the inauspicious debut, January turned out to be a better month. "The weather has actually cleared up for a couple of days," marvelled young Lieutenant Sinclair of the 13th (Royal Highlanders of Canada) Battalion, "and life around the lines has become almost worth while again. We're getting in lots of work, particularly musketry, and march from two to eight miles to the ranges every day."[88] The infantry staged large-scale manoeuvres, including mock battles, as twenty-two-year-old Pte. Albert Smith of the 3rd (Toronto) Battalion recalled:

> Once during our training in England we had to engage in a sham battle on a huge hill near Salisbury Plains. Little did we know that the farmers had just cleared away their sheep to make ready for our mock exercise. When we arrived, we were ordered to crawl, sprint, and jump down again. The trouble was that the hill was covered with sheep's manure. As we diligently cleaned and scrubbed our uniforms that night we vowed we would never forget what we came to call "The Battle of Lamb Shit Hill."[89]

The infantry also worked to become proficient with their bayonets – "in practising bayonet exercises," read the orders issued the Canadians, "the men must not be opposed to each other with rifles, either with bayonets fixed or unfixed"[90] – and at digging trenches, always being careful to fill them in and replace the turf when finished, like well-trained golfers.

There were, certainly, persistent problems. Limited facilities, which the Canadians had to share with British troops, meant that time on the firing ranges was restricted. Each infantryman fired 155 rounds while at Salisbury and additionally "practised charger-loading and rapid fire with dummy cartridges for ten minutes or more daily."[91] Similarly, the artillery of the Canadian Division had to compete for time and facilities with batteries from six British divisions and was able to fire only a fraction of its allotted ammunition in January.

(The gunners, at least, were more comfortable by now. The Canadian artillery and cavalry had been billeted at the beginning of January in private homes in surrounding villages. The arrangement resulted in many long-term friendships between British civilians and Canadian soldiers, in addition to improving the contingent's public relations. "Everything possible was done by the inhabitants," remarked the war diary of the 2nd Field Artillery Brigade, "to make the men comfortable.")[92]

Moreover, there was an air of unreality about the whole thing. The Canadians – like everyone else, on both sides – were being prepared for the wrong kind of war. Columns of infantry forming into successive waves, standing shoulder to shoulder, then charging with fixed bayonets; horse-drawn artillery limbers careering around the conveniently open country-side; glittering, galloping cavalry swooping across the plain in an irresistible charge – all of these made for sights that stirred the soldiers' blood, veterans and rookies alike. Although this type of training was useful in some ways, such as engendering the necessary discipline with which to conduct a battle and teaching the various arms to co-ordinate their efforts, it was of little value in view of the trench warfare that was evolving on the Western Front, a war in which the machine-gun dominated the battlefield, in which cavalry would have no significant role, in which the artillery seldom moved.

"I know now that we never did train," recalled a Canadian cavalryman, Pte. A.G. Jacobs of Lord Strathcona's Horse. "I didn't know then. We rode around. We knew how to form patrols. We were taught how to charge a battery, but we never had any detailed training."[93] They would have to learn the hard way – in combat.

The Canadians completed their organization as a division in January 1915. In virtually all respects, the division was modelled on the British formation of that period. Two-thirds of its authorized strength of 18,636 was composed of infantry, organized in three brigades, each consisting of four battalions. Each battalion numbered thirty officers and 996 other ranks, organized in four companies.

British indecision had caused considerable confusion for the Canadians. They had organized at Valcartier in eight-company battalions, but on 1 November the War Office ordered them to organize four companies to a battalion. This had no sooner been done than the War Office reversed itself on the seventeenth, and the Canadians reverted to eight-company battalions. On 10 December the British decided that four companies were more practicable; four days later, this was again reversed. At last, on 16 January, the final decision was handed down: the Canadians would go to France in four-company battalions. "I have to start in now & reorganize the Battn," fumed the former Quebec City journalist turned battalion commander, the 2nd's Colonel Watson, who clearly would have liked to fire off a fierce editorial on the subject. "Terrible confusion & discontent owing to these repeated changes."[94]

The artillery was also reorganized. The Canadians had come to England with each field brigade consisting of three six-gun batteries, after scrapping the militia's four-gun units at Valcartier. However, in mid-November, the War Office decreed its preference for four-gun batteries, four to a brigade, a switch that entailed the renumbering of the Canadian batteries and the juggling of unit commanders.

The contingent shed several formations that had accompanied it overseas. One of these was the Canadian Cavalry Brigade, formed on 1 February under the command of a former British cabinet minister, Col. J.E.B. Seely, whose appointment by Lord Kitchener displeased Prime Minister

Borden, who felt that there were capable Canadians who should have filled the position. "I shall see to it," Sir Robert vowed, "that the next Mounted Corps that goes from Canada is placed in command of one of our own men as Brigadier."[95] In any case, the Canadian Cavalry Brigade served under British jurisdiction for most of the war. As part of the Cavalry Corps, the Canadian horsemen would spend the bulk of their time grooming their animals and polishing their swords and saddles, waiting for the dramatic moment when they would charge into battle with pennants flying. Except for isolated incidents, they would have to wait until 1918 – when they discovered to their regret that they had become obsolete.

The Newfoundland contingent had also departed. For a while, the authorities toyed with the idea of breaking up the Newfoundlanders and adding them to Canadian battalions. "Naturally," recalled one of the islanders, "we didn't like that"[96] – a not surprising view, considering that Newfoundland was still a separate colony and would remain so for another thirty-five years. In early December the newly formed Newfoundland Regiment was shipped to Scotland for garrison duty and was later added to the British 29th Division. Ahead lay, among other campaigns, the twin trials of Gallipoli, in 1915, and the Somme, in 1916. The regiment was virtually annihilated in a single day at the Somme. Attacking near Beaumont Hamel on 1 July – a day still mourned on the island – the Newfoundlanders went into action with 801 officers and other ranks; within hours, 710 were dead, wounded, or missing. In early 1918, King George granted the title "Royal" to the Newfoundland Regiment, the only unit to be so honoured during the Great War.

Another departing unit was destined to become one of Canada's most famous regiments. Princess Patricia's Canadian Light Infantry was the brain-child of a Montreal millionaire and militia major, Andrew Hamilton Gault. A McGill-educated veteran of the South African War, thirty-three-year-old Gault had offered on the eve of the war to raise a regiment at his own expense; Ottawa accepted the proposal. At the suggestion of the governor-general's military secretary, Lt.-Col. Francis Farquhar, the PPCLI was composed almost entirely of veterans, making it unique, certainly in Canada and probably in the entire Empire. Of its 1087 officers and other ranks, 87 per cent were British-born; three-quarters had been decorated for valour. With none other than Colonel Farquhar its commanding officer and Major Gault its second-in-command, the PPCLI left Salisbury Plain in the middle of November to join the British 27th Division, arriving in France on 21 December. The men of the PPCLI were thus the first Canadians to reach the front in the Great War.

In addition, one slight change was made in the make-up of the Canadian Division. It occurred in the Second Brigade, where the 6th Battalion was converted to a reserve cavalry regiment, reverting to its famous name, the Fort Garry Horse. In its place came the 10th (Calgary-Winnipeg) Battalion from the Fourth Brigade, which was to remain in England as a reinforcement and training depot. The Second's brigadier, Col. Arthur Currie, vigorously opposed the selection of the 10th Battalion, fearing that his formation's efficiency would be impaired. Expressing a strong preference for the 11th, another prairie battalion, Currie argued that "in no instance has anyone, outside the 10th Battalion, claimed that the 10th was ever the equal of the 11th."[97] But it was to no avail, and the transfer was completed by 21 January.

Currie lost the argument in this case, but he was a winner in most other matters. Having already impressed his superiors at Valcartier, Currie continued the trend at Salisbury. It was hard work, but he thrived on it, as he explained in a letter to his mother in Strathroy, Ontario:

> I believe I'm getting along well. I am working hard and attending close to business. I take little leave and am morning, noon and night on the job. I have been complimented by the general on parade. I want so to act here that you will be proud of me and even my enemies will have cause to respect me. . . . I shall not spare myself, and if a good example is worth anything I shall do my best.[98]

His efforts soon paid off. British regulars attached to the Canadian Division – and there were many, because Canada had a mere handful of trained staff officers when the war began – regarded him highly. "I recognized that here in Currie," remembered Lt.-Col. G.C.W. Gordon-Hall, at divisional headquarters, "is a man who is going to be a great asset to the force." A fellow staff officer, Col. T. Birchall Wood, a thirty-year veteran, concurred:

> Currie from the first was an outstanding figure; by his manner and physical stature he created an atmosphere for himself. His sincerity and forcefulness were marked. . . . In approach he was good-natured, natural, imperturbable. He impressed me at first sight by his cheerfulness in the most depressing circumstance.[99]

Clearly, good things were expected of Currie. Asked in December by the Duke of Connaught to assess the Canadian brigadiers, General Alderson emphatically replied: "Currie is out and out the best."[100] As yet, the possibility of having a Canadian command the Canadians had crossed no one's mind – save Sam Hughes, who would have placed himself at their head if it could have been arranged. But it soon would be under consideration, at the War Office and in Ottawa, because Currie was about to live up to his rave notices where it counted, on the battlefields of France and Flanders.

It mattered not that Currie hardly looked like a soldier. At six-foot-four, the 250-pounder from Victoria had trouble finding uniforms to properly fit his pear-shaped body. Yet this modest look and calm demeanour masked the dreadful secret of his impropriety involving regimental funds back home. The possibility of being discovered and returned to Canada continued to haunt him, even as final preparations were being made to move the Canadian Division to the front. It was, he later wrote, "the last thing I thought of at night and the first thing in the morning."[101]

Throughout January, rumours flew as to the future of the Canadian Division. As early as the twelfth, the 2nd (Eastern Ontario) Battalion's Colonel Watson noted in his diary: "I hear today that we will be in France within 3 weeks."[102] This report, which would prove to be extremely accurate, suited the troops – officers and other ranks alike – just fine. Toronto's D.H.C. Mason, a 3rd Battalion captain, later commented that he found the time spent at Salisbury "very tedious. The general feeling was, 'For heaven's sake, let's get over to France and get into this thing.' "[103]

They would soon get their wish. On 2 February proof of the Division's imminent departure arrived in the form of an announcement: a royal review was scheduled for Thursday the fourth.

King George's inspection was a great success. It was held at Knight Down, within sight of Stonehenge, where the Canadian Division was drawn up in an array that stretched for more than two miles. "It was the most glorious sight I have ever seen," raved Colonel Watson, the former Quebec City newspaperman, "& the Canadians were very rightly congratulated afterwards. . . . It had been raining, but turned out beautiful & fine as the King was inspecting, a Happy augury."[104] His Majesty, accompanied by Lord Kitchener, walked the length of the Canadian alignment, often stopping to talk to various commanding officers. Colonel Creelman, the gunner with the inebriated servants, was honoured when the King shook hands with him "and had a bit of a chat about artillery firing. H.R.H. said that my guns would have sufficient practice across the channel to make up for what we have not had here."[105] The King told Col. John Currie, commanding the 15th Battalion from Toronto: "You are going abroad in a few days."[106]

The King's farewell message was later read to the troops:

At the beginning of November I had the pleasure of welcoming to the Mother Country this fine contingent from the Dominion of Canada, and now, after three months' training, I bid you God-speed on your way to assist my Army in the field.

I am well aware of the discomforts that you have experienced from the inclement weather and abnormal rain, and I admire the cheerful spirit displayed by all ranks in facing and overcoming all difficulties.

From all I have heard and from what I have been able to see at to-day's inspection and march-past, I am satisfied that you have made good use of the time spent on Salisbury Plain.

By your willing and prompt rally to our common flag, you have already earned the gratitude of the Motherland.

By your deeds and achievements on the field of battle I am confident that you will emulate the example of your fellow-countrymen in the South African War, and thus help to secure the triumph of our arms.

I shall follow with pride and interest all your movements. I pray that God may bless you and watch over you.[107]

The Canadian Division began its departure on Sunday, 7 February. Appropriately, it rained that day, and no one regretted seeing the last of Salisbury Plain. Between the seventh and twelfth, ninety trains carried the Canadians and their equipment to the port of Avonmouth near Bristol, where transports awaited them for the journey to France.

The officers and other ranks left behind were understandably upset to watch their comrades leave without them. An officer deleted from the roll of the 14th (Montreal) Battalion wrote: "Saw my dear Regiment off to the front. How badly I feel to see them go and leave me here."[108] Col. Richard Turner, the Third Brigade's scholarly-looking commander, should have been left in England as medically unfit. He had been involved in a serious car accident in January, and had broken his collar-bone and several ribs. But the slim, bespectacled colonel kept silent about his injuries, knowing that they would cost him the opportunity to lead his brigade into action.

That kind of spirit was typical. Pte. Alexander Sinclair captured the mood of the men when he commented in his diary on 9 February, the date his 5th (Western Cavalry) Battalion was due to depart:

There's an expectant stir in camp this morning, and there's more bustle than usual. For we are expected to leave this afternoon for somewhere. La belle France is to be our destination; via which port, we know not; nor shall we until we actually get there. But we are going, and that, to us, is much.[109]

They might have found it amusing to know that, as far as the newspapers back home were concerned, the Canadians were already across the Channel. The Calgary *Daily Herald* had carried the story on its front page on 6 February, under the banner headline, CANADIAN TROOPS LANDED IN FRANCE, with a smaller headline below: Bulk of First Contingent Already Located in France. The report mistakenly informed readers that the contingent had gone to Le Havre and was now billeted in nearby Rouen. This was no surprise to informed media observers, because recent reports had "indicated that Rouen would very probably be the base of the Canadian expeditionary force in France." Of course, the *Herald* or any other paper could not be wholly faulted for the misleading report. It was undoubtedly planted by the War Office, which heavily censored all news stories, in a bid to deceive the Germans about the actual timing and location of the Canadian movement.

The *Herald* did better in an editorial a few days later. Noting the sense of detachment with which most people viewed the war, the paper issued a grim warning:

> We have seen soldiers drilling, we have said goodbye to friends and relations, and are preparing to say goodbye to more, but it is still hard to comprehend from this distance that the greatest war in the world's history is raging on the continent of Europe.
>
> It is with the first news of fatalities to our Canadian soldiers that we begin, only, it is true, to a slight extent at first, to get a touch of the real consequence of war and for what we must be prepared for in future.[110]

"Decent Soap Is Hard to Get"

If Avonmouth – on the west coast of England – was a strange sailing point for France, the Canadians' destination, far to the south on the French coast, was equally inconvenient. Located on the Bay of Biscay at the mouth of the River Loire, Saint-Nazaire had been selected as the point of entry because of a renewed German submarine threat in the English Channel, which precluded the more direct route from Southampton to Le Havre. Under normal conditions, the trip from Avonmouth to Saint-Nazaire should have required thirty-six hours. But conditions in mid-February 1915 were far from normal, and many of the Canadians were forced to spend up to five days crammed in the cold, dark holds of small cargo vessels.

Their ordeal was caused by a storm that swept across the Bay of Biscay, the worst storm in recent memory, with fierce westerly gales howling off the Atlantic and heavy seas pounding any vessel rash enough to be at sea. While experienced skippers stayed in harbour, the nineteen ships conveying the Canadians to France plunged through hell. Colonel Watson of the 2nd (Eastern Ontario) Battalion, on the tramp steamer *Blackwell*, remarked in his diary, "I never put in such a night as last night, such rolling & pitching . . . & at times was pitched from one side of the deck to the other. The officers were greatly excited, some thought the ship was going down."[1]

The storm peaked on the twelfth and thirteenth. The 13th (Royal Highlanders of Canada) Battalion's Lieutenant Sinclair, on board *Novian*, commented that the wind was "blowing like a young hurricane. . . . All ranks have put in a most abominable four days and the poor transport horses have been fairly standing on their heads in the lower decks."[2] There were fatalities, and not just among the animals. A cook belonging to the 9th Field Artillery Battery succumbed to a fractured skull suffered when he was thrown against a stanchion on the steamer *Maidan*. But the losses among the horses were much greater. J.W. Ross, an artilleryman who was also on *Maidan*, never forgot the heart-breaking experience. "The waves were so terrific that they came right over and knocked the horses down on the steel deck." He recalled that many were beyond help, and "we'd just shoot them and throw them overboard."[3]

Col. Arthur Currie,* the Second Brigade's guilt-ridden commander, endured a comedy of errors. Arriving in Avonmouth on the afternoon of the tenth, he boarded the decrepit *City of Dunkirk*, which was scheduled to sail early the next morning. But a boiler broke down and the ship's departure was delayed for twenty-four hours. In the meantime, one of his staff officers came down with pneumonia and had to be rushed to hospital. Then a soldier fell overboard. The reason for the mishap emerges from the colonel's diary: "Came up after 10 minutes in water with life preserver in one hand and bottle of whiskey in other." Finally sailing on the twelfth, *City of Dunkirk* was caught by the storm. "I did not miss a meal," Currie wrote, "but most everyone was ill. Not enough men to mount a guard." *City of Dunkirk* arrived off Saint-Nazaire on the morning of the fourteenth and tried to negotiate the River Loire without a pilot. This was a mistake. Running aground, the ship was unable to dock until late that night.[4]

Five days is a long time to spend on rough waters, and most of the men were very much worse for the wear by the time they set foot on French soil. On *Mount Temple*, a Toronto man, Pte. C.E. Longstaff of the 15th (48th Highlanders of Canada) Battalion remarked that "as the fellows came up out of the hold to go ashore they looked green, absolutely green, and their uniforms was one terrible mess."[5] A rousing welcome by French civilians made them feel better. According to Lieutenant Sinclair, "we pulled up to the quay amid a roar of cheers and simply showers of delicious oranges and flowers."[6] The civilians were thrilled, in turn, when the French-speaking members of 4 Company of the 14th (Montreal) Battalion assembled on the dock and marched through Saint-Nazaire singing "Alouette."

One prairie battalion was in trouble as soon as it landed. The 10th, from Calgary and Winnipeg, had had a miserable trip aboard the tramp steamer *Kingstonian*; even under ideal weather conditions, it would have been a torture test. "The capacity of the boat was somewhere around four hundred and thirty passengers," recalled Sgt. Chris Scriven, a long-time militiaman who had never seen this kind of organization, or lack of it. "That's all they were allowed to carry, but they packed on our own unit

---

*Currie had been promoted to full colonel on 4 February, along with the First Brigade's Malcolm Mercer and the divisional artillery chief, Harry Burstall. The Third Brigade's Richard Turner, complete with broken ribs and collar-bone, already held that rank.

plus a small unit of Army Service Corps men" – well over a thousand troops. Running aground in the Loire forced them to spend another day on board. When *Kingstonian* finally tied up, the sharp-eyed Canadians were quick to spot an unguarded barrel of rum sitting on the dock. The rum disappeared before the 10th departed the next day, and while Sergeant Scriven strongly denied that the battalion had anything to do with it, the army had no doubt about who was responsible. The 10th was later fined heavily, over the protests of the adjutant, Maj. Dan Ormond, a lawyer unused to the ways of the army, who demanded evidence of the battalion's guilt.[7]

Nevertheless, the arrival of the Canadian Division was significant. It was the first nonregular British division to reach France. Raised, equipped, and trained in only six months, the Division was now en route to the front, where it would be welcomed by the British Expeditionary Force in which it would serve. After the battles to hold up the German advance, there were alarmingly few of the "Old Contemptibles," the regulars who had done most of the fighting on Britain's behalf during 1914. Now the load would be shouldered by civilians from all over the Empire, and the Canadians were chafing for the chance to prove their mettle. That opportunity would come all too soon.

But before they did any fighting, another test of endurance awaited the Canadians. Disembarkation was completed by the evening of the fifteenth, and the troops boarded trains at Saint-Nazaire for the forty-three-hour, five-hundred-mile journey to the front. Officers were allotted regular passenger cars – which Colonel Watson from Quebec described as "miserable";[8] the other ranks were packed into boxcars with a supposed capacity of eight horses or forty men. These boxcars – especially the ones that had previously held horses – were not pleasant: they were overcrowded, and sanitation arrangements were primitive. "You couldn't lie down in any comfortable position," remembered Pte. Cuthbert Johnson of the 14th (Montreal) Battalion, "that somebody wasn't lying over your legs or something like that."[9]

As always, spirits remained high. Col. John Currie, the Toronto member of Parliament who commanded the 15th (48th Highlanders of Canada) Battalion, apologized to his men for the uncomfortable conditions. "That's all right, sir," they replied. "That's what we are here for."[10]

Frequent stops made the trip bearable. While the horses were watered, the soldiers enjoyed French hospitality, as one young Canadian commented in a letter home:

We had a great time getting off at the stations and singing to the crowds that gathered at every place all the way through. They couldn't understand what we were singing about, but they clapped just the same, and gave us apples, pears, onions, cider, wine, and all sorts of things. Wine is very cheap here, and you can get a quart bottle for a franc – viz., a shilling.[11]

Detraining after five hundred miles near Hazebrouck, in French Flanders, the Canadians were billeted in nearby villages and farms. The surroundings were familiar. "The mud here is as thick and much stickier than at Salisbury Plains," noted Col. John Creelman of the 2nd Field Artillery Brigade, "but nobody minds now."[12] This was due to their proximity to the front, which lent an air of excitement to the situation. "Guns bursting in the firing line about 10 miles away keep us interested," reads the diary of Winnipeg's William Alldritt, an 8th Battalion sergeant, "while at night the search lights flicker like tongues of flame."[13] Senior officers were equally fascinated by the sights and sounds, according to the 2nd Battalion's Colonel Watson: "At night watched the heavy star shell fire & the heavy gun bombardment."[14]

Because they had not yet tasted life in the front lines, there was, seemingly, nothing special about their billets. But they would soon grow to appreciate the comparative luxury of these accommodations far from the battle zone. They would return to places like this between front-line tours, to bask in the pleasure of a hot shower – sometimes as often as once a week – and enjoy an issue of fresh underwear, before turning to the task of chipping the accumulated mud from their clothing and kit. And there was the glorious chance to sleep in relative comfort, on a straw mattress under a roof, even if it was only a barn roof. Other pleasures included brothels, and even the smallest village had an estaminet where the soldiers could buy weak beer or strong coffee, or a plate of "eggs and chips," a refreshing change from army food. The prices were already high, but the Canadians forced them even higher, because the French peasants were quick to learn that these "colonials" earned five times as much as British troops. When Canadians were in the neighbourhood, prices escalated from exorbitant to extortionate, causing more than a little bitterness on the part of the underpaid British Tommies. To keep prices under control, the army eventually set up canteens, as did the Young Men's Christian Association and the Salvation Army.

But all of that lay in the future. For the moment, the Canadians were mere spectators in this terrible war, although they were by now a step closer to the action.

The Canadian Division was attached to Lt.-Gen. William Pulteney's III Corps, in General Sir Horace Smith-Dorrien's Second Army. The British Expeditionary Force (BEF) by now consisted of two field armies, totalling sixteen divisions, plus the Indian Corps. The BEF's commander-in-chief, Field-Marshal Sir John French, inspected the Canadians on Saturday, 20 February. Sir John was acquainted with them, having commanded Canadian troops in the South African War and reported on the state of Canada's military in 1910. Now he addressed them glowingly: "If you fight as well as you look, you will acquit yourselves well."[15] This was not mere puffery on the field-marshal's part. "They appear to be a fine lot of men," he told his diary, "and I like the look of the Division."[16]

The Canadians were not to be entrusted with their own section of the front lines just yet. First they had to prove themselves, and the Division was broken up for training purposes – the legendary confrontation between Sam Hughes and Lord Kitchener notwithstanding. Divided into brigade groups – each of the three infantry brigades formed a group, supplemented with artillery, engineers, and other support services – they were attached to British formations for a short period of instruction, training and assessment. Colonel Mercer's First Brigade Group trained with the British 6th Division between 17 and 23 February, being replaced by Colonel Turner's Third Brigade Group until 2 March; Colonel Currie and his Second Brigade Group served with the British 4th Division from the twenty-first until the twenty-eighth. The 4th Division was holding the line northeast of Armentières, while the 6th Division held the sector on its immediate right. Here, the Canadians received their introduction to the strange, deadly world of trench warfare.*

It was supposed to be a short war. At least, that was the expectation of the so-called experts, who predicted that it would amount to little more than, as one historian put it, "six weeks' autumn manoeuvres with live ammunition."[17] In Berlin in early August 1914, Kaiser Wilhelm assured his departing legions: "You will be home before the leaves have fallen from the trees."[18]

Germany had long prepared for this conflict. In 1905, Count Alfred von Schlieffen drew up a detailed memorandum dealing with the prospect of a future two-front war, with Russia in the east and with France in the west. The Schlieffen Plan, as it came to be called, advocated maintaining a holding action on the Eastern Front while concentrating the bulk of the

---

*As before, when the contingent had crossed to France, the newspapers in Canada jumped the gun. On 15 February, two days before the first Canadian troops went into the trenches, the Calgary *Daily Herald* carried a front-page bulletin under the headline, CANADIANS IN TRENCHES: "Members of the Canadian contingent are now at the front, and a certain brigade of Canadian infantry moved to their positions in the trenches last Saturday night."

German army against France. Schlieffen proposed to mass three-quarters of his western forces on the right wing and deliver a decisive blow via neutral Belgium, rolling irresistibly across northern France, scooping up Paris, and outflanking the French armies to the north and east of the capital.

Most historians mistakenly view the Schlieffen Plan as a masterpiece of military planning, a blueprint for certain success had it been followed to the letter. In fact, it was, according to the American historian S.L.A. Marshall, a "logistical absurdity,"[19] demanding superhuman feats from the ordinary German foot-soldiers who would have to execute it. The plan remained essentially intact by 1914, although it had been modified by Schlieffen's sixty-six-year-old successor, Gen. Helmuth von Moltke, who weakened the right wing to reinforce his left and centre. Still, the right wing was sufficiently strong for the task assigned it, and despite the short-comings of the Schlieffen Plan it might have worked, had not Moltke made a further, and fatal, change once the war was well under way.

France's master plan was even more flawed. Plan XVII – it was the seventeenth in a series formulated since 1875 – was not very imaginative. "A piece of back-stairs jobbery" is how one noted historian, J.F.C. Fuller (the same Fuller who was so appalled at the Canadians when they arrived in England), later described it.[20] Relying on the élan and offensive esprit de corps cultivated by the French army in the wake of the Franco-Prussian War, Plan XVII called for a major attack in Alsace and Lorraine, the two provinces lost to Germany after that war. Plan XVII was to be carried out regardless of German intentions or actions.

The French were, in many ways, woefully out of touch with the realities of modern warfare. While the German army had adopted field-grey uniforms, and the British wore khaki, France's army was still clothed in Napoleonic finery: bright red trousers and dark blue coats. Relying primarily on the individual infantryman's bayonet, they had fallen far behind in technical developments and as a consequence suffered a considerable disadvantage in firepower. Except for the rapid-firing 75-millimetre field gun, which was unexcelled, the French went to war lamentably weak in artillery, the one arm that was capable of producing decisive results on the trench-scarred battlefield. Indeed, Napoleon, a gunner by training, would have been appalled by the state of the French army in 1914.

The first few weeks of the war proceeded almost predictably. The Germans swiftly smashed the little Belgian army, its resistance centred on powerful fortifications in and around Liège, which were pulverized by heavy howitzers. While the Belgians withdrew to Antwerp, the right wing of the German armies rolled onward, seemingly invincible, as the French played into their hands. Blindly adhering to Plan XVII, two of the five French armies plunged into Alsace-Lorraine on 14 August, reaching the River Rhine at one point. But success was both fleeting and costly. The Germans, effectively employing their enormous advantage in firepower, quickly crushed the attackers. Undeterred, the French commander-in-chief, Gen. Joseph Joffre – a big, amiable engineer, nicknamed Papa by his adoring troops – threw two more armies into the Ardennes, farther north, on the twenty-second. This attack was routed even faster than the earlier offensive in Alsace-Lorraine, and as August wound down it was finally beginning to dawn on Papa Joffre that he was in serious trouble.

The Germans were jubilant. "The Kaiser is radiant," one observer commented as the Battle of the Frontiers swung clearly in Germany's favour. But his commander, General Moltke, was less certain. The French had been defeated, it was true, but they had not been completely crushed. "Don't let's deceive ourselves," he warned, noting that "the victor [should have] prisoners. Where are our prisoners?"[21]

A rude surprise awaited the Germans in Belgium, not far from the French border. On 22 August, near Mons, they collided with elements of Field-Marshal French's newly arrived BEF, 100,000 strong. That "contemptible little army," Kaiser Wilhelm called the BEF, and the British professionals were happy to refer to themselves as "Old Contemptibles." The British troops fought furiously in the face of enormous odds throughout the twenty-third before reluctantly retiring with the neighbouring French on their right, pursued by three-quarters of a million Germans. But before they pulled back, the British Tommies put on a dazzling display of what was still called musketry, firing fifteen rounds a minute from their Lee-Enfields, and convincing the Germans that they were facing massed machine-guns.

The last week of August and the early days of September took on the appearance of a chase as the Germans raced to catch the British and French retreating across northern France. The weather was unusually warm, and the sweat-soaked soldiers choked on the great clouds of dust kicked up by millions of marching feet.

On 4 September Moltke made his fatal mistake. According to the Schlieffen Plan, the German right wing was supposed to swing west of Paris and take the French armies to the north and east by the flank and rear. However, Moltke instructed his two right-hand armies to cut in front of Paris. In moving east of the capital, he presented his own vulnerable flank to the newly created French Sixth Army, which was defending Paris, and the BEF.

The Allies did not miss this golden opportunity. On 7 September they counter-attacked as the German spearheads crossed the River Marne. The Battle of the Marne marked the end of the enemy invasion, and the Germans subsequently withdrew behind the River Aisne.

The defeat cost Moltke his job. On 14 September he was replaced by Gen. Erich von Falkenhayn.

While the Germans dug in and consolidated their gains, the race west to the sea ensued. Both sides attempted to outflank the other, extending their lines towards the North Sea. As they repeatedly clashed and dug in, they gradually created the unbroken Western Front. This was something new in war, a line of opposing trenches stretching more than four hundred miles between the coast and neutral Switzerland.

On 10 October Antwerp fell, but not before the remnants of the Belgian army escaped and fled along the coastline, where they helped the Allies hold the small corner of Belgium that remained outside Germany's clutches.

The Germans made the first major effort to break the deadlock. On 20 October General Falkenhayn launched an offensive against the ancient Flanders town of Ypres, in a belated bid to capture the French ports on the English Channel. The German attack crashed head-on with the BEF, which was attempting to extend its own line in the area. The result was the First Battle of Ypres, three weeks of ferocious fighting that produced a quarter-million casualties. For all intents and purposes, the battle destroyed the cream of Britain's prewar professional army – arguably the best in the world at that time – and killed so many young Germans that it was named *Der Kindermord von Ypren*. The battle left the British holding a big bulge deep in the enemy lines: the soon-to-be-infamous Ypres salient.

Exhausted, both sides paused to lick their wounds for the winter. Few realized it, but the war of movement had ended; siege warfare had begun.

As the war went on, the defences on either side became increasingly sophisticated. But during the winter of 1914/15, conditions were incredibly primitive, reflecting the prevailing but sadly mistaken belief that this was merely a temporary state of affairs:

A "trench" was a slight narrow excavation with steep sides and six to nine feet wide traverses, lacking duck-boards and drainage and revetment worth the name. A "dug-out" was merely a hole in the ground with splinter-proof covering. A "trench mortar" was a length of brass tubing, inaccurate and dangerous to the firer. A "hand-grenade" was a similarly improvised weapon, set in action by a match or cigarette, or, at best, by a friction lighter.[22]

In addition to claiming millions of lives, the trenches condemned soldiers of all nations to four years of unimaginable filth and squalor, suffering and misery.

"Gentlemen, you are about to face a cruel, cunning, and unscrupulous enemy," General Pulteney, commanding III Corps, warned a group of Canadian officers preparing to go into the front lines for the first time. "If you make a mistake you will not get a chance to make a second one."[23]

The Canadians were given a relatively gentle indoctrination. Small groups of officers and other ranks from the infantry and engineers joined British battalions in the trenches for forty-eight-hour tours. After everyone had been initiated, Canadian platoons were assigned to their own front-line sectors, under the strict supervision of British officers and NCOs.

In the process, the Canadians gained new respect for their British cousins. Calgary's Walter Critchley, a lieutenant in the 10th (Calgary-Winnipeg) Battalion, admitted that he was "scared stiff" the first time he went into the line, but the stiff-upper-lip attitude of the British soldiers accompanying him quickly calmed him down. "They were a very hardy bunch," he later said of them, "extremely brave men."[24] Victor Lewis, a private in the same outfit, never forgot their words of encouragement. "Come on now, straighten up," they told the Canadians. "Nothing to be afraid of."[25] Of course there was plenty to be afraid of, but no one wanted to embarrass himself or his unit by actually showing fear.

The artillery's experience was somewhat different. Whereas all of the infantry were being indoctrinated, only selected gunners were undergoing training in the battle zone, for the simple reason that the guns were too valuable to endanger through careless or amateurish mistakes. Therefore only brigade and battery commanders, accompanied by small parties of NCOs, were attached to British formations, before returning to their own units to instruct them "in digging emplacements, concealing guns from aerial observation, and in methods of artillery communication."[26] Only when they had mastered these techniques were Canadian guns allowed into action. As a result, not until 10:15 A.M. on Tuesday, 2 March, did a gun of the 1st Field Battery fire the first round for the Canadian army in the Great War.[27]

Even in these early days, there were casualties – slight by later standards, but no less distressing. The Second Brigade Group, for example, lost four officers and other ranks killed, and twenty wounded in its first week in the trenches. The death of one of the officers was particularly painful for the brigadier, Arthur Currie. Lieut. Herbie Boggs of the 7th (British Columbia) Battalion, killed on 26 February, was the son of Currie's neighbours on Alston Street in Victoria West. Currie was distraught, because he had known the Boggs family for years. He attended the lieutenant's funeral the following day and "wired Boggs and wrote him a letter." After the war, Currie sought out the young man's gravesite.[28]

Death was a constant companion in the trenches. Artillery was an around-the-clock threat; possibly two-thirds of all casualties in this war were caused by the big guns. The Canadians were quick to learn the nicknames given the enemy's shells. High explosives were dubbed Black Marias, slang for English police patrol-wagons, Jack Johnsons – after the American heavyweight boxer – or coal boxes. Shrapnel shells were Whizz Bangs or Whistling Willies. Trench mortars (*Minenwerfen*) delivered rum jars. Whatever the name, the exploding shells caused terrible, often untreatable injuries, decapitating and maiming luckless victims with jagged pieces of steel, or burying them beneath tons of dirt.

Snipers were deadly, too. An officer of the 14th (Montreal) Battalion remarked: "The snipers are the very deuce. They pick our men off whenever they get a chance."[29] An unidentified sergeant added:

> In fact, all of the boys who have been hit have been hit in the head, mainly through not being cautious enough. The Tommy out here has a most wholesome respect for the German sniper – we also have now – and laughs when he reads [in the newspapers] of the bad shooting of the German infantry. The Germans certainly have brought sniping down to a fine art.[30]

According to Ian MacTavish, a twenty-four-year-old Vancouverite in the 16th (Canadian Scottish) Battalion, "the German soldier is by no means to be despised. Their shooting is accurate."[31]

The Canadians were no slouches, either. One sharpshooter in the 8th (90th Winnipeg Rifles) Battalion "pinked" three German snipers in these early days in the trenches. As the war went on, Canadian marksmen would prove to have few peers, and it was no coincidence that Native Indians were among the best. Two members of the 8th Battalion, a metis named Patrick Riel – a relative of Louis Riel, whose 1885 rebellion was quelled with assistance from this battalion's forerunner, the 90th Winnipeg Rifles – and Philip McDonald, an Iroquois from Ontario, accounted for more than a hundred Germans between them, before their deaths a few days apart in January 1916.[32] Johnson Paudash, a Mississauga Indian, killed eighty-eight Germans as a member of the 2nd (Eastern Ontario) Battalion. A Cree, Henry "Ducky" Norwest, of the 50th (Calgary) Battalion, amassed 115 kills prior to his death at the hands of an enemy sniper in August 1918. Best of all, of course, was Francis "Peg" Pegahmagabow from Ontario's Parry Island Band, now of the 1st (Western Ontario) Battalion, and probably the deadliest shot in any army on the Western Front, who picked off as many as 378 Germans.[33]

Animosity was noticeable by its absence. Although they were trying to kill each other, the soldiers on either side had not yet cultivated grudges. These would, however, develop in the course of coming events. Just a few weeks earlier, at Christmas, British and German troops had openly fraternized in no man's land, that desolate strip of ground between the opposing lines; in the British army, fraternization with the enemy was an offence punishable by death. The Canadians inherited this charitable attitude from the British who supervised them. "I have seen more hostility and bitter feeling displayed between two football teams," commented a Winnipegger in the 8th Battalion, "than appears to exist between the Germans in front of us and ourselves."[34]

Still, the Canadians were quick to learn the derogatory nicknames given the Germans, who were referred to, usually in the singular, as the Hun, Heinie, the Boche, Jerry, Kraut, and Fritz.

They also soon learned that routine dominated trench life. Each morning, a half-hour before dawn, the men would stand to arms, in anticipation of possible attack. "After breakfast," related an officer of the 15th (48th Highlanders of Canada) Battalion, "everyone started in to clean the trenches, pump out water, which in some places was quite deep, and generally settle down."[35]

Water and mud seemed to be everywhere. "This Flemish mud is of a gooey sticky consistency which is hard to beat," complained Hamilton's Capt. Harry Crerar. "I never saw anything like the way it sticks. After I've been walking ten minutes, I have at least five pounds of it on either foot."[36] An officer of British Columbia's 7th Battalion commented: "In the trenches themselves one has to look out, as there is lots of water under the narrow planks which have now been put down, and a false step means you go over the top of your gum boots in water which does not smell exactly like eau-de-cologne."[37] As one veteran later suggested, "We did not know what mud was on Salisbury Plain."[38]

Because of the ever-present danger from enemy snipers, only minor chores could be performed in daylight; it was at night that major work was undertaken, by both sides. At dusk the troops would stand-to once again; this would be followed by supper and an issue of rum. Each man in the British army was entitled to a daily ration of a quarter-ounce of "Service Rum, Diluted" – the initials S.R.D. were stamped on the ceramic jugs in which the liquor was delivered to the trenches. Misadventures involving rum abounded. One platoon of Montrealers in the 14th Battalion had to do without its rum on its first night in the front lines, when the man carrying the ration fell down and broke the jug. "He wasn't popular that night," recalled Sgt. W.R. Duncan.[39] Eventually, the men reinterpreted s.r.d. to mean "Seldom Reaches Destination." This practice of issuing rum caused predictable problems with the temperance people back home, but Canadian soldiers continued to receive the rum ration throughout the war.

It was a small comfort amid almost unrelieved misery. The men wallowed in cold water and mud for days on end, and no one suffered more than the Highlanders in their khaki kilts. Pte. Andrew Rae of the 16th (Canadian Scottish) Battalion remembered those early days in the trenches:

> You were so cold you would feel almost the marrow was frozen in your bones. We were wearing a kilt, and at night time you would freeze into the ground and when you rose up you would have to pull part of the earth away with you. You had some trouble getting the earth loose from your kilt.[40]

The accommodations left much to be desired. "In some of the places," the former lawyer Maj. Dan Ormond of the 10th (Calgary-Winnipeg) Battalion recalled, "the men had got doors off ruined buildings and had built up mud or sandbags and then that was looked on as a dugout. It probably was a slight protection from the weather, but no other protection."[41] Taking a cue from the British, the Canadians dignified their dugouts with names like Vermin Villa, The Ritz-Carlton, Maple Leaf Hotel, and Yonge St. Mission.[42]

Personal hygiene was a lost cause in these conditions. Lice became a fact of life. One Canadian Highlander, K.C. Hossick of the 13th Battalion from Montreal, recalled making his way towards the trenches for the first time and being greeted by a British soldier inquiring, "Are you lousy, Jock?" When Hossick shook his head, the other replied, "Well, by God, you will be in the morning" – and so he was. The words of one battalion commander came back to haunt him at this time: the 3rd (Toronto) Battalions Lt.-Col. Robert Rennie, a fifty-two-year-old businessman, had sternly lectured his unit at Salisbury on the need for personal cleanliness, warning, "I will not take one lousy man to France." Itching and scratching within hours of entering the trenches, the men of the 3rd Battalion laughed as they recalled Rennie's remark.[43]

Food was always a soldier's major concern. Behind the lines, field kitchens provided plain but substantial meals of stews, roast beef, and mutton. The troops in the trenches cooked their own meals, a practice discontinued in the next year because smoke from the braziers drew enemy shell fire and because supplying coal and wood for fuel became increasingly difficult. Edmonton's Pte. Harold Peat, now a member of the 3rd (Toronto) Battalion – he had transferred just before the unit left Salisbury Plain – felt that the food was both plentiful and good. "Regardless of any, we are the best fed troops in the field." He described the type of rations issued:

> [W]e receive some tea and sugar, lots of bully beef and biscuits. The bully beef is corned beef and has its origin . . . in Chicago, Illinois, or so we believe. It is quite good. But you can get too much of a good thing once too often. So sometimes we eat it, and sometimes we use the unopened tins as bricks, and line the trenches with them. Good solid bricks, too! We get soup powders and yet more soup powders. We get cheese that is not cream cheese, and we get a slice of raw bacon.

The little Edmontonian even offered a recipe for stew: "A stock of weak tea, some sugar, salt, some bully beef, biscuits crumbled down, the whole well stirred and brought to a boil, then thickened by several soup powders. . . . Of its appearance I say nothing."[44]

Glimpses of trench life can be gleaned from letters home. Two members of the 16th (Canadian Scottish) Battalion wrote vivid descriptions of their adopted lifestyle. One, a Vancouver lad – unidentified for censorship reasons, presumably – assured his family that there was plenty to keep him busy, including the never-ending "work of construction, sentry duties, cooking, cold feet, and also 'old women's' gossiping parties," adding:

> Everything one touches is muddy, and it is hard to keep clean. The government supplies rubber boots up to the knees, and we keep dry so long as the mud water is just so deep. We get socks when we want them, also tobacco, cigarettes and rum are issued daily. While in the trenches we had all we could eat; in fact we left some behind in the trenches. We cook our own meals in braziers. What with starting the fire and nursing it till it is good enough to cook with, and doing our own cooking, trench life is fairly busy. Decent soap is hard to get.[45]

Another unidentified private in the same kilted unit tried to convince the people at home in Vancouver that the trenches were "not so bad." But the rest of his letter hardly supported his contention:

> Our clothes are simply awful from mud, but I have given up worrying about such matters. One important thing is, don't make yourself a target for the Germans.

It is impossible to write in the trenches. There is no light and no room, and one's fingers are too cold to hold the pencil. Don't worry if you don't hear for a whole week. Your biscuits and jam were welcome. We get fresh eggs at five cents each, and milk at two cents per cup, so we are O.K.[46]

After dark, the trenches buzzed with activity. "Everyone is on the go," wrote a 7th (British Columbia) Battalion officer. "Working parties out in front fixing the [barbed] wire, others working on the parapet, and so forth. Fatigue parties bringing in rations and fuel, and listening posts and patrols coming in reporting if there is any movement in the enemy's trenches."[47] The adverse conditions made it exhausting work. "The trenches are in a horrible state of mud," one young sapper complained. "We shore up the banks with sandbags and hurdles, build dug-outs, etc., and get back to billets about 3 A.M., generally 'all in.' We spend next day in scraping mud off boots, coats, rifles, etc."[48] Complicating matters was a perpetual shortage of materials, including spades. Even sandbags were in short supply, but a veteran militiaman, Sgt. Chris Scriven of the 10th (Calgary-Winnipeg) Battalion, found a solution. "We used to listen at night until we could hear a German work party working," he recalled, "and then we used to go out and swipe their sandbags, and the first piece of trench I ever built was built with stolen sandbags from Fritzie."[49]

No man's land was a busy place, indeed. In a 23 February letter, a weary engineer described his experience:

Our job was to put up wire entanglements outside and we worked for about two hours, with the Germans about four hundred yards away and nothing in between. In the bright moonlight we felt a good mark, but nothing came our way. The truth is the Germans had a working party out on the same game, and by a sort of mutual agreement we let each other alone. . . . Beyond . . . the continual sniping there was not much doing. It is hard work carrying wire about and being hampered by an overcoat and ammunition. I got very hot and cross and was covered with mud when I was finished.[50]

This live-and-let-live attitude was sometimes perplexing. Fred Arnold, a private in the 7th (British Columbia) Battalion, recalled spotting a German work party in no man's land one bright night and raising his rifle to fire on them. A British soldier grabbed his arm and told him not to shoot, because the Germans would retaliate. "Well, I thought, this is a devil of a war," Arnold remarked. "Come six thousand miles to shoot Germans, and the first ones I had a look at I couldn't shoot them."[51]

Patrolling could be nerve-racking work. Some, like the 10th Battalion's Sgt. John Matheson, a thirty-year-old Scots-born banker from Medicine Hat, considered patrols in no man's land "exciting,"[52] but few would have agreed with him. "I was on a no-man's-land patrol," recalled another banker, Yorkton's R.L. Christopherson, "and I was never so scared in my life."[53] Similar sentiments were expressed by Pte. C.E. Longstaff of the 48th Highlanders. He and a fellow Canadian were taken by a British scout to set up a listening post within a few yards of the German trenches. "Don't do anything unless I tell you," the scout hissed before crawling off to his own post nearby.

Longstaff and his companion waited. Then, in the moonlight, they spotted an approaching enemy patrol. His heart pounding, Longstaff scrambled over to the scout. "What do we do now," he asked, "do we fire?"

"For God's sake, no," replied the scout. "Keep quiet. Tell your partner to keep quiet, too."

Returning to his post, Longstaff and his buddy kept their heads down. The Germans came closer and closer, until it seemed certain that they would walk right on top of the Canadians. At the last moment, they veered away and soon disappeared from sight.

The next thing Longstaff recalled was a voice from behind; a British sergeant-major who had good news. "We're going to take you in now. We brought out the relief."

"Well," Longstaff answered, "you wouldn't believe how relieved I am."[54]

The Canadians were soon adept at this type of warfare. It was a rapid and remarkable transformation. "I think it made you feel that you'd changed over from a boy to a man," remembered a 14th (Montreal) Battalion subaltern, Henry Campbell. "You learned more in twenty-four hours in the front line than what you'd learned with all your training that you'd had previously." To Sgt. George Twigg, a British veteran now serving with the 4th (Central Ontario) Battalion, it was marvellous to witness. "What I was surprised at," Twigg later said, "was we had youngsters, seventeen or eighteen, that never even saw a rifle until they went over there and the way they behaved. They came up just perfect."[55]

Certainly the divisional commander, General Alderson, was pleased. "I am very glad to be able to say that they are doing remarkably well," he informed newly knighted Sir George Perley, Canada's acting high commissioner in London. "I knew they would do well, but they have done much better than I expected."[56] The commander-in-chief was no less impressed. Sir John French wrote of the Canadians to an inquiring Lord Kitchener:

They presented a splendid and most soldierlike appearance on parade. The men were of good physique, hard and fit. I judged by what I saw of them that they were well enough trained and quite able to take their places in the line of battle. Since then the Division has thoroughly justified the good opinion I formed of it.[57]

Even before the Canadians had completed their period of indoctrination, it was decided that the Division could safely hold its own sector. On 26 February orders were issued accordingly: the Canadians would relieve the British 7th Division near Fleurbaix, joining Lt.-Gen. Sir Henry Rawlinson's IV Corps in Gen. Sir Douglas Haig's First Army. They arrived in time for a front-row seat to Neuve-Chapelle, the first major British offensive since the advent of trench warfare.

The takeover began on 1 March, when troops of the First Brigade shifted to the new front. At 11 A.M. on Wednesday, 3 March, General Alderson took command of the Canadian zone. As his men moved in, he addressed them in fatherly fashion:

My old regiment, the Royal West Kent, has been here since the beginning of the war and it has never lost a trench. The Army says, "The West Kents never budge." I am proud of the great record of my old Regiment. And I think it is a good omen. I now belong to you and you belong to me: and before long the Army will say, "The Canadians never budge." Lads, it can be left there, and there I leave it.[58]

CHAPTER SIX

"The Tricks of the Trade"

As the Canadians took over from the British occupants of this sector, they occasionally encountered anticolonial prejudice. Montreal's Andy McNaughton was ordered to establish his 7th Field Battery near Fleurbaix, where he had to deal with what he called a "stuffy British Horse Artillery colonel." The tension was perceptible, until McNaughton learned that the colonel was a Stephen Leacock fan. When McNaughton mentioned that he knew Leacock personally from his McGill days, the colonel's demeanour improved at once, and "a very difficult takeover became smooth and friendly."[1]

This sector was relatively quiet. Not far from the front, stolid French farmers tended to their fields, ploughing and seeding, with only an occasional shell burst to disturb the peace. It was sodden, flat countryside, bereft of notable physical features. The Canadians held a stretch of trenches 6400 yards long, flanked on the left by the British 6th Division and by the 8th Division on the right. Each of the three Canadian infantry brigades held a share of the front, each with two battalions in the line and the others echeloned to the rear, in reserve. On 4 March Canadian Division headquarters issued a document, "Principles of Defence," which declared that "*the cardinal principle of the defensive scheme of the Division is a determination to hold the front trenches at all costs.*" Where a trench was lost to the enemy, it was to be regained by a counter-attack "carried out promptly and with resolution." At the same time, the Canadians were urged to be aggressive – holding a trench did not necessarily mean "that we are on the defensive" – and to conduct "bold patrolling, persistent and accurate sniping, and prompt enterprises against any sapheads." All of these actions were intended to maintain the Canadians' moral "ascendancy over the Germans."[2]

This was clearly a war like none before it. The First Brigade's commander, Toronto's Brig.-Gen. Malcolm Mercer (promoted on 4 March along with the Canadian Division's other brigadiers, Currie, Turner, and

Burstall, to make the senior Canadian ranks conform to the British) remarked in a letter home on the "very queer" conditions that existed on the Western Front. "My brigade is holding a bit of the line – about 2,000 or 2,500 yards," the former Toronto lawyer explained. "The lines at one point are only some 65 yards apart, at another 85 yards, average distance from 200 to 350 yards, and this sort of thing prevails for hundreds of miles."[3]

Meningitis was still a problem. On 5 March, Pte. Gerald Patterson of the 4th (Central Ontario) Battalion contracted the disease. Three days later the twenty-two-year-old bank clerk from St. Catharines was dead.[4] However, the epidemic had run its course, and while it would be evident throughout the war, meningitis would soon be overshadowed by other health hazards, such as trench foot, an ailment similar to frostbite, the result of prolonged exposure to cold, wet conditions.

On 7 March the Canadians instituted an organizational change that reflected the reality of static warfare. Every brigade in the BEF created a grenade company, 120 strong, expert throwers, or "bombers", who handled the primitive hand grenades then in use. One type was a jam can filled with scraps of iron and a half-pound of explosive, with a fuse. The need for specialists was obvious, and baseball-playing Canadians were ideal for what was a tough job. An officer of the 13th (Royal Highlanders of Canada) Battalion observed that the grenades "seem to be about as dangerous to the throwers as to any body else."[5]

Neuve-Chapelle came soon afterwards. Originally planned as a joint Franco-British offensive, the French cancelled their participation at the last minute, and the BEF proceeded on its own. The attack went in at 8:05 A.M. on Wednesday, 10 March, by four divisions of the First Army in which the Canadian Division was serving. Initial objectives were quickly taken, but the British were slow to exploit this success, and the Germans were able to limit their advance to a maximum of 1200 yards on a 4000-yard front. It was both frustrating and disappointing for the British, whose opening bombardment of thirty-five minutes' duration had blasted a mile-wide hole in the enemy defences. General Haig, the First Army's commander, later attributed the failure to exploit the success to an "inexcusable" lack of initiative by officers who refused to move without first receiving "specific orders to do so from their immediate superiors."[6] The offensive was renewed the following day, without success, and operations were finally cancelled on the twelfth.

The Canadians had no direct part in this action. Their task was to distract and deceive the enemy opposite them. "We kept up supporting fire all day," the Second Brigade's General Currie told his diary. "Terrific cannonading and rifle fire."[7] Other veterans never forgot the experience. A Montrealer, Capt. Thomas Morrisey of the 13th Battalion called it "the biggest noise I'd ever heard," while Pte. Fred Arnold of the 7th (British Columbia) Battalion recalled years later that "the ground just rocked."[8]

The artillery was hampered by a shortage of shells that plagued the entire BEF.* General Burstall, the Canadian Division's artillery commander, issued instructions before the battle: "It is more important that while we create the belief that we are about to assault, we should at the same time husband our ammunition, and from ten to fifteen rounds per gun should suffice for this task." In the event, the Canadians fired more than twice their allotment of ammunition. But afterwards the daily ration of shells per 18-pounder field gun was reduced from ten to just three. It was a strange way to fight a war.[9]

The infantry, too, had problems. By now, the flaws in the Ross rifle were painfully evident. "That was the first time we had the chance to use them for rapid fire," remembered Sgt. W.R. Duncan of the 14th (Montreal) Battalion. "And when we started rapid fire, it jammed there. You [had to] take your foot and bash the bolt down."[10] General Currie noted in a 16 March memorandum to divisional headquarters that his troops had

> reported that the Small Arms Ammunition of British manufacture does not work as well in the Ross Rifle as the ammunition of Canadian manufacture. They find, after firing a few rounds, that the shells seem to stick in the bolt and are not easily extracted, in fact, more than the ordinary pressure must be applied. . . . This seems to me to be a point where the most rigid investigation is necessary, as a serious interference with rapid firing may prove fatal on occasions.[11]

Another problem arose when the Ross was fired with the bayonet fixed. The bayonet had a disturbing tendency to fall off, forcing the owner to retrieve it from the front of the parapet after nightfall.

The Canadian Division held the line at Fleurbaix for an unusually long time. A scheduled 17 March relief was postponed by a German attack near Saint-Eloi, south of Ypres, forcing the Canadians to remain in the trenches for twenty-four days. Fortunately, the relative calm made it bearable; there were even some humorous moments. "Germans put up toy horse on parapet, we knocked it down, they put it up again bandaged round neck and hind legs," General Currie wrote in his diary.[12] One

---

*Actually, the problem was a shortage of fuses. By the end of August 1915, there were 25 million shells stockpiled in Britain awaiting the fuses without which, of course, they were useless.

highlight came on the seventeenth, the so-called Battle of St. Patrick's Day, described in a letter home by an officer of Winnipeg's 8th Battalion:

> We have just had a rather amusing day . . . the men had to celebrate St. Patrick's Day somehow. They started off by sticking the Irish flag, the Union Jack, and the [French] tricolour on the parapet. Where they conjured them from the Lord only knows! They then sang the National Anthem, the Marseillaise, the Maple Leaf, and Wearing o' the Green. They riddled the tricolour with bullets, but left the other two alone.[13]

For some, this sector was too quiet. The gunners, their ammunition strictly rationed, had little to do, as Montreal's Colonel Creelman complained in his diary:

> There is a mild Spring rain falling and the winter's accumulation of manure in the court yard is smelling to Heaven but we have to keep the window open for air. Plowing is finished and harrowing almost so. Flowers are growing here and there and in an occasional pasture are cows grazing after the winter spent in barns. Things are deadly quiet and we are very much bored. In six whole days my Brigade has fired only 22 shells.[14]

The Canadians found themselves the objects of considerable interest. Canada's frontier image fascinated Europeans, who expected the Canadians to be mostly cowboys and Indians. "Why, they're *white*!" one resident of Plymouth had exclaimed as the Canadians marched through town when they arrived in England the previous October.[15] Such misconceptions were fostered by British and French journalists. "The Canadian troops at the front have discovered a novel use for lacrosse sticks," reads one fanciful British report that reached Canada, "namely, throwing hand grenades into the German trenches. They are able in this way to throw them farther, more accurately and with less risk than otherwise."[16] A French writer, Maurice Barrès, promoted the frontier aspect with a series of stories about the Canadians, which included a feature about "a Red Indian soldier who had just died, like the last of the Mohicans, for the honour of his people."[17]

Not until 25 March did units of the British 8th Division begin relieving the Canadians. At 10 A.M. on the twenty-seventh, General Alderson relinquished command of the sector, overseeing the northward move of his Division to billets in the vicinity of the River Lys. In twenty-four days in the front lines, the Division had suffered 278 casualties, about the normal rate of attrition in the trenches at that time. The Canadians had also won the firm respect of top British generals. Sir Henry Rawlinson, in whose IV

Corps they had served in early March, told Lord Kitchener: "I am very pleased with the Canadians. They are magnificent men, as you know, and they are very quick to pick up new conditions, and to learn the tricks of the trade of trench warfare."[18] Field-Marshal French was equally happy with their performance. He considered that at Neuve-Chapelle "they had rendered valuable help by keeping the enemy actively engaged in front of their trenches" and concluded that the Canadians "have so far splendidly upheld the traditions of the Empire."[19]

A short but intensive period of training awaited them. A 13th (Royal Highlanders of Canada) Battalion officer, writing home to Montreal, remarked: "We are working harder than ever before. We are being taught the finer points in the game of mining, grenade throwing and wire cutting, and also putting up wire entanglements. We do from six to eight hours a day at this work, so you see we are not idle."[20] A tired member of the 1st (Western Ontario) Battalion grumbled: "We are supposed to be in a rest camp, but if this is rest, give me the trenches."[21] One soldier, after watching his battalion practise an attack, was reminded "of the pictures one used to see of the storming of castles in the Middle Ages. Ladders are carried, bridging material, explosives, etc."[22] The ever-present water hazards made the experience that much more challenging. "While practising to-day," wrote one unfortunate, "I fell into a ditch of slimy water up to the waist, which did not add to my comfort."[23]

By now, the Canadians had undergone a subtle yet noticeable change. A young soldier remarked on it in a letter to his parents:

> Our six months' training, I think, has strengthened and trained our minds and spirits even more than our bodies. Certainly we're very different in our outlook and behaviour from the gang that were at Valcartier. . . . Heaven is very near, and hell, too. But I think we're all quite tranquil. I know I may get killed the next minute, but I don't worry in the least about it. It's a great relief to be able to be like that.[24]

The Canadian Division was destined to make an early return to the trenches. On 1 April, in the midst of its latest training program, General Alderson received orders that the Division was to be reassigned to Gen. Sir Horace Smith-Dorrien's Second Army, joining Lt.-Gen. Sir Herbert Plumer's V Corps in the Ypres salient. Smith-Dorrien was so pleased to have the Canadians return to his jurisdiction that he personally greeted them during a formal inspection on Sunday, 11 April. He made a positive impression; one Canadian described him as "a very fine little man with a determined looking jaw" who offered "some good advice."[25] Smith-Dorrien informed them: "You are soon to take over from the French in the

Ypres salient, a most important part of the line, and there I know you will comport yourselves as becomes such an excellent fighting force."[26]

The inspection left no doubt in his mind as to the morale of the Canadians. Smith-Dorrien paused to speak to a man who seemed to be rather elderly for active service. "How old are you?" he asked.

"Thirty-seven years, sir."

"How many years have you served?"

"Forty-one, sir."

"How do you make that out?" wondered Smith-Dorrien.

"Well, sir, actually I am fifty-seven years of age, but I was allowed by the Department of Militia and Defence to enlist as at thirty-seven years. I have four sons now at the front."[27]

Soon afterwards, the Canadians began moving to the Ypres salient. The were bussed – in London double-decker buses – by brigades to Vlamertinghe, then marched by battalions at half-hour intervals through the old mediaeval towns of Ypres and Wieltje, which showed more wear from the past five months than the previous five hundred years. There they were met by guides who took them into the front lines of the French 11th Division. The Canadian Division was allocated a sector 4250 yards long, on the left of v Corps, whose other two divisions, the 27th – which included Princess Patricia's Canadian Light Infantry – and the 28th, held the balance of the British army's ten-mile share of the salient. To the left of the Canadians were two French divisions, the 45th (Algerian) and 87th (Territorial), of the Groupement d'Elverdinghe. General Currie's Second Brigade moved in first, on the night of 14/15 April, followed the next evening by General Turner's Third Brigade; the First Brigade under General Mercer remained in reserve about Vlamertinghe. General Alderson assumed command of the area at 10 A.M. on Saturday, 17 April, establishing his headquarters in the luxurious Château des Trois Tours, a couple of miles northwest of Ypres.

The salient was a deep curve that measured seventeen miles, from Steenstraat, north of Ypres, to Saint-Eloi, to the south. Across its eight-mile base ran the Canal de l'Yser, which constricted movement in and out of the salient. Battered Ypres was the focal point, as all roads in the vicinity passed through the old town like spokes on a wheel. Long ago, Ypres had been the heart of the flourishing Flanders cloth industry, represented by the massive Gothic-style Cloth Hall that overlooked the Grand Place, or main square. At its peak, in the mid-thirteenth century, Ypres rivalled London and Paris as commercial centres. By the end of the fourteenth century, however, the cloth trade was in decline, and Ypres went with it. As its population dwindled, the Cloth Hall gradually became the home to farmers' markets. This was a troubled land, too, and during the next few hundred years, Ypres was alternately besieged, bombarded, and pillaged by the English, French, Spanish, and Austrians.

Now, in April 1915, Ypres was a mere shadow of its former self. Perhaps half of its prewar population of 22,000 remained. The seventeenth-century fortifications built by Vauban were very much in evidence, reminders of the city's violent past – although, in the moat that enclosed the ramparts, swans still swam serenely, blissfully ignorant of the carnage going on around them. "It is quite a large city," commented Sgt. William Miller of Toronto, a member of the 15th (48th Highlanders of Canada) Battalion, "and although a great part of it including the famous Cloth Hall was in ruins from shells, other portions remained intact and business was going on as usual."[28] Many of the Canadians had trouble pronouncing the town's name, and, like their English equivalents, corrupted it to the easier "Wipers." Other local place names to suffer this indignity included Ploegsteert, which became "Plug Street," Wytschaete, "White Sheet," Poperinghe, "Popinjay," and so on.

There were few other large communities in the Canadian sector. Saint-Julien, northeast of Ypres, was the largest; its 1914 population had been 950, but it was now a virtual ghost town. Some other villages were Saint-Jean, Wieltje, Potijze, Fortuin, and Gravenstafel, each little more than a handful of houses and a church.

At first glance, the area seemed to be flat and featureless. But closer examination revealed a series of long, low ridges, the most important being Gravenstafel Ridge, which lay one to two thousand yards behind the Canadian front line, and Mauser Ridge, which overlooked the left-rear from the neighbouring French zone. The gently rolling countryside was criss-crossed by several creeks, notably the Stroombeek and Haanebeek, which flowed on either side of Gravenstafel Ridge. There was only one large wood in the Canadian sector: Bois de Cuisiniers, or Kitcheners Wood, immediately west of Saint-Julien, where two Canadian battalions would win immortality within a few days.

In strict military terms, there were no valid reasons for holding the salient. The Germans, on the high ground around Passchendaele, six miles northeast of Ypres, enjoyed nearly perfect observation over the whole area, and because they had their guns ranged on three sides, could shell the salient from all three directions with impunity. Historians, with the benefit of hindsight, maintain that the salient should have been evacuated by the French and British, who could have held the much more defensible line along the Canal de l'Yser. Such an argument overlooks the fact that Ypres stood in the heart of the one small part of Belgium that had not fallen to the Germans, and as such it was a symbol of Allied determination – and symbols are important in wartime.

The first Canadians to enter the front lines, four miles northeast of Ypres, would never forget the experience. One party of the 7th (British Columbia) Battalion got "gloriously lost," as Sgt. Raymond MacIlree wrote his parents in Victoria. "Soon a Frenchman found us, for it was a French Regt. we were relieving, and he steered us over all kinds of obstacles, shell holes polka dot the whole place, some so big that a Frenchy drowned in one, also there were dykes and ditches galore."[29] A private in the kilted 16th (Canadian Scottish) Battalion, twenty-year-old John Lockerby, wrote home to Vancouver in a similar vein:

> We got into single file about two paces apart (for the bullets were already beginning to come uncomfortably near) and turned off the hard road into the unknown fields, with a French guide to lead us, who only knew a few words of English.
>
> Our troubles then started in right shape. We were loaded so heavily that it made us quite awkward, and every time one of us stepped into a hole, which was always full of water and, owing to the extreme darkness, impossible to escape, he simply fell in with his load headlong into the filthy mire.
>
> We all began to wish we were at our destination, especially when our guide, after taking us around in circles, over ditches, through barbed wire entanglements, over old fallen trees, along muddy communication trenches and through ruined houses in which corpses had been lying unburied for months, announced suddenly that he had lost his way. It was well for him, and perhaps us too, that we could not speak French.[30]

A shock awaited them in the trenches. They had been warned to expect poor conditions; on 14 April, v Corps headquarters had informed General Alderson that, because the French employed different defensive measures, "it has been found that in taking over trenches from them the parapets generally require strengthening and thickening in order to be bullet proof" and "that there must be no delay in undertaking any work necessary to provide proper cover for the troops manning the trenches."[31] It was a reflection of the French army's disdain for defensive fighting, which they regarded as temporary, a pause between dashing offensive operations. In the event of an enemy attack, the French retired from their lightly held front lines and relied on their excellent, rapid-firing 75-millimetre field guns to prevent a breakthrough. The British, on the other hand, preferred a more secure position, prescribing defence in depth, which involved tooth-and-nail defence at the front trenches. This clash of philosophies always caused headaches for British troops who relieved French formations.

The Canadians discovered that actual conditions exceeded their worst expectations. The French handed over a series of shallow, short, unconnected stretches of trench, protected by the flimsiest of barbed-wire entanglements. British Columbia's 7th Battalion occupied a position that, according to Sergeant MacIlree, "we found to be a mere breastwork, bullet proof for about two feet up, no cover behind, and no traverses."[32] Proper entrenchments called for a continuous line, with a high, bullet-proof parapet in front, a parados (earthen parapet) at the rear to protect occupants from shell bursts behind them, and a zig-zag design, which had the twofold purpose of minimizing the effects of direct hits and of preventing enemy troops who might gain access to the trench from firing along its full length.

Not only were the front-line fortifications pitifully weak but support positions – other than isolated, partially built strongpoints a short distance to the rear – were as good as nonexistent. The war diary of the 10th (Calgary-Winnipeg) Battalion summed up the situation: "We did not see how it could possibly be held if a determined effort was made to take it by a strong force."[33]

Two officers of the 10th had a misadventure the very first night. After dark, Maj. Joseph MacLaren, a thirty-one-year-old Manitoba schoolteacher who served as the battalion's second-in-command, set out with the adjutant, Maj. Dan Ormond, the Portage-la-Prairie lawyer, to explore the position. They knew that the German lines were only eighty yards away, but so ill-defined was the 10th Battalion's location that the two majors, recalled Ormond, inadvertently "went right through our line before we knew it, and we kept on going. And the first thing we knew, a Boche sentry stopped us, and he was thirty feet away!" MacLaren and Ormond threw themselves to the ground, then scrambled back to their own trenches.[34]

Sanitary conditions were terrible, too. "The French have used the trenches as latrines," wrote Sgt. J.L. Stevens of the 8th (90th Winnipeg Rifles) Battalion, in great disgust. "There is a dead German with his feet sticking out of the walls of the trench and there are a lot more in front of the trenches, the whole place stinks to say the least."[35] The 7th Battalion's Sergeant MacIlree complained in a letter to Victoria "that all under my Section is one huge grave, and when you dig you find bodies in all positions, right at the head of my Bivy, a foot was sticking out."[36] The 10th Battalion from the prairies took over the trench that featured "a hand dangling through the parapet." Maj. Dan Ormond recalled that "the men used to shake hands with it."[37]

Things were only slightly better behind the lines. Colonel Creelman, escaping from the farmhouse with the stinking manure pile, established the headquarters of his 2nd Field Artillery Brigade in a dugout near Fortuin, a crossroads four miles east of Ypres. "We relieved a French Brigade two days ago," the unlucky Creelman wrote on 20 April, "and already everyone is itching and scratching. The place was absolutely filthy when we took it over. The straw used for bedding had not been changed in months and was lousy to the limit."[38]

The French also left a misleading impression. "You have come to a quiet spot," they told the incoming Canadians. "We have not been shelled for months."[39]

That was about to change. The Germans gave the Canadians a warm welcome to Flanders Fields, as Sergeant MacIlree wrote his parents in Victoria:

> The trenches were badly made and the Germans could enfilade them, of course we work all night fixing them up. . . . Do not get nervous, it is just bad luck if you get hit by shell fire. The moral effect is supposed to be the worst part. There were over 500 shells pitched into our three [front-line] companies, and the hits were few considering the trenches.[40]

In its first five days in the front lines, MacIlree's 7th Battalion lost four men killed and twenty-six wounded.[41] The neighbouring 8th Battalion from Winnipeg endured a two-hour bombardment during which 260 shells hit its positions. One blast caved in a dugout, "filling up the entrance and entombing three of my men," wrote Sergeant Stevens. "I had to remove the sandbags from the entrance in order to release them."[42] The shelling became so severe that General Currie soon recommended restrictions on daylight movement in the Canadian sector east of Wieltje.[43]

As if they did not have enough to contend with, the Canadians came under friendly fire on at least one occasion. "Shells from British guns explode within our lines," reads the 15 April entry in the Second Brigade's war diary, but there was little damage, and no casualties were reported.[44]

A far more serious threat was posed by snipers, who remained as deadly as ever. The 8th (90th Winnipeg Rifles) Battalion's first fatalities included a young private named Donald Gordon, who was hit by a German marksman on 15 April. Among Private Gordon's personal effects was a diary with the inscription, "Goodbye, Mother, Forgive me"; Gordon had enlisted without his parents' permission.[45] Maj. Harold Mathews, a company commander in the same unit, related how one of his officers, taking pot shots at a low-flying German aircraft, rested his rifle on the sandbagged parapet to steady his aim. According to Major Mathews, "a German sniper spotted it and put a bullet through the woodwork protecting the barrel. This shows what a sharp look out they kept and what clever shots they were, aided of course by telescopic sights."[46]

The Canadians worked hard to upgrade their defences. Nothing was done during the day – the troops were warned "not to show ourselves in the daytime," according to Sergeant Stevens[47] – but at night the soldiers, supervised by engineers, sweated to link up the trenches, raise the parapets with sandbags, and thicken the barbed-wire obstacles in no man's land.

Far from being "quiet," the Ypres salient was a hot spot, as the Canadians were finding out. On 17 April the British attacked Hill 60 (designated by its height in metres) on the southern end of the salient, taking and holding it in a small but bloody four-day battle that featured repeated enemy counter-attacks. Canadian troops were alerted for a possible part in this furious fighting; on 21 April General Mercer was warned to have his First Brigade, in reserve about Vlamertinghe, ready to move to Hill 60 on an hour's notice. Meanwhile, the Germans had stepped up their shelling across the salient, including, on 20 April, the long-distance bombardment by 17-inch howitzers of Ypres itself. The one-ton shells created enormous craters: one, in a field, measured thirty-nine feet wide and fifteen feet deep. "You could put three ambulances into it," claimed a Canadian stretcher-bearer.[48] At senior headquarters the bombardment caused no undue alarm; it was accepted as due retaliation for the capture of Hill 60.

There were, however, more ominous signs that all was not well. The earliest of these came to the Canadians on 15 April, when General Currie wrote in his diary: "Attack expected at night to be preceded by the sending of poisonous gases to our lines and sending up 3 red lights (reported by prisoner who came into French lines)."[49] There was no attack, but continued heavy shelling of the Canadian sector cost Currie's brigade twenty-five casualties.

The prospect of an attack involving "the sending of poisonous gases" was puzzling. Maj. Victor Odlum, second-in-command of the 7th (British Columbia) Battalion, recalled discussing the possibility with his commanding officer, Lt.-Col. William Hart-McHarg. Neither had "the faintest idea" what it meant, said Odlum, the Vancouver newspaperman.[50] "We could not visualize an attack with gas, we could not guess where the gas would come from or how we could recognize it when it did come, and we did not know what were the necessary precautions. And no one could tell us."[51]

Six foot four, fluently bilingual and already a millionaire, Guy Melfort Drummond was 23 and enjoying his socially admired role as an officer in Montreal's 5th Royal Highlanders when this portrait was taken. Three years later he was one of the many young men from the city's leading families who rushed to enlist in the summer of 1914.

(NOTMAN PHOTOGRAPHIC ARCHIVES, McCORD MUSEUM, McGILL UNIVERSITY)

From all parts of the country, and from family homes as diverse as the Drummond mansion on Montreal's Sherbrooke Street (top) and this prairie homestead (below), the eager Canadian volunteers lined up to enlist.

(GLENBOW ARCHIVES, CALGARY/NA-4725-1)

One hundred troop trains left for Valcartier in the summer of 1914. The departure of the 10th Royal Grenadiers from Toronto's Union Station (top) brought out throngs of well-wishers, a brass band, and an overwhelming mood of fervent patriotism and naive optimism. Below, the 48th Highlanders marched bravely off, unaware that at Ypres they would sustain heavier losses than any other Canadian unit in any battle of the war.

Opposite above: Newly arrived at Valcartier, the young Canadians received shaves and haircuts as part of their transformation from citizens to soldiers.
(HORACE BROWN COLLECTION/NATIONAL ARCHIVES OF CANADA/PA-107280)

Opposite below: The eccentric, flamboyant Minister of Defence, Sam Hughes (centre) inspecting the troops at Valcartier. From the beginning, Hughes's style was unorthodox and controversial, but he succeeded in raising and equipping the largest armed force Canada had ever assembled.
(HORACE BROWN COLLECTION/NATIONAL ARCHIVES OF CANADA/PA-107281)

Above: The convoy carrying the first and largest ever Canadian contingent – over 30,000 men and 7,000 horses – across the Atlantic to England sailed at 3 p.m. on Saturday, October 3, 1914. Tragically few of these 30,000 eager young men would make the return trip.
(NATIONAL ARCHIVES OF CANADA/PA-22731)

(GLENBOW ARCHIVES, CALGARY/NA-4927-1)

The Canadians headed for Salisbury Plain, where they were to endure day after day of raw, cold wind and rain. These photos show the men on a route march past the ruins of Stonehenge (top) and (below) in the legendary mud.

(NATIONAL ARCHIVES OF CANADA/PA-22705)

Brig.-Gen. Richard Turner won the Victoria Cross in South Africa and was so courageous that he concealed his broken ribs to get into action at Ypres. But commanding the Third Brigade from the exposed HQ at Mouse Trap Farm he revealed a dangerously weak grasp of military strategy.
(NATIONAL ARCHIVES OF CANADA/ PA-6315)

Lt.-Col. David Watson was 46, a militiaman and former Quebec City journalist. As commander of the 2nd Battalion he once carried a wounded private for half a mile through enemy fire.
(NATIONAL ARCHIVES OF CANADA/ PA-2116)

Brig.-Gen. Malcolm S. Mercer, the 55-year-old former Toronto lawyer, was given little opportunity to prove himself as commander of the First Brigade in this battle. He was killed as a major-general in action on June 2, 1916 at Mount Sorrel in the Ypres salient.
(NATIONAL ARCHIVES OF CANADA/ PA-7443)

Major Andy McNaughton, the brilliant young scientist who got married while at Valcartier, rose to prominence as the commander of the Canadian Corps heavy artillery, and then survived Ypres to command the Canadian army in World War II.
(NATIONAL ARCHIVES OF CANADA/ PA-34150)

Brig.-Gen. Arthur Currie, a militiaman who had never before been in combat,
proved himself to be a natural leader. In sharp contrast to the other four
generals in the Canadian Division, Currie won rave reviews for his performance
at Second Ypres. In November 1918 Currie returned to Canada with an
impressive array of honours and awards, including a knighthood, and was
eventually promoted to full general, the first Canadian to achieve that rank.
(GLENBOW ARCHIVES, CALGARY/NA-1715-1)

This is not to say nothing was done. General Currie, as baffled as anyone, arranged for the 18-pounders of Colonel Creelman's 2nd Field Artillery Brigade to search the enemy lines for gas supplies. Maj. Andy McNaughton, whose 7th Battery received a special allotment of ninety shells for this purpose – at a time when British 18-pounders were limited to routine expenditure of three rounds per day – later called it "one of the best days I had in the war,"[52] because it gave him the opportunity to test some of his scientific theories for accurate shooting. (McNaughton even carried a thermometer so that the temperature of the shells could be taken into account in calculating ranges.) But the shelling of the German trenches and rear areas produced nothing unusual that might have lent credence to the reports of a pending gas attack.

So, with each passing day, the concern diminished. This was unfortunate, because the threat was real. The Germans had been plotting the destruction of the Ypres salient for some time. To succeed, they intended to introduce a terrible new weapon – poison gas.

As early as December 1914, plans had been drawn up to eliminate the salient. Gen.-Col. Duke Albrecht of Württemberg, whose Fourth Army was responsible for the Ypres sector, considered a limited, corps-sized operation to take Langemarck and Pilckem in the northern part of the salient. Although these plans came to naught, they were revived in January 1915. On the twenty-fifth of that month, General Bertold von Deimling, who commanded xv Corps in Duke Albrecht's army, was summoned to General Falkenhayn's headquarters. There, Deimling, whose corps held the southern half of the salient, learned that his superiors "were going to put into service a new weapon of war, toxic gas, that it was in my sector that they had thought to make the first attempts." Deimling admitted that the idea "disgusted" him, but he set aside his personal revulsion, arguing that war "knows no laws."[53]

There was, of course, nothing unique about the concept of chemical warfare. Its origins can be traced as far back as several centuries before the birth of Christ. The Greeks were famed for it. In 429 BC, for example, the Spartans attempted to capture Plataea by employing clouds of sulphur fumes to disable the city's defenders. More famous was the so-called Greek fire, an incendiary mixture delivered in pots thrown by catapults; introduced as early as 424 BC, Greek fire and its variations were used well into mediaeval times. During the Middle Ages, defenders of besieged castles poured boiling oil and molten lead on the unfortunate heads of their attackers. In 1485 Belgrade was saved from the rapacious Turks by an alchemist who created a toxic cloud from burning chemicals. As recently as the American Civil War, the United States government had entertained proposals for liquid-chlorine gas shells.

In the early 1900s Germany had conducted considerable research into the use of poison gas, in spite of international treaties specifically prohibiting it. A special Hague Declaration in 1899 forbade "the use of projectiles the sole object of which is the diffusion of asphyxiating gases," and The Hague Convention, 1907, banned the employment of "poison or poisoned weapons" in wartime.[54]

The Germans had not been alone. During the first weeks of the war, the French employed gas-filled cartridges fired by special rifles, as well as grenades containing an irritant that could be lethal in sufficiently large quantities. The British, too, had considered contravening the accepted rules of war. Lord Kitchener had already rejected the use of incapacitating gas as unsuited to land warfare, but the Admiralty had studied the effects of nonlethal gases during the winter of 1914/15. As late as 11 March 1915, Sir Douglas Haig, commanding the BEF's First Army, wrote of a visit by a prominent personage:

> Lord Dundonald arrived from England, he is studying the conditions of war in the hopes of being able to apply to modern conditions an invention of his great grandfather for driving a garrison out of a fort by using sulfur fumes. I asked him how he arranged to have a favourable wind.[55]

Even in Canada, the Department of Militia and Defence had dealt with private proposals for the use of poison gas. In November 1914 it had been suggested "that tubes of CS_2 highly charged with cacodylcyanide be thrown to burst in the enemy's trenches," while another patriotic individual wrote in February 1915: "I have invented a four inch cartridge which explodes when fired, giving off from one hundred fifty to two hundred cubic feet of extremely poisonous gas. Tests show that it is so poisonous that one deep breath of it will prove fatal." The militia department replied: "The use of asphyxiating or deleterious gases is not allowed by the International Declaration signed at The Hague, 29th July 1899."[56]

German research had been renewed in the fall of 1914, at General Falkenhayn's insistence. The results left something to be desired. In late October a nontoxic sneezing powder, contained in artillery shells, was fired at British troops in the Neuve-Chapelle sector. This proved to be an invention not to be sneezed at. "It speaks volumes for the shells' effectiveness that the victims did not realize that they had been victimized till they read about it after the war."[57] The search for more lethal means led to shells filled with xyxyl bromide. This gas was used against Russian troops on the Eastern Front in January 1915, but its effect was negated by the extreme cold. After some modifications, it was used on French forces on the Western Front in March, but again it went unnoticed.

Research in another area offered better prospects. Germany's large dye industry manufactured a lethal by-product, chlorine gas, which could be produced "in sufficient quantities without encroachment on the national production of munitions." Scientists proposed to concentrate this gas in cylinders that would discharge a deadly cloud that the wind would carry over the enemy lines. The Germans later justified its use on the grounds that it "was a discovery of German war research and in no way contravened earlier international agreements. Moreover the precepts of humanity did not forbid introduction of the gas weapon."[58]

The attack on the Ypres salient would serve two purposes. In addition to enabling the Germans to test the chlorine-gas cloud, it would serve as a diversion for their main effort in 1915, an attack on the Russians, in Galicia.

Preparations proceeded quickly. By late February, the first gas cylinders had been installed along the front of General Deimling's xv Corps. Random British shell fire destroyed several cylinders, causing casualties among German troops, who were then issued with primitive respirators to cover their noses and mouths: proper gas masks were still far in the future. By 10 March, six thousand cylinders had been put in place. But the weather failed to co-operate. Either there was no wind, or it blew in the wrong direction. The army commander, Duke Albrecht, waited impatiently for two weeks before ordering a change in plan: he would strike the northern part of the salient, between Steenstraat and Poelcappelle. By 11 April 5730 cylinders had been installed in that sector, but General Falkenhayn was unhappy with the lengthy delay. On the tenth, he told Albrecht that he wanted the attack executed as soon as possible to cover the imminent departure of the troops taking part in the Galician offensive. Albrecht set 15 April as the date, but the wind let him down again. Rescheduled for the twentieth, the attack once again had to be postponed because there was no breeze. Albrecht selected a new date: 22 April.

It was to be a strictly limited operation. Carried out by two corps, xxiii Reserve and xxvi Reserve, on a four-mile front. Their objective was "the seizure of the [Pilckem] ridge marked by the road Boesinghe-Pilckem-Langemarck-Poelcappelle"; following its capture, "the troops are at once to dig in, arranging for mutual flanking by means of supporting points."[59] The Germans believed that the capture of this high ground would make it "impossible for the enemy to remain longer in the Ypres salient."[60]

Because the operation was limited, Albrecht had few reserves available to exploit success. To compensate for this shortcoming, the general-colonel created a special force. On 5 April he thinned out the front of his XXVII Reserve Corps, and the ten battalions procured in this manner were banded into Stürmbrigade Schmieden, named after its commanding officer. The formation was withdrawn and its troops underwent "special training in the attack on trenches and in open warfare." On the fifteenth they were inspected by Kaiser Wilhelm, who "stood each man a litre of beer out of his own private purse."[61]

Security was abysmal. As early as 30 March, the French Tenth Army, holding the line immediately south of the Ypres salient, captured a number of prisoners who revealed that "there is a large supply along the whole front in the neighbourhood of Zillebeek of iron cylinders, 1.4 metres long, which are stored a little in rear of the trenches in bomb-proof shelters or even buried. They contain a gas which is intended to render the enemy unconscious or to asphyxiate him."[62]

Then there was Pte. August Jäger. A member of the 234th Reserve Regiment of the 51st Reserve Division, XXVI Reserve Corps, Private Jäger deserted late on 13 April, surrendering to French troops near Langemarck. Jäger gave his hosts full details of an impending attack involving "asphyxiating gas." The gas cloud would be discharged upon "a given signal, 3 red rockets fired by the artillery," said Jäger, and would be "carried by a favourable wind towards the French lines. This gas is intended to asphyxiate the men who occupy the trenches and to allow the Germans to occupy them without loss." He added that the attackers had been equipped with respirators to enable them to breathe safely.[63]

Jäger's warning was heeded by at least one senior French officer. Gen. Edmond Ferry,* commanding the 11th Division – the formation relieved by the Canadians – alerted his front-line brigade and sent a staff officer to warn the British "to exercise the greatest vigilance and to seek suitable means to prevent inhalation of gas." The French high command, however, did not share Ferry's concern. A liaison officer from Grand Quartier Général – the French equivalent of the British army's General Headquarters, or GHQ – told Ferry that "all this gas business cannot be taken seriously" and reprimanded him for issuing a warning to the British: "A divisional commander has not the right to communicate direct with allied troops."[64] Ferry's immediate superior, Gen. Henri Gabriel Putz, was

*Private Jäger's name was kept confidential until it was revealed by General Ferry in a 1930 magazine article. In December 1932 a German court sentenced Jäger to ten years' imprisonment for his betrayal.

openly sceptical of Jäger's information. In view of the deserter's "great knowledge of the German position and defence arrangements," General Putz concluded that the private "had been primed and sent over with the intention to deceive."[65]

But there were other warning signs. A French agent learned of the tentative date of the attack, 15 April, and a Belgian spy reported: "Passages have been prepared across old trenches to facilitate bringing up of artillery. Germans intend making use of tubes with asphyxiating gas. They are placed in batteries of 20 tubes per 40 metres along front of XXIV [sic] Corps. A favourable wind necessary." The following day, Belgian intelligence discovered that the Germans had placed in Ghent "a rush order of 20,000 mouth respirators" soaked in a special liquid.[66]

Perhaps the most convincing evidence was provided publicly by the Germans. On 17 April a press communiqué accused the British of using "shells and bombs with asphyxiating gas" near Ypres. This was typical of "the German mentality," says the British official history, "that the Germans intended to do something of the kind themselves, and were putting the blame on their opponents in advance."[67]

In the meantime, another deserter clouded the picture for the Allies. Julius Rapsahl, a disgruntled former NCO – he had been demoted for striking an officer – with the 4th Landwehr Regiment of the 52nd Reserve Division, XXVI Reserve Corps, crossed no man's land on the fifteenth and surrendered to troops of the French 11th Division. Rapsahl denied the possibility of a pending gas attack by the Germans, explaining that the cotton packet in his possession had been issued to protect him against the Allied use of poison gas.[68]

With the evidence inconclusive, even contradictory, the French and British high commands remained sceptical. Not only was the concept of a gas attack utterly foreign but it was inconceivable to these generals that the Germans would actually attempt such a flagrant violation of the accepted rules of war – which speaks highly of their respect for the German military. Nevertheless, it would have been irresponsible to ignore the possibility altogether, and the British defenders of the salient were repeatedly alerted. General Plumer, commanding V Corps, passed along all available information to his divisional commanders, "for what it was worth" – a reflection of his own scepticism. Aerial reconnaissance on 15 April revealed no unusual activity in the enemy's rear areas that might indicate preparations for an attack, but on the eighteenth Plumer predicted that "the Germans will endeavour to take some kind of offensive action against some part of the line" within a few days. "Such action will probably include a heavy artillery bombardment and possibly a mine explosion followed by an attempt to rush one or more of our trenches." Although there was no mention of poison gas, the British were at least braced for an attack, which is more than can be said for the French, who remained content with a passive pose, much as they had in this sector for the past few months. The opportunity to discover the enemy's intentions was there, but the French permitted it to pass.[69]

This was an anxious time for the Germans. Their offensive was now solely dependent on the weather, over which they had no control. General Falkenhayn continually urged Duke Albrecht to "make the attack at the first possible favourable opportunity,"[70] but the Fourth Army's commander could do nothing without a breeze blowing in the right direction. That they found themselves in this predicament seems surprising – especially considering the German reputation for efficiency – because any competent meteorologist could have told them that the prevailing winds in this part of Europe blow from west to east, rather than east to west as the Germans required. It was also a significant consideration if the Allies chose to retaliate with their own poison-gas clouds. The Germans, it might be said, were starting to throw stones from a very exposed glass house.

Thursday, 22 April, dawned warm and sunny, a beautiful spring day – but without a breath of wind. The German attack, scheduled for 5:45 A.M., was postponed at 5:30 until later in the day.

In the trenches, the grey-clad German infantry, densely packed in their attack formations, had no choice but to sit and wait. Any movement might give them away to the enemy, and there were already enough telltale signs to fret about. Along a three-and-three-quarter-mile front, 160 tons of chlorine had been assembled, each of the 5730 cylinders connected to its own hose draped over the parapet and hanging in no man's land. Moreover, German engineers had already cut passages through their own barbed wire. If any of these preparations were noticed by the French troops along the northern face of the salient, the Germans would be doomed, slaughtered with ease by the deadly 75-millimetre field guns of the French. Just as haunting was the possibility of a random hit by enemy artillery shells on one or more of the gas cylinders: since there were not enough respirators to go around, only the leading waves had been issued them, and the rest did not have to be told the terrible consequences they would suffer with the accidental release of the gas. It was not only the seventy-degree temperatures that made the Germans sweat on that fateful April day.

Late in the afternoon, a light wind sprang up. And it was blowing in the right direction. Shortly after four o'clock, the German artillery opened a furious bombardment of the French entrenchments, and the Fourth Army's headquarters issued new orders: the gas would be discharged at 5

P.M., followed twenty minutes later by the infantry, attacking with bayonets fixed and rifles unloaded.

The first great gas attack in the history of modern warfare was about to become a horrific reality. And Canadians were destined to play a leading part in the bloody fight that lay ahead.

CHAPTER SEVEN

"A Great Day for Canada, Boys"

It started out as a typical day in the Ypres salient. The Canadian Division's 4250-yard-long sector was still being held by two brigades, the Second under General Currie on the right and the Third under General Turner on the left. The Second Brigade had two battalions, the 5th (Western Cavalry) and 8th (90th Winnipeg Rifles), in the front line, with the 7th (British Columbia) in close support near Fortuin and the 10th (Calgary-Winnipeg) in divisional reserve back at Ypres. The Third Brigade's front was held by the 13th (Royal Highlanders of Canada) and 15th (48th Highlanders of Canada) battalions, supported by the 14th (Montreal) in Saint-Jean and the 16th (Canadian Scottish) in divisional reserve, also at Ypres. The First Brigade, billeted in and around Vlamertinghe, was in V Corps reserve.

The weather was gorgeous. "On that April day," wrote Lt.-Col. George Nasmith of Toronto, "the very essence of spring was in the air; the hedges of northern France were beginning to whiten with bloom, and the wild flowers were thick. . . . It was the time back in Canada when the spring feeling suddenly gets into the blood, when one throws work to the winds and takes to the woods in search of the first violets."[1]

In the trenches, life went on as usual. Most of the men spent the daylight hours trying to rest from the previous night's work on the defences, saving their energy for the coming night's toil. Still, there was a need for recreational diversions, even in the front lines, as divisional headquarters answered a Third Brigade request for certain items: "There are one hundred mouth organs at divn'l HQ for you. Please call for them. No cards available just now but will send you some out of next consignment."[2] The reserve units were more fortunate, the officers taking advantage of the sunshine to play polo, the other ranks engaging in rough-and-tumble games of soccer. Some were even making arrangements to attend a cockfight, "a popular local diversion novel to most Canadians."[3]

But even in this pastoral setting, the harsh reality of war was ever-present. Throughout the day, the Germans continued their long-range destruction of Ypres, until "a dark red pall of dust and smoke lay heavy on the town."[4] There was cause for concern in a report from v Corps headquarters that aerial reconnaissance had detected an unusual amount of activity in the enemy's rear, including a quarter-mile-long column of troops at Poelcappelle.[5] Unfortunately for the Allies, French vigilance was not as pronounced as that of the British, and the painfully obvious preparations by the enemy opposite the northern part of the salient went unnoticed.

At five that afternoon, everything changed. General Alderson, the divisional commander, had ridden his horse, Sir James, to Wieltje, then dismounted and walked forward to inspect a Canadian gun position near Saint-Julien. There his attention was drawn by the sound of heavy rifle fire in the French zone to the north – so common was shelling in the salient that he paid no heed to the Germans' preliminary bombardment. "Directly afterwards," Alderson wrote, "two clouds of yellowish-green smoke appeared. . . . These clouds spread rapidly, laterally, until they appeared to merge into each other."[6]

This smoke was chlorine gas, although the Canadians were slow to realize it. At least one senior officer attributed it to "a new powder the French were using."[7] And while most accounts agree that the cloud was yellow-green, Canadian observers reported a number of variations, ranging from "brownish yellow" to "bluish grey" to "greeny-red."[8]

Immediately to the left of the Canadian section, the French of the 45th and 87th divisions bore the brunt of the gas attack. Precisely at 5 P.M., the Germans had changed the history of war by setting the chlorine hissing from the thousands of assembled cylinders. Forming a huge cloud half-a-mile deep, the deadly vapours drifted steadily at five to six miles an hour across no man's land towards the French trenches. A medical officer in the 45th Division recalled that the fumes "burned in my throat, caused pains in my chest, and made breathing all but impossible. I spat blood and suffered from dizziness." Few other Frenchmen stayed around to feel the effects. A French army medical report later stated that only 625 men were treated for gassing, and of these three died.[9]

If the impact of the gas was mainly psychological on 22 April, its results were nonetheless devastating. "Even before it reached them," the German official account says of the French, "the enemy could be seen to waver before it after firing a few shots."[10] When the German infantry attacked at 5:20 P.M., they found only isolated pockets of French resistance. The French field artillery went into action promptly, but by seven o'clock the guns had fallen silent: fifty-seven had been captured, and the rest had withdrawn amid the panic-stricken rout of the two defending divisions.

The Canadians had a clear view of the impending disaster. At Pond Farm, near Fortuin, the Second Brigade's General Currie soon "saw a great many French soldiers, a few of whom were wounded, come running past Report Centre from the North saying that all was lost and the Germans coming."[11] The scenes were equally alarming elsewhere. General Alderson, riding hard for his headquarters at Château des Trois Tours, found the crossings of the Canal de l'Yser already congested with fleeing French troops. Lt.-Col. Edward Morrison, the former Ottawa newspaperman whose 1st Field Artillery Brigade had been moving towards Ypres in the late afternoon en route to positions in the salient, witnessed the following:

> The French troops were absolutely in rout and were coming across country in a very demoralized condition. Ambulances loaded with unwounded men, ammunition wagons, transport vehicles crowded with infantry, were galloping across country through hedges, ditches, and barbed wire. In many cases artillery horses had been unhooked from guns and limbers, and were being used for quick transportation, sometimes with two and three men on their backs. After this rabble came men on foot, without arms, singly and in groups, alternately running and walking, and only intent on getting away. At the time nothing was known regarding gas and the fugitives were quite unable to explain the cause of their terror.[12]

Two Canadian medical officers were among the first to diagnose the problem. One was Colonel Nasmith, whose four-foot-six height precluded combat duty and who so eloquently described the springlike conditions in the salient prior to the attack; the other was a close friend, Capt. F.A.C. Scrimger, the thirty-five-year-old medical officer of the 14th (Montreal) Battalion. Nasmith, an analytical chemist from Toronto, met Scrimger near Ypres, and they watched the mysterious cloud advance. "It looks like chlorine," Nasmith surmised, and Scrimger, a surgeon at Montreal's Royal Victoria Hospital, agreed.[13] (Later analysis showed the gas to be "largely chlorine but with probably some bromine present."[14] Within a few days, Nasmith had put his skills as a chemist to work and had developed a remedy, a pad soaked in hyposulfite of soda, which was issued to the front-line units in the salient.)

In the meantime, Scrimger, who was to win the coveted Victoria Cross in the course of the battle, came up with a more immediate solution to the menacing yellowish-green cloud now drifting silently towards the Canadian lines. No doubt using more direct language, he instructed the men of his battalion "to urinate on your pocket handkerchief [and] tie it over your mouth."[15] This unpleasant emergency measure, which caused the chlorine to crystallize, saved countless Canadian lives during the next several days.

As they peered out at the gas, the Canadians knew that its effects were ghastly. Capt. Paul Villiers of Victoria, at Third Brigade headquarters at Mouse Trap Farm, recalled seeing the fleeing Algerians "suffering the agony of the damned, grey-green in the face, and dying from suffocation."[16] On the west bank of the canal, Colonel Morrison saw them, too, "many suffering from the gas and tearing madly through the crush of fugitives with staring eyes and their faces flecked with blood and froth. Frequently these men would fall down under the feet of the mob, and roll about like mad dogs in their death agonies."[17]

The Canadians who received mild doses of the gas were able to sympathize with the terrified French. The fumes drifted through the ranks of the 7th (British Columbia) Battalion near Fortuin, "causing eyes to smart and water, noses to run, and breathing to become difficult," reported Maj. Victor Odlum, the second-in-command.[18] Lt.-Col. John Currie, the officer commanding the 15th (48th Highlanders of Canada) Battalion, endured a slight gassing in the village of Saint-Julien. "When it is first breathed," Colonel Currie later wrote, "it is not unpleasant, smelling not unlike chloroform, but very soon it stings the mucous-membrane of the mouth, the eyes, and the nose. The lungs feel as if they were filled with rheumatism. The tissues of the lungs are scalded and broken down, and it takes a man a long time to recover, if he ever does fully recover."[19]

Civilians, most of them from Ypres, soon joined the exodus from the salient. There were heart-breaking sights for the watching Canadian soldiers. Pte. Nathaniel Nicholson of the 16th (Canadian Scottish) Battalion recalled that "people were running hither and thither. As a matter of fact, I saw one woman carrying a baby, and the baby's head was gone, and it was quite devastating."[20] The 14th (Royal Montreal Regiment) Battalion's Lance-Cpl. Hugh Brewer added: "I can see them now. There was one youngster, probably fifteen years old, carrying his grandmother on his back, and there was a little baby, about five years old, in the doorway across the street, deserted and crying."[21] Young and old, they carried their few worldly possessions on their backs or in small carts pulled by dogs or mules. Colonel Morrison, the gunner from Ottawa, observed that "it was not uncommon to see ladies, hatless and wearing high-heeled slippers, sometimes carrying babies in their arms, and with younger children hanging to their skirts, while their mothers' feet were already bleeding from tramping over the rough cobblestones."[22]

The human flood almost swept away the Canadian batteries heading towards the front on the road into Ypres. "So great became the crush,"

Morrison later reported, "that a wedge of horsemen had to be formed at the head of the brigade column to prevent it being broken and overrun."[23] In the early evening, the Canadian guns were moved into adjacent fields to cover the approaches to the canal.

Although spared the worst of the poison gas, the Canadians in the forward zone had plenty to keep them busy. The Germans subjected them to a brief but furious bombardment that one officer said was "simply indescribable."[24] In Saint-Julien, Lt.-Col. John Currie considered himself lucky to escape. "The rain of heavy shells made it impossible for any human being to move around the streets. A number of my men were killed, three of them while I was walking up the street." Reaching his battalion headquarters, Colonel Currie ordered staff officers to remove papers and valuables. The village, he noted, was already being peppered with small-arms fire.[25]

Although several hours passed before a clear picture emerged, it was immediately obvious that the French had suffered a serious defeat and that a similar fate threatened the more than fifty thousand British defenders in the southern half of the salient. From the left of the Canadian Division, on the Poelcappelle road, to the Canal de l'Yser, stretched an undefended gap of eight thousand yards – over four miles. Save for a few small groups rallied by the Canadians, there were no organized French units east of the canal by nightfall. Indeed, there were pitifully few formations of any description standing in the path of the advancing Germans. The largest was the Canadian garrison at Saint-Julien: two companies, one each from Montreal's 13th and 14th battalions, fewer than five hundred men in all. Five hundred yards north of Saint-Julien stood a Canadian field battery, while to the west, in Kitcheners Wood, was a battery of British heavy guns. Unless these scattered units could be reinforced and the gap filled – and quickly – the Ypres salient was doomed.

The situation was critical, but for a long time it appeared to be even worse than it really was. Confusing and often erroneous reports flew back and forth across the battlefield, and by the time they reached v Corps headquarters at Poperinghe, things must have seemed utterly hopeless. As late as ten o'clock that night, it was believed that both Saint-Julien and Wieltje had been captured and that most of the Canadian Division had been routed along with the French. In fact, the Canadians had not been directly attacked and were still holding their original front-line positions. The surprise is evident in the war diary of v Corps, written at noon on the twenty-third: "It appears that the Canadian Div. are still in all their fire trenches."[26]

Much of the confusion can be attributed to an age-old problem, "the fog of war." Communications, even in 1915, were primitive: wireless radio had not yet been adapted for use in combat, and the field telephone was the primary instrument of communication, as it would remain throughout the war. However, telephone lines were vulnerable to shell fire, and interruptions in service were commonplace. Human messengers, "runners," were employed on those occasions, but it was hazardous work, and more than a few reports and orders failed to arrive at their destinations in the bullet- and shell-swept battle zone around Ypres.

Human failings were apparent, too. In this case, two officers can be singled out, both of them at Third Brigade headquarters: General Turner (the man who had concealed his fractures in order to be there) and his brigade-major, Lt.-Col. Garnet Hughes, who happened to be the son of the minister of militia and defence – a connection that did not hamper his rise through the Canadian military hierarchy, although his capabilities were openly questioned. Turner and Hughes were inexperienced, as were all the senior Canadian officers, and they failed to get a grip on the situation right from the start of the battle. They were, to be sure, acting under extreme duress at all times. It did not encourage cool deliberation that their headquarters, at Mouse Trap Farm, were now virtually in the front lines, and by seven that evening had come under small-arms fire from the Germans holding Mauser Ridge, a scant five hundred yards away.

Whatever is said about Turner's ability as a combat commander, none can doubt his personal bravery. Slender and bespectacled, Turner looked more like a mild-mannered schoolteacher than a war hero, but that is what he was, having won the Victoria Cross as a subaltern in the South African War. His courage did not fail him now, with enemy bullets whining off the brick buildings at Mouse Trap Farm. Turner, "buckling on his revolver, [declared] that he was quite prepared to die there, but surrender, he would not."[27] Later in the fighting, a shell burst showered him with dust and debris as he was writing out an order. "Pretty close," he muttered, then coolly concluded his message.[28]

Turner and Hughes displayed their incompetence early in the battle. The flurry of erroneous reports from them began at 6:32 P.M., when the following was sent to the Second Brigade: "The left of our left section is retiring having been driven in. Will you be ready to support us?" Within minutes, Hughes dispatched an even more alarming message about their Third Brigade to divisional headquarters: "Our left driven back and apparently whole line forced back towards St. Julien." And at 7:10 P.M.: "We are forced back on GHQ line" – a reference to the partially completed support position known as the General Headquarters line.* At this time,

---

*Formally known as the GHQ second line, it will be referred to as the GHQ line in this text, simply because there was no GHQ first line.

the Third Brigade's position was not only intact but it had not even been attacked yet. It was eight-thirty before Turner and Hughes discovered the correct state of affairs and relayed the information to General Alderson at divisional headquarters.[29]

If nothing else, these inaccurate reports helped to galvanize higher commands to act with urgency. At eight o'clock, General Plumer released two battalions, the 2nd (Eastern Ontario) and 3rd (Toronto), of the First Brigade from V Corps reserve and sent them to Alderson. "You must endeavour to make your left secure," Plumer told the Canadian Division commander. "Make certain of the second line of defence [i.e., the GHQ line] at any rate."[30] Plumer also placed at Alderson's disposal a British battalion, the 2nd East Yorkshire, which was stationed near Brielen, just north of Ypres, to guard the canal crossings; it was the first of thirty-three British battalions that would come under Alderson's jurisdiction during the battle. Other reinforcements were on the way, too. The 28th Division, on the immediate right of the Canadians, had three reserve battalions billeted near Saint-Jean. Two of these, the 2nd East Kent (the "Buffs") and 3rd Middlesex, deployed along a two-thousand-yard front (with their left flank touching) to the canal; the other, the 5th King's Own Royal Regiment, remained in reserve.

No Canadian unit was in worse shape than Montreal's 13th (Royal Highlanders of Canada) Battalion, which was responsible for the Third Brigade's left-front trenches as far as the Poelcappelle road. The French on the left of this battalion had all but disappeared, leaving the Canadian flank totally unprotected. As soon as it became clear that the French were in trouble on the left, the commander of 1 Company, Maj. D. Rykert McCuaig, wasted no time in forming a new flank along the road, thinning out his front line and freeing a few troops, plus a handful of Algerians, to man the new position. Several hundred yards to the rear, beyond the Lekkerboterbeek, Maj. Edward Norsworthy, second-in-command of the 13th Battalion, posted two platoons and also rallied a number of Algerians. Major Norsworthy was much admired; one NCO called him "the finest officer in our battalion."[31]

Norsworthy and his party out near the Lekkerboterbeek were doomed. The little group of Canadians and Algerians stood in the path of a determined German effort to cross the Poelcappelle road and outflank the Canadian front line. In a short, sharp, one-sided fight as darkness descended, the enemy overwhelmed Norsworthy's little force. All the defenders were killed or captured; Norsworthy was among the dead. With him fell Capt. Guy Drummond, the young millionaire from Montreal's "Square Mile", who took a bullet in the neck. The man who had been groomed as a future prime minister now lay dead in the gathering Flanders dusk, killed at the outset of the first Canadian action of the war.

But their brave stand in their first action had not been wasted. With daylight starting to fade, the Germans, having suffered heavy casualties and growing concerned about the intentions of the defenders facing them, halted their advance and dug in for the night.

Meanwhile, the road to Saint-Julien was wide open, save for four Canadian field guns. These 18-pounders belonged to Maj. William King's 10th Field Battery and were posted in an orchard midway between Keerselaere and Saint-Julien. With the demise of Major Norsworthy's party, the 10th Battery was the only organized force in the mile-wide gap between the front lines and Saint-Julien. But the four guns had already proven their potency. In the early evening, a group of Germans occupied a nearby house, which Major King, a thirty-seven-year-old South African War veteran from Ontario, spotted through his binoculars. "That house is full of Boche," he called to his gunners. "Watch me blow them out at point blank." He scored a direct hit with his first shot, and the Canadians cheered as they watched the enemy soldiers scramble for safety amid the rubble and smoke.[32]

An even more tempting target presented itself a short time later. A French sergeant who had joined the battery gripped Major King's arm, pointed, and muttered one word: "Allemandes." There, on the other side of a hedge west of the Poelcappelle road, marched an enemy column, oblivious to the presence of the Canadians. King quickly swung his guns around and opened fire over open sights – point-blank range. The carnage was incredible as the shrapnel shells ripped huge holes in the grey-clad ranks of the German column. The stunned survivors scattered. But soon they returned the fire, and the Canadian gunners were showered with leaves as bullets shredded the willow trees around them.[33]

The Germans eventually withdrew, but King knew that he had only gained a little breathing-space; his guns were dangerously exposed and would be easy pickings for the swarms of German foot-soldiers once darkness had fallen. Before then, however, help arrived in the form of sixty Canadians from Saint-Julien. Among them was a machine-gunner, Lance-Cpl. Frederick Fisher of the 13th (Royal Highlanders of Canada) Battalion. The nineteen-year-old student from Toronto and his four-man crew swiftly set up their Colt machine-gun. Again and again in the fading light, the Germans advanced towards the vulnerable Canadian 18-pounders, but each time, Fred Fisher and his gun drove them back. "All four of Fisher's crew were shot down, but Fisher, not content with the work he had done towards saving the battery, moved his machine-gun forward to a still more advanced position, where it was fully exposed to the fire of shrapnel, machine-guns, and rifles, and where he stayed, fighting with his gun, until he was shot dead." Corporal Fisher was rewarded with a posthumous Victoria Cross, the first awarded to a Canadian soldier in the Great War.[34]

Thanks to Fisher's sacrifice, Major King extricated his precious 18-pounders, but only by the narrowest of margins. The battery was almost surrounded by Germans, making it impossible to bring up the horses to haul the guns away; so King's gunners and infantrymen, under fire, man-handled the 18-pounders back to the horses. Once they were limbered, King instructed his drivers to head in the darkness for the west side of the canal, "any way you can get out."[35]

Darkness was a godsend for the Canadians. With the withdrawal of Major King's battery, there was no organized resistance left in the mile between Saint-Julien and the Canadian front lines. The Canadians could also consider themselves lucky that by encountering King and his gunners the Germans had stumbled into the only defenders in the entire gap on the evening of the twenty-second; the bloody, confused fighting in semidarkness left the enemy convinced that they faced stronger opposition than was actually the case. This gaping hole remained unoccupied by Canadians for several more hours, but the Germans, no doubt mindful of the damage caused by King's guns and Fisher's machine-gun, and reluctant to meet similar defences everywhere, made no effort to exploit it.

Throughout the evening, the two front-line Canadian brigades tried to shore up the line. General Turner, to his credit, wasted little time in summoning his nearest reserve, three companies of the 14th (Montreal) Battalion, billeted near Saint-Jean – the battalion's other company formed part of the Saint-Julien garrison. The 14th set off shortly after six o'clock, but progress was slow, as one NCO later related:

A steady stream of humanity – the most mixed and miserable lot of people I have ever seen – moved by us in the direction of Ypres, leaving us barely room to squeeze through in the direction of the enemy. Most pitiful were the civilian population – mostly women and children – all utterly demoralized and passing in seemingly endless procession. . . . And, of course, there were the wounded – hundreds of them – and the main body of French colonial troops in retreat, some of who[m] had been gassed, with yellow faces and gasping for breath.[36]

The reserves of the 14th Battalion quickly occupied the GHQ line near Mouse Trap Farm, the location of Turner and the younger Hughes's Third

Brigade headquarters. This partially constructed position consisted of a series of well-sited redoubts, a few hundred yards apart, protected by six-foot-wide barriers of barbed wire, gapped in places to permit the passage of friendly troops – but no work had been done on the trench that should have linked the strong points, except for the removal of the turf to show where it should be dug. The GHQ line ended on nearby Mauser Ridge, and, as the Canadians would soon discover, it could be outflanked with ease.

Already, an unknown number of enemy troops were holding Mauser Ridge. Two patrols of Montreal's 14th Battalion were sent out to determine the exact position of the Germans, but only one returned. In the descending darkness, Company Sgt.-Maj. Charles Price (who ended the war a lieutenant-colonel in command of the 14th Battalion) and Cpl. Stuart LeMesurier set out to scout the enemy lines. They soon encountered two figures; when Corporal LeMesurier challenged them, he was shot through the hand. "So then, just instinctively," Sergeant-Major Price recalled, "I put up my rifle and I shot both of them."[37] Price and the wounded LeMesurier then returned to the battalion, which kept up a sporadic fire with the enemy for most of the night.

Meanwhile, over to the right, the Second Brigade's commander, General Currie, had called up his support unit, the 7th (British Columbia) Battalion. The 7th was ordered to Locality C, on Gravenstafel Ridge. Locality C was important, but not impressive. It consisted "chiefly of a rather poor trench, 200 yards long, facing north-east, built in the usual French thin parapet style, with no depth, no thickness and no parados [rear parapet]. . . . Along the front, ten yards away, was a barbed wired fence."[38] The 7th Battalion reached the position after dark, and began digging in.

Information was sketchy. Lt.-Col. William Hart-McHarg, the officer commanding the 7th, was worried about the uncertainty of the situation on his left, knowing that Currie's Second Brigade headquarters had made repeated attempts during the evening to determine the Third Brigade's status from Turner and Hughes; all of these requests were to go unanswered until just before midnight.[39] In the hope of forming some kind of picture, Colonel Hart-McHarg sent his second-in-command, Maj. Victor Odlum, to survey the scene.

Major Odlum, the wealthy Vancouver newspaperman who had gone to war looking for adventure, set out at ten-thirty to reconnoitre the Third Brigade's lines. "The left of the line I found to be open, resting on the St. Julien–Poelcappelle road, with the enemy advancing behind them on the west side of that road."[40] Odlum worked his way into Saint-Julien, arriving at the headquarters of the garrison commander, Lt.-Col. Frederick

Loomis of the 13th (Royal Highlanders of Canada) Battalion. It was a grim, chaotic scene, recalled Odlum, with casualties lying everywhere.

> The shrieks and groans, the smell and din were awful. Loomis was so much upset that he did not welcome me. He almost treated me as a German spy. I could get nothing from him but a tale of the officers who were killed and the disasters that had been and still were overwhelming. He could not [even] tell me where his companies were.[41]

Having risked his life for these small shreds of information, Odlum left Saint-Julien just after midnight. Dodging shells and bullets in the vacant fields to the south, he reported to Second Brigade's advanced headquarters at Pond Farm, where he described the situation to General Currie, before rejoining the 7th Battalion at Locality C.

By this time, an important event had occurred elsewhere on the battlefield: the first major Canadian attack of the war.

The orders for the Canadian counter-attack had been issued shortly after dark. Around eight o'clock, a French liaison officer reported to Canadian Division headquarters at Château des Trois Tours and told General Alderson of a planned attack by the French 45th Division towards Pilckem. This operation failed to materialize because the 45th had more or less ceased to exist; most of its artillery had been lost, and its surviving infantry were still hopelessly disorganized in the wake of the gas attack. However, Alderson was in no position to question French intentions or their ability to carry them out. (It was not until the next morning that he learned, through V Corps headquarters, "that no formed units of French troops were left on the East bank of the Canal, that their troops were suffering from the effects of gas, and were incapable of resistance.")[42] Agreeing to co-operate in this phantom attack, he sent orders at 8:25 P.M. to the Third Brigade's General Turner that he was to aid the French by clearing Kitcheners Wood.

Two battalions were available to Turner: his own 16th (Canadian Scottish) and the 10th (Calgary-Winnipeg), which belonged to the Second Brigade. Both battalions had been released from divisional reserve and had returned to their respective brigades in the early evening, although communication problems delayed transmission of the necessary orders until nearly eight o'clock. In fact, General Currie had not waited for permission to move the 10th, alerting it at 5:45 P.M. to be ready to march for Wieltje. Currie's message arrived during a meeting of the battalion's officers run by Lt.-Col. Russell Boyle, the big, tough Alberta rancher. Boyle's officers were somewhat shaken by a shell burst that shattered every window in the little farmhouse that served as their headquarters. But their marching orders generated genuine excitement, offering the prospect of giving the Germans a taste of their own medicine.

This was not the first time that the 10th Battalion had been shelled in this area. Until two days before, the prairie unit had been billeted in Ypres, but had moved to this farm to get away from the long-range bombardment begun by the enemy on 20 April. Every six minutes, a one-ton shell exploded in or around the city. This was dubbed the Wipers Express, because the screaming shells reminded the troops of London subway trains.[43]

Shortly before seven that evening, the prairie lads of the 10th Battalion hit the road. Khaki caps perched jauntily on their heads (steel helmets were not worn by Canadian soldiers until 1916) and burdened by fifty-eight-pound packs filled with ammunition, rations, and personal belongings, the troops sang "O Canada" and "The Maple Leaf Forever." According to a former Calgary contractor, Sgt. Charlie Stevenson, they were "feeling as gay as if going to a picnic or a ball game."[44] Like all the other units moving up, however, they were delayed by crowds of fleeing soldiers and civilians, and it was after seven-thirty when the 10th finally reached Wieltje. Colonel Boyle went ahead and reported to General Currie at Pond Farm, where he learned that his battalion of Westerners was assigned to assist the Third Brigade, in response to General Turner's pleas for help. "Col. Boyle 10th Bn. has received instructions to get in touch with you," Currie informed Turner, suggesting that the 10th might be used to fill the gap between Mouse Trap Farm and Saint-Julien.[45] At the time, Currie was unaware that Boyle's battalion was to be used not for defensive measures but in a costly counter-attack.

The prairie boys of Boyle's 10th reached Mouse Trap Farm some time after nine o'clock, well after nightfall. Deploying in a nearby field, the battalion waited for further instructions from Third Brigade headquarters. It was an uncomfortable wait for Pte. Wally Bennett, the twenty-year-old accountant from Calgary. The smell of chlorine was still strong, and he found it "kinda choking you, getting in your eyes – my eyes were sore for days afterwards – and your throat was kinda rough there for days."[46]

The 16th (Canadian Scottish) Battalion started much later than the 10th. Although ordered to stand-to around five-thirty, more than two hours passed before it received its marching orders from the Third Brigade. The intervening time was not wasted. "As soon as the battalion had stood to arms," wrote its commanding officer, Lt.-Col. R.G. Edwards Leckie, the forty-five-year-old South African veteran and Vancouver mining engineer, "the constant stream of fugitives from French regiments crossing the bridges on the canal led me to believe that the Allie[d] line had been broken, and on my own responsibility, I deployed the battalion along the bank of the canal on the west side and had them dig themselves in behind the hedges, thus protecting three crossings of the canal." Instructions to move forward arrived at 7:40 P.M., and as the battalion assembled in columns of four, extra small-arms ammunition was distributed, so that each man was carrying 220 rounds.[47]

It was not an easy march. "We had a lot of difficulty getting up that road," Pte. Harry Oldaker related. "You see, there was only the one road going up there, and there was artillery traffic and supplies and civilians and ambulances coming back."[48] Pausing for a fifteen-minute rest near Wieltje, the Canadian Highlanders "could not understand why our eyes and nostrils smarted so much. Later we realized that poisonous gas was the cause, and this is a matter of three or four hours after the attack and a good mile and a quarter behind the trenches."[49] The heavy-laden 16th left its greatcoats and packs here; the Germans, mistaking them for a troop concentration, shelled the field the next day.

It was nearly ten o'clock before Leckie's 16th Battalion arrived at Mouse Trap Farm. By this time, the Third Brigade had issued its orders for the counter-attack, confirming them just before eleven. "10th and 16th Bns. in that order will counter-attack at 11.30 P.M. . . . Attack on frontage of two companies. Remaining 6 companies in close support at 30 yards distance on same frontage."[50] It was a formation that Napoleon might have used a century before, long before the invention of the machine-gun, but it was the formation that they had practised earlier and that was in vogue in the British army at the moment. "I regretted placing 10th in front," General Turner later explained, "but they arrived first, and I prepared them to make the counter[-attack] if necessary alone. Time was urgent."[51]

Guided by a Third Brigade staff officer, Boyle's 10th Battalion assembled in a field five hundred yards northeast of Mouse Trap Farm. Each company of 200 men formed two ranks, twenty yards apart, with thirty yards separating each two-company wave. The 10th was ready by 11:10, and Leckie's 16th, perhaps already missing their greatcoats as the night grew cold, moved in behind soon afterwards, forming up in the same manner. At 11:30 officers of the two battalions synchronized their watches; the attack was now scheduled for 11:45 P.M. Five hundred yards away loomed their objective, Kitcheners Wood, a dark shadow in the bright moonlight.

The advance would involve fifteen hundred Canadians, about three-quarters of the combined strength of the two units. No battalion ever took all its men into action; a certain number of officers and other ranks were designated "left out of battle," providing a solid core around which the battalion could rebuild in the event of a disaster. In this instance, the 10th took 816 officers and other ranks into the fight;[52] the balance came from the 16th.

There was no scarcity of encouraging words. "We have been aching for a fight," Colonel Boyle told his troops, "and now we are going to get it."[53] Even more inspirational was Montreal's Canon Scott, who strode up and down the ranks saying cheerfully, "It's a great day for Canada, boys."[54]

An honorary major, Scott was adored by the troops. He was supposed to have stayed behind at Salisbury, but disregarded orders and slipped across to France, where he simply attached himself to the first unit he came across, which happened to be the 15th (48th Highlanders of Canada) Battalion. Now, just two weeks after his fifty-fourth birthday, Scott had seen the Highlanders of the 16th Battalion on the road from Ypres and tagged along. The men were glad he did. One later called him "one of the best and bravest men I have ever known," and another contended that "had it not been for the kind and cheerful words of encouragement given to me by our beloved padre, Canon Scott, I am sure I could not have faced the new ordeal."*[55]

By now, Colonel Hughes himself had arrived from Third Brigade headquarters to oversee the final arrangements. Youthful – he had celebrated his thirty-fifth birthday earlier in the day – tall, and ruggedly handsome, Hughes had not inherited his father's passion for oratory. He merely pointed out the objective, ordered Colonels Boyle and Leckie to follow the North Star, and told them to advance when they were ready.

Because of the hasty preparations, there had been no time for reconnaissance, an oversight that would deprive the attackers of the essential element of surprise. There was limited artillery support, too, with only thirteen guns from four British and Canadian batteries arrayed to back the assault. An error by Colonel Boyle compounded the difficulties. To the left stood Oblong Farm, which was held by the enemy; machine-guns posted there could inflict terrible damage. Boyle's adjutant, Maj. Dan Ormond, the Portage-la-Prairie lawyer, recalled: "Some of us strongly advised that the farm . . . should be taken by at least one platoon, however Colonel Boyle . . . decided not to do this."[56] Clearly, the big rancher was counting on surprise to get his prairie battalion safely across the open, moonlit field in front of Kitcheners Wood.

---

*Throughout the war, Scott could be found in or near the front lines. He led a charmed life until September 1918, when, as chaplain of the First Canadian Division, he was severely wounded in action near Cambrai.

At 11:48 P.M. the order to advance was issued,[57] via whispered commands rather than the usual method of whistles blown by the officers. "Believe me there was some excitement in the ranks," the 10th's Sgt. John Matheson later wrote. The former Medicine Hat banker went on: "We didn't seem to realize what we were up against."[58] Fifteen hundred Canadians, bayonets fixed, shoulder to shoulder in eight lines, started forward. "The moon shone out," recalled a subaltern of the kilted 16th Battalion, "and I was thinking what a picture the flashing bayonets made in the moonlight."[59]

Kitcheners Wood was five hundred yards away. The freshly ploughed field absorbed the tramp of the Canadians' boots; "not a sound was audible down the long waving lines but the soft pad of feet and the knock of bayonet scabbards against thighs."[60]

Four hundred yards. The silence was broken only by the occasional burst of small-arms fire and by the Canadian and British shells bursting in the far side of the wood.

Three hundred yards. The Canadians were nearly halfway to the objective, and "the long dark lines of men could be seen keeping their formation perfectly," according to Colonel Leckie, the old South African veteran.[61] There was nothing to indicate that the enemy was aware of their presence: complete surprise seemed assured.

And then, chaos. Two hundred yards from Kitcheners Wood, the Canadians encountered a hedge, four to six feet high, with a thick strand of barbed wire woven through it; they were about to reap the bitter harvest sown by the failure to reconnoitre. "There was no talking, not a word," commented Major Ormond, admiring his men's discipline, though the snapping twigs and branches and the clatter of "entrenching tool[s] and bayonet scabbards and the rifle butts . . . made a great deal of noise."[62] The front rank of the 10th Battalion broke through the barrier, reformed into straight lines, and resumed the steady advance. The following ranks did likewise, but the jig was up.

A flare shot up from the enemy lines. As it arched slowly into the sky, it turned night into day for agonizingly long seconds, clearly revealing the two Canadian battalions in the open field to the German riflemen and machine-gunners defending Kitcheners Wood. The Canadians instinctively dropped to the ground, but Maj. James Lightfoot, a 10th Battalion company commander, shouted, "Come on, boys, remember that you're Canadians."[63] At this, the troops gave what Sgt. Charlie Stevenson called "a real British yell," and charged.[64] Moments later, they were engulfed in a storm of small-arms fire.

None of the survivors ever forgot that charge. "The wood seemed to be literally lined with machine guns," wrote the 10th Battalion's Sgt. John Matheson, "and they played these guns on us with terrible effect. Our men were dropping thick and fast."[65] Lieut. Henry Duncan of the 16th, a twenty-two-year-old from Seattle, Washington, said that "the fire was awful, coming, it seemed, from all directions, making a steady roar."[66] A 10th Battalion sergeant likened the sound to a "hailstorm on a zinc roof," noting that "somehow a few of us were missed, while other fellows were cut in half by the stream of lead."[67] To Pte. Gerald Hardman of the 16th, the fire was "so intense that it seemed nothing could live in it. We went down in hundreds."[68] A 10th Battalion NCO added:

> The machine guns mowed our boys down like grass, but we stayed with it and came out on top. I went through the charge, but with my proverbial luck was not touched. Why, I do not know. Men fell all around me. It was a ghastly sight. Our dead and wounded were lying in heaps.[69]

"When we had gone about fifty yards," an officer of the 16th wrote, "the rank in front of me seemed to melt away."[70]

A 16th Battalion subaltern later wrote:

> Men on each side of me were crying out in pain, and still we went on. I personally felt I must surely be hit, the hail of bullets was so thick. The cracking of the bullets close to the ears made them sing, and it was impossible to make oneself heard even to one's nearest neighbour.[71]

One survivor of the 10th Battalion marvelled at his brush with death:

> What a life! what an escape! Really I ought to be a stiff – way out there on our battlefield – because I said my prayers and prepared for the inevitable bullet to do its worst, but nothing came except one clean through my hat. I saw stars with a jerk, thought I was hit, but nothing doing.[72]

Irresistibly, the Canadians rushed on. Lieut. William Lowry of the 10th was proud that his battalion of prairie men "charged just as coolly as if it was doing the thing on parade."[73] The 16th's Lieutenant Duncan was just as proud of his Highlanders: "Enough cannot be said for the men. They behaved like veterans, never wavered for an instant, and took whatever came without a word of complaint."[74] They were inspired by officers like Capt. John Geddes of the 16th, who, although mortally wounded, crawled forward on hands and knees, calling out to his men, "Come on!"[75]

The losses were appalling, with tragically few survivors – but enough to take Kitcheners Wood. Along the southern edge of the wood, the

Germans had constructed a shallow trench, and the Canadians swarmed over it. According to a Canadian Scottish survivor, "the struggle became a dreadful hand-to-hand conflict. We fought in clumps and batches, and the living struggled over the bodies of the dead and dying. . . . The clashing bayonets flashed like quicksilver [in the moonlight], and faces were lit up as by limelight." In minutes the trench had been captured. "Here all who resisted were bayoneted; those who yielded were sent to the rear."[76]

There was no stopping the Canadians now. City boys and farmers, loggers and fishermen, bank clerks and ranchers, schoolkids and business-men, they proved to be more than a match for the grey-clad products of Germany's mighty military machine. At the edge of the trees the two battalions were hopelessly intermingled, the kilted figures of the 16th leaping amongst the men of the 10th, and although most of their officers lay dead or wounded in the field behind them, they swept on, into the wood.

The fighting here was no less vicious. German star shells and flares lit up the sky, casting ghostly shadows among the splintered oak trees. "Many Germans were encountered in the woods, some of whom surren-dered, but the majority were bayoneted or shot," related Colonel Leckie, a long way from his Vancouver mining engineer business. "Many, however, escaped by dodging through the underbrush."[77] Throughout Kitcheners Wood, the Germans had constructed little sandbag forts defended by machine-guns; around these, dozens of desperate, individual struggles took place. Pte. Sid Cox of the 10th (Calgary-Winnipeg) Battalion vividly remembered his own experience:

> It was all so mixed up you just didn't know for anything. That's where I got the biggest scare of my life. I went into a bit of a hut there. I went to go in it, and a great big German stepped out, and he may have been going to surrender – I couldn't tell you – but I got out of there in a hurry. I pulled the trigger and ran.[78]

A surprise awaited them in the wood. Among the shadows were those belonging to four artillery pieces. "Judging from the direction in which they were pointing," wrote Colonel Leckie, "I came to the conclusion that they were guns abandoned by the French."[79] In fact, they were British, of the 2nd London Heavy Battery. The 4.7-inch guns had been disabled before their crews had abandoned them the previous evening. "They were piled high with dead – British, Turcos and German," commented the 10th's lawyer-adjutant, Major Ormond. "In my opinion it would have been impossible to have recovered and removed these guns."[80] An attempt was made, however: a message was sent to the 3rd Field Artillery Brigade to send up teams of horses to haul out the 4.7s. The motorcyclist entrusted with the request got lost, "and the message came back the following day undelivered," when it was too late to do anything more.[81]

The Canadians quickly cleared most of Kitcheners Wood. But it took time to establish some semblance of order among the two battalions. Indeed, at first it was even difficult to find them. The 10th Battalion's Private Cox, still a nervous wreck after his first meeting with the enemy, came out the far side of the wood with a couple of buddies, and they "couldn't find anybody." For a while, he recalled, "we thought we were alone." There were no Germans around, and few Canadians. But Cox and his colleagues did find a horse, "a lovely packhorse. Belonged to a German colonel or something, and there the poor devil was tied up, and when I let him go, we didn't know what we were going to do with him. 'Gee, it would be nice to have this to ride.' Lovely animal. I don't know what happened to him."[82]

Elsewhere beyond the wood, two 10th Battalion NCOs had gone looking for the enemy. Sgt. Chris Scriven and Cpl. Jack Wennevold, a tough ex-U.S. Marine, had little trouble finding them. As they crossed a field, the two Canadians were almost blinded by the sudden light of a flare fired immediately in front of them. Freezing, they were horrified to see a German officer, flare gun in hand, a mere ten feet away. Incredibly, the officer failed to spot the two NCOs, and as soon as the light flickered away, they made a mad dash for the safety of the woods. Both men knew that where there was an officer, there had to be troops nearby.

They were right, and some of these soldiers opened fire, shooting blindly in the direction of the noise made by the fleeing Canadians. As the bullets flew, Corporal Wennevold staggered. "I'm hit," he grunted, and fell into Sergeant Scriven's arms. Scriven was appalled by Wennevold's wound. The bullet had left him "ripped open from stem to stern," across the stomach. The sergeant carried the corporal into the shelter of some trees, then stuffed field dressings into the gaping hole in his stomach. He then unwound the corporal's puttees from around his ankles and wrapped them tightly around his midsection to hold the bandages in place. Thanks to Scriven's handiwork, Wennevold recovered – to be killed in action just six weeks before the end of the war.[83]

By now only a few hundred strong, the attackers were gradually sorting themselves out. The Highlanders of the 16th Battalion manned a hedge along the northern edge of the wood, while to the left, the prairie boys of Boyle's 10th occupied a shallow trench that faced directly north. It did not take a genius to realize that they would be hard-pressed to hold this position if the Germans counter-attacked.

The 16th's Colonel Leckie was already calling for help. Scribbling a brief report describing the success of the attack and the situation as it stood, Leckie handed the pencilled message to his adjutant, Maj. Gilbert Godson-Godson, who had been wounded in the throat. The major delivered the good news to Mouse Trap Farm around two in the morning – the first word that General Turner had received since the operation was launched two hours earlier.

Other wounded men arrived at Mouse Trap Farm as the night wore on. A dressing station had been established in the barn, and dozens of men, their khaki uniforms tattered and bloodied, stumbled and crawled to it. One of them was a 16th Battalion subaltern from Vancouver who was so badly hurt that he had to drag himself along the ground all the way from the captured trench to the farm, a distance of more than half a mile. The lieutenant was Reginald Tupper, and he was the son of a former prime minister, Sir Charles Tupper.

By now, Colonel Boyle's 10th Battalion was under its third commanding officer. The popular former rancher had been wounded soon after the wood fell to the Canadians. Switching on his flashlight to read a message, the big Albertan drew fire from a German machine-gunner and fell mortally wounded, his thigh shattered by five bullets. Bleeding to death, he was evacuated by the battalion's second-in-command, Maj. Joseph MacLaren. The former schoolteacher from Manitoba was himself hit in the leg during the assault and had to be sent behind the lines for treatment. There, he was killed by a shell burst as his ambulance passed through Ypres; Colonel Boyle died in hospital three days later. Command of the 10th devolved on the adjutant, Major Ormond, the lawyer from Portage-la-Prairie.

Ormond was soon put to the test. After helping Colonel Leckie sort out the troops on the far side of the wood, the major returned to the south-side trench, which was under fire from a German strongpoint in the wood's southwestern corner. "We have you surrounded: surrender," the enemy shouted, in good English.[84] Unimpressed, Ormond rounded up a party of thirty-four men and stormed the redoubt. Twice, the Canadians tried to outflank it, and twice the German machine-guns drove them back with heavy losses: half of Ormond's force was killed or wounded. The Germans attempted to reinforce the position – once with "at least 800" troops, by Ormond's estimate[85] – but they were driven back by Canadian rifle fire. Having reached a stalemate, Ormond ordered his men to dig in at right angles to the trench, facing the strongpoint.

The moonlit counter-attack by the 10th and 16th battalions had succeeded, but it was becoming increasingly doubtful whether the ground taken at such great cost could be held. The Canadian position was extremely vulnerable, as Colonel Leckie – now in overall command by virtue of his seniority – well realized. In taking Kitcheners Wood, the

Canadians had driven a thousand-yard wedge into the enemy lines. But, as a result, they found themselves under fire from almost every direction, with the stubborn strongpoint in the southwestern corner of the wood particularly dangerous. Fortunately, help was on the way.

Two fresh battalions had arrived at Mouse Trap Farm shortly after midnight. These were the 2nd (Eastern Ontario) and 3rd (Toronto), which had been allocated to General Turner by Canadian Division headquarters late on the twenty-second. "They should be used primarily to prolong your left and fill gap between you and French," read General Alderson's instructions.[86] But instead, Turner kept both battalions near his headquarters, pending word of the counter-attack. When news of its success came via the wounded Major Godson-Godson, Turner ordered the 2nd Battalion, under Lt.-Col. David Watson, to move up and reinforce the 10th and 16th battalions.

Colonel Watson set out promptly. At forty-six, the former manager of the Quebec City *Chronicle* was perhaps a little old for this sort of thing, but he gamely made his way through darkness and sporadic small-arms fire to Colonel Leckie's headquarters. The HQ was located at Juliet Farm, in the field where the 10th and 16th battalions had so recently attacked. The farm was also serving as a dressing station, and so it was amid the screams and groans of the injured and dying that Leckie outlined the situation for Watson. The two colonels agreed that it was essential to shore up the flanks, and Watson handed different assignments to each of the three companies he had arranged to join him at Juliet Farm. One company, under Maj. George Bennett, would go to the left and, crossing the field now soaked with the blood of the 10th and 16th battalions, take the troublesome redoubt in the southwestern corner of Kitcheners Wood. Another company would swing farther left, its objective Oblong Farm. The remaining company would shift to the right to shore up that exposed flank in the direction of Saint-Julien.

The manoeuvres could have been completed before dawn, but there were delays. The battalion was held up in its march to Juliet Farm, hampered by darkness, narrow, winding roads, and fields intersected by hedges and soggy, weed-choked ditches. And when the company commanders were finally given their instructions, one of them complicated matters by spending too much time reconnoitering the lay of the land. This was Major Bennett, whose task was to take the redoubt in the wood. First he sent out patrols to locate the enemy's position; when they failed to come back, he went out himself to have a look. Night was just giving way to day by the time he returned and gave the order to fix bayonets.

The delay proved fatal. Instead of making a night attack, Major Bennett and his men were about to cross in broad daylight the same deadly ground as the 10th and 16th battalions. Bennett called, "Number One Company, charge" and, waving his walking stick, led the assault. According to one of his men, Pte. Jack Booker, the major "only got about ten feet when down he went."[87] Most of the company shared his fate. The beleaguered survivors of the 10th Battalion watched in horror as the enemy machine-guns cut down the 2nd Battalion troops who were to reinforce their position. "Not more than 10 to 15 ever even got to our trenches," Major Ormond noted sadly.[88]

Colonel Watson was mortified when he found out what happened to Bennett's company. "My God! What an awful night we have had," he wrote in his diary later that day. "Lost almost 200 men & 6 officers of No. 1 Coy."[89]

Their sacrifice was not totally in vain, however. The futile and bloody attack on the redoubt distracted the defenders long enough to permit the other parts of the 2nd Battalion to succeed in their attacks. Capt. Geoffrey Chrysler, with 3 Company, captured Oblong Farm, while Capt. Claude Culling's 2 Company occupied farm buildings on the right of the line, at the cost of two killed and one wounded.

But the 2nd Battalion had come too late to enable the 10th and 16th battalions to hold Kitcheners Wood. As daylight approached, Colonel Leckie decided that it would be too costly to retain the exposed position on the far, north side of the wood, and he ordered the two battalions to pull back to the captured trench on the south side. This withdrawal was carried out just before dawn, between three and four in the morning. Thanks to the efforts of working parties from both units, the trench was in slightly better shape now, "about 1½ to 2 feet deep," according to Major Ormond, "with a good parapet in construction consisting of dirt and sand bags."[90]

The remnants of the two battalions were in rough shape. Not only were they "exposed to a bad rifle and worse shell fire," said the 16th's Private Hardman, but "we had neither water nor food."[91] Their greatcoats and packs had been discarded behind the lines, so they lacked both comfort and warmth. They were also understandably nervous. "Frightfully tired and discouraged," was the way one Canadian Scottish diarist described his buddies. "Suddenly word came along that the Germans were attacking, and before they could be stopped almost every man was up on the parapet firing away as fast as he could." No attack materialized, and "we were a little ashamed of the excitement."[92]

Dawn also brought a horrible sight. Strewn across the fields to the south lay the dead and wounded, some clad in trousers – 10th Battalion victims – and some in kilts – the Highlanders of Leckie's 16th Battalion. The 10th's Sergeant Stevenson never forgot the scene:

> I looked back across the field we had crossed the previous night, and I could see what havoc had been wrought on our boys, for all around were the dead bodies of men who, a few hours before, had been singing Canada's national song. They died with it on their lips, but their memory will live for many a day and year to come. For they made a name for the Dominion that will live in history.[93]

A roll call that morning told the tale in stark statistics. The 10th Battalion went into action with 816 men; only five officers and 188 other ranks answered their names. The 16th, with approximately the same strength, was reduced to five officers and 263 other ranks.[94] Among the dead was young Pte. Frederick Lidiard. "I must tell you," he had written to his mother just a week before, "I was never in better health in my life. I am getting fat as a pig, and now the spring is here I am getting sunburnt. . . . I expect to come home soon, as in my opinion the war is pretty nearly over. I am convinced that the Germans are beaten."*[95]

The tally of dead, wounded, and missing stands as mute testimony to the hazards of hasty preparations. The worst of these, as far as the 10th and 16th battalions were concerned, was the failure to reconnoitre the ground – a failing that not only cost them the complete surprise they sought but also denied the artillery appropriate precise targets: the gunners had to randomly lob a few shells into the wood, with minimal effect. There was also a woeful lack of communications between the attackers and Turner's Third Brigade headquarters, which was supposed to be directing the operation. This delayed the arrival of reinforcements. And the use of mass formations against machine-guns was in itself a dreadful lesson in modern warfare.

Its execution can be questioned, its military merits debated, but there can be no doubt that the assault by the 10th and 16th battalions, the first major offensive operation conducted by Canadian troops in the Great War, was a success, although all of the objectives could not be held.

---

*While it is almost impossible to determine German casualties in the battle for Kitcheners Wood, they "must have been very severe," in Colonel Leckie's opinion. He later wrote: "I observed his dead lying in considerable numbers beyond the trenches and in the woods. I had no means of counting the prisoners as they were forwarded as taken to Brigade Headquarters. The majority of these were wounded and all received proper medical attention. Several of their wounded were killed by their own shells during the bombardment of my Headquarters on April 23rd" (PAC, MG30 E46, volume 4, file 7, "Account of the Charge of the Canadian Scottish").

Moreover, it proved to be the only successful attack by Allied forces during the Second Battle of Ypres, which was a tribute to the training, discipline, and esprit de corps of these inexperienced young Canadians, who were richly applauded for their efforts. The Second Army's General Smith-Dorrien declared that these two battalions "did everything to restore the situation and confuse the enemy," in the process "maintaining the high tradition of the British Army."*[96] Ferdinand Foch, the French general who would emerge later in the war as the Allied supreme commander, called this counter-attack "the finest act in the War."[97]

The Canadians had also won the grudging respect of their enemies, whose leaders had so recently dismissed them with contempt. A German officer captured by the 10th Battalion muttered as he was led away: "You fellows fight like hell."[98]

While brave young men from Canada were fighting for their lives in far-off Flanders, 22 April had been just another day for most Canadians on the home front. The only war news in the papers concerned the battle for Hill 60, in which no Canadian troops were involved. Sam Hughes did manage, however, to make a spectacle of himself that day in Toronto, where he reviewed more than five thousand soldiers. "Characteristic of General Hughes, he stopped a column and ordered the band-master to change the tune played, as he did not like it."[99]

Earlier in the day, fire destroyed the Lakeside Home for Little Children, a landmark on the Toronto Island.[100] In politics, there was talk of a snap election in Quebec and speculation that British Columbia's ailing premier, Sir Richard McBride, would soon step down. But most Canadians were concerned with getting ready for summer.

On the prairies, while ten thousand out-of-work Winnipeggers protested in front of the Legislature in the Manitoba capital, the spring auction of bulls was front-page news in Calgary, involving "one of the most exciting bidding matches in the history of the local sales."[101]

All too soon these events would be disregarded as the news from France brought war into thousands of Canadian households.

---

*In 1934 the Calgary Highlanders and the Winnipeg Light Infantry, perpetuating the 10th Battalion, and the Victoria-based Canadian Scottish Regiment, perpetuating the 16th Battalion, were authorized to wear a special badge consisting of an oak leaf and acorn, symbolizing Kitcheners Wood.

CHAPTER EIGHT

"The Gates of Hell"

Historians profess puzzlement at the conduct of the Germans on 22 April. After blasting a four-mile-wide hole in the Allied lines, they had easily captured their limited objectives by nightfall. But the infantry, on the verge of a really decisive victory, stopped and contentedly dug in, awaiting supplies and reinforcements.

They were ordered to stop in at least one instance. At six o'clock that evening, XXVI Reserve Corps told its 52nd Reserve Division "for the moment not to go beyond the southern slope of Pilckem Ridge," which left them digging in along Mauser ridge, overlooking Saint-Julien and Wieltje. At the same time, the 51st Reserve Division was lamely instructed to take Saint-Julien, "if possible."[1] A combination of factors frustrated the enemy here, including the uncharacteristic lack of aggression and initiative that the grey-clad infantrymen would exhibit throughout the battle. Attempting to cross the Poelcappelle road to reach Saint-Julien and roll up the Canadian front line, the 51st ran out of daylight. The Germans were also unlucky, having the great misfortune to run into the only two points of resistance facing them: Major Norsworthy's brave band of Montreal Highlanders and Algerians, and Major King's deadly 18-pounders.

There were other factors to take into account. Although flushed with success, the Germans were also very tired after spending a hot, nerve-racking day in their trenches in constant fear of detection, then advancing several thousand yards through the French defences. No fresh reserves were immediately available to exploit this success. As well, the Germans were dogged by the same communications difficulties that plagued the Allies.

Duke Albrecht's plans for the next day, 23 April, reflected his confidence. The Fourth Army commander presumed that victory was a foregone conclusion and chose to stretch his modest resources in hopes of maximizing his gains. Albrecht ordered XXIII Reserve Corps to strike across the Canal de l'Yser towards Poperinghe, six miles to the west, while XXVI Reserve Corps continued the southward advance against the flank and rear of the Canadian Division. Significantly, Albrecht informed XXVI Reserve Corps that he regarded "the undertaking against Poperinghe as the main operation" on the twenty-third.[2] He clearly expected the salient to fall with ease.

The duke's confidence was justified. By lopping off the top of the Ypres salient and driving the French across the canal, his forces had – to anybody with the least understanding of military matters – rendered the Canadian and British positions to the south quite untenable. In the early morning hours of 23 April, it seemed that the fate of the salient was sealed: with a 5–2 advantage in manpower and a 5–1 preponderance in artillery, the Germans had everything in their favour against outflanked defenders in hastily prepared positions.

But Duke Albrecht committed a cardinal sin. He underestimated his opposition.

As Thursday gave way to Friday, the situation in the salient was chaotic. Joining the westbound stream of soldiers and civilians seeking safety beyond the canal was the diminutive Toronto chemist Colonel Nasmith, who had been ordered to the rear. Nasmith remembered glancing over his shoulder and seeing " the red glow of fires burning in different parts of Ypres. . . . All around the salient star-shells flared into the sky and remained suspended for a few minutes as they threw a white glare over the surrounding country, silhouetting the trees against the sky like ghosts before they died away and fell to earth."[3]

The roads were choked with people and horses and transport of all descriptions: wagons, trucks, motorcycles, bicycles, even baby carriages. Much of this traffic was headed out of the salient, but a considerable amount was swimming against the current and moving into it – infantry reinforcements, artillery, and supplies of food and ammunition. All of the traffic crossed bridges that had been wired for demolition. By nine-thirty Thursday night, Canadian engineers had rigged every bridge in their sector, along with several in the French zone, with explosive charges.

No one was busier than the medics that night. As would be the case during the entire battle, it was impossible to evacuate the wounded until after dark: movement in daylight was tantamount to suicide in the bullet- and shell-swept salient. Injured men were given first-aid in the regimental aid posts in the front lines, but more sophisticated treatment was available only far to the rear. The walking wounded and stretcher cases – Canadian, British, French, as well as German prisoners – were funnelled through the advanced dressing stations at Wieltje and Mouse Trap Farm, the main dressing stations in Ypres and Vlamertinghe, all the way to the casualty clearing stations in Poperinghe, Hazebrouck, and Bailleul. Early in the fighting, the Canadian Division faced a critical shortage of stretchers, which the chief medical officer, Col. G.L. Foster, blamed on the French, who perfidiously removed their wounded without returning the borrowed stretchers.[4]

Canadian doctors and stretcher-bearers were up to their elbows in blood and gore. Medical facilities were swamped. The 3rd Canadian Field Ambulance, for example, treated 5200 injured men in the course of the battle. The first of these began arriving in the late afternoon of the twenty-second. They were tended by a staff that laboured mightily, shocked by what they saw. Pte. Bert Goose told his diary:

> 1,800 was put through inside 24 hours, many of my chums have been through. The wounded came at such a great pace, it was a great job to attend them all.
>
> Some awful wounds were attended to, gashes large enough to put your fist in, many came with bullet wounds, many poor boys will have to have there arms or legs taken off. Other poor fellows will never live to tell the tale. As fast as possible we take the wounded a distance of 6 miles to Poperinghe, ready for a departure to the base, England or elsewhere.
>
> The battle is still raging on. . . . If it's possible I will have a sleep as have only had an hour when chance came my way.

As it turned out, Private Goose would get little sleep; a short time later he wrote "5 days and my boots are still on."[5]

Not all the life-saving was performed by experts. Among the men on the Ypres–Vlamertinghe road that first night was a transport driver from Toronto, a member of the 15th (48th Highlanders of Canada) Battalion. Badly wounded by shrapnel, he was being carried on horseback, swept along by the momentum of the crowd around him. Recovering from his delirium, he noticed a pregnant woman lying at the roadside, ignored by the passing throng. He gallantly stopped, slumping off his horse to assist her. The woman was in labour and soon gave birth. The injured driver did what he could, then put mother and infant on his horse and led them to a nearby aid station. There, moments after handing the baby to a doctor, he collapsed and died.[6]

By dawn on Friday, 23 April, the Canadian Division had staved off disaster for another night. The rout of the French forces on its left had, in a matter of hours, nearly tripled the Division's frontage. The original trenches, between Gravenstafel and the Ypres–Poelcappelle road, were not an immediate concern; still strongly held by two battalions each from the Second and Third brigades, these defences had not yet been tested by the enemy. Much more worrisome was the four-mile stretch between the original front line and the Canal de l'Yser. For most of the night, it had been held by a handful of troops – the small garrison of Saint-Julien and the mixed force in and about Kitcheners Wood – in hastily dug, shallow trenches dominated by the enemy holding the high ground to the north. The wide gaps separating these units posed grave dangers. But steps had been taken to deal with them.

The first had been made by divisional headquarters. At 12:30 A.M. on 23 April, General Alderson created a provisional British brigade, under Lt.-Col. A.D. Geddes, the officer commanding the 2nd East Kent Regiment. This temporary formation, dubbed Geddes's Detachment, initially comprised four battalions – the 2nd East Kent, 3rd Middlesex, 5th King's Own, and 1st York and Lancaster – but grew to as many as seven in the subsequent six days. Deployed with its left on the canal and its right on Saint-Jean, where Colonel Geddes established his headquarters, Geddes's Detachment was viewed by Alderson as "a precautionary measure, as the actual position of the French was doubtful."[7]

What has never been explained was Alderson's decision to ignore a more senior Canadian officer for the task. Near at hand was the First Brigade's General Mercer, with only two of his four battalions still under command, and his complete staff; Geddes, by contrast, had to improvise a staff to oversee his detachment. Although the British colonel was undoubtedly well qualified – he was a career officer, a graduate of the Staff College, and a veteran of the 1914 campaign – Alderson's choice can only be construed as a vote of nonconfidence, in Mercer personally and perhaps in Canadian officers generally.

Colonel Geddes was quick to respond to a call for help from the Third Brigade. Throughout the night, its 13th (Royal Highlanders of Canada) Battalion was in a precarious position. Major McCuaig's company, holding the apex of the Canadian line, had been reinforced by two hundred Algerians, but his left flank, extended along the Poelcappelle road at right angles to the original trenches – the mile between here and Saint-Julien – was undefended. "The Germans attacked a couple of times," McCuaig later wrote, "but our fire was too intense for them and they were driven back. In fact, the firing was incessant the whole night." McCuaig knew that he and his Montreal Highlanders were in trouble; flares fired periodically by the enemy indicated that "they had penetrated for a considerable distance and were working round in rear of us."[8] With the approach of daylight, and no help in sight, McCuaig withdrew his kilted company three hundred yards, but this had no sooner been carried out than reinforcements arrived. Maj. Victor Buchanan, second-in-command of the 13th Battalion, brought with him Capt. C.J. Smith's company from his own unit's garrison in Saint-Julien and a company of the 2nd East Kent, under Capt. F.W. Tomlinson, from Geddes's Detachment. McCuaig quickly reoccupied the position along the road, but he remained painfully aware that his situation was only marginally better.

It would have been even worse, had it not been for the intervention of troops from the Second Brigade on the right. Things had been relatively quiet on General Currie's front, and at midnight the three battalions still under his command – the 5th, 7th, and 8th – "reported all supplies and ammunition received,"[9] although in at least one case rations did not arrive until nearly dawn. Currie's front-line units, the 5th and 8th battalions, worked hard to improve their flimsy defences. "During the night," reported Maj. Harold Mathews, a company commander with the 8th (90th Winnipeg Rifles), "a very vigilant watch was kept, every other man being on sentry duty and the reliefs employed strengthening the trench. . . . Reconnoitring patrols were constantly sent out . . . but no activity on the part of the enemy was discovered."[10]

At two in the morning, Currie heard from his Third Brigade counterpart, the courageous ex-regular General Turner. "Active support urgently needed," pleaded Turner, pointing to the wide gap between Saint-Julien and his 13th (Royal Highlanders of Canada) Battalion. Currie responded by rushing to Keerselaere three companies of the 7th (British Columbia) Battalion. (Its remaining company, under Capt. John Warden, stayed at Locality c.) This move was executed smartly in the darkness, and by 3:20 A.M. the 7th reported that its left was in touch with the Saint-Julien garrison and its right had contacted the 15th Battalion's support troops. However, a thousand-yard gap still existed between the right of the 7th and the left of the 13th.

Currie's prompt response to Turner's request can only be admired. Within the past few hours, he had sent two of his four battalions to the aid of the Third Brigade. He was still unaware that the 10th under Colonel Boyle had been almost completely destroyed in the counter-attack on Kitcheners Wood. His first inkling came at six-thirty that morning, when Turner sent a message of thanks: "Feel situation now well in hand. . . . Wish to thank you for your assistance. Without it feel our line would have been cut. 10th Battalion led the assault and did splendid work under Col. Boyle despite heavy casualties."[11] Nearly twenty-four more hours would pass before Currie discovered just how heavily the 10th had suffered.

Turner, meanwhile, had devoted much of his time and attention to the centre of his new line between Saint-Julien and Kitcheners Wood. The borrowed 2nd Battalion of Ontario boys had helped out considerably the previous night, although it lost most of one company in the ill-fated attack on the strongpoint still holding out in the southwest corner of the wood. At the same time, two other companies had fared better, one managing to seize Oblong Farm and extend the brigade's line towards the canal, the other clearing some trenches and farmhouses east of the wood. One farmhouse became known as Hooper's House, occupied by a platoon under Capt. William Hooper, while the other, Doxsee's House, was held by Lieut. William Doxsee's platoon, reinforced by a machine-gun crew of westerners from the 10th Battalion. The remainder of this company manned the captured trenches, reversing the parapet and making the position more defensible, all the while keeping up an early-morning gunbattle with the Germans. A Canadian sniper, Sgt. Harry Ablard, accounted for eighteen of the enemy – "They lay exposed where they fell and could be readily counted" – near Doxsee's House. A nearby trench remained in enemy hands, and at dawn its occupants tried a ruse that nearly worked. Capt. George Richardson described how "some twenty Germans, unarmed, had climbed out over their parapet and claiming to be French (their dress in the dim light gave colour to their assertions) invited our men over to have coffee. Our men got as far as shaking hands," but Lieutenant Doxsee ordered the Canadians to cover "and opened fire on the hastily retreating Germans."[12]

Another gap, of about five hundred yards, had to be filled between these 2nd Battalion troops and Saint-Julien. General Turner dispatched two companies of the 3rd (Toronto) Battalion from Mouse Trap Farm to fill it. This force, under the 3rd's second-in-command, Maj. Arthur Kirkpatrick, set out shortly after dawn and had to run a gauntlet of small-arms fire. "The machine gun fire was hellish," related little Harold Peat, the Edmontonian who had transferred from the 9th Battalion just days before the 3rd left Salisbury. "It seemed as though no one could live in such a hail of lead." Losses mounted rapidly; one company suffered fifty-seven casualties while moving into this crucial gap. Capt. John Streight was an inspiration to his men: wounded in the leg, he led them by crawling ahead. One survivor commented: "I'd have followed him to Hell and then some!"[13]

Even after all of these moves had been carried out, the Third Brigade's left flank was still dangerously exposed on 23 April. West of the 2nd Battalion force holding Oblong Farm was a gap of three thousand yards, or nearly two miles, only partly covered by Geddes's Detachment.

To stabilize the situation, another Canadian counter-attack was planned. General Plumer, commanding v Corps, had discussed the operation with General Alderson shortly after midnight. The French, adamant that their 45th Division was capable of offensive operations, promised Plumer an attack shortly after dawn. At Plumer's insistence, Alderson reluctantly agreed to co-operate, apparently ignorant of the French failure to attack the previous night, which had left the 10th and 16th battalions unsupported in their assault on Kitcheners Wood. For the task Alderson selected the two First Brigade battalions of Ontario recruits still under the command of General Mercer. Alderson's orders were issued at 3:47 A.M. and received by Mercer a half-hour later: "At 5 o'clock two French battalions are to make counter-attack against Pilckem with their right resting on Pilckem–Ypres road. You will co-operate with this attack by attacking at the same time with your left on this road."[14] Several more hours would pass before Alderson discovered that the French were incapable of living up to their promises.

Mercer, the fifty-five-year-old Toronto lawyer who commanded the Queen's Own, was rather old for battlefield action, but he promptly rode off to execute his orders. Near Brielen, he met his battalion commanders, the 1st's Lt.-Col. Fred Hill, the former mayor of Niagara Falls, and Lt.-Col. Arthur Birchall, a forty-year-old British-born regular who led the 4th Battalion. Mercer designated the 4th Battalion to lead the assault, with two companies of the 1st in close support.

The Ontario men were in a lively mood. They had moved up to the canal during the night, and Colonel Morrison, the gunner from Ottawa, had been impressed:

> The troops appeared to be in great spirits, laughing and roaring choruses of marching songs. Sometimes they jested with the fugitives and shouted words of encouragement to them in very bad French or cheery English. It was a fine sight to witness the splendid morale of these men, and it had a great effect in soothing the terror of the civilians.[15]

The lads from Ontario quickly crossed the pontoon bridge, located their assembly point in the semidarkness, and formed up along a two-hundred-yard front. By the time they were ready, the sun was beginning to rise on the eastern horizon, but there was no sign of the French forces that were supposed to be taking part in the operation, who were in fact supposed to be the moving spirits in the attack, with which the Canadians were to "co-operate." Five o'clock came and went, and there was still nothing to be seen of the French. But in the dawn's early light, the Canadians could clearly see the Germans on Mauser Ridge, fifteen hundred yards away, feverishly digging in and laying barbed-wire entanglements. Long, gentle slopes led to the enemy positions atop a ridge that stood barely thirty feet above the surrounding fields.

The Germans could see the Canadians, too; there was no possibility of surprise, and the khaki-clad "colonials," standing shoulder to shoulder, presented the enemy machine-gunners with magnificent targets. The attack had all the makings of a suicide charge.

The minutes ticked by, and for a while it seemed unlikely that it would be attempted at all. Just before five-thirty, however, the impatient Colonel Birchall spotted through some trees a troop movement near a farm about a mile away. Assuming this to be the French finally getting into position to attack, Birchall gave the signal to advance. Whatever it was that he saw, he was gravely mistaken; the French attack never occurred, and Birchall's reinforced battalion charged up Mauser Ridge all by itself.

It was, to some, a grand sight. Peering through binoculars, General Mercer proudly watched his troops advance "in most perfect order as if on parade." Bayonets fixed and flashing in the sunlight, the six companies of Canadians passed Foch's Farm, where "the farmer's untouched supper stood cold on the kitchen table and cows lowed in the yard for a milker fled."[16]

The Germans held their fire, allowing the attackers to clear the farm first. When they did begin shooting, the effect was devastating. "They opened the gates of hell," said one survivor of the 4th Battalion, "and pushed us in."[17] Rifle and machine-gun bullets riddled the ranks of the Canadians, and within moments German shrapnel shells joined the bloodshed. Cpl. Edgar Wackett of the 1st Battalion later wrote: "It did not seem possible that any human being could live in the rain of shot and shell that began to play upon us as we advanced. . . . For a time every other man seemed to fall."[18]

One man who lived through this hell-on-earth was the 1st Battalion's Pte. George Bell. He later described the nightmare:

"Forward," command our officers ahead of us. We keep on going. Ahead of me I see men running. Suddenly their legs double up and they sink to the ground. Here's a body with the head shot off. I jump over it. Here's a devil with both legs gone, but still alive. A body of a man means nothing except something to avoid stumbling over. It's just another obstacle. There goes little Elliot, one of the boys from the print shop where I worked in Detroit, only ten yards from me. Poor devil. There's nothing I can do for him. What's one man, more or less, in this slaughter?[19]

The Canadians were, almost literally, cut to pieces. Seeing one of his company commanders go down, Colonel Birchall, waving his walking stick, rushed forward to lead the charge. "I am going to lead you, boys," he called. "Will you come?"[20]

They did, but to no avail. "It seemed that every soldier in the enemy's ranks had a machine gun," remarked J.M. McKinley, a 4th Battalion lieutenant from Toronto, "and the air was literally filled with bullets."[21] The German fire was simply too heavy for flesh and blood to endure, and there was too little artillery support – only sixteen Canadian and British 18-pounders – to make a significant impression on the defenders of Mauser Ridge. The Canadian soldiers were soon forced to hug the ground, many crawling behind small piles of manure, which proved to be "better ranging marks than protection."[22] On the right, where the attackers received help from two companies of British troops belonging to the 3rd Middlesex, they came to within four hundred yards of the enemy lines. But that was the farthest point in the advance.

On the left, the assault was stopped along a row of willow trees on the valley bottom; from there Maj. Albert Kimmins of the 1st Battalion made several attempts to contact the neighbouring French, hoping to get some help. After two runners dispatched across the bullet-swept fields failed to return, Major Kimmins set out by himself; he, too, was killed.

With Major Kimmins was a lance-corporal, Edward Mockler. The nineteen-year-old Irishman was so severely wounded that it took him six agonizing hours to crawl back to his lines. Eventually evacuated to England, he died of his wounds on 7 May, and was buried in his hometown of Ballinderry, County Antrim, Ireland.[23]

By seven-thirty that morning, the attack had stopped dead. But Colonel Birchall was not prepared to give up just yet. After appealing for assistance from the 1st Battalion, he was given most of the two companies still at Colonel Hill's disposal. These veered to the right, where they joined men of the 3rd Middlesex in storming Turco Farm. A company commander, Maj. George Wilkinson, recalled that the British and Canadians took the farm "at the point of the bayonet, surprising Fritz somewhat, because I don't imagine he thought we were able to do it. The centre of that old farm . . . was a regular shambles. I saw more wounded and dead men in a radius of about fifty yards than I think I ever saw before or hope to see again."[24]

It was a bad day for Pte. Goldwin Pirie of Toronto. Eleven days past his twenty-first birthday, Private Pirie was formerly a clerk at the Yonge and Eglinton branch of the Canadian Bank of Commerce. Normally at this hour he would have been getting ready to hop a streetcar that would take him to work. Instead, he was lying in a shell hole, his pelvis smashed, his right arm shattered by German bullets. Pirie was only vaguely aware of his own plight, much less that of his comrades in the 1st Battalion. Sadly, three full days would pass before he was pulled, unconscious, from this shallow crater. Evacuated to England, he would undergo several operations, before succumbing to his injuries on 1 July.[25]

Meanwhile, seeing his men being slaughtered with no sign of the French had sent General Mercer out on the warpath. He went looking for the officer who was supposed to be in command of the French operation, Col. Jacques Mordacq, the commander of the 45th Division's 90th Brigade. Colonel Mordacq assured the Canadian general that he had now assembled five and a half battalions, and his attack would commence shortly. Sceptical and disgusted, Mercer rode back to watch the continuing slaughter of his First Brigade. He waited until eight-thirty, and when the French had still not moved, he sent orders to the two battered battalions to dig in. Not until midday did any French forces make an appearance west of the Pilckem–Ypres road; even then no attack materialized.

The surviving Canadians were in a desperate plight. Singly and in little groups, surrounded by the dead and wounded, they hugged the exposed ground with the enemy only three to six hundred yards away. But the Germans failed to take advantage of the situation. "My God," exclaimed one 4th Battalion sergeant, "if they had any sense at all, or any guts at all, they'd come over here and they wouldn't have to fire a shot. They could just take us all prisoners."[26] So the exposed Canadians continued to hug the ground, pinned down, unable to do anything but hope and pray for relief.

It proved to be a long, hot day along the entire front of the Canadian Division. Shelling started soon after dawn, even as Ontario's 1st and 4th battalions stormed Mauser Ridge. Periodically thereafter, the Germans deluged various parts of the line with terrific bombardments, concentrating their enormous firepower on certain sectors, then shifting to others. These barrages lasted anywhere from a few minutes to a few hours.

Shell fire was one of the worst experiences a soldier could have. The mind-numbing, near-deafening noise and bone-rattling vibrations from even distant explosions were bad enough, but the wounds were worse – much worse. "At its worst [a bursting shell] could disintegrate a human being, so that nothing recognizable – sometimes apparently nothing at all – remained of him," writes noted historian John Keegan. "Less spectacular, but sometimes as deadly, shell blast could create over-pressures or vacuums in the body's organs, rupturing the lungs and producing haemorrhages in the brain and spinal cord." But the majority of injuries came from splinters and shrapnel balls. According to Keegan:

> Such projectiles . . . often travelled in clusters, which would inflict several large or many small wounds on the same person. The splinters were irregular in shape, so producing a very rough wound with a great deal of tissue damage, and they frequently carried fragments of clothing or other foreign matter into the body, which made infection almost inevitable. Very large shell fragments could . . . amputate limbs, decapitate, bisect or otherwise grossly mutilate the human frame.[27]

None of this had to be explained to the thin khaki line of Canadians on 23 April. Huddled in their hastily dug, shallow trenches, caps pulled down for imaginary security, they had no choice but to sit there and endure the bombardment. Anyone attempting to flee would have been a target for enemy snipers and machine-gunners – as the many wounded Canadians lying in the open knew all too well.

Casualties mounted steadily. As if they had not suffered enough in their heroic attack the night before, the 10th (Calgary-Winnipeg) and 16th (Canadian Scottish) battalions, holding the line along the southern edge of Kitcheners Wood, were especially hard-hit. "It was very trying to the men in the trench," commented Colonel Leckie, "as they had practically no cover."[28] Major Ormond called it "an anxious day," reporting that the two battalions were "losing 3 and 4 men at a time" to enemy fire.[29]

The barrage was, indeed, hard to take. The 10th Battalion's Sgt. John Matheson, the Medicine Hat banker who so enjoyed patrolling no man's land, wrote that "it was more nerve-racking than the bayonet charge itself, as all around us were the dead and wounded."[30] The 16th's Lieut. Henry Duncan, the volunteer from Seattle, considered it "an awful day. Men blown out of the trench was a common occurrence, leaving nothing but possibly a boot or a Glengarry."[31] Another officer of the 16th recollected his experience:

> One shell blew some men out of the trench; one burst overhead and the shock of it alone seemed to kill men for there was no scratch on them. The terrible long day dragged on, and the shelling stopped. We lifted the dead bodies behind the trench as we were so crowded. The wounded we made small traverses for, and left them there until night. I never remember being so glad of darkness.[32]

Amid the bombardment inflicted on the 10th, Pte. Sid Cox, who had had such a memorable night during the attack on the wood, witnessed the strange death of a comrade. This fellow, Private Cox recalled, simply dropped dead in midsentence. "And we took every stitch of clothing off him, and we couldn't find a mark. Not a mark. I don't know what killed him. He just suddenly, in the middle of a word, rolled right forward. Didn't have a bruise on him." The battalion's medical officer later speculated that the victim had had a weak heart.[33]

Cox found one practice instituted this day deeply disturbing. In order to keep track of how many men they still had, the officers would periodically have the troops "number off." Cox recognized the necessity, but he was also quick to realize that "every time you numbered, you were a lower number than you were the time before. You didn't feel so good about that."[34]

In the midst of the ongoing bombardment, a 10th Battalion corporal from Calgary was conducting a one-man battle. It had not started out that way. Around dawn, English-born Cpl. William Baker had led sixteen bombers into the new trench facing the troublesome German redoubt in the edge of the wood. Corporal Baker's party engaged the enemy with rifles and grenades in a running fight. As the day progressed, the Canadians were picked off one by one, until only Baker was left. Using his fallen men's grenades, Baker kept up the fight for the remainder of the day and through the night. He was later awarded the French Croix de Guerre for his efforts.[35]

In the middle of the morning, an attempt was made to reinforce the thin line at Kitcheners Wood. General Turner sent in two companies of the 14th (Montreal) Battalion, but when it became apparent that they would suffer unacceptably heavy losses crossing the open fields, the effort was abandoned. The gantlet of enemy fire also meant that neither food nor ammunition could be delivered to the men in the front line; nor could the wounded be evacuated. Fortunately, the Canadians recovered a considerable quantity of German rations in the captured trench, and these were "fairly good," in Lieutenant Duncan's opinion.[36]

All day, there were worrisome signs of an impending German attack. Shortly after eight o'clock that Friday morning, the 2nd (Eastern Ontario) Battalion's Col. David Watson reported "that reinforcements numbering from 500 to 1,000 are being brought up" opposite his position; an hour later, the ex-journalist estimated that twenty-five hundred Germans had been assembled behind Kitcheners Wood.[37] General Turner immediately sent a warning to Canadian Division headquarters: "We will not be able to hold trenches . . . unless counter attack regains lost French line."[38] The situation grew more alarming as the morning progressed. Colonel Loomis, the garrison commander in Saint-Julien, warned Turner at Third Brigade H.Q. shortly before eleven: "Enemy in great force. Convinced that something must be done quick."[39]

During the day no fewer than four German attacks on Saint-Julien were repulsed by Canadian small-arms fire, and the original front lines in both the Second and Third brigade sectors were also attacked. In a late-afternoon assault on the Highlanders from Montreal and Toronto in the 13th and 15th battalions, the Germans employed tear gas. "Irritating fumes from shells very bad," wrote Capt. George McLaren of the 15th (48th Highlanders of Canada). "All the men coughing, eyes and noses running. Wet handkerchiefs seemed to help this."[40] When the Germans finally attacked, they "were subjected to such a heavy rifle fire that they retreated and only about a dozen of them reached their trenches again," claimed the 15th's Lt.-Col. John Currie. "Hundreds of the enemy were killed."[41]

The 8th (90th Winnipeg Rifles) Battalion also turned back an enemy venture that had ominous overtones. Maj. Harold Mathews, the company commander who had been so impressed by German snipers, reported that around five in the afternoon "the sentries on the left noticed a few Germans creeping out from a port in their parapet and crawling back along the front of their own trench." Battalion snipers swiftly put an end to the activity. Some of these enemy soldiers, said Major Mathews, "appeared to be wearing black masks, and as later events proved, I think they were attempting to complete their plans for sending the asphyxiating gases over us just before dark, in the same way they had treated the French line the evening before. However, we managed to temporarily spoil their plans."[42]

Near Keerselaere, the 7th (British Columbia) Battalion underwent a ferocious bombardment during the afternoon. One officer recounted: "Four shells with gas burst, and more than half the company . . . were laid prostrate by the fumes. I was laid out for about twenty minutes." Recovering his senses, he endured another shelling, this time "with shrapnel. I got a smack on the head from a splinter. Shortly afterwards I got another piece through my leg."[43]

The day's action cost the British Columbia battalion its commander. At forty-six, Irish-born Lt.-Col. William Hart-McHarg was one of the best officers in the Canadian forces. A world-class shot, a veteran of the South African War, and a Vancouver lawyer, Hart-McHarg was, in spite of his square-jawed good looks, in very poor health. In fact he weighed only 140 pounds due to chronic indigestion that often restricted him to a diet of milk and biscuits.[44] Despite the milksop diet, the colonel was a fighter. No sooner had he led his 7th Battalion to Keerselaere that morning than he requested permission from General Currie to attack the Germans nearby. Currie refused: "I ordered him to dig well in."[45]

In view of the severe shelling, Colonel Hart-McHarg decided to seek a more secure position. Around four o'clock, accompanied by his second-in-command, Major Odlum, and Lieut. D.M. Mathieson, he set off to reconnoitre the ground in front of his unit. After surveying the area, he and Odlum agreed that the 7th's existing line was "the most suitable one,"[46] but before returning, the colonel decided to investigate some houses three hundred yards from the battalion's position. From these ruins, Odlum recalled, the three officers spotted "large numbers of Germans about a hundred yards from us, and they saw us too." As the Canadians beat a hasty retreat, the Germans opened fire on them. Odlum rolled into a shell hole and the colonel fell on top of him, groaning, "I don't want to get it again!"

"Get what?" asked Odlum.

"Get hit," Hart-McHarg replied. "I'm wounded in the stomach."[47]

Odlum crawled out and fetched the battalion medical officer, Capt. George Gibson, who patched up the colonel as well as he could. But it was impossible to move him until after dark, and by then it was too late. Hart-McHarg died in hospital the following day. "As a man and as a soldier," wrote his brigadier, Arthur Currie, "he was all that could be desired and his place will be very hard to fill."[48] (In 1921 a bronze tablet was unveiled in Vancouver's Christ Church "by his comrades as a tribute to a brave soldier and a gallant gentleman.")[49]

Odlum, who succeeded Hart-McHarg in command of the 7th Battalion, was devastated by the death. "It almost broke my heart to lose him," he explained in a letter to the colonel's mother. "We have got along so well together, and he was such a splendid type, that I had learned to love him. His loss almost totally unnerved me."[50] The wealthy Vancouver newspaperman would suffer more heartbreak before the battle ended, when his brother and a cousin, both members of his battalion, were killed in action.

Tragedies of a similar nature were distressingly commonplace on this battlefield. Toronto's Lieut. Arthur Ryerson of the 9th Field Battery spent much of the day hauling ammunition to his guns, positioned a thousand yards southwest of Mouse Trap Farm. "Imagine my horror," he wrote, "when, just in front of me, I came across the dead body of my brother George," a captain and company commander in the 3rd (Toronto) Battalion, killed by a shell burst early that morning. And Lieutenant Ryerson's grief did not end there. He was wounded a short time later and eventually ended up in hospital in England. His mother, intent on visiting him, boarded the liner *Lusitania* in New York bound for Liverpool; she was among the 1198 people who perished on 7 May when the vessel was torpedoed by a German submarine off the coast of Ireland.[51]

Sadly, the litany of misfortunes was to continue at Ypres on 23 April.

Another suicidal counter-attack on Mauser Ridge was about to be attempted.

Sir John French's inclination was to abandon the Ypres salient. The dapper little field-marshal had no great opinion of his French allies to begin with, and the rout of 22 April merely confirmed his views. "Although the gas no doubt had something to do with the panic," he informed Lord Kitchener, "this would never have happened if the French had not weakened their line a good deal too much."[52] By Friday morning, Sir John was in no mood to sacrifice British troops to restore the reputation of the French army.

He changed his mind, however, after a meeting with the French general Ferdinand Foch. These two men were a study in contrasts. Now sixty-three, Field-Marshal French had made his name as a cavalry commander ranging over the veldt in the South African War, but he was clearly over his head as commander-in-chief of the BEF, "the classic example of a man who had risen above the level of his competence."[53] Foch, on the other hand, was a born leader. At sixty-four, the loquacious Frenchman was still superbly fit; more to the point, he was still a proponent of *l'offensive à outrance* – attack to the limit – a doctrine that had cost the French army dearly during the first months of the war and would continue to bleed it until well into 1917. Although he ended the war as the Allied supreme commander, Foch was not really much of a general. He was, in the words of the eminent historian Sir Basil Liddell Hart, "a natural disorganizer," who lacked understanding of "the needs and principles of either organization or training."[54]

Foch's command was a curious one. It was broken into three parts by the presence of French's BEF and the small Belgian army under King Albert I. Under his jurisdiction were the French Tenth Army, which held the line below the Ypres salient; the Groupement d'Elverdinghe, which was responsible for the northern sector of the salient; and the Groupement de Nieuport, which held the front between the Belgians and the coast. The latter two formations were under an intermediate commander, Gen. Henri Gabriel Putz, a fifty-six-year-old veteran who was rarely intimidated by Foch.

Sir John French was less resistant to the strain of Foch's persuasion. Through a combination of charm, bluster, and argument, Foch was invariably able to manipulate the British commander-in-chief, and 23 April was no exception. French arrived at Foch's headquarters at Cassel that morning intent on giving up the salient; but by the time he departed, he had not only agreed to hold on but to co-operate in the counter-attacks that Foch assured him would win back the ground lost the previous day. French summarized the meeting:

> General Foch informed me that it was his intention to make good the original line and regain the trenches which the French Division had lost. He expressed the desire that I should maintain my present line, assuring me that the original position would be re-established in a few days. General Foch further informed me that he had ordered up large French reinforcements, which were now on their way, and that troops from the North had already arrived to reinforce General Putz.[55]

French had no way of knowing that Foch was deliberately misleading him, that the "large reinforcements" summoned by the Frenchman amounted to a single fresh division.

The two commanders then went their separate ways, Foch rushing to urge the reluctant Putz to exert his best efforts to regain the original French front line, Sir John travelling to the Second Army's headquarters to ensure that General Smith-Dorrien co-operated fully. While Putz half-heartedly responded to Foch's theatrics by preparing a feeble counter-attack for the middle of that afternoon, Smith-Dorrien was promised plenty of help in the forthcoming fight. French instructed the Cavalry Corps to concentrate at Poperinghe as a mobile reserve for General Plumer's V Corps. French also ordered up from GHQ reserve Maj.-Gen. W.F.L. Lindsay's 50th (Northumbrian) Division, which was to be bussed to Vlamertinghe and added to V Corps reserve. Two other divisions, the 4th and Lahore, billeted at Bailleul and Merville respectively, were alerted to be ready to move to Ypres at short notice.

Earlier in the day, Smith-Dorrien had released from Second Army reserve the British 13th Brigade, under Brig.-Gen. R. Wanless-O'Gowan, and given it to Plumer, who in turn allotted it to the Canadian Division. Plumer instructed General Alderson to "endeavour to push back the enemy northwards on the east side of the canal working in co-operation with the French."[56] To emphasize the importance of holding the Ypres salient, Smith-Dorrien arrived at noon at Alderson's Canadian headquarters at Château des Trois Tours, personally ordering him to employ the 13th Brigade in an attack between Kitcheners Wood and the Canal de l'Yser that afternoon.

Alderson issued his orders accordingly. The British 13th Brigade was told to "form up and attack in the direction of Pilckem [with] its right on the Pilckem–Ypres road." The pinned-down 1st and 4th Canadian battalions, still hopelessly clinging to the southern slopes of Mauser Ridge, were somehow to support the British assault, along with Geddes's Detachment. It was an ambitious plan: "After the capture of the Pilckem line the attack will be continued and the old French line reoccupied."[57]

It was also a terribly flawed plan. Consistent with the earlier Canadian attacks, there was, as the British official history points out, "little opportunity . . . for reconnaissance or preparation, and hardly time to write orders."[58] The haste was evident in other ways. The attack was scheduled for 3:30 P.M., half an hour after the French had gone into action. But the 13th Brigade was assigned the same objectives as Colonel Mordacq's 90th Brigade of the 45th (Algerian) Division. The French did not object, believing that the British were aiming for Langemarck, farther east.

The First Brigade's General Mercer was one of the first to recognize the potential conflict. Noting the similar objectives, the former Toronto lawyer asked Canadian Division headquarters whether it might be advisable to cancel the smaller French operation. "No," came the perplexing answer, "let French commence their attack and if possible you might cooperate as far as possible and then let 13th Bde. go through you."[59] Mercer must have wondered what was going on at divisional headquarters: his men were east of the road and the 13th was west of it, and nowhere did the battle plan state that the British were to "go through" his two battalions.

At the same time, there were other disturbing signs that Alderson and his staff were not quite in control of the situation. Receiving erroneous information from the French, Alderson dispatched at 1:20 P.M. a message to Mercer and the Third Brigade's General Turner. "French report that Germans are apparently running short of ammunition," it read. "They have been ordered to advance. Divisional Commander wishes you to seize this opportunity to push forward." At that moment, the Third Brigade was being battered by a bombardment that indicated that the Germans were far from "running short of ammunition." Turner, after nearly twenty-four hours of being showered with debris at Mouse Trap Farm, can be forgiven for disgustedly scribbling on his copy: "An example of the value of information received from the rear."[60]

Co-ordination between the services was noticeably absent once again. At 2:45 P.M., the artillery opened fire at Mauser Ridge, in the belief that the 13th Brigade was to attack at 3:00, instead of 3:30. By the time this mistake had been rectified, the Canadian and British batteries had expended most of their immediate stock of shells; this meant that when the 13th did attack, the British troops would have virtually no artillery support.

No one more anxiously awaited the arrival of these fresh forces than the Canadians who had survived the early-morning counter-attack by Ontario's 1st and 4th battalions. Huddled in shell holes or hiding behind the little manure piles that offered no protection whatever, these men had endured day-long sniping, shelling, and machine-gunning by the Germans who overlooked them from the crest of Mauser Ridge. The blazing-hot sun seemed to be suspended overhead as these Canadians came to grips with new enemies: hunger and thirst. "What wouldn't I give for a drink of cold water?" the 1st Battalion's Pte. George Bell thought, lying among so many of his dead and wounded comrades. "Even bully beef and hard tack would taste good. If only the artillery would stop long enough so a man could rest. It's enough to drive one nuts!"[61]

Three o'clock came and went with no sign of the promised French attack. But the British operation was also being delayed. At 3:45, fifteen minutes after his attack was supposed to have been launched, General Wanless-O'Gowan, the brigade commander, informed Canadian Division headquarters that he would need at least another half-hour to get into position. It turned out that the 13th Brigade had taken a circuitous route to avoid congested roads in its five-mile march from Vlamertinghe, in addition to making a lengthy stop for lunch, at Wanless-O'Gowan's insistence. The morale of these British troops was very high – a Canadian transport driver who saw them remarked that they were "in great spirits, singing, and some of them almost on the trot"[62] – but there were not many of them. The 13th had suffered 1362 casualties in the battle for Hill 60, at the southern end of the salient, a few days before and now mustered fewer than three thousand bayonets. Crossing the canal, Wanless-O'Gowan deployed three battalions: two – the 1st Royal West Kent and 2nd King's Own Scottish Borderers – to lead the assault, and the 2nd King's Own Yorkshire Light Infantry in close support. All three were regular-force units.

Their attack, launched at 4:25 P.M., was doomed. The tough British regulars suffered the same fate as the earlier Canadian attackers. Without effective artillery support, they were attacking an entrenched enemy in daylight and crossing flat fields devoid of cover, except for scattered clusters of willow trees. It was not a recipe for success. To make matters worse, the French finally showed up. A battalion of Zouaves, colourful in their distinctive red-and-blue uniforms, crossed the canal and proceeded to march in front of the British line of advance, forcing the two leading battalions in the 13th Brigade's advance formation to veer to the right, causing overcrowding along the road and presenting the German machine-gunners with even better targets. Having disrupted the British advance, the French halted and dug in, to take no further part in the attack.

The British regulars advanced into a maelstrom of small-arms fire. Their neat, shoulder-to-shoulder ranks were decimated. The Canadians huddled below Mauser Ridge saw the full horror of it at close range, as the thinning British ranks approached. Pte. James Fraser of the 4th (Central Ontario) Battalion recalled that "they were just simply bowled over like ninepins."[63] In spite of the galling fire, the British stolidly continued their advance. Pte. Victor Trowles, also of the 4th Battalion, saw a British soldier fall nearby. "He was hit in the shoulder, and I went over and got his field bandage out and patched it up," related Trowles. "Hadn't more than tied it and he was hit in the same place again."[64]

Inspired by this courageous display, the few able-bodied Canadians jumped to their feet and gamely joined the attack. It was a futile effort: they could move forward no more than a few yards before being forced to hug the ground. The two beleaguered Canadian battalions accomplished nothing, except to add to their already enormous casualty lists. The 4th also lost its British-born commanding officer. Colonel Birchall, cane in one hand and revolver in the other, was riddled with bullets as he led a charge on the nearest German trench.

The attack was extended to the east by four battalions of Geddes's Detachment. The 2nd East Yorkshire and the 1st York and Lancaster, aided by the 3rd Middlesex, somehow pushed to within a couple of hundred yards of the enemy lines; one small party of British soldiers made it to within thirty yards. But that was the closest anyone got to the defenders of Mauser Ridge. The 9th Royal Scots and 2nd Duke of ~~Connaught's~~ Cornwalls Light Infantry were stopped cold – indeed, the Scots came under such heavy fire that they had to withdraw three hundred yards to find cover.

The débâcle was over in an hour and a half. By then the slopes of the ridge were littered with khaki-clad corpses. After dark, the exhausted survivors of the two Canadian and eight British battalions staggered back and dug in six hundred yards from the enemy's powerful position. There was considerable confusion in the cloudy, moonless night; some of these exhausted men dug in facing the wrong way.

The casualties on 23 April had been terrible. The two Canadian battalions were especially hard-hit, the 1st losing 404 men, the 4th, 454, including its British-born colonel and its second-in-command, Lt.-Col. William Buell, a forty-seven-year-old lawyer who had been mayor of Brockville.[65] Also among the 4th's dead were two notable lieutenants. One, Cameron Brant, from Hamilton, was a descendant of the great Mohawk chief, Joseph Brant. The other was the handsome, athletic, pipe-smoking Alf Bastedo, the militiaman from Milton who had spent part of the previous summer in Pembroke with his University of Toronto classmate Ramsey Morris. Just returned from leave in England, Lieutenant Bastedo had written a happy but somewhat formal love letter to Ramsey's sister, Grace, the tennis-playing girl who had seen him off the day after war was declared. In his last letter Bastedo wrote:

> I have been enjoying life rather well of late, haven't been working too hard but expect to get into it a bit harder before long. . . .
> I guess we won't have much tennis this year. By the way, I'm getting to be quite a French linguist. I manage to make out most of what is said to me and get them to understand. I hope to be quite efficient before long and then when I see you again, I'll be quite too much for you. I would be very glad to hear from you if you would be so kind.[66]

By happy contrast, Maj. Alfred Hunter was only injured, and his sense of humour remained intact. In peacetime a prominent Toronto lawyer, Major Hunter wired home assurances that he was all right: "Shrapnel bounced off. Head as usual unreceptive. Convalescent."[67]

British losses were just as shocking; no battalion suffered fewer than two hundred casualties. The 1st York and Lancaster lost 425 killed and wounded, including its commanding officer, Lt.-Col. A.G. Burt. The 2nd East Yorkshire had 383 casualties, and the 3rd Middlesex was so weak at the end of the day that it was reorganized into a single company. Among its dead was its commander, Lt.-Col. E.W.R. Stephenson.[68]

Afterwards, General Alderson sent a note of appreciation to General Wanless-O'Gowan. "Words cannot express," said Alderson, "what the Canadians owe the 13th for their splendid attack and the way they restored confidence."[69] Alderson's remarks must have been scant consolation for Wanless-O'Gowan as he surveyed his brigade's casualty returns. The brigadier probably came to the same scathing conclusion as the British army's official historian: "No ground was gained that could not have been secured, probably without casualties, by a simple advance after dark."[70]

Nothing better sums up this operation than the pathetic sight a Canadian gunner witnessed in its wake. Gunner John Armstrong of the 3rd Field Battery, which had attempted to support the 13th Brigade's attack, recalled seeing a horse wandering about the battlefield. "For three days after the attack he went around with just the lower part of a man's body in the saddle. From the waist up there was nothing. A good-sized shell had hit him."[71]

Friday, 23 April, had been a disappointing day for the Germans. Nothing had worked out the way Duke Albrecht had planned. Worst of all, Ypres remained in Allied hands in spite of the advantages in position and numbers enjoyed by the Germans. Albrecht knew, too, that this was as much a result of German inaction as of the suicidal counter-attacks carried out by the British and Canadians.

Albrecht himself had spent most of the day looking beyond the Canal de l'Yser, and Poperinghe, six miles to the west, remained his main objective until late Friday, when the high command bluntly told him "that Poperinghe did not primarily enter the question at all as an objective and that for the present it was strictly a matter of cutting off the salient."[72] Poperinghe was beyond Albrecht's very limited resources, but by allowing himself to be distracted by an unrealistic goal, he had lost his best chance to realize the more attainable goal of crushing the salient.

The German infantrymen were uncharacteristically passive. This, too, can be traced to poor leadership, for the orders from senior officers lacked urgency; the overconfidence of the generals spread to the foot-soldiers, and there seems to have been widespread reluctance to make sacrifices in a battle presumed to have been won. It is a poor commander who blames his men for failure, but at least one formation, XXVI Reserve Corps, under a general named von Hugel, attempted to do this when its war diary complained of the rank and file:

> Unfortunately the infantry had become enfeebled by trench warfare and had lost its daring and its indifference to heavy losses and the disintegrating influence of enemy fire effect. The leaders and the brave-hearted fell, and the bulk of the men, mostly inexperienced reinforcements, became helpless and only too inclined to leave the work to the artillery and trench mortars.[73]

This failing was most noticeable near the apex of the Canadian Division's line. A gap of nearly a thousand yards, between the left of the 13th Battalion and the right of the 7th, faced the Germans all day, but no attempt was made to exploit it; by Saturday morning the gap was gone.

Regardless of the reasons – the bravery and savagery of the British and Canadian counter-attackers or the weak German performance, or a combination of both – a whole day had been wasted by the enemy. Duke Albrecht belatedly realized that the fighting was far from finished and that the salient was not going to fall into his hands like a ripe plum dropping from a tree. Clearly a serious, and vigorous, effort would have to be made to crush the Canadian Division.

On Friday night Albrecht prepared to do just that. He marshalled all his available forces – thirty-four battalions, twenty of them fresh – opposite the eight Canadian battalions between Gravenstafel and Kitcheners Wood. The Fourth Army would mount its operation in two stages on

Saturday. In the first, an early-morning attack would be mounted against Belgian-held Lizerne, five miles north of Ypres, by XXIII Reserve Corps, which would then drive towards Vlamertinghe and cut off the British army's main line of retreat from the salient. The second – and main – stage would begin at 4 A.M., when a converging attack by XXVI Reserve Corps, supported by XXVII Reserve Corps, would smash the stubborn Canadians.

To ensure success, Duke Albrecht resorted to the trump card that had proved so effective against the French two days earlier. Saturday morning's attack on the Canadian Division would be preceded by poison gas.

So far, no one in Canada knew what was happening to their fathers and husbands, brothers and lovers, in Flanders. Thanks to severe censorship, Friday's newspapers at home were still devoting extensive coverage to the Hill 60 battle. But there was a new, if incorrect, twist to the story. "Canadians have won golden spurs there," one unidentified British officer was quoted as saying in the Calgary *Daily Herald*'s front-page report. "Details are tantalizingly scarce," the correspondent admitted – not surprisingly, since the Canadians were in action not at Hill 60 but several miles to the north. The *Herald* also reported the authoritative verdict offered by *The Times* of London: "The victory at Hill Sixty, following Neuve Chapelle, proves the offensive is passing over to us. The German troops are not as good as they were."

More astute readers might have noted with alarm a small item at the very bottom of the *Herald*'s front page. Date-lined London, it concerned a wireless report from Berlin. The headline read, GERMANS DENY USING SHELLS TO ASPHYXIATE.

It was a long night for the Canadians in the salient. Few, if any, were able to sleep. In some cases, this was due to frayed nerves seeing phantom attackers in the dark. "All that night," wrote a 16th (Canadian Scottish) Battalion platoon commander, "it was a case of 'stand to' every half hour, the cry being 'they're coming.' "[74] But there was also a lot of work to be done, and the salient buzzed with activity after dark:

> the infantry adjusting dispositions, strengthening parapets, building traverses and digging cover; the transport and ration parties carrying supplies and even letters and parcels from home to some of the most exposed trenches; the engineers assisting with material and skill; the field artillery bringing up and unloading ammunition, an arduous task when batteries were firing from six to sixteen tons in twenty-four hours.[75]

Typical was the experience of 2 Company of the 8th (90th Winnipeg Rifles) Battalion, which was holding the Second Brigade's left-front trenches. The company commander, Maj. Harold Mathews, later described the work that went on in his sector:

The night was very dark. . . . We kept a very careful watch all night, two officers being always on duty, and no man allowed to be in the dugouts on any pretext whatever. Captain McMeans and Lieut. Paget took turns to go out with Creeping Patrols and except for two or three false alarms, nothing untoward happened.

We had great difficulty in getting sufficient stretchers to carry our wounded out during the night, but eventually succeeded and very late some of the rations and a few boxes of ammunition arrived. We also managed to get all the water-bottles and dixies filled and repaired the damage done to the parapet and continued under difficulties the construction of the parapet.[76]

The 8th Battalion took one precaution that would save many lives on Saturday morning. "In expectation that we might be gassed," wrote Major Mathews, "dixies of water had been placed at intervals along the trench, handkerchiefs and empty bandoliers had been wetted hoping that by keeping something damp over our mouths and noses the effect of the poisonous gas would be nullified to some extent."[77]

The neighbouring 5th (Western Cavalry) Battalion awaited the coming trial with the utmost confidence. "Situation perfectly quiet," the 5th's Lt.-Col. George Tuxford reported at midnight. "Perfectly prepared."[78] Tuxford, the Welsh-born farmer from southern Saskatchewan, who had made the cattle drive to the Yukon, was a good man to have around in a fight.

The Third Brigade, meanwhile, had finally done something about the dangerous gap in its line, between the 7th (British Columbia) Battalion at Keerselaere and the 13th (Royal Highlanders of Canada) Battalion in the original trenches. The divisional commander, General Alderson, had recommended earlier in the day that General Turner abandon the 13th's trenches, suggesting that "some sort of line might be dug by the supports and your troops fall back on it."[79] Turner concurred, and at ten o'clock on Friday night the 13th – mostly Montrealers, but including the reinforcing company of the 2nd East Kent Regiment – executed a perilous manoeuvre. It withdrew in the dark from its exposed position under the very noses of the enemy and occupied a new line at right angles to the 15th (48th Highlanders of Canada) Battalion. The new trench featured a number of sandbagged machine-gun posts, and reinforcements arrived in the form of two companies of the 14th (Montreal) Battalion, under that unit's second-in-command, Lt.-Col. W.W. Burland. (The officer commanding the 14th, Lt.-Col. Frank Meighen, had been placed in charge of the miscellaneous troops in the GHQ line, where he was to remain for the duration of the battle.)

Although the enemy made no attempt to interfere with these adjustments, a sense of foreboding gripped some Canadian soldiers. This anxiety was pronounced in the 15th Battalion, the unit based around the 48th Highlanders of Toronto, which now held the apex of the V-shaped Canadian line. "German flares appear to be going up in almost a complete circle around us," wrote a company commander, Capt. George McLaren, who noted "also two fires to be seen behind us."[80]

Captain McLaren's worries were shared by his superior, Col. John Currie, the Toronto politician-cum-soldier. Currie, who had insisted that double rations and extra ammunition be issued to his battalion, had ordered his men "to hold their parapets at all costs and if they lost them they would have to take them with their bayonets. If ammunition gave out they were to rely on their bayonets."[81] But these defiant words could not conceal Currie's concern. "I confess," he later wrote, "I thought our chances of ever getting out were very slim."[82]

CHAPTER NINE

"Their Damned Rifles"

Saturday, 24 April, dawned warm and cloudless. "A very gentle N.E. breeze drifted from the German lines to us," wrote the 8th (90th Winnipeg Rifles) Battalion's Maj. Harold Mathews, who had spent the night preparing for an enemy attack. "In fact it was a perfect spring morning, nature was so calm and still it would have been quite impossible to imagine the sun could rise on the awful tragedies so soon to be enacted." At 3 A.M. the Canadians stood-to, alerted by the rumble of the German attack on the Belgians to the north – Lizerne had fallen at one-thirty, but the German attack in that quarter quickly stalled – and, as four o'clock approached, all was quiet on the Canadian front, and "we began to think nothing would happen at all."[1]

The situation changed dramatically at 4 A.M. The 15th (48th Highlanders of Canada) Battalion's Captain McLaren spotted a stationary balloon behind the enemy lines. "Three red lights were dropped from it," wrote McLaren, "immediately we noticed men (perhaps 2 or 3) appear over the German parapet, they appeared to have helmets on much like those worn by divers, with hoses in their hands from which came a heavy green gas."[2]

Thus began what the Canadian official history calls "a great and terrible day for Canada."[3]

The Germans had amassed cylinders of chlorine gas on a twelve-hundred-yard front opposite the 8th and 15th battalions, in the original Canadian front line. The release of the gas was accompanied by a ten-minute bombardment by guns of all calibres, which tore apart Canadian parapets and caved in dugouts. The screams of the wounded were drowned by the innumerable explosions that rocked the Canadian positions.

Despite the turmoil caused by the shelling, the approaching poison gas was the immediate chief concern. Major Mathews vividly described its effect on the 8th Battalion's defenders from Winnipeg:

This wall of vapour appeared to me to be at least fifteen feet in height, white on top, the remainder being of a greenish yellow colour. Although the breeze was of the lightest, it advanced with great rapidity and was on us in less than three minutes.

It is impossible for me to give a real idea of the terror and horror spread among us by this filthy loathsome pestilence. Not, I think, the fear of death or anything supernatural, but the great dread that we could not stand the fearful suffocation sufficiently to be each in our proper places and able to resist to the uttermost the attack which we felt sure must follow, and so hang on at all costs to the trench that we had been ordered to hold.[4]

Cpl. William Thornton, one of Mathews's men, saw the gas cloud coming across no man's land. "Well, when I saw it coming," he explained in a letter to his father back in Winnipeg, "I was not curious to find out what it was, but just grabbed a towel, which was a big, thick one, soaked it in water and covered my face, so I came off lucky."[5]

Others were not so lucky. "When the fumes were full on us," related Major Mathews, "breathing became most difficult, it was hard to resist the temptation to tear away the damp rags from our mouths in the struggle for air." All around him, "men were coughing, spitting, cursing and grovelling on the ground and trying to be sick." But Mathews proudly pointed out that in his company "there was not a single officer or man who did not do his duty by manfully fighting down to the best of his ability the awful choking sensation and trying to stick to his post."[6]

The deadly fumes drifted across Gravenstafel Ridge to the rear of the Canadian trenches. The 8th Battalion's commander, Lt.-Col. Louis Lipsett, at his headquarters at Boetleer Farm, reported that "the gas had a most paralysing effect on one, leaving one almost helpless and gasping for breath."[7] As soon as he learned of the gas attack on his left, the 5th Battalion's Lt.-Col. George Tuxford called Lipsett on the telephone for further details. The Moose Jaw rancher later wrote that Lipsett "replied personally, choking and gasping in such a manner that I thought he was done for."[8] At nearby Locality c, Capt. John Warden's company of the 7th (British Columbia) Battalion was "almost overcome by the fumes," which were so potent that "two men died from the effects of the gas in my trench at this time."[9] The gas cloud even reached the Second Brigade's report centre near Fortuin, and General Currie described how it "made the nose and eyes run and our heads ache."[10]

Close behind the cloud came the German infantry, the leading ranks equipped with rudimentary respirators. The gas release had been so successful, and the wind so obliging, that the attackers confidently expected a repeat of Thursday's easy victory, when the gas had routed the French from their trenches, and they had simply strolled to victory. This time, however, the 8th Battalion had a nasty surprise in store for them: the "Little Black Devils" were about to live up to their name.

Cpl. John Simpson found himself surrounded by men who were "coughing and spitting, and gasping for breath, and blind as well." Knowing that the enemy would soon attack, Simpson crawled to the top of the trench, "and as the heavy mist disappeared, leaving a greenish haze, I saw the Germans climbing over their parapet, so I called to all who could get up and 'fire rapid.' We killed all who got over, and no more attempted it."[11]

Dragging himself up to fire in another part of the trench was Pte. J. Carey. He recalled his experience:

> Of the hundreds of Germans directly in front of me, I see one big fat fellow aiming. I get him and he limps like a big pack rabbit performing in a pantomime. I laugh as I see him come down on his shoulder with his heels sticking up and wiggling funnily. But, nevertheless, I fire again and the wiggling stops.

At the height of the fighting, Private Carey heard someone strike a match. Thinking that rather odd, he turned to the fellow beside him to remark on it. Carey recoiled in horror as he realized that the sound had been caused by a bullet smacking his neighbour in the head.[12]

Major Mathews estimated that, on his company's front, "fifty or sixty Germans were killed, and the attack absolutely collapsed. They were really too easily beaten off, the men wanted to kill and go on killing, and it was hard to prevent them climbing out of the trench and making an attack on the enemy."[13]

The Little Black Devils had stood their ground. As the brigadier, General Currie, later observed, the 8th Battalion was "the only regiment in the British service to date that, after being gassed, held their trenches."[14] The battalion had managed this even though many of its Ross rifles jammed during rapid firing, a problem that would become more pronounced as the battle progressed. The 8th also enjoyed the generous assistance of the 5th Battalion to their right, which had poured deadly enfilade fire into the ranks of the advancing Germans, as well as excellent support from the guns of the 2nd Field Artillery Brigade, which replied to an SOS signal with shrapnel at the rate of half a ton a minute.

Still, the poison gas took its toll. Major Mathews described the gruesome effect:

I don't suppose the worst of it lasted more than ten minutes, but we could not have stood it much longer. After the excitement was over the symptoms chiefly noticed were coldness of the hands and feet and great weakness, the lungs seeming to refuse to do their duty. When I say that the men's bayonets looked as though they had been dipped in a solution of copper it is possible to realize to some extent what the effect on human beings would be.

Many of the men lay down at once and went into a deep sleep. Very few were fit for sentry duty but those that were bravely stuck to their posts. The majority of them gradually recovered and were fairly fit again by noon. The worst cases, however, were just as bad twelve hours after and it was very difficult to get them back from the trench, the least exertion bringing on choking fits almost like convulsions.

Lying down proved to be the worst thing to do, for the gas, being heavier than air, soon settled on the ground. "Consequently," reported Mathews, "anyone lying on the ground would be much more seriously affected than others standing up or manning the parapet."[15]

While the Little Black Devils were standing firm, the 48th Highlanders of the 15th Battalion on their left were not so fortunate. The gas concentration there was somewhat heavier, and the effects on the boys from Toronto were even more pronounced. "Imagine Hell in its worst form," wrote Sgt. William Miller, "and you may have a slight idea what it was like."[16] Capt. George McLaren, whose company held the centre of the battalion's line, later reported that "the gas soon rose to about 10 feet and we could not see through it and it struck our trenches in a very short time. It was impossible to breathe in it, giving the effect of having cotton batting in one's lungs. All the men were terribly affected by it and we had no protection, wet handkerchiefs being of no use."[17] One of McLaren's subalterns, Lieut. Herbert Scott, elaborated:

> A great wall of green gas about fifteen to twenty feet high was on top of us. Captain MacLaren gave an order to get handkerchiefs, soak them and tie them around our mouths and noses. (Some were able to do that and some just urinated on their handkerchiefs.) Some managed to cover their faces. Others, myself included, did not, owing to a scarcity of the necessary articles . . . we just lay in bundles at the bottom of the trench, choking and gasping for breath.

Lieutenant Scott, a descendant of the novelist Sir Walter Scott, was later helped to the rear by two of his men, who "coaxed, dragged and pushed me over the most uncomfortable four miles I had ever gone. I wanted to lie down every twenty yards to get my breath back." Scott eventually reached the hospital at Saint-Omer, where he recovered from the gassing.[18]

Not only was the gas thicker here but the Toronto Highlanders at the apex of the Canadian line did not have the kind of help enjoyed by Winnipeg's 8th Battalion on their right. There was nobody who could deliver enfilade fire on the masses of German soldiers swarming across no man's land, and there was no artillery support. The infantrymen were baffled and angered by the silence of their own guns. "Our own Artillery," complained Sergeant Miller, "for some reason or other seemed to be standing cold."[19] The reason was tragically simple, as the 3rd Field Artillery Brigade informed the 15th Battalion at 4:01 A.M.: "We have to admit that it is impossible for us to respond to your SOS and along the entire original front, as the trenches are out of range from our present positions."[20]

The result was nearly catastrophic. Capt. Archie McGregor's 1 Company, on the right of McLaren's 3 Company, was virtually annihilated. Captain McGregor died along with most of his men; the Germans who took the trench called it "a grave."[21] Out of two hundred men who went into action with 1 Company, only six answered a roll call the next day.

Among the many young men of this battalion who would not be going back to Toronto was Pte. Norman Gillespie. The twenty-three-year-old Irish-born Gillespie had quit his job at the Yonge and Queen branch of the Canadian Bank of Commerce the day after the war started and had enlisted in the 48th Highlanders. Badly injured, Gillespie was lifted from the corpse-filled trench by German stretcher-bearers and taken to a field hospital. He died there the next day.[22]

With the 15th Battalion's front ruptured, McLaren's company was forced back to its reserve trenches. They were closely pursued by victorious Germans, who were severely punished by a pair of Colt machine-guns. But the Canadians, too, lost heavily in the withdrawal, which to the watching Winnipeggers in the 8th Battalion took on the appearance of a rout. Pte. Tom Drummond recalled seeing "the men on our left leaving the line, casting away equipment, rifles and clothing as they ran." Many, said Drummond, fell "writhing on the ground, clutching at their throats, tearing open their shirts in a last struggle for air, and after a while ceasing to struggle and lying still while a greenish foam formed over their mouths and lips."[23] The ones who made it to the rearward entrenchments "were practically useless," reported McLaren. "Many were so weak they could not hold a rifle and others died in the trench from suffocation." McLaren himself was in no better shape. Sick and disoriented, he set out to report to the battalion's senior officer in the front line, Maj. James Osborne –

who had been wounded and would soon be captured – but McLaren got lost and ended up in the 7th (British Columbia) Battalion's position. "As I was by this time entirely unfit for anything," he admitted, "I was sent to the rear to a dressing station and finally to hospital in Boulogne."[24]

The Canadians clearly had a crisis on their hands. By sheer weight of numbers – one estimate suggests that the Germans had a 10–1 numerical edge here[25] – in addition to their overwhelming advantage in artillery, not to mention the poison gas, the enemy had breached the 15th Battalion's line and now seemed set to pour through the breach and swamp the entire Canadian Division.

The Little Black Devils of the neighbouring 8th Battalion roused themselves to another effort to minimize the German gains. Colonel Lipsett, aware that his left flank was completely exposed, immediately dispatched to the danger point his only reserve, two platoons under Capt. Arthur Morley. Within minutes, Captain Morley, a thirty-four-year-old Winnipeg lawyer, had led his half-company to the far end of the 8th Battalion's trench, where he discovered the defenders to be in rough shape. "They were all badly affected with gas," he noted, "and very few could man the parapet." Things were even worse in the 15th Battalion's sector, where the Canadians, he discovered, "were all gone. Their former trench was full of Germans who had put up their flag on the parapet. From there they were bringing an enfilade fire on our left trench." Morley skilfully deployed his men at right angles to the main line, where they kept up a running fight with the enemy for the next several hours.[26]

The breach in the 15th Battalion's defences endangered the entire Canadian position. By six-thirty this dreadful Saturday morning, the Germans had reached the Stroombeek, overrunning a handful of Highlanders who rallied for a last stand on the banks of that inconsequential little stream, seven hundred yards behind the Canadian front line. The forces on either side of the breach were in grave peril. To the left, the Germans were in the rear of the 13th (Royal Highlanders of Canada) Battalion; with a vigorous push, the enemy could easily roll up the Highlanders from Montreal and encircle the other battalions defending Saint-Julien, the 7th (British Columbia) and 14th (Montreal). To the right, the Second Brigade's original trenches had been outflanked, and enemy troops were within three hundred yards of Locality c atop Gravenstafel Ridge. If the ridge was lost, General Currie's front-line battalions would be cut off.

Help was on the way. The Third Brigade's General Turner was the first to offer assistance, although he did so for the wrong reasons. Believing that the Second Brigade's line had been "driven in"[27] – as his brigade-major,

Colonel Hughes, informed divisional headquarters – Turner ordered the
10th and 16th battalions to withdraw from Kitcheners Wood, from the
positions they had won so dearly in the night attack two days earlier. The
Highlanders of the 16th were to report to the GHQ line and the Prairie boys
of the 10th were to head for General Currie's advanced headquarters at
Pond Farm. Troops of the 2nd Battalion would replace them.

It was not easy for these two battalions to extricate themselves. As the
10th's Lieut. Walter Critchley pointed out, "it was broad daylight. In full
view of the Hun we had to individually get out and race across this
ploughed field and reassemble."[28] Once again, impeding their progress
was the damned hedge that had ruined their surprise attack. But by now
holes had been chopped in the hedge, and with the smell of hawthorn and
gunpowder in their nostrils, they did it, and with only a handful of casualties. Led by Major Ormond, the pitiful remnant of rancher Boyle's 10th
Battalion marched to Fortuin: three officers and 171 other ranks – less
than 20 per cent of its original strength. It must have been a shock for
Currie to see so few of them, but he "gave the men a cheery word,"
according to Ormond. Then he instructed them to reinforce the defenders
at Locality C atop Gravenstafel Ridge, where they were to come under
Colonel Lipsett's orders.[29]

Currie had great faith in Lipsett. The forty-year-old Irishman had
been a British career officer who was seconded to the Canadian army to
train militia officers. One of his staff-course students in early 1914 had
been Currie, then a lieutenant-colonel commanding the 50th Gordon
Highlanders of Canada, when he was not struggling to sell real estate in
Victoria. Lipsett had been impressed, calling Currie "an excellent officer
who, if war broke out, would, I think, be the type of man who could not be
held back."[30] Currie felt the same way about Lipsett, describing him in a
report the militia minister, Sam Hughes, as "eminently satisfactory in
every particular."[31]

Now, Currie was counting on Lipsett to restore the situation. He gave
the colonel responsibility for Locality C, which was held by Capt. John
Warden's company of the 7th (British Columbia) Battalion, soon to be
joined by the company-sized remains of the 10th. Currie also sent him the
brigade's sole reserve, a company of the 5th (Western Cavalry) Battalion,
which Lipsett deployed near his headquarters at Boetleer Farm, eight
hundred yards east of Locality C. Although Lipsett told Currie at 4:50
A.M. that he considered "the situation in hand,"[32] he had no illusions
about his prospects. Between his front line and Locality C was a gap of
thirteen hundred yards, and Lipsett knew that "I could not hope to stop a
determined attack" on this vulnerable point with the forces at hand.[33]

That attack soon began, with another furious bombardment of the entire Canadian line. The defenders were caught in a cross-fire, as the Germans brought to bear every available gun in a bid to blow the Canadians out of their trenches with high explosive and shrapnel. The shell fire was so loud, according to Pte. Arthur Corker, a 7th (British Columbia) Battalion machine-gunner not a stranger to noise, that "it made me deaf."[34] Lt.-Col. John Currie, in command of the badly-mauled Torontonians in the 15th Battalion, had a close call at this time. "My adjutant [Lieut. Joseph Dansereau] who had gone into the left section of the supporting trenches was struck in the head and Coy. Sergt. Major Vernon was blown to pieces. A shell dropped alongside me and killed Lt. Shoenberger, my Signalling Officer."[35] Casualties along the Canadian line mounted steadily.

Then, at eight-thirty, came the German infantry. Their immediate objectives were Saint-Julien and Locality c – the heart of the Canadian position. At Locality c, Captain Warden's company of British Columbians, which had been reinforced by a few kilted stragglers from the 15th Battalion, prepared to meet the onslaught. At that crucial moment, Major Ormond and the tattered survivors of Boyle's 10th (Calgary-Winnipeg) Battalion arrived, doggedly filing into the shallow trench to the left of Warden's men to take their place in the firing line.

One of the Calgarians, Lieut. Walter Critchley, recalled that "all we could see was masses of Germans coming up in mass formation. Their officers were still on horseback then. They were just coming right up."[36] Three times the Germans stormed Locality c, and three times they were repulsed, as the resilient Major Ormond remembered:

> We stood up on our parapet and gave them three ruddy cheers and shook our fists at them. We gave them everything we had, and they figured it wasn't worth while and they just turned around and went back. They did that again and we did it again. We were quite happy about it. So then they did it a third time. When they went back the third time, we thought we'd won the war.[37]

The Canadians prevailed, here as elsewhere on the battlefield, in spite of continued problems with their Ross rifles. "Instead of getting off twelve or fifteen rounds a minute," recalled Ormond, "we could only get off two or three. They were jamming and men would have to lay down and take their heel to force the bolt open."[38] Outnumbered and almost surrounded by the enemy, pulverized by his artillery, it was a difficulty the Canadian soldiers did not need. One of Ormond's sergeants, Chris Scriven, a long-time militiaman, was particularly bitter about the failings of the Ross rifle:

It wasn't even safe to send a fourteen-year[-old] kid out rabbit-hunting in the fields with, never mind going into battle with. I laid in a shell hole with four other men for a day and a half, and out of five Ross rifles in that hole, it took four of us to keep one of them working, banging the bolts out. As soon as you fired a round, you had to sit down and take the entrenching-tool handle to bash the bolt out, to get the [expended cartridge] out, before you could load it again.[39]

At one point, the Germans tried trickery. In Captain Warden's section the Canadians were approached by "a long line of men dressed in British uniforms," with "the enemy pretending to drive them along with their bayonets towards us." The ruse almost worked, as Warden later wrote:

As there was now a Highland Major in command of my trench, I waited for his orders to fire. Not receiving any, and as the enemy were getting within 50 yards and outnumbering us, I should say 10 to 1, I ordered the men myself to fire.

This Major (I do not know his name or Battalion) ordered the men to cease firing, as he said we would shoot our own men in front of the Germans. I shouted, "They are not British Soldiers – they are Germans dressed in British Uniforms," and again gave the order to fire. Again he stopped those near him firing.

I ordered my own men to open rapid fire, which they did and succeed[ed] in driving back the enemy. Those in British Uniforms, who were right up to our entanglement and could have come into our trench had they wished, turned and ran back even faster than the rest, which was sufficient proof that they were not British Soldiers.[40]

Locality c had been saved, for the time being, but only by the narrowest of margins. The few defenders had been greatly assisted by the 8th (90th Winnipeg Rifles) Battalion's long-range machine-gun fire, which caught the advancing enemy forces in the flank and rear, where they were most vulnerable.

But the position of the 8th Battalion – still affected by the gas attack it had withstood – remained harrowing. "By six o'clock," reported Capt. Arthur Morley, the Winnipeg lawyer in charge of the little group trying to shield the battalion's exposed left flank, "my casualties had become very serious." Welcome reinforcements arrived shortly afterwards, in the form of two platoons from the battalion's small reserve, and it was here that the second Canadian Victoria Cross was won, by Company Sgt.-Maj. Frederick Hall, a thirty-year-old Irishman. In Flanders, with bullets flying everywhere, the former Winnipeg clerk risked his life to save other men. During the move to the flank, the reinforcing platoons had suffered several casualties, and the Belfast-born sergeant-major had twice scrambled into the open to rescue the wounded. Around nine o'clock that morning, another injured man was spotted, and Captain Morley watched the valiant efforts of Sergeant-Major Hall and his comrades:

> My Servant, Tug Wilson, had been hit coming up but he ran back to get the wounded man and was hit again – I am sorry to think fatally. Then L/Cpl. [Henry] Payne [Pain] who was also wounded walked out to the wounded man and attempted to rescue him but Payne too was hit again and fell this time. Then CSM Hall ran towards him but he too was hit with a bullet in the centre of his forehead and instantly killed.[41]

Hall, who had deliberately run into the demonstrated danger, was awarded a posthumous VC .

There was heavy fighting, in the meantime, on the northwestern face of the Canadian line, held by the westerners of the 7th Battalion, Montreal's 13th and 14th battalions, and the Ontario-based 2nd and 3rd battalions. Earlier, the Germans had attempted a gas attack here. "The enemy liberated gas fumes on our front," the 7th (British Columbia) Battalion's Major Odlum noted, "but owing to the direction of the prevailing wind we escaped the full effect of them."[42] The gas cloud did, however, drift to the left, over the lines of the 3rd (Toronto) Battalion, dug in between Saint-Julien and Kitcheners Wood. "We lay down flat and covered our mouths with wet cloths, waiting for the Germans to come up," recalled twenty-three-year-old Pte. Frank Ashbourne. "They came slowly, thinking we were all dead from their gas, but not so. It drifted slowly over us and showed the Germans about seventy-five yards away. We were suddenly ordered to rapid fire, and I don't think more than a dozen Germans got away alive."[43]

The Germans attacked repeatedly that morning. A 3rd (Toronto) Battalion major, Peter Anderson, who was celebrating his forty-seventh birthday, was enraged by the constant problems with the Ross rifles. "The Ross Rifle Company got the money; our brave men died for the aforesaid company's greed," he charged. Anderson, an Edmontonian who had recently transferred from the 9th Battalion, which remained in England, took action to meet the crisis. As the rifles jammed, he ordered that marksmen only should fire, while the others worked at unjamming and loading rifles for them.[44]

Desperate, bloody battles were fought around the two farmhouses held by the 2nd Battalion between Saint-Julien and Kitcheners Wood. At Hooper's House a shortage of small-arms ammunition briefly threatened disaster, but after the supply was replenished, Captain Hooper confidently informed battalion headquarters that he "could hold out for two more days."[45] The defenders of Doxsee's House drove off a half-dozen attacks during the day, but the first one was costly. "The attack was repulsed with severe loss to the enemy who left many men scattered across the fields in front, but Lieutenant Doxee [*sic*], to whom we owed so much of our success, was killed."[46] Capt. George Richardson, who had witnessed the enemy's earlier attempted ruse, assumed command of the house for the balance of the battle.

By eight-thirty that morning, the 3rd Battalion, an Ontario unit built around the Queen's Own Rifles, had survived the enemy's most punishing blows. Manning the shallow trenches between Hooper's and Doxsee's houses, the battalion blocked the German attempts to break into Saint-Julien from the north. "We are holding on nicely," Major Kirkpatrick coolly reported. "Every time enemy starts something he goes back before he comes close, but we have been lucky, as the enemy's artillery has left us alone fairly well."[47]

But not for long. With the failure of these attacks, the Germans resumed their devastating artillery fire. At Locality C the shelling was "terrific," in Captain Warden's opinion,[48] while Major Ormond later related that he and the battle-weary survivors of Boyle's 10th "were being lifted right out of the ground" by the explosions.[49] The shell fire ranged as far as Fortuin, where General Currie had already been forced to evacuate his advanced headquarters at Pond Farm, after enemy shells had set the farmhouse on fire.

Nowhere was the shelling more severe than along the line northeast of Saint-Julien. There, the 7th and 13th battalions, reinforced by half of the 14th, endured a holocaust of high explosive and shrapnel. The enemy's accuracy was uncanny "as almost every shell hit," complained Colonel Meighen of the 14th, the one unit in the Highland brigade that was not kilted, but boasted a fair complement of French-Canadian troops. "After about two hours of this shelling the men of the two battalions [13th and 14th] were forced to retire having been literally blown out of the trenches."[50] Their difficulties were complicated by the German troops in their rear, where the 15th Battalion's line had been breached.

A more or less organized withdrawal was attempted. At eight-thirty orders were issued to the 13th (Royal Highlanders of Canada) and the two companies of the 14th reinforcing it to pull back to a more secure position several hundred yards away, on the west end of Gravenstafel Ridge. By now, all four of the battalion's machine-guns had been knocked out, and the Germans were pressing on three sides. Unfortunately, the withdrawal order did not reach the far end of the line, where the determined Maj. Rykert McCuaig found himself cut off, along with two other officers and forty enlisted men, as well as the survivors of the company of the 2nd East Kent Regiment that had joined them earlier. McCuaig's party made a desperate bid for freedom, running a gantlet of small-arms and artillery fire. In this race back to their own lines, Lieut. Charles Pitblado, who was already wounded, accompanied McCuaig. The major later described what happened:

> We were going back together when I was wounded in the knee but was able to proceed. I was shortly after shot through both legs and rendered helpless. Pitblado in spite of my protests refused to leave me and bandaged up the wounds in my legs under a very heavy fire. He was then wounded a second time in the leg, which finished his chances of getting away. I was subsequently wounded four more times while lying on the ground.
>
> We both remained there until picked up by the Germans an hour or two later. Their firing line passed us about ten minutes after we were wounded.[51]

McCuaig was later awarded the Distinguished Service Order; Pitblado won the Military Cross. Both spent the rest of the war in enemy prison camps. Few of their men escaped, and almost none of the British company, which was forced to surrender at nine o'clock, having run out of ammunition and being completely surrounded.

The collapse of the 13th Battalion, added to the earlier withdrawal of the 15th, left the 7th in serious trouble. The acting commander, Major Odlum, had been uncomfortable for several hours, sending a worried message to his brigadier, General Currie:

> Shelling continues heavily and attack on right is apparently being pressed. Many men of 15th Batt., mostly wounded, are streaming through. Col. Currie, OC 15th Batt., is here collecting stragglers. Unless reinforcements are received the situation on the right may become worse. If the line here gives way my battalion will be cut off.[52]

That was before seven o'clock in the morning; now, less than three hours later, Odlum's worst fears were being realized.

Odlum was addressing his concerns to the wrong brigadier, and he knew it. At 5:15 A.M., General Currie had placed the 7th at the disposal of the Third Brigade, since it was holding the centre of that brigade's line, and since Currie knew it was important "to prevent confusion of orders."[53] There was no confusion, because there were no orders. Although General Turner, pacing painfully around his HQ at Mouse Trap

Farm, and young Hughes, his second-in-command, had been informed of the change, the Third Brigade failed to exercise its jurisdiction over the 7th, despite repeated pleas by Odlum for instructions. "It nearly broke my heart," Odlum later wrote. "We were not in touch with the 3rd Bde. HQ, had no telephonic or other communications, and did not even know where it was. We had no information as to plans or intentions. We were in a position particularly precarious . . . and we were orphans."[54]

This state of affairs was symptomatic of a much larger and more serious problem. At this crucial juncture, the Canadian command structure in the salient was breaking down.

It was a warm, sunny Saturday, but the fog of war had once again enveloped the Canadian Division's palatial headquarters at Château des Trois Tours. There was a lamentable lack of information, since communications were notoriously slow. For instance, it was not until after seven o'clock in the morning that General Plumer at V Corps headquarters learned of the break in the Canadian front line. Four more hours passed before Plumer received additional word, and that came not from General Alderson but from Maj.-Gen. Thomas Snow, the crusty commander of the British 27th Division, which was holding the sector to the right of the 28th Division, on the Canadian right. General Snow was none too impressed with his Canadian Division counterpart, as indicated by the tone an early-morning wire addressed to Alderson:

> If my guns assist you today as I hope they will, please arrange more definite targets than yesterday. Yesterday we were asked to fire at our extreme range on certain areas. After sighting I found out target was about 2500 yards behind enemy's position. Possibly that was what you wanted but I doubt it.[55]

To blame Alderson alone would be unfair. He was at the mercy of his subordinates and, as had happened late Thursday and early Friday, he was receiving contradictory news from his front-line brigadiers, Currie and Turner. The most detailed, and accurate, reports came from Currie, whose first message to Canadian Division headquarters – timed 5:15 A.M. but not received until nearly an hour later – indicated clearly that the Second Brigade's position was intact but that the "Germans have entered trenches in Section III [the 15th Battalion's sector]."[56] At six-thirty, Currie followed with an even more complete picture:

> Germans have broken through Highlanders [the 15th Battalion] trenches about 1000 yards left of Section II (8th Battn). I regard the situation . . . as critical. Can I get any reinforcements to report at

Fortuin via Wieltje to be used as necessary? They have shelled Sections II and III again with gas-emitting shells. Telephonic communications between Brigade Headquarters and Battalion Hqrs broken.[57]

Turner, on the other hand, for all his personal bravery and South African experience, was utterly ignorant of the actual situation. His brigade-major, Colonel Hughes, informed divisional headquarters at 4:55 A.M.: "Left of Second Bde. section trenches has been driven in."[58] Turner and Hughes remained unaware that the crisis was within their own Third Brigade lines, rather than the Second Brigade's; as late as 6:50 A.M. Hughes assured Alderson, "We do not feel uneasy"[59] – and this was nearly three hours after the 15th Battalion's front had been smashed in the initial gas attack.

Reality abruptly intruded on the Third Brigade's headquarters a few minutes later. At seven o'clock Lt.-Col. Frederick Loomis, the Montreal businessman commanding the Saint-Julien garrison, dispatched an eye-opening report to Turner and Hughes:

> Quite a number of stragglers coming back, evidently line broken. Just received message from [Colonel] Burland [second-in-command of the 14th Battalion] saying breaking through on our right. I will endeavour to collect stragglers and delay retirement quick. If any supports will be available please let me know.[60]

At last, the realization of impending disaster dawned on Turner and Hughes. They responded with a flurry of meaningless and, at times, ridiculous orders. Colonel Loomis, warned that "St. Julien must be held," was told to "counter attack with two companies at once."[61] Poor Loomis was baffled: to obey these orders would mean leaving Saint-Julien defenceless. To clarify his instructions, Loomis dodged bullets and shells and reported to Mouse Trap Farm for a face-to-face interview with Turner. The proposed counter-attack was cancelled, and Loomis, still fuming, returned to Saint-Julien.

Equally irrelevant orders were delivered to the 15th (48th Highlanders of Canada) Battalion's Col. John Currie. His reaction can only be imagined when he read the following:

> Reported that impression exists in your regiment that they are to retire on GHQ line. This must be corrected at once. You are to hold your front line. If driven out, collect your men, organize counter attack, and regain it. You are *on no account* to retire on GHQ line.[62]

This message was dispatched at 7:15 A.M., by which time the 15th Battalion had, for all practical purposes, ceased to exist. Isolated bands of kilted

Highlanders, their ammunition exhausted and rifles jammed in any case, had already been overwhelmed on the Stroombeek by the advancing German hordes. The 15th Battalion's losses in the German attack were later calculated at 671 – the most by a Canadian unit in such a short period in the entire Great War.[63] Obviously, a counter-attack by the 15th was out of the question, except in the confused minds of Turner and Hughes.

Yet, another half-hour passed before they relayed a realistic report to Canadian Division headquarters. "Our line is broken," reads their 7:05 A.M. admission. "Organising at St. Julien and occupying GHQ line. No troops in rear. Support needed." The message was repeated half an hour later with the added plea: "Is there any prospect for help?"[64]

By then Alderson had finally acted. Even if Turner did not seem to know what was going on, the reports from Currie were simply too serious and alarming to ignore any longer. Since three-thirty that morning, Alderson had had at his disposal the four battalions of the 150th (York and Durham) Brigade, which belonged to the recently arrived 50th (Northumbrian) Division. At seven-thirty – three and a half hours after the German gas attack – Alderson ordered Brig.-Gen. J.E. Bush, commanding the 150th Brigade, to rush two of his battalions to the GHQ line. An hour later General Bush was told to take the rest of the brigade across the canal and "get into communication" with the Second and Third Canadian brigades. "You will act as reserve to these two Brigades as required," read Alderson's vague instructions.[65] In the meantime, Currie and Turner, both starved for reinforcements, were told: "Brigadier [Bush] has been directed to help you if necessary. Get in touch with him."[66] These politely worded orders were open to interpretation, and each of the three brigadiers would interpret them to his own advantage.

The effect would be needlessly tragic for the Canadian soldiers fighting for survival in the front lines, unaware that their generals were letting them down.

By midmorning the Germans had achieved a partial victory. Thanks to the poison gas, they had succeeded in smashing the apex of the Canadian Division's line, but the results had fallen far short of what they had anticipated. Their penetration had been limited to a maximum of a thousand yards on a half-mile front, after five hours of hard fighting. Now, with superb artillery support and a huge numerical superiority, the Germans continued to apply relentless pressure on the remaining Canadian positions between Gravenstafel and Kitcheners Wood.

Yet the Second Brigade's original trenches remained impervious to repeated attacks. The German infantry advanced under cover of "a high mustard crop" in the fields in front of the Winnipeg men in the 8th Battalion. They stormed the Canadian line again and again, but the survivors of the first gas attack continued to stand firm. Each assault received a rude reception from the Canadians, according to one of the Little Black Devils, Company Sgt.-Maj. G.W. Gorman:

> The Germans clambered over their trenches, and with nervous little cries grouped themselves for a charge. Fire was reserved from the Eighth position until its effect would be most deadly at short range. A bugle blurted. With cries of "Neuve Chapelle, Neuve Chapelle," the grey clad figures came forward many deep. Then the Regiment cut into them with a low fire, every bullet must have gone home. The masses broke once again and fled back.[67]

"There were 4 distinct attacks during the day time," reported Colonel Lipsett, "and one at night on this trench." The Irish-born regular noted laconically that "once a few attackers reached the wire."[68]

Each time, the neighbouring 5th (Western Cavalry) Battalion rendered outstanding assistance. While Lt.-Col. George Tuxford rushed his support company to Lipsett, who used it to bolster his exposed left flank, the riflemen and machine-gunners of the 5th – "Tuxford's Dandies," these dismounted cavalrymen from western Canada called themselves – responded with deadly enfilade fire that ripped the enemy's ranks. As usual, their Ross rifles repeatedly jammed during rapid fire. Tuxford, the former trail boss, was sympathetic to his men's frustration with this unreliable weapon:

> I have seen strong men weep in anguish at the failure, with a useless rifle in their hands and the enemy advancing in full sight. We instructed the men to lay the handles of their entrenching tools alongside them on the trench, so when the jam occurred, by sharply hitting the bolt, it might be released. If this failed, as a last resort the man placed the butt of the rifle on the ground and stamped hard on the bolt with his heel.[69]

The Canadian field artillery had a fine day, too, aiding the Second Brigade. The gunners worked tirelessly to help the infantry hold the line, manning their 18-pounders at such short range that they came under small-arms fire. Maj. Andy McNaughton, soon to be wounded in action, recalled seeing the waves of grey uniforms and spiked helmets – the *pickelhaube*, made of hard leather, was a prized souvenir in the Great War, but a rarity by the end of 1915, when it was replaced by steel helmets – as the four guns of his 7th Field Battery fired "over open sights down to eight or nine hundred yards with shrapnel."[70] Major McNaughton's 18-pounders fired a daily average of 248 shells per gun, a far cry from the three-a-day rationing in effect at the beginning of the battle. The Canadians fired their own shells, as well as ammunition obtained from the neighbouring 27th and 28th divisions, whose guns were usually too far away to assist the Canadian Division. Montreal's Lt.-Col. John Creelman, happy at last, later reported that his 2nd Field Artillery Brigade expended "more than twelve thousand rounds" on 23 and 24 April.[71]

It was a stifling hot morning at Locality C. The battered 10th Battalion, survivors of the night attack, the retreat from Kitcheners Wood, and some of the toughest fighting of the morning, had by now dwindled to 146 officers and other ranks, out of the 174 who had reported to General Currie earlier in the day. "The shell fire was terrific," Major Ormond wrote. At one point, he reported, "we saw . . . at least 3000 troops to our left front, formed up, [and] we opened fire at 700 and 800 yards." The situation soon grew desperate.

> We were being blown up 5 and 6 at a time, the sand from the parapet filling the rifles with dirt, the rifles jammed *fearfully*, the [enemy] troops twice attempted to advance, but twice retired and deployed. Finally, a number in extended order came up to some buildings about 100 yards to our front and were sent back by our fire, but one M.G. [machine-gun] got in the building and made a great dust on our parapet, the wind blowing this on to us. Their artillery was superb, and very heavy.[72]

Locality C was fast becoming untenable. The defenders had to contend with fire not only from the front but from the flank and rear as well. Late in the morning Captain Warden, the man who had spotted the fake British prisoners' ruse, decided that the northwest end of the trench had to be abandoned, and Major Ormond agreed, withdrawing the handful of 10th Battalion survivors to the road at the foot of the ridge. The Germans quickly seized the vacated trench, but went no farther. According to Warden, "we barricaded the trench where it made a fairly sharp curve which acted as a traverse and gave us some protection."[73]

Even so, by noon Warden's little force was all but surrounded. The captain sent out three patrols to reconnoitre the ground towards Saint-Julien, but none returned. Besides Warden, the only surviving officer was a lieutenant, Howard Scharschmidt; all NCOs, except Company Sgt.-Maj. William Gilson, had been killed or wounded. Out of the 234 officers and men Warden had taken into action on 22 April, the captain estimated that "I only had about 50 men left. . . . We were very short of ammunition and kept our supply up by relieving the wounded and dead of theirs."[74]

Just to the west, the remainder of the 7th (British Columbia) Battalion was engaged in a death struggle near Keerselaere. They were still receiving no orders from Turner and Hughes, and Major Odlum's fear of being cut off was turning into grim reality. At eight-thirty Odlum heard the sound of small-arms fire from the rear and, thinking it was his reserve company, the Vancouver newspaperman went back to stop it, only to discover that the shooting was being done by Germans three hundred yards behind his battalion. All the while, the 7th was also being battered by a massive frontal assault. According to Odlum's front-line company commanders, Maj. Percy Byng-Hall and Capt. Thomas Scudamore, "the enemy were advancing in very large numbers . . . but were being cut down in masses by rifle fire." The confident Canadians "had no doubt of their ability to hold their position against any frontal attack."[75]

The carnage, however, was sickening. "The wounded and the dead were lying everywhere," remembered Pte. Perley Smith, "and there was everything in the German Army coming towards us over the fields for miles."[76] Pte. Arthur Corker, the machine-gunner who had been deafened in the previous day's bombardment and was about to be captured, never forgot the scene:

> They came over in masses. You couldn't miss if you could fire a gun. If our guns had been working, or just if we had good rifles – some fellows picked up Lee-Enfields and threw the Ross away. There were some fellows crying in the trenches because they couldn't fire their damned rifles.[77]

"Their damned rifles." It was a familiar refrain for a weapon plagued with the same problems noted on that fateful day at Quebec City in 1901. Excellent for target practice, it was unsuitable for combat because of its tendency to jam during rapid fire. No one will ever know how many Canadians were killed or captured here because they were holding a rifle that would not work – and neither Sir Charles Ross nor Sam Hughes was there to see the results of their handiwork. "Those who were in the line with that rifle will never forget," wrote one of Odlum's front-line captains, Tom Scudamore of Vancouver, "whilst those who were not will never be able to understand what it was like to be charged by the flower of the German army, confident of victory, and be unable to fire a shot in return."[78]

Somehow, the British Columbia battalion held on. When their weapons failed them, inspirational leadership helped to fill the void. Sgt. Hugh Peerless rallied his platoon with the sturdy western shout: "Give the sons of bitches hell, boys!"[79]

Major Odlum, at his headquarters in a nearby farmhouse, experienced his own horror. Among a party rushing small-arms ammunition to the embattled front line, he noted a familiar face: his brother Joseph, a corporal. "I stood watching the group on its way, when a shell landed in the midst and my brother, amongst others, simply ceased to exist."[80]

The major, perhaps fortunately, had no time to dwell on the tragedy, since his headquarters were now under heavy fire. "Bullets poured through the doors and windows," he later wrote. "Many of the HQ personnel were wounded there."[81] At nine-thirty Odlum was forced to shift his headquarters to a dugout. Anticipating the worst, he posted two platoons of his reserve company well to the rear "to support whatever troops of the 3rd Brigade there might still be in that direction."[82]

By ten-thirty the situation had deteriorated. Odlum learned that the two platoons at the extreme right of his front line "had been wiped out, and that the enemy were in possession of their position."[83] In desperation, he dispatched a message to Turner and Hughes at Third Brigade headquarters:

> Enemy have appeared between 200 & 300 yards from my rear. . . . Have lost all contact with troops on right. Right of my line surrounded and wiped out. Stragglers report that all troops on my right & behind me have retired. Am under heavy shell fire and covered from machine guns. . . . My position becoming desperate. Unless reinforcements hurried up, my batt. will be cut off. Can only get out with difficulty by way of St. Julien. Instructions please.[84]

Since coming under the Third Brigade's jurisdiction five hours earlier, Odlum had not received a single reply to his many messages. This one was no exception.

Odlum had only two alternatives: save the battalion by pulling back, or lose it by staying. He decided to withdraw, a decision reached with help from Colonels Currie* and Burland, who were nearby at Enfiladed Crossroads, rallying survivors of the 14th and 15th battalions. The three officers

---

*Col. John Currie's subsequent actions were rather curious. By his own account, he returned to Ypres "to look up any stragglers in the city and send them forward" (Currie, 258-59). However, during the afternoon, he stumbled into General Currie's Second Brigade report centre near Fortuin, where he had to be "manhandled out" by a staff officer. Eventually, the colonel ended up in Boulogne, on the coast, where he was tracked down by an irate General Turner, who wired him: "Return at once or you will be placed under arrest" (PAC, MG30 E8, notes by A.F. Dugald).

It was no coincidence that Colonel Currie was shipped back to Canada soon afterwards. In his defence, it should be said that he was probably suffering from the effects of shell-shock, which was not at that time recognized as a valid medical problem. But Currie was to spend much of the rest of his life defending himself against whispered accusations of cowardice.

agreed to take up a new line three hundred yards back, between Saint-Julien and Locality C, and Odlum hurried back to organize the withdrawal of the 7th.

It was almost too late. The Canadians, with the enemy all around and very close, could extricate themselves only with considerable difficulty. The bulk of those who escaped did so by moving to the left, via Saint-Julien. Others, in small groups, tried to fight their way out, but few of them succeeded. Capt. Tom Scudamore, accompanied by six soldiers and two stretcher-bearers, was among the unlucky ones. When his group was pinned down by German fire, Scudamore, who had earlier been wounded in the head, fainted dead away. He awoke to find himself a prisoner of war. A German soldier snatched Scudamore's Ross rifle as a souvenir, and "I told him he was welcome to it."[85]

Another party under the other front-line company commander, Maj. Percy Byng-Hall, nearly got away. Passing through a hail of shells and bullets, Byng-Hall and his men reached a reserve trench of the 13th Battalion manned by survivors of Capt. George Alexander's company. Hot on their heels, the Germans swarmed to the attack, and after a half-hour battle Byng-Hall chose to withdraw. This movement was under way when, according to Captain Alexander, they discovered "that the enemy had occupied the bushes and houses in our rear, and were capturing the men" as they left the trench. At twelve-forty-five, Byng-Hall and Alexander and thirty-eight others surrendered.[86]

They were roughly handled by their captors. Pte. W.C. Thurgood of Vancouver recalled that, as the motley crew of Canadians stood with their arms in the air, the Germans "started to wipe us out. Three of our men were bayonetted before an officer arrived and saved the rest of us." Even so, Private Thurgood complained that he and his comrades were struck with rifle butts and kicked as they were marched into captivity.[87]*

That anyone belonging to British Columbia's 7th Battalion escaped can be attributed in large part to the bravery of two men. On the gentle rise overlooking the crossroads behind Keerselaere was a machine-gun

---

*There were other reports of atrocities by the Germans. "The enemy shot our wounded unmercifully," the 10th Battalion's Major Ormond claimed, "and with some sort of a projectile that set fire to their clothing. These had the velocity of bullets, some exploding in the air, these I observed myself" (PAC, RG9 III C3, volume 4919, war diary, 10th Battalion).

The most famous, or infamous, incident was a masterpiece of wartime propaganda, the Canadian Golgotha. According to rumours, in the course of this battle a Toronto sergeant was "foully crucified . . . on a barn door" (Currie, 238). The story was repeated so many times that it came to be accepted as a matter of fact, but a postwar investigation proved it to be unfounded.

post. There, Lieut. E. Donald Bellew and Sgt. Hugh Peerless made their last stand, buying valuable time for the rest of the battalion. They made an unlikely pair. While the tough-talking sergeant had already made his mark on the battle – rallying his troops by shouting "Give the sons of bitches hell, boys!" – Don Bellew was a mild-mannered thirty-seven-year-old engineer from Vancouver. Each manning a Colt machine-gun, Lieutenant Bellew and Sergeant Peerless allowed the grey-clad enemy to approach within a hundred yards before they opened fire. The effect was terrible; dozens of Germans fell to the ground amid the hail of bullets. The skilled soldiers on the other side recovered quickly, bringing concentrated small-arms fire to bear on the little Canadian machine-gun post. Soon, Peerless was killed. Bellew was wounded, but he kept firing until he ran out of ammunition. Disabling his gun, the lieutenant picked up a rifle and took on the swarming Germans at bayonet-point until he was overpowered and captured. Bellew was later awarded the Victoria Cross, the third won by a Canadian in the past two days.[88]

At his new position along the road between Saint-Julien and Fortuin, Major Odlum, his private grief carefully kept out of mind, collected a hundred men of the 7th, along with a few from various other units. But this location was not tenable, "owing to the terrific shell fire,"[89] and at one in the afternoon Odlum withdrew another few hundred yards, occupying a trench near Fortuin, not far from General Currie's advanced headquarters. After reporting his new whereabouts to Currie, Odlum spent the rest of the afternoon there, collecting stragglers from his own and other battalions. But by nightfall he could account for "only some 350 of the battn."[90]

The Germans, in the meantime, had turned their full fury on Saint-Julien. During the late morning, they hammered the defenders in a series of attacks, striking directly at the village along the Poelcappelle road and trying to break the thin line of the 2nd and 3rd battalions between Saint-Julien and Kitcheners Wood.

The fighting was furious. The 3rd Battalion's Major Anderson recalled that "the firing was terrific; just one continuous hiss. The air seemed red-hot. The poor fellows fell around me in heaps." While the poor fellows from Ontario farms or university campuses dropped around him, Anderson seemed to be leading a charmed life: although his clothing was riddled with bullet holes and a piece of shrapnel had smashed his wrist watch, he remained unscathed.[91]

Six times the Germans stormed Doxsee's House, and six times they were repulsed. The handful of defenders under Capt. George Richardson, reinforced by a 10th (Calgary-Winnipeg) Battalion machine-gun crew, held on stubbornly. Captain Richardson later described the awful scene in the battered two-storey house:

Our whole position was shelled and machine guns played on the house, until the shots penetrated all three walls. At times men lay on beds and boxes while the machine gun bullets swept the floors. Again, they hugged the floor while the bullets passed over their heads.[92]

Upstairs, a twenty-year-old clerk from Calgary, Pte. Wally Bennett of the 10th Battalion, was manning a Colt machine-gun. Protected by a barricade of bricks and tiles, Private Bennett fired through a shell hole in the wall. He never forgot the lingering stench of chlorine in the air, the screams of the wounded and dying. There was no food, the men having long since eaten their rations of bully-beef and biscuits, and no water – "the water in the well was slimy and rank," according to Bennett.[93] The situation looked grim. "I never expected to get out," he later admitted.[94]

At nearby Saint-Julien, the enemy's steady pressure was finally having an effect. Under concentrated artillery fire from what seemed to be every direction, the defenders were driven out of their trench astride the Poel-cappelle road. Withdrawing into the village proper, the garrison – two companies of the 14th (Montreal) Battalion and one from the badly gassed Highlanders in the 15th – fought a bloody street battle in the face of enormous odds. The last message from the garrison, timed 11:30 A.M., came from Capt. Wilfred Brotherhood of the 14th Battalion: "Enemy have shelled us out and are advancing from our left and front. Will hold every traverse if we have to retire to our right."[95] Within the hour, Captain Brotherhood was dead, and most of the little garrison killed or captured.

The coup de grâce was delivered at noon. Twelve German battalions assembled in the open fields across the Stroombeek, then mounted a steady advance towards Saint-Julien. Some of the enemy carried what appeared to Canadian observers to be white flags; they were, in fact, range-markers for the artillery. This mass formation was impressive, but it provided an excellent target for one of the 2nd Battalion's machine-guns in Doxsee's House. According to Captain Richardson, the Canadian bullets, despite the long range, inflicted terrible damage. "We estimated that, at least, three hundred of them fell."[96] Canadian artillery shells tore great gaps in the neat lines of *feldgrau*, but the Germans advanced inexorably into Saint-Julien, where a desperate struggle – street to street, door to door, room to room – took place.

Reinforcements were rushed to the scene, but they were turned back. A party of the 3rd (Toronto) Battalion, dispatched to Saint-Julien by the Third Brigade's headquarters, was intercepted on the outskirts by a fellow Torontonian, Capt. Robert Cory of the 15th (48th Highlanders) Battalion. Coolly aware that the one-sided fight had only one possible outcome, and that there was no point in swelling the Canadian casualty count in a lost cause, Cory simply turned the men around. "There is nothing to be done here," he told the newcomers. "You had better beat it." Then Cory – who had been married earlier in the month while on leave in London – calmly walked back to rejoin his men in Saint-Julien, where he was captured shortly afterwards.[97]

It is difficult to determine precisely when Canadian resistance in the village was snuffed out. Although the worst of the fighting had ended by one o'clock that afternoon, it was three before the Germans could claim to have undisputed control of Saint-Julien, shell-marked, bullet-riddled, and blood-stained, and shrouded in smoke from burning buildings. But this was news to General Turner at Mouse Trap Farm; as late as 8:45 P.M., he believed that it remained in Canadian hands: "Some of our troops still are in St. Julien surrounded, this number originally 700 now possibly 200."[98]

The enemy's presence in Saint-Julien spelled trouble for the troops of Ontario's 2nd and 3rd battalions, stationed west of the village, towards Kitcheners Wood. The 3rd (Toronto) Battalion had two companies in the line at this point, and Capt. John Streight, so badly wounded that he could not walk, was never so proud of his men. "We were gassed, we were charged, we were bayoneted, and shelled out unmercifully," he later wrote. "We were blown from out of our position by the high explosive shells, many buried alive, many torn and wounded, while many were blown to eternity, yet we kept smiling and held our position."[99] Major Kirkpatrick, the battalion's senior officer here, reported at 12:35 P.M.: "I fear Streight's right flank will be turned. Enemy have secured all front trenches in St. Julien. We will drop back on right flank and hang on." When this report reached Third Brigade headquarters, General Turner rushed out specific orders: "Do not lose touch with St. Julien. Hang on."[100]

Even as he sent this message from Mouse Trap Farm, Turner must have begun to realize that the prospects for his Highland brigade were very bleak indeed.

"Every Man for Himself"

Canadian Division headquarters continued to be plagued by uncertainty on Saturday, 24 April. General Alderson had belatedly ordered two battalions of the British 150th (York and Durham) Brigade to move from their reserve billets near Vlamertinghe to the GHQ line, in support of the Second and Third brigades. Unfortunately, Alderson's vague instructions did not specify how the British were to assist the beleaguered Canadian formations in the front line. Soon afterwards, Alderson sent the rest of the York and Durham Brigade into the salient, and informed General Turner at 9:15 A.M.: "The whole of the York & Durham Bde. has now been sent to GHQ line and directed to get into communication with you."[1]

Both Canadian brigadiers, Currie and Turner, looked upon the British brigade as their salvation. Even at this late hour, disaster might well be averted if these fresh troops arrived soon enough. But the two Canadian generals were due to be disappointed. Unable to make up his mind what to do with the four York and Durham battalions, Alderson sent Turner new instructions at ten-thirty: "If absolutely necessary call on Brigadier, York and Durham, for assistance of one Bn. but do not do so unless absolutely necessary as it is hoped to use this Bde. to relieve yours this evening."[2]

Turner had good reason to question this message. Unless the situation improved drastically, and soon, there would be nothing left for the York and Durham Brigade to relieve. The Third Brigade, strung out along a rough arc from Oblong Farm on the left to Gravenstafel Ridge on the right, was not only being pummelled by infantry attacks and artillery bombardments; it was getting precious little help from its own field guns. "Our artillery," Turner complained to Alderson, "cannot reach the enemy's guns."[3] Of the four batteries of the 3rd Field Artillery Brigade, which was supposed to be supporting Turner's troops, only one, the 9th, was actually doing so. The others were out of range, one having retired to a position a half-mile south of Saint-Jean, the other two having moved west of the canal.

Then Alderson changed his mind again. The situation in the late morning seemed to be so serious that he decided to commit his British reserves after all, informing Turner at eleven-thirty: "Two Bns. of York and Durham Bde. are placed at your disposal for a counter attack to restore situation on your right. This attack must be energetically pushed."[4] At noon the British commander, General Bush, arrived at Turner's bullet-swept headquarters at Mouse Trap Farm to discuss the operation. Several minutes later, Bush departed to organize the counter-attack towards Saint-Julien.

Before it could get under way, Alderson called it off. Uncertain and overcome by caution, he relayed his new orders to Turner via a senior staff officer, Col. Cecil Romer, who spoke to the brigadier by telephone at one o'clock, then dispatched a written message: "As Germans seen massing near [Keerselaere] you must not counter attack but utilise Bns. of York and Durham Bde. to strengthen your line and hold on."[5]

Confusion begat confusion. While by "your line," Romer had referred to the Third Brigade's present position, Turner interpreted his instructions to mean the GHQ line, to his left-rear. He remained under this impression in spite of another phone conversation with Colonel Romer thirty-five minutes later. Turner accordingly issued orders to the Canadian and British battalions under his command: "You will hold GHQ line from St. Jean–Poelcappelle road south."[6]

Ordering a withdrawal in the midst of a battle is one thing; carrying it out is something else entirely. Due to difficulties in communications, it took up to two hours for the orders from Third Brigade headquarters to reach parts of its firing line, and in some cases they failed to get through at all; in other cases, it was impossible for the hard-pressed Canadians to disengage with the enemy swarming all over them.

These difficulties are illustrated by the fate of the 2nd and 3rd battalions, which had been placed under Turner's jurisdiction during the first night of the battle. The 2nd Battalion's Colonel Watson issued his own order to retire at 1:55 P.M., and the Quebec City publisher was none too happy about it. "It was during this retirement that we sustained our heaviest casualties," Watson later noted, stressing that the withdrawal "was *not compulsory*, the enemy having been repulsed with heavy losses, on their repeated attempts to advance."[7]

It was a difficult and costly withdrawal, and not uniformly successful. As always, the problem of disengaging a skilful and numerous enemy proved, at times, to be insurmountable. In the centre of the battalion's position, along the southern edge of Kitcheners Wood, the Ontario troops pulled out under the covering fire of a one-man rearguard, Maj. Herbert

Bolster, who was never seen again. Nevertheless, these Canadians came under heavy enemy fire, as seventeen-year-old Pte. Ferdinand Hardyman was able to testify. Uninjured to this point, the former bank clerk from Sault Ste. Marie was hit four times during the withdrawal, in the chest, left leg, and twice in the right arm. "I had to run, after receiving my wounds, about eight hundred yards to the reinforcement trench to escape from the Germans, and from there I crawled [a mile] to the dressing station." Passing out on arrival, Private Hardyman woke to find that his war was over; he was later evacuated to England, then invalided home to Canada.[8]

Hardyman was luckier than many of his comrades in the 2nd Battalion. On the left, at Oblong Farm, the defenders received the order to pull out, but it was meaningless. Virtually surrounded by Germans, and with every escape route covered by enemy fire, these men had no choice but to fight it out to the bitter end, which is what they did. Like the garrison of Saint-Julien, all were killed or captured.

East of Kitcheners Wood, Doxsee's House continued to be the vortex of furious fighting. The Germans used the cover of a nearby hedge to assemble for each assault, but every time they were decimated by Canadian small-arms fire. Calgary's Wally Bennett, the machine-gunner in the upper storey, vividly recalled the last attack of the day:

> I watched till they broke through the hedge, and they had over a hundred yards to cross over to get to our farmhouse. We saw them breaking through the hedge, with their bayonets fixed, and they were going to come right at us, at the front. And, as near as I can remember, I held my fire, because we were short of ammunition, you know. We couldn't have stopped another attack – we didn't have the ammunition, we'd run out.
>
> So I had to wait until they got through the hedge and let them get a few yards . . . before I opened up on them. I just cut 'em down. For once, the gun didn't jam. We beat them back – some of them we killed, some of them were lying there kicking, you know, you could hear them [screaming]. . . . Those that could get back, crawled back, and carried some of their wounded back.[9]

Around three-thirty, the order to retire reached Doxsee's House. "It was every man for himself," Bennett recalled. To get away, they had to cross seventy-five yards of open ground, to reach a trench that had been dug at the rear of the house. Carrying his machine-gun, Bennett made a run for it along with a few others; but only two made it:

> The bullets were coming both ways – two or three of the others went down. And I got near this trench – say, ten or fifteen yards – and a

fellow fell in front of me, wounded – he was hit in the leg. He fell down in front of me; I ran past, put the machine-gun in the trench, crawled back on my belly, got his good leg, and pulled him in the trench. . . . I don't even know who he was.[10]

Besides Bennett, only a handful of the garrison of Doxsee's House managed to escape, including the officer in charge, Capt. George Richardson.

Less fortunate were the defenders of Hooper's House. There, as at Oblong Farm, the men under Captain Hooper waited too long to evacuate and were overwhelmed by the enemy.

By the time the withdrawal was completed, the 2nd Battalion had been cut to pieces. Its casualties were tabulated at 544, all ranks. Out of the twenty-two officers who had led the battalion into action, only seven were still standing. The dead included the young yachtsman from a distinguished Toronto family, Capt. Leslie Gordon, who, with the 3rd Battalion's Lieut. W.D.P. Jarvis, had thrilled the Royal Canadian Yacht Club by sailing *Nirwana* to win the international George Cup the previous July.[11] That night, licking its wounds in the GHQ line, the 2nd was reorganized into two composite companies, both understrength. Fittingly, the last member of the battalion to get away was the commanding officer, Colonel Watson, who carried an injured private on his back for half a mile to a dressing station.

For Toronto's 3rd Battalion, the retirement was equally disastrous. Its two companies east of Kitcheners Wood were overrun, and few escaped. "All you could see in the woods was a succession of spiked helmets," recalled Eric Seaman. "And there were hordes of them came at us there."[12] Seaman was shocked when a buddy, John Hewitt, was hit in the head by a bullet. Hewitt collapsed, covered with blood, and Seaman assumed that he was dead. But a short time later Hewitt stirred, then struggled to his feet. Seaman was very surprised and asked him how he felt.

"Oh, I feel as though I had been on a drunk for a week," replied the injured man. "That's all."[13]

Hewitt survived but, like Seaman, spent the rest of the war as a prisoner.

The end came around three-thirty. With their only machine-gun out of action, "surrounded and outnumbered, our ammunition all but gone," Major Kirkpatrick surrendered in order "to save useless waste of lives."[14] The decision to surrender came too late for one young subaltern, W.D.P. Jarvis. The bearer of a proud Toronto name, with a grandfather who fought in the war of 1812, the Toronto yachtsman met the same fate as his crewmate from the previous summer, Captain Gordon of the 2nd Battalion.[15] Only forty-three members of the two companies eluded capture; most of them were wounded, and two were totally blind.[16]

Among the prisoners was the officer with a healthy respect for snipers, Maj. Peter Anderson, whose wrist watch had been smashed to smithereens earlier. Although unwounded, he was twice knocked unconscious by shell blasts. The second time, he awoke to find himself in enemy hands. "I was awfully dazed," he later wrote. "I have a hazy recollection of a German trying to take my pistol." As his head cleared, he belatedly realized his situation. "I was now a prisoner of war. What an awful feeling; what a humiliating position to be in. What will people at home think about me? A prisoner of war, and not wounded." It was a depressing way to spend his forty-seventh birthday.*[17]

The agony of defeat was eased somewhat by the comment of a German officer. Surveying the heaps of German dead and wounded lying around the khaki-clad Canadians, the officer asked Anderson in tones of admiration and despair: "You do not mean to tell me that you did all this damage with these few men?"[18]

Another prisoner was twenty-four-year-old Cpl. Jack Finnimore of

---

*Major Anderson was not a prisoner for long. Along with the other Canadian officers captured at Ypres, he was shipped to a prison camp at Bischofswerda, near Dresden, in central Germany. Life as a prisoner of war was not particularly hard – officers were paid 100 marks per month, could play sports such as tennis, and received mail, food parcels, and newspapers and magazines from home – but Anderson, driven by his feelings of humiliation, immediately began collecting the clothing, money, and food he would need to escape, something he intended to do at the earliest opportunity.

His chance came on 28 September 1915. During a bath parade at the edge of the camp, Anderson managed to slip into a well, where he hid for seven hours, until darkness allowed him to scramble over the single barbed-wire fence. The Danish-born Anderson naturally headed for Denmark, six hundred miles away. Travelling cross-country, camping in secluded spots, he began to grow impatient at his slow progress on foot. Eventually, he got up the nerve to purchase a train ticket, posing as Pete Jansen, a Swedish immigrant from the neutral United States.

Remarkably, Anderson had only one close call. Not far from the Danish border, a German soldier eyed him suspiciously and demanded his identification papers. Somehow, Anderson befriended the soldier and got him drunk enough to forget about Anderson's papers. Soon after this episode, the train crossed into Denmark, and Anderson made his way to England via Sweden and Norway. He arrived in London at 11:30 P.M. on Friday, 22 October, less than four weeks after breaking out of the camp in Bischofswerda.

As the only Canadian officer to escape from captivity in Germany during the Great War, Anderson was rewarded with an audience with King George and a promotion to lieutenant-colonel. He spent the rest of the war in England, in an administrative capacity (PAA, Peter Anderson papers, unpublished memoirs).

Toronto. Shot in the leg, Corporal Finnimore could not walk and had no choice but to await the arrival of the Germans. Expecting the worst, Finnimore was pleasantly surprised by his treatment. "One of the German soldiers handed his rifle to his comrade, found a wheelbarrow in a deserted farmyard, placed me on it and pushed me through to the rear lines." Had it not been for their kindness, Finnimore was convinced, "I would have died at the side of the road in a mudhole."[19]

It had been costly, but the Third Brigade had completed its chaotic withdrawal. By midafternoon, a rag-tag collection of troops from the 2nd, 3rd, 13th, 14th, 15th, and 16th battalions was digging in along the GHQ line. In one sense, it had been a remarkable achievement, executed under the most difficult circumstances.

In another sense, though, it was a recipe for disaster. In saving the Third Brigade, General Turner had endangered General Currie's Second Brigade on the right. With several hours of daylight still available to the enemy, the Third's withdrawal had opened a gap two and a half miles wide between the Second's original trenches and the GHQ line to the rear. Only a few Canadians stood in this space, including the determined defenders of Locality c and the pitiful remnants of the 10th Battalion at the foot of Gravenstafel Ridge and the 7th at Fortuin. Currie's beleaguered brigade, having fought so brilliantly and bravely to defend its line, was now faced with the possibility of total destruction.

CHAPTER ELEVEN

"Give Them Hell, Give Them Hell"

General Currie's worst fears about his left flank were fast being realized. Ever since the enemy's initial attack early that morning, he had been concerned about the situation on his left and had devoted all his efforts to finding reinforcements to shore up the front line and fill the gap caused by the breach in the 15th Battalion's defences. Later, Currie made no effort to hide his pride in the performance of his men. "The 8th Battalion were subjected to exactly the same bombardment as the 15th Battalion," he noted, "but never left their trenches."[1]

For Currie, a hazel-eyed, brown-haired gentle giant, this was to be a day of great stress, and one that would push his personal courage and leadership skills to the limit. In the early hours of the morning he got a whiff of the poisonous fumes that enveloped his brigade's front lines, but emerged unhurt. Then his report centre at Pond Farm came under long-range shelling and, at seven in the morning, was set ablaze. Even as the farmhouse burned down around him, Currie scribbled a hasty plea for help addressed to the neighbouring British 85th Brigade – "Have you anybody to spare?" he asked, receiving a negative reply[2] – before grabbing a few private belongings and fleeing to the nearby headquarters of Montreal's Colonel Creelman, who commanded the 2nd Field Artillery Brigade a few hundred yards south of Fortuin. Creelman, who seemed to have as much bad luck with his accommodation as he did with his servants, compared his dugout to "a huge boiler, sunk in the ground and covered with several feet of hard earth."[3] It was cramped, but it would have to do.

Here, Currie learned of the worsening state of affairs on the left. Captain Warden, at Locality C, reported at seven-thirty that "14th Battalion have retired past our line. . . . We are now in firing line, must send someone to stop the 14th and support." Currie had nothing to offer Warden except words of encouragement.[4]

Good news arrived soon afterwards. At eight-fifteen, Currie learned from divisional headquarters about the two battalions of the York and Durham Brigade that were en route to the GHQ line. After waiting impatiently until nearly ten o'clock, he finally sent his orderly officer, Lieut. Murray Greene, with a note for the British brigadier, General Bush: "Please send me four companies [i.e., one battalion] to help me re-establish line broken by retirement 3rd Brigade. The bearer will guide them."[5]

This was the start of a frustrating experience for Currie, not to mention Lieutenant Greene, who safely passed through the hail of bullets to reach the GHQ line, only to find no sign of the British battalions. He returned with that disappointing report, but Currie sent him back to Wieltje to await their arrival.

Things were going from bad to worse for the Second Brigade as the morning wore on. Wreathed in smoke and dust, the 5th (Western Cavalry) and 8th (90th Winnipeg Rifles) battalions continued to cling tenaciously to their front-line trenches. How much longer they could hold out was anyone's guess: they were outflanked; some enemy machine-gunners had slipped in behind them; and the German artillery fire, coming from three directions, was growing heavier by the minute. To make matters worse, communications with General Turner at Third Brigade headquarters were unreliable. A 9:10 A.M. request for information – "how you appreciate the general situation from my left flank"[6] – went unanswered. An hour and a half later, Currie called for help, which brought the prompt but predictable reply from Turner and Hughes, embattled at Mouse Trap Farm: "Have not substantial reinforcements at my disposal to reinforce your left."[7]

By eleven Currie was forced to consider what had previously been unthinkable: the Second Brigade might have to abandon its position. He sent a warning to the commander of the neighbouring British 85th Brigade, Brig.-Gen. A.J. Chapman: "Am still holding front line trenches and I think Locality C but third Bde. has apparently retired. May have to evacuate trenches as left is very much exposed [but] I will not order retirement for some time yet."[8]

In the trenches, the situation facing the 8th Battalion, the Little Black Devils who had fought off the original gas attack, was getting more desperate with each passing minute. "My trench was now a shambles," wrote a company commander, the Winnipeg lawyer Capt. Arthur Morley. "In 50 yards I had 50 or 60 casualties with many killed, the parapet blown in in several places, and some men had used as many as 3 or 4 rifles."[9] The 8th's commanding officer, Currie's trusted Colonel Lipsett, warned "that the Germans were working around his left rear" and asked for a company to fill the potentially disastrous gap between his front line and Locality C. "I could send no help," Currie later wrote, "our reserves were all used up." At the same time, Lipsett assured his brigadier that the 8th would hang on for as long as possible, reporting that his three company commanders in the trenches, including Captain Morley, "have stated they are prepared to stick to their positions . . . to the last."[10]

But Currie knew that it would take more than brave words to save the situation. He needed reinforcements, and quickly.

It was late in the morning before the leading battalion of the York and Durham Brigade reached Wieltje, where Lieutenant Greene was anxiously waiting. This unit was the 5th Durham Light Infantry, and Greene promptly greeted its commander with Currie's summons. To Greene's disbelief and disgust, the British colonel refused to act, stating that this was beyond his authority and that he intended to wait at Wieltje "for further instructions." Greene hurried back to Currie with the bad news.[11]

It was nearly noon, and Currie was preparing for the worst. At 11:45 A.M. he sent instructions to Colonel Lipsett: "As the 3rd Bde. are falling back on GHQ 2nd Line you will have to retire on the Gravenstafel Ridge and hold there. The OC 5th Battn [Colonel Tuxford] is being told to conform with this. . . . No re-inforcements available."[12] He subsequently informed the 85th Brigade's General Chapman:

> Owing to my left flank . . . being entirely unprotected and having been informed that no reinforcements are available, I have ordered the 8th Battn. . . . to retire by its left on the Gravenstafel ridge, the 5th Battalion . . . to conform to the movement of the 8th Bn. but to maintain contact with your left. Will endeavour to establish line from [Kitcheners Wood] – St. Julien – Locality C – Gravenstafel ridge.[13]

The withdrawal proved to be unnecessary. At noon things took an unexpected turn for the better, thanks to the enemy. "Just heard," reported Colonel Lipsett, "German advance against our left seems to have slackened and come to a halt. I am not uneasy about being able to hold my line if the Germans are prevented walking round my rear." But the Irishman made it clear that it was still "a very bad situation," with "only 20 men" defending the critical gap on his left flank.[14]

Shortly afterwards, Lieutenant Greene appeared with his disappointing report. Far from being discouraged – and this is a measure of Currie's ability as a leader – the brigadier concluded that there was a way to save his brigade: a counter-attack carried out by the British units assembling in the GHQ line. Unaware that Canadian Division headquarters had already authorized such a measure, Currie dispatched a message to General

Turner: "It is understood that you intend to hold GHQ 2nd line to the last but I suggest that a local counter attack in the direction of St. Julien . . . will do much to restoring the situation. I would be glad if you would consider this and let me know your decision." Ten minutes later, at 12:20, he was informed of the planned counter-attack by the York and Durhams.[15]

Time was of the essence. Currie's impatience and anxiety are understandable: four hours had passed since he had been told that two British battalions were en route to help him, and they had only recently reached the GHQ line, well to the rear. There seemed to be a lack of urgency, and Currie decided to act. As he later wrote, "my staff were urging me to go to them and bring them forward, it being thought that they might move for me when unlikely to move for officers of lesser rank." After discussing the situation with the dependable Colonel Lipsett, who "urged me to go and hurry," Currie decided to go back and personally fetch the recalcitrant British.[16]

Before departing, Currie ordered Lipsett "to hang on to his front trenches as long as possible instead of carrying out a retirement on Gravenstafel Ridge."[17] Leaving Lipsett in command of the battle zone – although the 5th Battalion's Lt.-Col. George Tuxford was the senior officer – Currie also wrote out an order for Lipsett to withdraw, which Lipsett was not to use unless necessary. "As he was the man on the spot," Currie explained, "I left it to his judgment, and Lipsett and myself had a very clear understanding."[18]

In leaving his report centre, Currie was risking his career. It is usually inadvisable for a general to leave his headquarters – even, as in this case, his advanced headquarters – in the heat of battle. But Currie was convinced that he could do more to help his brigade by going to the GHQ line than he could by sitting in his overcrowded dugout.

He was also risking his life. To reach the GHQ line, Currie had to pass on foot through extremely dangerous territory. At the Second Brigade's main headquarters in Wieltje, Capt. Ross Napier watched the brigadier's approach:

> I was astonished to see General Currie approaching alone across the open. The roads were being heavily shelled and the open was searched by rifle, machine gun and shrapnel. As he drew near, a salvo of heavies intended for the road burst immediately in his line of approach, but he reached the comparative shelter (from rifle fire at least) of the ruined cottage where I was – making, as he did so, a jocular remark as to the comparative salubrity of Salisbury Plains.[19]

Currie's good humour was soon to be severely tested. It was about one o'clock, and he quickly sought out the nearby British unit. "It would not move," Currie later wrote of the 5th Durham Light Infantry, "and there it was joined by its Brigadier (Brig. General Bush). General Bush was ready to make a counter-attack, but he desired to wait for another of his battalions which he said was on its way to the GHQ line by way of Potijze." While Bush set off to look for that unit, the 4th Yorkshire, Currie waited impatiently at Wieltje.[20]

Naturally in this tragi-comedy of errors, the 4th Yorkshire showed up soon after Bush's departure. Currie went to the two battalion commanders "and I urged them to advance towards St. Julien." Both colonels refused to act in Bush's absence.[21]

Worse news followed. Currie encountered a Third Brigade staff officer, Capt. Harold McDonald, who was carrying a message from General Turner: "Have instructed troops to hold GHQ line. Orders for counter attack cancelled."[22]

Currie was thunderstruck. The withdrawal to the GHQ line meant that a gap of nearly three miles was being opened behind his brigade, which, to all appearances, was being abandoned.

The Canadian general refused to let that happen. He sought out General Bush, who had now established his headquarters in a nearby farm. "I pled with him," Currie recounted, "to move these two battalions, but he by that time had received orders that the battalions were not to be used as formerly intended and apparently had been ordered to increase the large bodies of troops protecting Potijze."[23]

By now, Currie was getting desperate. "My sole concern," he later wrote, "was to move troops to fill the gap." Before leaving Bush, he learned of the presence of a British divisional headquarters a few hundred yards away, at Potijze. Currie hurried over there, where he met Maj.-Gen. Thomas Snow, commanding the 27th Division, in a hastily constructed dugout. Excavated to a depth of only two feet, its walls were made of planks and earth, and with a few sheets of corrugated iron for a roof, it was neither shell- nor bullet-proof.[24] If the surroundings were shabby, so was the treatment Currie was about to receive from the square-jawed, moustachioed General Snow, whom Currie discovered "had the reputation of being the rudest officer in the British Army." (Snow's earlier note to Alderson gave a hint of his style.) Writing in 1926, Currie related what happened during the meeting with Snow:

He at once asked me who I was. I told him and with the aid of a map proceeded to give him my appreciation of the situation. . . .

As soon as I mentioned that apparently there was a gap between the left of my 8th Bn. and the 3rd Brigade troops, he shouted at me and asked how dare I allow a gap to occur. To hear him one would have thought that I personally and solely was responsible for that gap, although every man of the 2nd Brigade was fighting in the line at that moment. He roundly abused me and told me to get out, shouting at me to "Give them hell, give them hell." When I considered the position of all the troops of the 2nd Brigade and my inability to move two battalions whom I thought had been sent to our assistance, I confess that at that moment I thought I had never heard a more stupid remark. I have thought about it many times during the past eleven years and am of the same opinion still.

I asked if I might send a message to the 1st Canadian Division, but had no sooner sat down at a table to write the message than he again shouted at me, saying that I was taking much too long over it. That was an insult and so at variance with the treatment which one officer should receive from another of superior rank that I was dumbfounded.[25]

Snow's version was much different. He later contended that Currie had already made up his mind to pull the Second Brigade out of the front line, and that Currie showed him a conditional order for the withdrawal: "If compelled to withdraw, do so to the GHQ line." Snow claimed that he angrily tore up the order and then "forcibly persuaded" the Canadian brigadier to keep his troops in their trenches.[26]

The extent of the volatile British general's fury is revealed by a statement he made later: "If Currie was an English Officer I would have had him put under arrest and he would probably have been shot."[27]

The one witness to this confrontation was a lowly Canadian engineer, Lieut. E.F. Lynn of the 2nd Field Company. The thirty-two-year-old Lieutenant Lynn had been posted outside Potijze that morning, ostensibly to work on entrenchments, but he soon found himself preoccupied with rallying and organizing several hundred stragglers, most of them Canadians from the Second and Third brigades. A staff officer of the 27th Division had ordered Lynn to report to General Snow for further orders, and he arrived in the midst of Snow's discussion with General Currie. "Genl. Currie was cool and adamant," Lynn observed, while "Genl. Snow, in contrast, was excited, raving, abusive and insulting." Indeed, Lynn believed that the Englishman "was very close to an attack of apoplexy, owing to his frenzy," and added: "It was obvious that of the two leaders Genl. Currie was the one to follow. He certainly commanded respect and confidence which was denied to his protagonist, Genl. Snow."[28] An incorrigible diarist, Lynn later reconstructed the generals' ten-minute exchange:

CURRIE: Your men are fresh and their assistance at the points mentioned would be of great value.

SNOW: Have you come here to teach me my profession and dictate to me how I shall handle my division?

CURRIE: There was no intention on my part to attempt to tell you your job or to advise you how to handle your division; but I have been in this sector for some time now and know it pretty well. My brigade has been in the line for ten days. They were in it when the attack was launched and have resisted every attack without relinquishing a foot of ground. They have counter-attacked and have been fearfully cut up. They are tired and hungry, and require support at many points before nightfall.

SNOW: Do you expect me to wet-nurse your brigade? You have got yourself and your men into a mess and you will have to get them out as best you can.

CURRIE: So much for your co-operation in this grave situation. I am not in a mess nor are my men. My men and I have held out against fierce onslaughts and will continue to hold out as long as any of us are left. As I have already stated, my men have not lost any ground despite the fact that they are played out, hungry, and decimated. The support of some fresh troops is essential for the safety of the line.

SNOW: Enough of this, I have heard enough of your harangue. Get out of here. Take care of your own line.*[29]

---

*This episode became the subject of a bitter British–Canadian dispute after the war. In preparing his volume concerning the Second Battle of Ypres, the British official historian, Sir James Edmonds, accepted Snow's version of the confrontation with Currie. The original draft written by Edmonds portrayed Currie as "terror stricken" and contended that "Currie and his staff made grave mistakes" in the course of the battle, and that his purpose in visiting Snow was to obtain the latter's help and advice in withdrawing the Second Brigade. This interpretation prompted a howl of protests from Canada, and no one was more indignant than Currie, who, in Edmonds's words, "begged for its deletion" (Travers, 1, 8).

Sir James was not surprised at the violent Canadian reaction, and Currie's in particular. "The publication of the whole story would ruin his position in Canada," but Edmonds denied that he was being unfair. Far from being biased against the Canadians, he argued, "I had . . . covered up a number of unpleasant incidents, and particularly the

General Snow's boorish behaviour was inexcusable, but it revealed his contempt – shared by many British professionals at the time, and later – for these amateur soldiers from the colonies. What is baffling is that Snow had already taken steps to deal with Currie's concerns but said nothing of them to the Canadian brigadier. Between noon and three o'clock, the approximate time of his meeting with Currie, Snow sent no fewer than five British battalions to the crucial gap in the Canadian Division's line, acting in his capacity as commander of all reserves in the salient, an appointment he had held since midmorning. In fact, just before Currie's appearance at his dugout, he had attempted to intervene in General Turner's withdrawal to the GHQ line. In a bluntly worded order, Snow had demanded that Turner "move every man you have" to block the German "advance from Fortuin," which he mistakenly believed had fallen. "Act with vigour," he added.[30] Turner chose to ignore Snow's instructions; twelve hours later he politely notified the British general, "I regret not having been able to comply with your request."[31]

Currie was not the only Canadian officer to feel Snow's wrath on 24 April. On his way out of the dugout, Currie met Capt. Paul Villiers, who had served with him in the 50th Gordon Highlanders in Victoria before the war. They chatted for a moment – "it struck me," Villiers later wrote, "that he had had a duce [sic] of a row with Snow and had found Snow bombastic and unsympathetic" – before going their separate ways. Villiers, the staff captain at Third Brigade headquarters, had been sent by

unsoldierly behaviour of General Currie and some of the higher officers" (*Ibid.*, 2).

That Edmonds initially accepted Snow's version is understandable, because he had served under him on the staff of the British 4th Division in 1914. But Sir James had ulterior motives, and they were far from honourable. It was his intention to use the British official history to belittle Canada's contribution to the war effort, to "get even" with them for the fine reputation they had acquired. Digging in his heels over Second Ypres, he privately confessed in 1926: "As the history proceeds, many and very serious difficulties with the Canadians will crop up – there was no limit to their lying as the war went on. It is important to make a stand now." Edmonds was not alone among senior British officers in his resentment of the Canadians. Sir Henry Horne, for example, complained in 1919 that the Canadians were "rather apt to take all the credit . . . for everything, and to consider that the BEF consists of the Canadian Corps and some other troops" (*Ibid.*, 12).

In the end, however, common sense prevailed. An official history is clearly no place to pursue the kind of malice Sir James had in mind. Unable to corroborate Snow's version of his meeting with Currie, and undoubtedly aware of the strong feelings the issue was generating on both sides of the Atlantic, Edmonds did not even mention the dugout dispute in his 1927 volume. The Canadian official history, published in 1938, mentioned it only in passing, prompting Sir James to comment approvingly: "The Snow–Currie part gives the incident most respectable burial" (*Ibid.*, 13).

General Turner to outline the situation now that the brigade had fallen back to the GHQ line. Giving his report to Snow, Villiers "found him quite civil though rather brusque in his manner." Then he mentioned Turner's plans for a three o'clock counter-attack towards Saint-Julien, which the brigadier believed was still holding out, though surrounded.[32]

At that, Snow "exploded and said that the order must be cancelled at once." Snow told Villiers to personally report to every battalion commander concerned and cancel the operation. The captain set off on his mission, "a bit of a nightmare" which lasted three-quarters of an hour. "I ran down the front line on top of the trenches by far the most frightened person in the whole of the War, shouting 'Troops will stand fast, orders for counter attack are cancelled.'" Eventually, Villiers made it back to brigade headquarters, where he explained to Turner what he had done. The brigadier, he recalled "was very upset about it at the time and, rather unreasonably I thought, questioned my right to do what I had done, but I pointed out to him that I was taking direct orders from General Snow, his superior officer." That seemed to calm Turner down, and he never again mentioned the matter to Villiers.[33]

While Captain Villiers was running back and forth, risking his life to endure verbal abuse, General Currie was dejectedly trudging back to Wieltje late that afternoon. He was saddened by the sight of literally thousands of British soldiers digging in around Potijze, far behind the embattled front lines where they were desperately needed. "I could not understand," he later wrote, "why they should be throwing up defences in an area unsuitable for defence and tactically worthless when they might have been much more usefully employed elsewhere." His mission to find reinforcements had apparently failed. The best he could do was round up some Second Brigade stragglers, whose presence nearby was mentioned by the helpful Lieutenant Lynn, the engineer who had witnessed his argument with Snow. There were "about 100" by Currie's count[34] – although Lynn put their number at "three hundred to four hundred in all"[35] – which he placed under the command of the 7th (British Columbia) Battalion's regimental sergeant-major, David Philpot, and sent off to the front. But that small group was, Currie realized, far from sufficient to save his doomed brigade.

Much had happened in General Currie's absence from his advanced headquarters. Almost miraculously, the Second Brigade was still holding its seemingly hopeless position, east of, and on top of, Gravenstafel Ridge. Outflanked, outnumbered, and outgunned by the enemy, these Canadians from the prairies and British Columbia simply refused to admit defeat. As far back as Valcartier, Currie had predicted that his brigade would "fight like Billy be damned" – and right he was.[36]

When Currie, arriving at his main headquarters in a ruined house in Wieltje, was told that his battered brigade still stood firm, he immediately set out to have a look for himself. En route to the front, he passed his report centre near Fortuin and ordered the staff officers there to return to Wieltje. It was dark by the time he reached Gravenstafel Ridge, where he met the dependable Colonel Lipsett, who briefed him on the events subsequent to his departure in the early afternoon.

Left in temporary command of the brigade's battle zone, Lipsett had decided to hold on for as long as possible. "The officers commanding companies in the trenches told me they would hang on and hold their trenches as long as they had a man to put on the parapet." Lipsett duly informed the commander of the 5th (Western Cavalry) Battalion, Colonel Tuxford, and the legendary cattle-driver "received my decision to remain with much delight."[37]

A stellar performance by the Canadian field artillery helped considerably. Around four in the afternoon, the Germans made another effort to exploit the opening between the 8th Battalion's front line and Locality c. When Lipsett called for artillery support to meet this threat, the 6th Field Battery sent two guns, under Lieut. H.F. Geary. The Canadian guns, under heavy small-arms fire, reached the critical location in the nick of time and "succeeded in causing serious losses to the enemy and forcing them to temporarily forsake their objective." Lieutenant Geary kept his guns in action here until all his ammunition had been expended; then he withdrew safely.[38]

Even more crucial was the timely arrival of the British battalions ordered into the gap by crusty old General Snow. The first to reach the scene were the 12th London Rangers and the 1st Suffolk Regiment, which Snow had commandeered from the reserve of the neighbouring 28th Division. Spread out in skirmishing order – a long, well-spaced line – these two units moved across the Second Brigade's rear, reaching Fortuin shortly after three o'clock. The brigade-major, Lt.-Col. Herbert Kemmis-Betty, and another staff officer, Maj. Chalmers Mersereau, led the British northward, deploying them below Locality c, with their left flank bent backward to minimize the effect of enfilade fire coming from the Germans in Saint-Julien.

The Suffolks and Rangers found themselves in a hot spot. They had to contend not only with enemy fire but with their own artillery; for British batteries to the south, unaware of the presence of the two battalions, shelled the area in the mistaken belief that it had been occupied by the

Germans. In short order, the Suffolks suffered 154 casualties, while the Rangers lost 59 men, including their commanding officer, Lt.-Col. A.D. Bayliffe. The Suffolks' Lt.-Col. W.B. Wallace took charge of both units.

Farther west, three more British battalions had entered the picture. The first to move in was the 1st Royal Irish, from the 27th Division's reserve, sent up at noon. Passing through the GHQ line, the Irish, only 370 strong, found Fortuin to be in Canadian hands – contrary to reports reaching General Snow at divisional headquarters near Potijze – and swung north towards Saint-Julien, which was undoubtedly in German hands. Stopped by heavy fire several hundred yards south of the village, the Irish dug in and awaited further developments in the early afternoon.

They did not have long to wait. Two battalions of the York and Durham Brigade, so long delayed by contradictory orders at the GHQ line – which was rapidly filling with troops from the Third Brigade – were finally moving into action. The 4th Yorkshire and 4th East Yorkshire were under the command of the senior officer, Lt.-Col. M.H.L. Bell, who had so recently rejected General Currie's pleas to advance into the gap and who now accepted orders from an unknown staff officer of the 27th Division "to make Fortuin good and stop the Germans" before they reached the GHQ line.[39]

These advancing battalions collided head-on with a major German attack. The enemy, fresh from conquering the Canadian defenders in and around Saint-Julien, charged across the open fields, only to recoil in the face of furious small-arms fire from the York and Durham units, which were both seeing combat for the first time. Canadian field guns came roaring to their assistance. In his dugout south of Fortuin, Colonel Creelman of the 2nd Field Artillery Brigade ordered half a dozen 18-pounders from three batteries to move up in close support of the embattled British Territorials. Creelman described the ensuing action:

> Soon Germans in long lines emerged from the line of trees [in Kitchen-ers Wood] and started across the open, each man on the sky line and silhouetted against the red glow of the setting sun. It was the most ideal target any of us had ever seen. Every man at every gun saw his objective. The order to fire was given and in a very few minutes two lines of Germans ceased to exist. Up to dark no third line had attempted to leave the woods.[40]

Still, it was a close-run action. The Canadian guns, firing twenty rounds a minute, soon ran short of shells. Just when it appeared that the shrapnel supply would run out, the welcome shout was heard above the din: "Four wagons of ammunition, sir." It was a subaltern and his drivers, fresh from an all-day ride from Vlamertinghe, six miles away; they had been kept busy dodging enemy fire for most of that distance.[41]

The German rout was complete. Believing that they were facing a major Allied assault, the enemy evacuated Saint-Julien in favour of the higher and more defensible ground to the immediate north. In the semi-darkness, the German exodus was mistaken for an Allied advance; at six-thirty it was reported: "Our troops advancing from St. Julien towards Kitcheners Wood."[42] But the British, instead of advancing, were actually getting ready to withdraw.

This was the handiwork of General Turner. After spending most of the battle under fire at Mouse Trap Farm, the Third Brigade's commander was by this time obsessed with defending the GHQ line, apparently convinced that it was the salvation not only of his brigade but of the entire Canadian Division. Having filled the GHQ line with all four of his own battalions and two First-Brigade battalions placed under his command, Turner, at great personal risk – again, no one can question his courage – set out in the late afternoon to find the units that General Snow had allotted to him. He found only the 1st Royal Irish, huddled in the open fields south of Saint-Julien, and instructed the commanding officer to pull back to the GHQ line at dusk, insisting that these troops were "unsupported."[43] The same orders were relayed to the two nearby battalions of the York and Durham Brigade, and at seven o'clock the three units withdrew. It was fortunate that Turner had not detected the presence of the 1st Suffolk Regiment and 12th London Rangers, but his action had partly reopened the dangerous gap between his brigade and General Currie's. (The Suffolk and London battalions would have withdrawn also, if the commander of the 28th Division had had his way. Maj.-Gen. E.S. Bulfin was enraged when he discovered that his only reserves had been diverted by General Snow, and in the late afternoon he demanded their return "at the earliest possible moment." Snow, however, refused to move them.)[44]

Not until late on Saturday afternoon did General Alderson, at Canadian Division headquarters, realize that Turner was trying to defend the wrong line. Years afterwards, one of Alderson's staff officers, Lt.-Col. G.C.W. Gordon-Hall, remarked bitterly on Turner's performance:

Turner began to sit on his reserves instead of using them to reinforce his forward position as directed by Div. HQ. This policy he pursued to the end and nothing Div. HQ or other commanders could order, or suggest, or implore, made him alter his policy, with of course disastrous consequences to all concerned and to none more than to his own troops.

I don't think enough is made of the overcrowding in GHQ line and to the resultant heavy casualties from hostile artilleryfire. It had a magnetic attraction for Turner in spite of the fact that it faced the wrong way and could be enfiladed.[45]

Alderson's problem in all of this was his assumption that Turner was acting in accordance with the scheme of defence issued when the Canadian Division moved into the salient. This policy required the Canadians "to hold the front trenches at all costs and in the event of any trench being lost, to counter-attack at once." The GHQ line, according to this plan, "acts as a support of the front trenches and as a basis for any required counter-attacks"; Turner, however, had turned it into his new front line.[46]

It was nearly midnight before Alderson found out what Turner was doing. His immediate superior, General Plumer at V Corps headquarters, sent a message berating Alderson for allowing the retirement of Canadian and British battalions that had been "ordered by Gen. Turner back to GHQ second line or to their division thus giving up all the ground for which such a struggle has been made to-day and leaving the second bde. in the air." Plumer demanded that "instant action be taken" to restore the situation.[47]

Alderson could hardly believe his eyes when he read Plumer's angry note. To find out precisely what was going on, he sent a senior staff officer, Colonel Gordon-Hall, to confer with the Canadian brigadiers and assess the situation. As Gordon-Hall made his way into the salient, he passed Turner, who was en route to Château des Trois Tours seeking an explanation for the orders he had been receiving – but ignoring – from the 27th Division's General Snow.

The meeting between Turner and Alderson went badly. As the Canadian official history points out, it "only served to develop the unfortunate, but partially correct, conviction in the mind of each commander that the other did not understand what was happening."[48]

With the battlefield blanketed in blessed darkness, the shooting gradually died down. After Saturday's bloodbath, both sides needed a rest. The luckiest Canadian troops were those in the GHQ line, where hot meals were being served. In the front lines around Gravenstafel Ridge, however, rations were few and far between; for the moment, ammunition supplies were getting priority treatment. Many of the men were too tired to care about eating anyway, and took advantage of the temporary quiet to sleep in the bottom of their shallow, shell-blasted trenches.

All night long, a steady stream of walking wounded and stretcher-bearers stumbled towards the rear. Every injured man was taken first to a regimental aid post, where his battalion's medical officer sorted out the wounded and administered first-aid. Then it was off to the dressing stations located in and around Ypres. The most serious cases were passed along to the casualty clearing stations farther back still, and to hospitals in centres such as Boulogne on the French coast. As always, the medical services performed valiantly, but there were strict limitations on what the doctors could accomplish. It was not until 1917 that blood transfusions were freely available on the battlefield, and because surgical techniques were still being refined, amputations were more common than they would be in the next world war. There was little that could be done about major abdominal, chest, or head wounds, and without antibiotics – not introduced until 1943 – nothing could be done about infections.[49]

The day's bloody fighting had left the Canadian Division in desperate straits. But things could have been worse. Employing an effective combination of poison gas and overwhelming numbers at the point of attack, the Germans had smashed the apex of the Canadian line and forced it back some distance. Their gains, however, were modest in comparison with the effort expended and casualties incurred – thanks to the fine defence thrown up by the Canadians. As the 15th Battalion's commander, Colonel Currie, the Toronto MP, wrote, his political rhetoric in full flight: "Bayonets, brawn, and bull-dog courage were all we had to match against all the resources of . . . our enemies."[50]

The Third Brigade had had a tough time. Pounded by German artillery for hours on end, the Canadian Highland brigade had been, as General Turner put it, "literally blown out of position after position."[51] By nightfall on the twenty-fourth, Turner estimated that he had assembled in the GHQ line "probably 3,500" men from four Canadian and five British battalions.[52]

In sharp contrast, the Second Brigade had performed brilliantly. It still held its original trenches, despite staggering odds. In General Currie's absence, Colonel Lipsett, displaying the resourcefulness and initiative that mark a good commander, had worked hard to bolster the 8th Battalion's weak line. Begging, pleading, cajoling, the Irishman had managed to collect an assortment of British troops – "about 1,000 men"[53] – from neighbouring units. These included a hundred men from the 2nd Northumberland Fusiliers, a company each from the 1st Monmouthshire Regiment and 2nd Cheshire Regiment, and two weak companies from the 1st Suffolk Regiment. Most of these were posted along an eight-hundred-yard front near Lipsett's headquarters at Boetleer Farm. Another key acquisition was the 8th Durham Light Infantry, under Lt.-Col. John Turnbull. The Durhams arrived in time to relieve two of Lipsett's three front-line companies; daylight prevented relief of the other.

If they were going to hold on, they would have to do it without the continued excellent close-range support of the field artillery. So far, the 18-pounders had performed prodigiously, as exemplified by Maj. Andy McNaughton's 7th Field Battery, which fired over eighteen hundred shells on Saturday. Major McNaughton had been hit in the shoulder by shrapnel, but remained to direct his guns for another twelve hours; often they fired at point-blank range, said McNaughton, "so we could get the greatest number of people in the line of fire." In the end McNaughton had to be carried out on a stretcher, but he survived to distinguish himself further in this war, and to command the Canadian army in the next one.[54]

But by ten o'clock that night the situation had become intolerable for Colonel Creelman's 2nd Field Artillery Brigade. His eight remaining guns had only sixty rounds of ammunition left among them, and the Germans were dangerously close, within six hundred yards.[55] The enemy's shell fire was raking the area with alarming accuracy, prompting Creelman to complain that "it was very disagreeable being shot at all the time day and night from about four-fifths of the circumference."[56] Regretfully explaining his reasons to Colonel Lipsett, Creelman ordered his guns to limber up and head for the relative safety of Potijze.

It was a hair-raising withdrawal, under heavy fire all the way, but Creelman was pleased to point out that it "was done with practically no loss." His guns escaped "by a road across the fields which I had reconnoitred several days before and had filled in the ditches, cut hedges and removed wire where necessary. In this game it is well to be prepared beforehand for a hasty getaway." Creelman's batteries were back in action early Sunday morning, but they were now too far back to assist in the Second Brigade's defence of its front lines.[57]

There was more bad news for the Second Brigade: Locality C had finally fallen, its 7th Battalion garrison relinquishing the blood-soaked strongpoint only after a fight of epic proportions. All day, the dwindling company of defenders had repulsed one attack after another by Germans who seemed to be swarming from all directions. Captain Warden, the tough British Columbian in charge here, had been wounded early in the afternoon, but he had stayed at his post until dusk, "assisting the men and encouraging those who were left – now about 35 I should say." When he was evacuated, Warden handed over the command to Lieut. Howard Scharschmidt. According to the lieutenant, the orders to retire came from Colonel Kemmis-Betty at brigade headquarters "about 4 in the morning," by which time Locality C had been completely surrounded. The wounded Scharschmidt escaped with twenty-two others under cover of a thick fog.[58]

With Locality C lost, the fate of Currie's Second Brigade appeared to be a foregone conclusion. Its left flank remained in the air, and to its rear was a gap of nearly three miles, defended only by a rag-tag collection of Canadian and British troops on and about Gravenstafel Ridge, while the 12th London Rangers and half of the 1st Suffolk Regiment were left with the task of manning a twelve-hundred-yard stretch southwest of the ridge.

It is a tribute to the tenacity of the defenders, Canadian and British alike, that the enemy failed to take advantage of this glaring weakness. There were no fewer than thirty-nine German battalions in the immediate vicinity, outnumbering the Canadians and their British cousins by 3 to 1 or more, and in theory they should have been more than sufficient to casually seize the remainder of the Canadian Division's position. But the enemy had already suffered immense losses. The fields north and east of Ypres were carpeted with grey-clad corpses; as the Canadian official history observes: "They had been fought to a standstill."[59]

The German official account of the battle praised the resistance that had been met on 24 April:

> The attack encountered strong opposition and progressed but slowly. Keerselaere, from which enemy machine guns were fired, held out particularly long. In the farms and hedges round St. Julien, too, the enemy resisted stoutly in spite of heavy artillery bombardment.[60]

The British had been no less impressed with the performance of the Canadian Division. Any concerns about its ability to function capably in combat conditions had been dispelled, and the BEF's commander-in-chief, Field-Marshal French, sent a telegram to General Alderson on Saturday afternoon expressing "to you and Canadian Troops my admiration of the gallant stand and fight they have made. They have performed a most brilliant and valuable service." King George said the same thing a few hours later, when he publicly declared his appreciation for "the gallant conduct of the Canadian Division in repulsing the enemy."[61]

The Canadians would have to continue to perform brilliantly, because another agonizing day of hard fighting lay ahead. The question was, could the Canadian Division survive another day like the twenty-fourth of April?

It had been a warm, bright day on the Canadian prairies. Laura Boyle took advantage of the fine weather that Saturday to travel into Calgary, thirty-five miles south of the 960-acre ranch she and Russell owned. Together with her two children, Annie, who was seven, and four-year-old James, Mrs. Boyle had arranged to have a family portrait taken. It would be a splendid way to mark the children's coming birthdays; James's was on 2 May, the next weekend, and Annie's was on the tenth of that month. The photograph would also be a nice keepsake for her husband, commanding the 10th Battalion overseas.

Laura Boyle had no way of knowing that, at the very moment she and the youngsters were briefly blinded by the photographer's flash, Colonel Boyle was lying on his death bed in a hospital in Boulogne, France.

She might have worried, though, had she picked up a copy of the Calgary *Daily Herald*. GERMANS ARE REACHING FOR THE SEA COAST, screamed the banner headline, while underneath was another disturbing headline: HEAVIEST CASUALTIES OF ANY ENGAGEMENT YET DURING PERIOD OF WAR. An accompanying story told of Thursday's gas attack on the French – "acid asphyxiating shells and bombs" and "gas grenades" – and the "glorious but costly" fighting that had involved "practically the whole [Canadian] division."[62]

The first intimation of Canadian involvement in a great battle had come earlier in the day, when the War Office in London issued a communiqué:

> The fight for the ground into which the Germans penetrated between Steenstraate [*sic*] and Langhemarq [*sic*] still continues. The loss of this part of the line laid bare the left of the Canadian division, which was forced to fall back in order to keep in touch with the right of the neighbouring troops. In the rear of the latter had been placed 4.7 [-inch] guns, which thus passed into the hands of the enemy. But some hours later the Canadians made a most brilliant and successful advance, recapturing these guns and taking a considerable number of German prisoners, including a colonel. The Canadians had many casualties, but their gallantry and determination undoubtedly saved the day. Their conduct has been magnificent throughout.[63]

It was old news, of course, and had been eclipsed by that very day's events. Interestingly, this was the first information received not only by ordinary Canadians but by their government leaders, too. Like everyone else, even the militia minister, Sam Hughes, had to rely on dispatches from the War Office to find out what was going on with Canadian troops. "They would never leave those guns in the hands of the Germans," he responded when quizzed by reporters outside his Ottawa office. "They have done what was expected of them, what we all knew they could do, and that was their duty. Yes, this dispatch makes us prouder than ever of them. I am sorry that the dispatch says there were many casualties, but we must be prepared for these."[64]

Not even the blustery militia minister was prepared for the kind of casualties the Canadian contingent had incurred to date.

"We Can Only Hang On"

In 1915 the Allied high commands remained lamentably out of touch with reality, fighting a twentieth-century war with nineteenth-century methods. Comfortably ensconced in their châteaux far to the rear, often beyond the sound of the guns, senior British and French generals clutched battle reports that were usually erroneous or out of date and struck attitudes in front of maps, pushing coloured pins representing units that had sometimes ceased to exist, defending positions that had long since been captured. They were experiencing a problem that would plague them throughout the Great War: they commanded huge forces without the communications needed to properly *control* them. Not until later, much later, when the generals realized that this was really "a platoon commanders' war," did they get better results by instituting a more flexible command system. But that innovation lay far in the future; in the meantime, the higher commands continued to direct battles that were beyond their scope to co-ordinate.

All day Saturday, 24 April, from GHQ at Saint-Omer, Field-Marshal French badgered the Second Army's General Smith-Dorrien to take decisive steps to stabilize the situation in the salient. "Every effort must be made at once to restore and hold the line about St. Julien," GHQ insisted, "or situation of the 28th Division will be jeopardised."[1] French believed that the Germans "are now numerically inferior to us as far as we can judge. In fact, there seems little doubt about it";[2] although the British were slowly but surely bringing to bear more battalions, this was a dangerous delusion.

During the afternoon of the twenty-fourth, Sir John agreed to co-operate with yet another proposed counter-attack by the French. The British commander-in-chief was sportingly living up to his agreement with the French commander, General Foch, to assist any and all operations designed to recapture lost ground, but he seemed oblivious to the fact that Foch had previously promised a number of attacks that had failed to materialize, at considerable cost to the BEF.

This time, Foch was planning a grandiose effort for early Sunday morning, "a vigorous offensive against the front Steenstraat, Pilckem, Langemarck and east of these places."[3] It would be carried out, he told Sir John, by two fresh divisions – one of which had been organized only ten days before. Foch's optimism can only be considered remarkable: with two new divisions, plus the two tired ones at the scene, supported by a few batteries of French, British, and Canadian field guns, he intended to take on four victorious German divisions, backed by an impressive array of artillery and strongly entrenched on a three-mile front, and drive them back three miles to the original French trench line.[4] That French agreed to co-operate seems just as remarkable; but at this stage of the war the British considered themselves junior partners of the French, who were, after all, the "home team," and they also deferred to a mistaken and exaggerated belief in French military prowess. That this prowess was mythical was being revealed in cold, stark terms on the battlefields about Ypres.

Not everyone at GHQ held such blind faith in the French. The chief of the General Staff, Lt.-Gen. Sir William Robertson, was an admitted francophobe. "Evidently," the feisty Robertson had told Smith-Dorrien early on Saturday, "not much reliance can be placed on the two French divisions on your left."[5] Their performance during the day confirmed Robertson's scepticism: they twice tried to recapture Lizerne, without success. In the afternoon, four battalions of Zouaves crossed the canal; their attack petered out quickly, and they merely extended the British line from Turco Farm.

In spite of the French troubles, to co-operate with their plans the British set about organizing a major counter-attack. Smith-Dorrien relayed French's wishes to General Plumer at V Corps headquarters, and Plumer in turn instructed General Alderson at Canadian Division headquarters to make "the strongest possible counter attack with the object of retaking St. Julien and driving the enemy in that neighbourhood as far north as possible so as to . . . re-establish our trench lines as far northward as possible."[6]

Dispatched at six-thirty on Saturday evening, the orders to counter-attack disrupted Alderson's own plans. His intention was to send the newly arrived 10th Brigade to relieve Geddes's Detachment and to replace his battered Third Brigade with the York and Durham Brigade. However, Plumer's instructions specified that many of these units were to take part in the counter-attack towards Saint-Julien. At eight o'clock that night, Alderson issued his final order: the attack, under the command of the 10th Brigade's Brig.-Gen. Charles Hull, would take place at 3:30 A.M. on Sunday, 25 April. General Hull would have at his disposal fifteen Canadian and British battalions.

Like each one preceding it, this counter-attack was poorly conceived, hastily prepared, and bravely executed – this last characteristic was not, unfortunately, sufficient to compensate for the first two. Right from the start problems were evident, with disturbing hints that General Hull, a forty-nine-year-old British professional whose wife was from Quebec, was not the best choice to command the operation. After receiving his orders from Alderson, Hull summoned the fifteen battalion commanders to a nine o'clock conference at his headquarters northwest of Ypres. Only one showed up; the rest either failed to get word of the meeting, were too far away to get there on short notice, or could not find Hull's headquarters, which he had moved without telling anyone. As a result, just before midnight Hull decided to delay the attack by an hour.

The operation was falling apart before it could get started. Instead of fifteen battalions, Hull ended up with just the five in his own brigade. Of the other ten, three were not immediately available, three were removed from his command at the last minute, two were already committed elsewhere, and two were too weak to take part. As if that were not enough, Hull had trouble getting his brigade forward, and shortly after three o'clock on Sunday morning he delayed the attack by another hour.

The operation was now radically different from what was originally planned. Far smaller than first proposed, it would be taking place in daylight instead of under cover of darkness. Moreover, the repeated postponements and poor communications combined to deliver another blow. At three-thirty, Canadian and British batteries, unaware of the delay, opened fire according to their most recent instructions. The bombardment not only eliminated the possibility of surprise but it announced to the Germans that Saint-Julien was unoccupied, and within the hour enemy patrols were taking possession of the shattered village.

To make matters worse, it was also a piecemeal effort. By five-thirty Hull's battalions were still getting into position; each attacked when it was ready, independent of the others.

The results were tragic. Four of Hull's five battalions – 1st Royal Warwickshire Regiment, 2nd Seaforth Highlanders, 1st Royal Irish Fusiliers, and 2nd Royal Dublin Fusiliers – were regulars, and they deployed in impeccably straight lines before advancing to their doom. They had to cross nearly a mile of flat terrain, with only a thin ground-mist to protect them. Within minutes the British were engulfed in a rising swell of rifle and machine-gun fire. Hull and other observers, watching from Mouse Trap Farm, soon saw the leading waves lying in neat lines. "Why do they stop?" asked an inexperienced officer, peering in bewilderment through his field glasses.

"They are dead," he was told.[7]

One young Canadian who witnessed the attack was appalled. Lieut. Walter Critchley, a Calgarian in the 10th Battalion, later commented, "I have never seen such a slaughter in my life," adding: "They were lined up – I can see it still – in a long line, straight up and the Hun opened up on them with machine-guns. They were just raked down. It was pathetic."[8]

Only one battalion, the 1st Royal Irish Fusiliers, came close to its objective, but it was stopped a couple of hundred yards from Saint-Julien. At 6:15 A.M., Hull attempted to renew the attack by committing two newly arrived battalions of the 149th (Northumberland) Brigade. But they encountered the same storm of fire and did little but swell the casualty lists. By seven Hull had to admit defeat, and he realigned his shattered units in a line roughly linking Fortuin and Mouse Trap Farm. The cost to the 10th Brigade for two hours of fighting: 2419 killed and wounded.[9]

Things might have been even worse had it not been for the yeoman work of the Canadian field artillery. Seven batteries of Canadian guns, informed at almost the last moment of the rescheduled assault, opened fire at five-thirty. "The artillery fire was good," General Hull later wrote, "but there was not enough of it to seriously damage the enemy who were entrenched in a very strong position."[10] In fact, the Canadian shell fire was most effective. The Germans had been assembling behind Kitcheners Wood for their own attack through Fortuin, in a bid to roll up the original Canadian and British trenches to the east. Catching the enemy in the open, the Canadians hit them with shrapnel that caused horrifying losses among the masses of enemy soldiers, inflicting such damage that it was fully ten days before the Germans attempted another attack from this location.[11]

The ill-fated assault by the 10th Brigade had one other, and no less important, result. The scattered survivors of the attack had all but closed the vulnerable gap to the rear of the Second Brigade, although at heartbreaking cost. But the Canadian brigade still faced a great struggle on this sunny Sunday in Flanders.

General Currie had had an eventful night. He had gone up to the front lines after dark and late that night had filed a situation report with divisional headquarters:

5th Battalion hold original trenches, Section I, 8th Battalion Section II. 2 battalions 28th Div. entrenched [east of Fortuin]. Have collected all I can find of the 7th Battalion and sent them to report to Col. Lipsett, OC 8th Battn. Balance of the 10th Battn. that can be located are in GHQ line.[12]

Returning to Wieltje around midnight, Currie attended the conference with Colonel Gordon-Hall, the staff officer sent by Canadian Division headquarters to determine the exact situation and to co-ordinate Canadian efforts with the planned counter-attack by the 10th Brigade. Currie sat in on the meeting with his brigade-major, Colonel Kemmis-Betty, the First Brigade's General Mercer, the Third's brigade-major, Colonel Hughes, and General Bush of the York and Durham Brigade. (General Turner was at this time en route to Château des Trois Tours for his unsatisfactory interview with General Alderson.) Familiarizing himself with the dispositions of these units, Gordon-Hall issued orders in Alderson's name. Bush was to secure Fortuin, while Currie extended his line west from Boetleer Farm; Mercer was to move two battalions, the 1st and 4th, onto Currie's left, and Turner was to make good the GHQ line.

Currie should have been exhausted by now. He had not slept since the gas attack on Thursday and, like Turner, should have been showing the strain. But he was a man of enormous energy and was able to revive himself with brief catnaps – a habit he was to pursue all through the war, never sleeping while his troops were in action.[13] Gordon-Hall recalled that Currie "raised no difficulties" after receiving his directions; he "walked out into the night" to carry them out.[14]

Nearby were remnants of two of his battalions, the 7th (British Columbia) and 10th (Calgary-Winnipeg). Both units had been decimated in the heavy fighting to date. The 10th had taken part in the costly counter-attack on Kitcheners Wood the very first night of the battle, and then had assisted in Saturday's dogged defence of Locality C on Gravenstafel Ridge; the 7th had come perilously close to complete destruction near Keerselaere. Both had lost their original colonels, Hart-McHarg of the 7th and Boyle of the 10th fatally wounded. The 7th's second-in-command, Maj. Odlum – still grieving over his brother's death the day before – remained in charge of that battalion, but the 10th had also lost its second-in-command, Major MacLaren, and the lawyer-turned-adjutant, Major Ormond, who had been wounded while leading the 10th back to the GHQ line for its first hot meal in four days. The 10th was now commanded by Capt. Geoff Arthur, a former secretary to the board of the Calgary General Hospital. The two battalions between them mustered a mere three hundred men, so Currie amalgamated them into a composite unit under Maj. Victor Odlum.

The big brigadier personally led the 7th/10th eastward towards the front lines. Around four in the morning, he deployed these tired, dishevelled troops on the western slope of Gravenstafel Ridge. The left flank of the composite unit was on the little stream called the Haanebeek, its right in touch with the defenders of Boetleer Farm. Dawn was already breaking as Currie positioned the men, and heavy small-arms fire greeted them. Currie ignored the enemy bullets, to the amazement of Pte. Sid Cox and others. "We thought he was crazy, standing up there with his red hat on," Cox recalled, "while we were taking all the cover we could till we got dug in."[15]

Currie then walked up to the Boetleer Farm, which served as Colonel Lipsett's headquarters. The place was "a shambles," according to Currie,[16] but he was pleased with Lipsett's defensive arrangements. Three of his 8th (90th Winnipeg Rifles) Battalion's companies and two of the 8th Durham Light Infantry had been posted in reserve behind the farm. The other company of the 8th – reinforced by the party of the 7th Battalion stragglers Currie had rounded up at Potijze the day before – and two companies of the Durhams now occupied the original trenches, which formed the apex of the Canadian Division's front line. Boetleer Farm was defended by a mixed force of British troops: Suffolks, Monmouthshires, Cheshires, and Northumberland Fusiliers.

Satisfied, Currie left soon after dawn for Gravenstafel, the headquarters of the 5th (Western Cavalry) Battalion's Colonel Tuxford. On the way, Currie found out just how exposed his brigade was when he came under machine-gun fire that forced him to dive for cover. Thinking he'd been fired on by Canadians, he angrily dusted himself off and stormed into the village smithy, which housed Tuxford's headquarters. "Tuxford," he fumed, "who the hell was that shooting at me?"[17] The rancher from Moose Jaw had considerable difficulty convincing Currie that the culprits were actually Germans who were occupying a house behind the Canadian front line. Afterwards, at breakfast, Currie recovered a spent bullet from his riding breeches, a souvenir of his brush with death.

The big brigadier spent the rest of the day at Gravenstafel, establishing his new report centre at Tuxford's headquarters. It was not the best place to be. The telephone line to his main headquarters was soon severed, and Currie later complained "that communication by runner was very slow and uncertain. On more than one occasion that day messages sent from either end were not received at the other." The little news he did get was, he said, "very alarming," notably the failure of the 10th Brigade's counter-attack, which he did not learn about until after one o'clock in the afternoon.[18]

The situation deteriorated steadily on Sunday morning. Currie described the men as "so tired." "The rifle, machine gun fire and shell fire was terrific," he related, "while no artillery support could be got," because the Canadian field guns were now out of range of the front lines. There was no sign of the First Brigade. Currie had left a staff officer, the luckless Lieut. Murray Greene, whose service recently had involved much standing and waiting, to guide General Mercer's men onto the left of the Second Brigade. But Lieutenant Greene's wait, in accordance with tradition, was a waste of time; he was wounded, and the 1st (Western Ontario) and 4th (Central Ontario) battalions, held west of Fortuin, never appeared. The York and Durham Brigade did reach Fortuin, but Currie, recalling with bitterness his inability to get help from that source on Saturday, was unimpressed: "This could not have been a hard task as the Germans had never been in it."[19]

Things were no better in the GHQ line, where the battered remnants of General Turner's Third Brigade spent this long spring day. The GHQ line was not very impressive, and Turner, who was obsessed with defending it, must have realized how weak it really was, because his headquarters were right in it. His staff captain, Paul Villiers, the former Victoria militiaman who had spent much of the previous day dodging both explosive and verbal blasts (the former courtesy of the Germans, the latter from his generals), described it as "a hastily constructed ditch making use of what hedges there were."[20] The GHQ line, running roughly north–south, protected both Potijze, a mile east of Ypres, and Wieltje, passed through Mouse Trap Farm, and ended on Mauser Ridge, which was in German hands, enabling the enemy to enfilade the flimsy defences. Casualties mounted steadily among Turner's Highlanders.

There was scarcely a square inch of the salient that was free of enemy fire. Even as far to the rear as Potijze, Lieut. E.F. Lynn, the Canadian engineer who had watched the confrontation between Generals Currie and Snow the day before, was amazed at the intensity of the shelling and small-arms fire sweeping the area:

> Gun fire was not concentrated on any one area continuously. It would be heavy for a time at one point and then would shift, apparently being directed by observation planes or balloons against advancing troops. The gun fire came from several directions and at all angles. Heavy machine gun and rifle fire to the North shifting about a good deal as if being directed against advancing troops were audible throughout the day.
>
> Again there would be a lull in the intensity of the fire and in

recording it I have this note in my diary – "I wonder if this lull means ground gained or lost." It was easy to tell our rapid rifle fire from that of the Bosche and our machine gun fire from theirs as those of the enemy had a different rattle and were or appeared to be more numerous.[21]

The enemy applied steadily increasing pressure on the Canadian and British defenders at the apex. At nine that morning, a furious bombardment broke out along the sector held by the British 28th Division, on the immediate right of the Canadian Division. For two hours shrapnel, high-explosive, and poison-gas shells rained down on the British troops manning a quarter-mile front. Then the enemy infantry poured across no man's land – only seventy yards wide here – and broke into the British trenches. Their success was fleeting; counter-attacks by the 84th and 85th brigades drove the Germans from all but a sixty-yard stretch of the front line.

Elsewhere, the Germans relied primarily on a sustained artillery barrage. They did not hesitate, however, to use deceit, as the 7th/10th Battalion's Major Odlum reported. Shortly after the composite battalion began digging in west of Boetleer Farm, Odlum's troops fired on two figures who ran from a ruined house in front of them. Someone called out that they were British soldiers, and when two Canadians went out to have a look, they were shot. More figures appeared, and a furious fusilade ensued, according to Odlum's account:

> Although the distance between the two lines was only about 200 yards, the morning was so misty that it was impossible to tell with certainty whether those in front of us were Germans or our own troops. I ordered firing to cease.
>
> One man (name unknown – a man belonging to the 2nd Canadian Battalion and picked with the stragglers), who could speak German, volunteered to go forward and find out who they were. He held up his hands and advanced, shouting out in German. When he had gone about fifty yards he was shot down.
>
> It was then quite evident that those in front were the enemy. They soon advanced in considerable numbers, but were held and driven to ground by rifle fire. Both lines then proceeded to dig in.[22]

For the rest of the morning the 7th/10th Battalion, which seemed to attract trouble wherever its troops went, was "subjected to very heavy shell fire," wrote Odlum, "which came from two opposite directions – from the neighbourhood of Passchendaele and from St. Julien."[23]

The shelling on the 8th (90th Winnipeg Rifles) Battalion's front was just as severe. "I am getting round shouldered from ducking," Cpl. William Thornton of the Little Black Devils complained in a letter home to Winnipeg.[24] "I should not call this war – it is slaughter," remarked Pte. Samuel Archer, who was wounded in the early afternoon, by a bullet in the arm and by shrapnel in the thigh. "I crawled half a mile to get my wounds dressed. . . . The shells were bursting all around me, and bullets coming in all directions over my head, while the dead were lying everywhere. No matter where you went you could see nothing but dead bodies."[25]

Incredibly, the shelling intensified during the afternoon, until it was almost impossible to move in the Second Brigade's battle zone without being hit by flying shell-splinters or bullets. The 7th/10th Battalion's Major Odlum begged for help at noon, asking General Currie to organize a counter-stroke to relieve the pressure on his front. Currie, still, had nothing to offer. "We must hang on," he replied helplessly, "at least to night fall." Odlum agreed to do his best. "We will hang on till night," he assured Currie. The men, who had been in action since the night attack on Kitcheners Wood, were, he reported "almost all in but are holding on well."[26]

But Currie knew that they could not hold on without help. He was told by General Alderson "that strong reinforcements are coming up to our assistance,"[27] and he hoped that the divisional commander knew what he was talking about. "We can only hang on," he told Alderson. "Can we get any artillery support and . . . where are 1st Brigade units? See nothing of them on our left."[28]

Help, alas, was not coming. As happened so often in this battle, Alderson was receiving incomplete and inaccurate reports, which slowed and sometimes paralyzed the decision-making process at Canadian Division headquarters, or produced poor decisions. In the early afternoon Alderson was handed information from the 5th and 28th divisions. The 5th indicated that Fortuin had apparently been lost,[29] while the 28th reported the appearance of German troops "in long columns" behind Gravenstafel Ridge.[30] Both reports were wrong; behind the ridge were not German but British soldiers, retiring to safer positions away from the heavy artillery fire. But Alderson understandably concluded that the ridge – and with it Currie's brigade – had been lost. He rushed a request to the fiery General Snow to move the 151st (Durham Light Infantry) Brigade up, not to the ridge, where Currie's brigade desperately needed help, but to the Fortuin–Passchendaele road, half a mile behind the ridge, to block the supposed enemy advance.

Several hours would pass before Currie realized that his brigade, stubbornly clinging to its exposed position, was being abandoned.

The storm broke in the middle of the afternoon. Around three o'clock, German infantry, spearheaded by the élite Stürmbrigade Schmieden – treated to beer at the Kaiser's personal expense before the battle – swarmed to the attack, striking the inverted-V-shaped Canadian line from two directions, with the main blow coming from the vicinity of Locality c.

On the left of the Second Brigade, the weary men from B.C. and the prairies who made up the composite 7th/10th Battalion were, in General Currie's words, "simply blown out of their position."[31] A sergeant, Raymond MacIlree of Victoria, described the grim battle in a letter to his parents:

> We were prepared to hold on forever when the order came to retire, as our flanks were turned. I took half my Platoon out along a hedge to cover the retreat of the Company, so I never saw them again.
>
> The Germans were coming in thousands, so we worked our way down the trenches to the left. In this way, we kept up a running battle . . . leaving one trench, and running across the open to another one in the rear. Our Artillery was so chivied about that they gave us no help, while we were being mowed down by shrapnel, machine guns, and rifles.
>
> It was sure a merry little hell . . . people kept getting killed, in such messy ways, that it became a nightmare. It is funny how calm you get. A man falls beside you, and you just heave him out of the way, like a sack of flour.
>
> Finally we reached the last trench, which was simply jammed with men from all our Regts.

Things were utterly chaotic, and Sergeant MacIlree contended that "at no time did we know what was happening elsewhere, and even now we have no idea how things are progressing."[32]

Boetleer Farm bore the brunt of the assault. The farm was a grim sight, according to Maj. Harold Mathews of the 8th (90th Winnipeg Rifles) Battalion, whose company had stood firm in the face of yesterday's gas attack. "The cellar was full of wounded and groaning men and any outbuilding that remained standing was being used for the same purpose. The place was getting a most unmerciful shelling and was a regular shambles."[33]

It was a short and bloody fight; by three-thirty the farm had fallen. The British defenders were overcome by the sheer weight of the enemy's numbers, as wave after wave of grey-clad soldiers swept around them. Colonel Lipsett, a shrapnel hole in his hat, narrowly escaped, but most of the wounded had to be left behind. Among them was Pte. Charles Sargent from Winnipeg, who had been injured the previous day when a shell fragment had partially severed his left arm. "Rather than stay there on the flat of my back, not knowing what was to become of me," Private Sargent later wrote, "I, with five others, tried to find my way out . . . and was surrounded by a large German patrol. Escape was out of the question."[34] Sargent's career as a prisoner of war was short-lived; after German surgeons amputated his arm, he was repatriated in October.

Now that Boetleer Farm was in enemy hands, Lipsett's task was to prevent a further advance by the Germans along Gravenstafel Ridge. To do this, he summoned his three small, weary companies, which had spent the day in reserve, resting in a nearby turnip field, to occupy an old trench below the fallen farm. This manoeuvre drew heavy fire. "The enemy must have seen us move up to this position," wrote Major Mathews, one of the company commanders, "for they got the range of us at once with high explosive, one shell dropped right in the trench and blew twelve men out at once, all of them being either killed or wounded."[35]

The breach at Boetleer Farm was patched up in other ways. The tireless Vancouver newsman, Major Odlum, rushed over from the neighbouring 7th/10th Battalion to prevent a rout, when he spotted retreating British and Canadian soldiers "pouring" down from the ridge. "With Major W.A. Munro of the 8th Battalion, I tried to stem the tide," Odlum related. "We succeeded in getting them turned back and returned to trenches near the crest."[36]

This improvised line had no sooner been put in place than the Manitobans in the 8th Battalion faced a new crisis: a shortage of small-arms ammunition. By this time few Canadian soldiers were having problems with their Ross rifles, for most of them had thrown the things away in favour of Lee-Enfields taken from British casualties. But even the reliable Lee-Enfield was useless without bullets, and for a while it appeared as though the feeble Canadian line would be swept away. The crisis was averted when the 5th Battalion on the right rushed 55,000 rounds to the front, which arrived in the nick of time.

For his report centre at Gravenstafel, Currie was sending out urgent pleas for help. "8th Battalion heavily attacked, hurry reinforcements. Disposition of troops is the same, will hang on. . . . Troops very tired."[37] That message was sent at 3:22 P.M., but it would be hours before Canadian Division headquarters received it – and by then it was far too late.

The original trenches were doomed. The warning signs of trouble came with unconfirmed reports that some members of the 8th Durham Light Infantry, which was in action for the first time, had broken and fled during the prolonged bombardment. The battalion commander, Colonel Turnbull, tried to reinforce the front line with one of his reserve companies, but the move ended disastrously. Shortly after four o'clock Turnbull reported to Currie that his trench on the extreme left "had all men killed or wounded. A reinforcing company was driven out by shell fire which is reported to have destroyed trench. . . . I have a small reserve of 100 men. Enemy do not appear to be pressing attack except by artillery fire."[38]

The end came soon after. The three front-line company commanders, two from the Durhams and Capt. George Northwood of 4 Company of the gallant 8th Battalion, which had held out against the previous day's gas attack had already agreed that, with the enemy on three sides, they would have to withdraw. They dispatched a message requesting permission to do so, and then, without waiting for an answer, began evacuating the wounded. This was a forlorn effort, as most of these men were shot trying to cross the open slope of the ridge to the rear of the trenches. Captain Northwood remained with the rearguard to cover the withdrawal, but few members of his company managed to get away; 4 Company's casualties included every officer and 139 other ranks, killed, wounded, or taken prisoner. Most of the Durhams were lost, too. Any who did escape owed their deliverance to the 8th Battalion machine-gunner, Winnipeg's Sgt. William Alldritt, who died at his post in the heart of the British lines. "The last that was seen of him," wrote Sgt.-Maj. G.W. Gorman, "was an heroic figure . . . automatically pumping away, on duty to the last."[39]

Currie was fast running out of options. His brigade was being crushed, piece by piece, and to save what was left of it, he made what seemed to be the only decision possible: to pull out. Shortly after five o'clock he had received a three-hour-old message from divisional headquarters suggesting that the Durham Light Infantry Brigade was digging in five hundred to one thousand yards to the rear of Currie's position. Earlier he had learned of the enemy's supposed presence "in long columns" to the west – a report that, he said, "naturally did not decrease my uneasiness." With the apex of his line, including Boetleer Farm, lost, Currie had a long list of factors to consider: the failure of the First Brigade to move onto his left flank, the repulse of the 10th Brigade's counter-attack, the lack of reinforcements and artillery support, and the relentless enemy pressure. "I concluded," he later wrote, "our position had been judged hopeless and ordered units to retire at dusk."[40]

Currie received strong support for his decision. "Within a few minutes of the issuance of the Order" – at five-fifteen – "I saw both Lipsett and Odlum in the trench at the western edge of Gravenstafel village, and both

Lt.-Col. Russell Boyle at 34 was a decorated veteran of the South African War and as commander of the 10th Battalion he threw off his coat and challenged malcontents to fight him. Many miles from Crossfield, Alberta, the big rancher was fatally wounded in the gallant and costly night assault on Kitcheners Wood. (GLENBOW ARCHIVES, CALGARY/NA-2362-38)

The town of Ypres, once the heart of the flourishing Flanders cloth industry,
was represented by the massive Gothic Cloth Hall overlooking the main square.
In 1914 Ypres was the base of the Canadians' salient.
(ARCHIVES OF ONTARIO/ACC. 11595)

Kitcheners Wood, the objective of the attack of the 10th and 16th Canadian
infantry battalions. Lt.-Col. Boyle's men took Kitcheners Wood, but with
staggering losses.
(NATIONAL ARCHIVES OF CANADA/PA-4564)

The village of Saint-Julien, made a wasteland by the dramatic house-to-house fighting between the Canadians and the Germans.
(GLENBOW ARCHIVES, CALGARY/NA-2880-1)

A panoramic view from Gravenstafel Ridge of the battleground over which the Germans advanced, after releasing poison gas April 24 and 25, 1915.
(NATIONAL ARCHIVES OF CANADA/PA-4499)

Lt.-Col. Louis Lipsett, a 40-year-old Irishman and commander of the 8th Battalion, impressed Arthur Currie as "eminently satisfactory in every particular." His men, consisting mostly of the 90th Winnipeg Rifles – "the Little Black Devils" – were the only unit to stand fast in the face of the gas attack. Tragically, Lipsett was killed in action less than a month before the end of the war. (NATIONAL ARCHIVES OF CANADA/ PA-7442)

A Vancouver lawyer and veteran of the South African War, Lt.-Col. William Hart-McHarg was a crack shot, having represented Canada in several international shooting competitions. But as commanding officer of the 7th Battalion of British Columbians he was killed in this first battle. (NATIONAL ARCHIVES OF CANADA/ C-51983)

The 40-year-old Lt.-Col. A.P. Birchall was a British-born regular. With walking stick in hand, he led the 4th Battalion of Ontario boys in the disastrous charge on Mauser Ridge, and, like most of them, died there. (NATIONAL ARCHIVES OF CANADA/ PA-28547)

At nineteen, Wally (later Sergeant) Bennett gave up his accounting studies in Calgary to join up with his friends: "We just went into it . . . thinking the war might be over before we got there." Bennett survived Ypres to pose as the machine gunner in Richard Jack's painting (on front cover), and was still hale and hearty when this book went to press. (GLENBOW ARCHIVES, CALGARY/ NA-4732-I)

The day I was presented to His Majesty the King. December 6, 1915."

The way I slept in the forests of Germany."

As the only Canadian officer to escape from captivity in Germany during the Great War, Maj. Peter Anderson was rewarded with an audience with King George and a promotion to lieutenant-colonel. Once free, he documented his adventures with studio photos – sometimes with unintended hilarious effect.

(PROVINCIAL ARCHIVES OF ALBERTA: PETER ANDERSON COLLECTION/ACC. 72.272/25a AND 20a)

Four Canadians were awarded the Victoria Cross for valour during the Second Battle of Ypres.

With his crew out of action, L/Cpl. Fred Fisher fired his machine gun again and again at the enemy swarming towards Saint-Julien. Before he was killed he managed to drive the Germans back, saving the vulnerable Canadian 18-pounders.
(NATIONAL ARCHIVES OF CANADA/ PA-7079)

At Flanders while the bullets flew around him, Company Sgt.-Maj. F.W. Hall from the 8th Battalion deliberately scrambled into the open, risking his own life to rescue other men.
(NATIONAL ARCHIVES OF CANADA/ PA-6767)

Lt. E.D. Bellew, a mild-mannered engineer from Vancouver, managed to buy valuable time for the rest of his 7th Battalion by fending off the approaching enemy, first with his machine gun and then with his rifle at bayonet-point, before he was overpowered and captured.
(NATIONAL ARCHIVES OF CANADA/ C-34940)

The 14th Battalion's medical officer, 34-year-old Capt. F.A.C. Scrimger, stood his ground amid exploding rounds at Mouse Trap Farm, directing the removal of the wounded. At one point, using himself as a shield, he dragged an injured officer through heavy shelling to safety.
(NATIONAL ARCHIVES OF CANADA/ PA-6771)

Left: A depiction of the Canadian Golgotha, the rumoured crucifixion of a Toronto sergeant on a barn door near Ypres by the Germans. The story came to be regarded as fact, but a postwar investigation proved it to be unfounded.
(ARCHIVES OF ONTARIO/ACC. 11595)

Below: The memorial to John McCrae, beside the cemetery where the Canadian major, looking out over this battlefield, composed his famous poem, "In Flanders Fields."
(DANIEL G. DANCOCKS)

After seventeen exhausting days of tending to the wounded at Ypres, John McCrae spent twenty minutes of precious rest time scribbling one of the most memorable war poems ever written.
(NATIONAL ARCHIVES OF CANADA/ C-19919)
(NATIONAL ARCHIVES OF CANADA/ C-128809)

In Flanders Fields
—

In Flanders fields the poppies blow
Between the crosses, row on row,
That mark our place; and in the sky
The larks, still bravely singing, fly
Scarce heard amid the guns below.

We are the Dead. Short days ago
We lived, felt dawn, saw sunset glow,
Loved, and were loved, and now we lie
    In Flanders fields.

Take up our quarrel with the foe:
To you from failing hands we throw
The torch; be yours to hold it high.
If ye break faith with us who die
We shall not sleep, though poppies grow
    In Flanders fields

John McCrae

"Punch"
Dec 8 1915

agreed with it."[41] While the weary Odlum sent an orderly to deliver the withdrawal instructions to his composite battalion, Lipsett took it in person, "exposing himself to great danger," as Odlum noted with admiration.[42] The 5th Battalion's Colonel Tuxford sent two officers to carry the word to his Saskatchewan boys in their original trenches – the last still in Canadian possession; Maj. Hugh Dyer and Capt. Edward Hilliam were both wounded en route, "Hilliam through the lung, Dyer within an inch of the heart," as Tuxford wrote. "Dyer, however, managed to struggle through to within 10 yards of the trenches, where he was hauled in by the men and the message was delivered."[43]

Currie intended to withdraw to "the switch line east and north of the Bombarded Cross Roads," a position supposedly being prepared by the Durham Light Infantry Brigade.[44] In fact, this new line was nonexistent, because General Snow, fearing another German attack on the 28th Division, had ignored General Alderson's request to move this brigade behind Gravenstafel Ridge.

Currie had no way of knowing this, but what he did know gave him much to worry about. Executing a withdrawal in conditions of close combat can be both difficult and dangerous, as the Third Brigade had learned the previous day. It proved to be particularly hard to extricate the 5th Battalion's two companies in the front lines. Colonels Tuxford and Lipsett had earlier agreed, "in the event of retirement, that we should do so in succession of Companies from the left," to provide mutual support. So Tuxford was shocked to see the 8th Battalion fall back "almost as a whole" around six-thirty. It was still quite light, and Tuxford knew that it would be suicidal to try to get his men out of their trenches unaided. Ignoring the bullets and shells sweeping the area, the old trail boss hurried to the rear and rallied a mixed-bag of stragglers, then led them back up the ridge to provide covering fire for his front-line troops. Tuxford had high praise for these men from B.C. and the prairies:

I now want to lay particular stress upon the magnificent morale of these men, some 5th, some 7th, some 8th and some 10th. They had retired to comparative safety, and, upon being ordered, immediately advanced up this half-mile slope, under heavy machine-gun fire at 400 yards, and then under most intense artillery fire, shrapnel [sic] and HE [high explosive], and as soon as I had put them in the trenches on top of the hill and had personally told all NCO's that we were going to hold the ridge till our two companies had retired and until they had arrived, when we would then retire altogether, these men immediately snapped their bayonets in and said, "Just tell us what to do, Sir, and we will do it," as cheerful as could be.[45]

By seven o'clock Tuxford's front-line companies could wait no longer to make their run to safety. With darkness near at hand, the Germans were threatening to cut them off; to wait would be disastrous. The shell fire had reached a new crescendo, until, according to Tuxford, "the noise was so intense that you had to shout to be heard." Tuxford watched with pride as his men calmly and coolly evacuated their trenches and started up the gentle slope of Gravenstafel Ridge. "I want to say here," the colonel later wrote, "that during this retirement, with the Germans yelling behind them, drums beating, and calling out – 'We have got you Canadians now' – I never saw a man quicken his step." Within minutes the 5th's two companies had reached the crest, and Tuxford deployed them here, "one man per yard." Hot on their heels were the Germans, countless ghostly shadows topping the crest in the rapidly descending darkness. "I expected a charge," recounted Tuxford, "and ordered rapid fire."[46]

The results were decisive. "We let go," recalled an 8th (90th Winnipeg rifles) Battalion survivor, Sgt. Aubrey Fisher, "and they must have thought the whole Canadian army was at the back of it. It was an absolute surprise to them. But we held them."[47] One sharpshooter, a 5th (Western Cavalry) Battalion sergeant named George Bowie, accounted for fourteen Germans in the ensuing slaughter.[48]

Regrettably, both battalions had had to abandon some of their wounded, so numerous that it was impossible to bring them all back under the circumstances. Among those of the 8th Battalion left behind were a nineteen-year-old sergeant, Thomas Ronaldson, and a twenty-one-year-old private, James Taylor. Both were from Fort Frances, Ontario, where they were employed by the Canadian Bank of Commerce. They were joined by the 5th Battalion's Joseph Leach, an eighteen-year-old private from Outlook, Saskatchewan, who was hit in the leg and unable to walk. Private Leach would eventually be interned in Switzerland, due to ill-health,* so he was luckier than one of his sergeants, twenty-seven-year-old James Stewart of Moose Jaw. Severely wounded, Sergeant Stewart died a month later in a German field hospital in Roulers, Belgium, where he was buried.

Finally, under cover of darkness, the Canadians completed their withdrawal. But Colonels Lipsett and Tuxford were in for some surprises once they led their exhausted men to the Haanebeek. To begin with, the new

---

*"The life of the prisoners in Germany was beyond all human exaggeration," he later wrote, "and had it not been for the food sent from England, I am afraid very few of the men would have returned; as it was, several hundred men died for no reason other than starvation and cruelty" (*Letters*, II/251).

line supposedly under construction by the British was nowhere to be found. Moreover, they found that their battalions had been the only ones to take part in the withdrawal. On the right, the 3rd Royal Fusiliers – a 28th Division formation – "had no orders to retire," recalled Tuxford, "and refus[ed] to do so."[49] On the left, the collection of British troops below Boetleer Farm – Suffolks, Monmouthshires, and Durhams, under Colonel Turnbull – were also holding their ground. Turnbull had received Currie's orders to withdraw, but rejected them, declaring that he was not under the Canadian's jurisdiction. As a result, the patched-together 7th/10th Battalion also remained in the firing line, a decision made jointly by the 7th's Capt. Stanley Gardner and the 10th's Maj. Percy Guthrie,* in the absence of the acting commander, Major Odlum.

Lipsett and Tuxford, the British regular and the rancher from Moose Jaw, acted quickly. Reassembling their tired and hungry men, the two colonels turned them around, back into the action, hastening back up the ridge, where they occupied their trenches near the crest. "It speaks well for the morale of the troops after the knocking about they had received," commented the 8th Battalion's Major Mathews, "when I say we had very little trouble in getting them back across the fire-swept zone to the trenches on the Ridge."[50] Here, they dug in once more and awaited further developments.

As the Second Brigade so narrowly averted disaster, a major reorganization of the British forces in the salient was belatedly getting under way. For the past three days the Canadian Division had been responsible for a front exceeding five miles, more than twice the average frontage for any division, British, French, or German, on the Western Front. Following the failure of the 10th Brigade's attack on Saint-Julien and Kitcheners Wood, the corps commander, General Plumer, decided to juggle divisional responsibilities and disentangle the confused brigade commands. Effective at 7 P.M. on Sunday, the Canadian Division's sector was reduced to the two miles between Turco Farm and the Fortuin–Saint-Julien road; the area east of the road fell into the jurisdiction of General Bulfin's 28th Division.

The change gave General Alderson a chance to relieve his front-line

---

*Major Guthrie, a prominent politician in his home province of New Brunswick, was the fifth officer to command the 10th Battalion since Colonel Boyle had fallen at the start of the battle. Stationed in England, Guthrie had been at Canadian Division headquarters on routine business when the fighting broke out and, hearing of the 10th's heavy losses, volunteered to join it as a junior officer. He ended up taking command of the Western unit.

troops. The 13th British Brigade took over from Geddes's Detachment, while the 10th filled in for General Turner's Third Brigade along the GHQ line. Although Turner's units had not had to repulse any attacks on Sunday, they had nevertheless had a trying time, being "fearfully shelled all day," according to Colonel Watson of the 2nd Battalion of men from Eastern Ontario.[51] Turner's headquarters at Mouse Trap Farm had been reduced to ashes late in the afternoon by concentrated shell fire, forcing him, Hughes, and the rest of the Third Brigade's staff to flee. In swimming the moat that surrounded the farm, they "lost their hats" and most of their personal belongings,[52] before dripping their way to a "small house" three hundred yards to the south.[53]

Another Victoria Cross arose from that episode. Mouse Trap Farm served not only as a headquarters but also as a dressing station. Worse, it also housed a small-arms ammunition dump. The heat generated by the burning buildings set off thousands of rounds, which discouraged the nearby enemy troops from trying to seize the place, but also sent splinters flying among the wounded being evacuated. Capt. F.A.C. Scrimger, a thirty-four-year-old Montreal surgeon who served as the 14th Battalion's medical officer, stood his ground amid the explosions, directing the removal of the wounded. He personally attended to a staff officer, Capt. Harold McDonald, who "was literally filled with splinters. One in the cheek, one in the eye, one in the shoulder, the right lung and in the neck."[54] Captain Scrimger half-dragged and half-carried Captain McDonald to safety through heavy shelling. At one point, six shells landed within a few feet of them, and Scrimger used his body to shield the injured officer. McDonald survived, though he lost an arm, and Scrimger was awarded the fourth and final Victoria Cross to be won by Canadians during the Second Battle of Ypres.[55]

During the evening, the First and Third brigades moved to the rear. General Mercer's Ontario battalions of the First Brigade crossed the Canal de l'Yser, where they were posted to guard the bridges, while General Turner's largely kilted Third Brigade concentrated in billets in La Brique, a village just north of Ypres. The troops were fed, then allowed to enjoy a well-earned sleep. Few of these gaunt, exhausted men – bankers and businessmen, clerks and college kids, farm-hands and lawyers, from Montreal and Ottawa and Toronto and scores of smaller centres in between – when they had enlisted in the midst of all the patriotic excitement a few short months ago could have even imagined the horrors of shelling and machine-gunning and sniping and poison gas that they had experienced in the past few days.

It was after nine o'clock that night when General Currie, huffing and puffing, arrived back at his headquarters in Wieltje. "Running the gaunt-let of the machine guns of the Germans" took two hours,[56] but he imme-diately sat down and wrote out a situation report for Canadian Division headquarters. Unaware that his withdrawal had been only partially com-pleted, he incorrectly informed General Alderson that as of 7 P.M. the Germans were in possession of Gravenstafel Ridge (when in fact the stubborn men who had marched back there with Tuxford and Lipsett still held the ridge). He did inform Alderson, correctly, that the remnants at the Second Brigade had been saved.[57] Currie was soon informed that his brigade had been placed under the command of General Bulfin of the 28th Division, "and it is hoped that you will be relieved by the 11th Bde. tonight."[58] Soon afterwards, units of the British brigade began passing through Wieltje, and Currie went out to meet the commander, Brig.-Gen. J. Hasler, and to discuss the relief of his tired troops.

The relief of the Second Brigade was a long, involved affair. The 11th Brigade, five battalions strong, was to deploy between Fortuin and Gra-venstafel, enabling the assortment of British and Canadian troops to the north to withdraw safely. The British brigade was delayed, however, by darkness and by unfamiliarity with the ground it had been instructed to occupy, and it was well after midnight before these battalions were finally in position.

It was a nerve-racking night for the haggard, hungry troops holding the front line. Major Mathews of the 8th Battalion recalled his anxiety as he and his company of Little Black Devils waited in the dark to be relieved:

> The Germans came up under cover of the slope and some woods and buildings in our front to within perhaps 400 or 500 yards of us, blow-ing a trumpet that sounded like a small hunting horn. We quite expected and hoped they would attack and charge our position, but evidently they had no idea of doing anything rash, and soon after we got an order to fall back.
>
> Our situation at this time was extremely precarious, and I for one never expected it would be possible to extricate ourselves. I buried all my maps, note book and papers in the bottom of the trench and ordered the other officers of my company to do the same.[59]

The final withdrawal was conducted between two and three-thirty on Monday morning. "This retirement . . . was not carried out in so orderly a manner as it might have been," wrote Major Mathews, who complained that "many of the men threw away their equipment unnecessarily."[60]

Considering that many of them had gone fifty or sixty hours without food or rest, enduring shell fire – enemy and friendly – from all directions, hand-to-hand combat, and poison gas, the strain on discipline is understandable. "All cohesion had vanished," observed a sympathetic Colonel Tuxford of the 5th Battalion. "It was pitiful to see these men, who had come from the very jaws of hell, staggering along absolutely dazed, gassed, hungry, and parched with thirst."[61]

If it lacked precision and form, the withdrawal went so smoothly and silently that the Germans had no idea that the troops facing them were slipping away. The thick fog enabled some Canadians to escape even when they were virtually surrounded. The 7th Battalion's Sergeant MacIlree could hear the Germans occasionally calling out to the encircled Canadians to give up. "Not caring to be made a prisoner, I decided to make a dash for it," the man from Victoria decided, and two members of his platoon followed. "None of us have any idea how we got out as the enemy were on three sides of us."[62] But somehow MacIlree and his companions reached safety.

In the confusion of the previous day's fighting, Canadian and British soldiers had become separated from their units and sometimes found themselves in the company of strangers. Such was the case of Pte. Sid Cox, a member of what little remained of the 10th (Calgary-Winnipeg) Battalion. Private Cox, who had come through the horrors of the counterattack on Kitcheners Wood and the bloody battle for Locality C, spent the night in an isolated trench with a handful of British troops. For whatever reason, the order to pull back did not reach this group, and their first realization of trouble came when they heard guttural German whispers in the misty darkness all around them. They were cut off! Leading to the rear was a shallow ditch, and for a few minutes Cox's comrades debated in whispers the merits of making a bid for freedom by following it. Cox was horrified when he heard that the consensus favoured giving up. His horror gave way to anger. "You can surrender if you damn well please," he hissed. "I'm going down the ditch!" Cox set off, and all but one of the British joined him. Fortunately, the ditch led them into the 11th Brigade's lines.[63]

It was nearly dawn on Monday, 26 April, when the movement was completed. General Currie was not pleased with the delay in getting his men out, later contending that it was primarily because of "the foggy weather on the morning of the 26th that some were able to get back at all."[64]

Passing through the British position to the rear, the Canadians formed into columns of four and marched towards Wieltje, where rest and hot food awaited them.

The Second Brigade, like its sister formations, was in sad shape. General Currie estimated that by dawn on 26 April, the formation that had consisted of four thousand eager young westerners just a few days earlier was now only "1200-1400 strong."[65] Feeling like hell, and looking it, too, unshaven and grubby, with torn, filthy uniforms, and many without their caps, these citizen-soldiers staggered down the road from Fortuin, past corpses and shell holes and the wreckage of war. Behind them, the sun was rising over the battlefield, and a new day's fighting had begun.

At Wieltje, behind the GHQ line, the troops were dispersed. Like their fellow-countrymen in the First and Third brigades the previous night, many joined long line-ups at field kitchens for their first hot rations in days; others, too tired to eat, threw themselves on the ground and slept. "Everyone looked forward to a march to rest billets beyond Ypres [later] in the morning."[66]

It was not to be. Unknown to them, General Currie had volunteered to lead his brigade back into battle.

Currie had set out for Fortuin that morning with General Hasler, when the British brigadier was handed a message informing him that the Germans had broken through the right of the 11th Brigade's line. According to Currie, "I offered to take the Brigade over to where the break was reported and to assist in restoring it."[67] Hasler agreed, and at eight o'clock, Currie's sleepwalking brigade was on the march once again. Within half an hour it was under heavy shell fire. "The fog had by this time lifted," related the 8th Battalion's Major Mathews, "and the sun shone bright and clear."[68]

The brigade deployed for its final advance across the Haanebeek. The Manitobans in the 8th Battalion moved up on the right of the Albertans in the 10th, with the 5th and 7th battalions from Saskatchewan and B.C. arrayed in reserve. An advance of three-quarters of a mile awaited these bone-weary survivors, and a new form of enemy harassment, as described by Major Mathews:

> As we moved forward across some ploughed fields a German aeroplane came over, and though we at once lay down it must have discovered us, for we were soon treated to a heavy shrapnel fire.
>
> However, we kept moving forward and escaped with very few casualties until we crossed a small stream and reached a line of farm houses.
>
> Pushing on towards the ridge we came under an oblique fire from machine guns at our left front, but soon the rising ground protected us.
>
> We found the ridge exposed to a cross as well as frontal fire of shrapnel and high explosive, and began to dig in behind the crest.

The major's battle ended a little while later. Crawling forward to the crest to reconnoitre, he was wounded in the leg by shrapnel. Evacuated that day, he was soon on his way to England, via Ypres, Vlamertinghe, Bailleul, Boulogne, and Dover.[69] He survived to end the war as a staff officer.

The Second Brigade's return to the battle zone was a waste of time. The reported break in the 11th Brigade's line was false, although a German attack had been narrowly repulsed early in the morning. Now in its new position immediately south of Fortuin, the Second was woefully exposed, and it was forced to endure what Currie called "extremely heavy shell fire, the heaviest yet experienced"[70] – which was saying something. During the two days that they remained there, the shelling took its toll of men and officers; among the casualties were two of Currie's senior staff officers, Colonel Kemmis-Betty and Major Mersereau.

The brigade remained here until Tuesday evening, 27 April. At five o'clock that afternoon, Currie received new orders: "Your Brigade will proceed after dark to Potijze and report to GOC 27th Division [General Snow] on arrival." Currie could hardly have looked forward to renewing his association with the astoundingly rude general and his staff, and he was not surprised by subsequent events. A staff officer sent to Snow's headquarters, Currie sourly noted, "was told they knew nothing of our movement and did not want to be bothered with us." At eleven that night, new orders arrived from Canadian Division headquarters: the brigade was to cross the Canal de l'Yser and bivouac near Vlamertinghe.[71]

Currie's western Canadian brigade deserved the rest. It had been the first to go into the salient, thirteen days earlier, when it had relieved French troops in the front lines northeast of Ypres. Now it was the last to leave, joining the other two brigades billeted across the canal. The troops were glad to make this move. "It was certainly cheerful news to us, and we were badly in need of a rest," recalled the young Calgary accountant, Pte. Wally Bennett, the 10th Battalion machine-gunner who had participated in the epic defence of Doxsee's House near Kitcheners Wood. They were "a tough looking lot" by now, recalled Private Bennett. "As for myself, I hardly knew my own face: I hadn't seen a razor for about seven or eight days, and my clothes were ragged and torn and still caked with mud!"[72]

No one was wearier than the brigadier himself. Currie, bringing up the rear, later told a friend "that his senses were so dulled that it hardly seemed worth while to pull himself out of direct range" of the enemy's guns.[73]

There was little real rest ahead, however, for any of the Canadians. Units of all three brigades were repeatedly put on alert in case they were needed again in the embattled salient. Fortunately, they were spared further fighting at this time, though they were kept busy in other ways. Working parties were constantly required to carry supplies forward and to assist in entrenching the battered British front line. One notable success was attained by troops of the First Brigade on the night of 28/29 April, when men from all four Ontario battalions dug a 1200-yard extension of the GHQ line, facing the Germans on Mauser Ridge. The trench was completed without casualties, and minimized the grim effects of the enemy's enfilade fire on the GHQ line.[74] Less fortunate was the Second Brigade, which lost ninety-one men to shell fire when the 5th (Western Cavalry) and 10th (Calgary-Winnipeg) battalions were assigned to guard the canal crossing until 5 May.[75]

One member of the 10th who very nearly became a casualty was Pte. Victor Lewis. The former CPR night watchman slipped out one night to steal a chicken from a nearby farm. Someone, possibly the farmer, took a pot shot at him, "and the bullet went through my hat, but it never touched me. I was lucky," he admitted, and added triumphantly, "I got the chicken anyway."[76]

Finally, on 4 May and continuing through the sixth, the three Canadian infantry brigades were relieved and marched back to billets in Bailleul, sixteen miles west of Ypres. It was "a very, very killing march," complained Walter Critchley, a lieutenant from Calgary serving in the 10th Battalion. "It was a forced march, which, really, I think, under the circumstances was unnecessary. They could have taken it a little easier."[77] Another Calgarian in the same outfit, Pte. Wally Bennett, agreed. "I'll never forget it," he recalled in later years. "Jesus, we were all in – no food, no water."*[78]

Other units endured the same kind of misery. A diarist with the 14th (Royal Montreal Regiment) Battalion wrote:

> It was a pretty sorry looking bunch that crept into Bailleul. We were all footsore and weary, but we found that our billets were two miles out of town. We managed to crawl that distance and reached our destination on the morning of May 5th. The march was the worst I ever experienced.[79]

The 16th (Canadian Scottish) Battalion was no happier on arrival in Bailleul. "Our guides were very bad and the billeting arrangements no

---

*Wally Bennett went on to achieve immortality in a small way. Wounded twice within the next year, Bennett, then a sergeant, was assigned to Lord Beaverbrook's Canadian War Records Office in London. There, in 1917, he posed as the machine-gunner in Richard Jack's famous painting, "The Second Battle of Ypres." Now in his early nineties, Bennett is believed to be the only surviving member of the 10th Battalion.

better," fumed one kilted subaltern. "Many men dropped during the march and slept by the wayside, and small groups were coming in all the next day." He added: "The strain on every person was almost at breaking point, for we got no rest day or night from shell fire."[80]

Grumbling aside, the infantrymen could consider themselves lucky to leave the salient when they did. The Canadian Division was relieved of front-line responsibilities on 4 May, when at 10 A.M. General Alderson handed over the sector to Maj.-Gen. H.F.M. Wilson and his 4th Division. But Canadian medics and gunners remained in action for several more days, under British jurisdiction.

The Canadian dressing stations throughout the battle faced a seemingly endless stream of injured soldiers: Canadian, British, French, and German. A stretcher-bearer with the 3rd Canadian Field Ambulance recalled the scene at the height of the battle:

> Wounded began to pour in, and when it dropped dark we went out to fetch those that could not walk in. Shells were flying around like rain. We had no time for meals, just snatch a bite when we could. We worked for sixty hours like this without sleep.
>
> Our officers are heroes; they worked like Trojans in the operating room. There was no time to use chloroform, and operations were done without a murmur from the patients.[81]

Another stretcher-bearer in the same unit, Pte. Bert Goose, went five days without sleep. "May came in a beautiful day," he wrote on the first of that month. "Had a grand sleep – what a joy at not hearing the guns."[82]

The Canadian artillery was also severely tested. Not until 9 May were the guns of the 1st Field Artillery Brigade allowed to rejoin the Canadian Division, after having "been constantly under fire night and day" since 23 April. In that period, reported Lt.-Col. Morrison, his brigade "had fired over a thousand rounds per gun."[83] One of his gunners, a veteran of the 4th Field Battery, later commented that the 18-pounders left behind piles of shell cases "as we have never seen in any of our subsequent battles."[84] Another gunner, in the 2nd Field Artillery Brigade, wrote at the height of the fighting to a sweetheart back in peaceful New Brunswick, "It certainly is awful here at times, shells bursting around us all the time and the only thing to do is look for safety which you cannot find. . . . I have up till now come through without a scratch but of course do not know how long I will be spared."[85]

Shockingly few had been spared by the end of the battle. The Canadian Division had suffered enormous losses in a short period: 6036, most of them on Saturday 24 and Sunday 25 April.[86] The infantry had borne the brunt of the casualties, with the three brigades losing surprisingly similar numbers: First, 1839; Second, 1829; Third, 1838.[87] The hardest-hit battalions were the Toronto Highlanders in the 15th, with 691 casualties, followed by the British Columbians of the 7th, which lost 650 all ranks;[88] the 10th, from the prairies, 619;[89] and the Little Black Devils from Winnipeg, 570.[90] Not far behind were the four Ontario battalions belonging to the First Brigade: 1st, 404; 2nd, 544; 3rd, 488;[91] 4th, 454.

In a single battle, the Canadian Division had lost half of its infantry.

It is difficult to determine how many were casualties of chlorine-gas attacks. Some sources indicate that the number was small: the 8th Battalion's Colonel Lipsett reported that "at least 4 died of the fumes" on 24 April,[92] and another report states that only 122 Canadians were admitted to hospital for treatment of gas poisoning, and eleven of these died – although these figures obviously do not take into account the dead in the trenches.[93] On the other hand, the Canadian official history reveals that 1556 men were evacuated for sickness, and many of these "were in fact suffering from the effects of poison gas."[94]

The artillery had suffered, too. The 1st Field Artillery Brigade went into action with sixteen 18-pounders; seven survived, and even these "guns were loose on their carriages," according to the commander, Colonel Morrison, "and the springs were so weak that they could scarcely take up the recoil, while the oil boiled in the buffers." The brigade's losses amounted to "nearly a hundred officers and men killed or wounded [and] 125 horses."[95] The 2nd Field Artillery Brigade suffered "approximately two hundred casualties, including seven officers, while . . . over four hundred killed or injured horses were replaced."[96]

The first parades after the battle brought home the full impact of the heart-breaking losses. "When the battalion lined up there were about three hundred who answered the roll call," wrote Lieut. Henry Duncan of the 16th (Canadian Scottish) Battalion. "A number of men broke down, some going off their heads."[97] Sgt. William Miller of the shattered 15th (48th Highlanders of Canada) Battalion lamented in a letter home to Toronto that "there were just a few old one[s] left."[98] Sgt. William Fidler, 8th (90th Winnipeg Rifles) Battalion, sadly surveyed his platoon. "Our spirits remained high," he wrote, "but we were reduced to a baker's dozen."[99]

Their grief notwithstanding, the survivors marvelled at their good fortune to be alive. Wrote Sergeant Miller: "How one of us got out alive, it is a puzzle to me."[100] Sgt. John Matheson wrote home to Medicine Hat:

How I have ever come through is a mystery to me. With the exception of being hit by a rifle bullet on the cheek and a piece of shrapnel in the side, I am still for it. . . . I have bullet holes in my hat, equipment and clothes, but evidently I am slated to do some more evil in this world yet.[101]

An unidentified officer of the 13th (Royal Highlanders of Canada) Battalion commented:

> God only knows why I am alive, as it does not seem possible for anyone to get through it. All my equipment I had to leave behind. My pack was blown to pieces by a shell, and twice I was buried under debris. Three pieces of shell bruised me, and I was temporarily knocked out by gas fumes.[102]

"It was only by a miracle that I escaped," wrote a 1st (Western Ontario) Battalion officer. "It was terrible to see one's friends fall all round one."[103]

CANADIANS MOWED DOWN LIKE SHEEP. That huge headline greeted readers of the Calgary *Daily Herald* on Monday, 26 April. Details of the battle were slow to reach Canada; by now, the Canadian infantry had been pulled out of the front lines in the Ypres salient, yet the news reports at home still centred on Thursday night's counter-attack on Kitcheners Wood. Below the grim headline was a black-bordered photograph of the 10th Battalion's Colonel Boyle, the popular rancher from nearby Crossfield. The picture was captioned, "Brave Alberta Soldier Dead," and a long accompanying story eulogized the colonel as "one of the best officers that ever fought for king and country."

Casualties, naturally, were the main concern, and these were prominently displayed. The *Herald*'s front page featured a short list of Alberta men, most of them members of the 10th Battalion, known to have been killed or wounded, along with a unit-by-unit breakdown of all other casualties. Additionally, most local soldiers, as well as notables from other parts of Canada, were given a brief obituary or, if they were wounded, an update on their condition. These items were occasionally accompanied by a small, grainy photograph of the citizen-soldier.

These few dozen names were merely the start. For days, even weeks, after Ypres, newspapers in every Canadian city would carry similar lists and stories; soon there would be too many to be accommodated on the front page, and they would gradually slip farther and farther back, among the editorials and classified advertisements. Only one thing was certain at first, as the *Herald* headline implied: the losses had been terrible. But actual numbers were hard to pin down. Monday's *Herald* warned that "over 500 Canadians had been killed or wounded" during the weekend fighting in Flanders. The next day, it quoted confidential sources that estimated the toll at "eight to ten thousand." By Wednesday, the figure was pegged at "2000."

For a long time, not even the military bureaucracy knew for sure. The small staff of clerks at the Canadian army's records office in London was swamped after Ypres, and it took two weeks to process the majority of the casualties and pass along the names to the militia department in Canada for publication. By the end of the year, the army was still trying to clarify the status of many of the missing men – some were prisoners of war, others had been killed in action.

It would be virtually impossible for people at home to compile anything remotely resembling a complete picture of the battle. The reason was censorship. Ruthless restrictions were applied to reporters, who were kept well away from the fighting front. News was funnelled through the War Office from official "eye-witnesses" – usually elderly soldiers or, in Canada's case, a politician, Sir Max Aitken, the future Lord Beaverbrook – and the resulting reports were sketchy and fragmentary. The intent was twofold. There was, of course, no sense in letting the Germans know how effective their shrapnel shells and machine-gun bullets had been. Equally important was the need to minimize the impact on the public in order to maintain morale – a what-they-don't-know-won't-hurt-them attitude. The piecemeal accounts were bad enough, but they were not nearly as dreadful as the whole story would have been.

Over the long term, it was impossible to hide the awful consequences of the Second Battle of Ypres. There were just too many parents and wives all across the country holding telegrams that began, "Deeply regret to inform you. . . ."* Scarcely a community anywhere in Canada was able to escape grief. And the full horror would be brought home by hundreds of invalid soldiers.

In the short term, however, the news of the battle paid unexpected dividends. That Monday after Ypres saw another rush to recruiting offices from coast to coast. "More men offering than ever before," was the word from Sam Hughes's militia department, which was overseeing the departure of the second contingent, now en route to England. In Calgary, for

---

*Not all families had to rely on official telegrams informing them of the death of loved ones. The wealthy, well-connected Drummond family in Montreal learned of the loss of the 13th Battalion's Capt. Guy Drummond via its Bank of Montreal connections. Helen Drummond, then thirteen, recalled that she was having dinner at 208 Drummond Street, the home of her uncle Hartley, when Sir Frederick Williams-Taylor, the bank's managing director, arrived, looking grave. Calling Hartley Drummond into the hallway, Williams-Taylor quietly informed him of his brother's death in Flanders. The convivial atmosphere of the dinner party gave way to grief. Helen remembered her own reaction: "This is going to be terrible for Mary," her Uncle Guy's wife. They had been married for one year, and now Mary Drummond was a widow. (Interview with author, 5/5/88.)

example, men began lining up outside the armoury on 14th Avenue East at seven o'clock in the morning, and by nine "they were standing four deep in a long line. A little later this line was broken, the men crowding around the door in their eagerness to gain admission."

Among the first to enlist were forty-year-old H.G. Gutteridge and his eighteen-year-old son Victor.[104] They would help to ensure that, for at least a little while longer, there was plenty of cannon fodder for the fighting that lay ahead.

CHAPTER THIRTEEN

"They Were Coming in Masses"

Fighting continued in the salient until the end of May. The Germans and British troops traded attack and counter-attack across the blood-soaked Flanders fields, accomplishing little aside from adding to the already extensive lists of casualties.

At a high-level conference on 25 April, the Allies had formulated a new plan. It called for another major French offensive to regain the ground lost in the northern half of the salient, with Belgian forces supporting on the left and the British on the right. Although the French commander, General Foch, had consistently failed to execute his previous plans, Field-Marshal French was unable to resist his latest persuasive pleas for co-operation. As a result, the Second Army's General Smith-Dorrien was instructed to strike northward on Monday afternoon, the twenty-sixth, with two brigades of the Lahore Division (recently arrived from India via Hong Kong), and the 149th (Northumberland) Brigade. The Indians were to attack between the Ypres–Langemarck road and Kitcheners Wood, while the Northumbrians stormed Saint-Julien, where so many British and Canadian soldiers had fallen in futile attacks.

If the ground was familiar, so, too, were the results. The Indians, weary from a thirty-mile march over congested roads to reach the salient, were stopped by a deadly combination of German artillery fire and poison gas. Routed, the Lahore Division lost 1829 men, including five battalion commanders. The Northumberland Brigade, attacking later in the afternoon fared no better, losing twelve hundred troops in two hours. Among the dead was the brigadier, J.F. Riddell. Other senior British officers to be killed before the battle ended included the 11th Brigade's General Hasler and Colonel Geddes of Geddes's Detachment. Meanwhile, the feeble French effort to the north had gone virtually unnoticed, both by the British and by the Germans.[1]

This sad story was repeated on the twenty-seventh. The French issued identical orders for their Tuesday operation and, yet again, expected full co-operation from the British. Shortly after noon, the Lahore Division was thrown into the battle once more, across the same ground as the previous day. Rocked first by concentrated artillery fire, then cut to pieces by German rifles and machine-guns, the turbaned Sikhs and fierce Gurkhas bravely pressed the attack to within two hundred yards of the enemy line. But they were unable to break through the barbed-wire entanglements, and the attack fell apart. The cost: twelve hundred additional casualties.

Nor was that the day's only sacrifice. At v Corps headquarters, General Plumer ordered another assault, this time in the early evening by a composite brigade of four small battalions. This attack was stopped almost before it got started; as darkness fell, the slopes of Mauser Ridge were again covered with khaki-clad corpses.

The British official history sums up the French contribution in a single sentence: "The French pinned to the ground by a heavy barrage put down on their infantry in its position of assembly did not make an attack."[2]

These operations had been carried out despite the misgivings of General Smith-Dorrien, who had already lost all confidence in the French. "Truly I don't want to be allies with the French more than once in a life time," he complained privately. "You can't trust them."[3] On Sunday night, after learning of the first proposed attack involving the Lahore Division, Smith-Dorrien had travelled to Saint-Omer to protest personally to Field-Marshal French. The commander-in-chief, Smith-Dorrien bitterly recounted, seemed unable to make up his mind in this meeting:

> [He] did not want to surrender any ground if it could possibly be avoided, but unless the French regained the ground they had lost, or a great deal of it, [he] realised that it might become impossible to retain our present very salient position in front of Ypres. It was essential, though, that the situation should be cleared up, and the area quieted down as much as possible, even if I had to withdraw to a more retired line, so that [he] might be able to continue [his] offensive elsewhere. [He] felt sure I should not take a retired line until all hope of the French recovering ground had vanished. [He] did not wish me to have any more heavy casualties, as he thought the French have got us into the difficulty and ought to pull us out of it.
>
> [He] mentioned that in any combined attack I was to be careful to see that our troops did not get ahead of the French.[4]

Smith-Dorrien obeyed his orders and launched the ill-fated attack on 26 April. The fiasco left him convinced that the French were leaving it up to the British to restore their position in the salient; that belief was confirmed when the French reissued their plans for the following day's operation, without in any way bolstering their attacking force. Smith-Dorrien was "horrified," and promptly appealed to GHQ:

If the French are not going to make a big push, the only line we can hold permanently and have a fair chance of keeping supplied, would be the GHQ line passing just east of Wieltje and Potijze with a curved switch line which is being prepared through Hooge . . . to join on to our present line about a thousand yards north-east of Hill 60.

Smith-Dorrien warned "that unless the French do something really vigorous the situation might become such as to make it impossible for us to hold any line east of Ypres."[5]

This protest sealed Smith-Dorrien's fate. A personality clash, which had first appeared the previous August when Smith-Dorrien defied orders and withdrew his troops from certain destruction at the hands of the invading Germans, was coming to a head in the last days of April. On the afternoon of the twenty-seventh, while the weakened Lahore Division was being sacrificed for a second time on the slopes of Mauser Ridge, Smith-Dorrien received a blunt message from the chief of staff at GHQ, General Robertson, himself not a notable admirer of the French military:

Chief does not regard situation nearly so unfavourable as your letter represents. He thinks you have abundance of troops and especially notes the large reserves you have. He wishes you to act vigorously with the full means available in co-operating with and assisting the French.[6]

A couple of hours later, Smith-Dorrien was, for all intents and purposes, sacked. Orders arrived from GHQ telling him to hand over responsibility for the salient to General Plumer. Field-Marshal French attempted to justify this decision in his diary:

Smith-Dorrien has, since the commencement of these operations, failed to get a real grip of the situation. He has been very unwise in his dealings with General Putz [his French counterpart]. He has acted quite against the instructions I have given him. . . . His messages are all wordy – and unintelligible. His pessimistic attitude has the worst effect on his commanders and their troops, and today he wrote a letter to Robertson which was full of contradictions and altogether bewildering. I have therefore been obliged to take the command of all Ypres operations out of his hands.[7]

It was the beginning of the end of Smith-Dorrien's career. Virtually reduced to a corps commander, Sir Horace endured the humiliation until

6 May, when he suggested that GHQ should transfer him to a different command. General Robertson visited him that very night and broke the bad news: " 'Orace, you're for 'ome."[8]

By then, the British had carried out a withdrawal similar to that proposed by Smith-Dorrien. Indeed, Plumer's orders the same day he assumed full responsibility for the salient required him "to prepare a line east of Ypres joining up with the line now held north and south of that place ready for occupation if and when it becomes advisable to withdraw from the present salient."[9] The following day, 28 April, Sir John French informed General Foch: "I cannot continue in the unfavourable situation in which I find myself."[10]

A major consideration in Sir John's thinking was a major Franco-British offensive scheduled for early May. It involved a French attack near Arras, where Vimy Ridge was one of their key objectives, while the BEF mounted a large diversionary attack on Festubert. The British commander-in-chief was reluctant to expend further resources, human or material, in a secondary sector such as the Ypres salient. So he put his foot down, giving the French notice that unless they restored the salient within the next few days, he would pull back to a more secure line. His lack of faith in the French is indicated by the fact that on 29 April General Plumer was allowed to issue preliminary orders for that withdrawal – "In case it should be considered necessary to shorten our present line east of Ypres"[11] – and when the French had made no appreciable progress by 1 May, he gave the order to proceed with the retirement to the new line, an arc running from the vicinity of Mouse Trap Farm through Frezenberg to Sanctuary Wood and Hill 60 in the south.

A German gas attack delayed the operation. On Sunday, 2 May, the enemy employed chlorine gas to support a big attack on the British lines between Saint-Julien and Berlin Wood. It was soundly defeated – the British had by now been issued with rudimentary respirators, forerunners of the gas masks that would soon be standard equipment for troops on both sides of the Western Front – although the fighting carried on into the following day.

The withdrawal to the new British line was conducted on the night of 3/4 May. It went flawlessly, and the Germans were unaware of it until daylight.

The enemy wasted little time in testing the new position. After a preliminary operation on 5 May, during which they recaptured Hill 60 at the south end of the salient, the Germans launched their main effort on Saturday, 8 May, when Duke Albrecht's Fourth Army threw three corps – XXVI Reserve, XXVII Reserve, and XV, from north to south – into battle, between Mouse Trap Farm and Bellewaarde Ridge. And once again, Canadian soldiers would play a part in thwarting the duke's designs.

The ensuing battle was highlighted by the magnificent stand of the only Canadian unit to take part in this phase of operations. Princess Patricia's Canadian Light Infantry, that élite volunteer group of veterans, had been detached from the first Canadian contingent after its arrival in England. As part of the British 27th Division's 80th Brigade, the PPCLI – or Patricias, as the men liked to call themselves – had reached France in late December 1914, moving into the trenches in early January 1915. Field-Marshal French described the Patricias as "a magnificent set of men."[12]

To the PPCLI had gone the honour of staging the first Canadian attack of the Great War. On the night of 27/28 February a party of one hundred Patricias set out from their waterlogged trenches under Major Hamilton Gault, the Montreal millionaire who had founded the regiment and now served as its second-in-command. When they proceeded to raid the German lines opposite, it marked an introduction to a type of warfare – the trench raid – at which Canadians were to show rare skill.

But the Patricias paid dearly for their aggressiveness. In the first three months of 1915, the regiment suffered 288 casualties, not counting the sick. In mid-March a German sniper claimed the life of the commanding officer, Lt.-Col. Francis Farquhar, the former military secretary to the governor-general. He was succeeded by another British regular, Lt.-Col. Herbert Buller.

Under their new commander, the Patricias moved into the Ypres salient on 5 April, ten days before units of the Canadian Division began relieving French formations farther north. The 27th Division, to which the PPCLI belonged, took over a sector east and slightly south of Ypres, with the 28th Division on its left; the Canadian Division, when it arrived, moved onto the left of the 28th. The PPCLI occupied trenches near Polygon Wood, about three miles south of the future front of the Canadian Division.

It was fairly quiet here, until 22 April, when the Germans launched their gas attack on the French divisions at the north end of the salient. During the next twelve days, shell fire cost the Patricias eighty casualties. On the night of 3/4 May, the regiment took part in the withdrawal to new positions to the rear – in this case, about two miles back. The PPCLI was posted on Bellewaarde Ridge, the last low rise east of Ypres. The area, like the rest of Flanders, was exceedingly flat; although primarily farmland, there were extensive woods east and west of the ridge, as well as to the south. The Patricias lost 122 men on 4 May, while digging in along

Bellewaarde Ridge. The next day Colonel Buller was wounded in the eye by a shell splinter; command of the regiment devolved on its intrepid founder, Major Gault, the wealthy Montrealer.

At seven o'clock in the morning on 8 May, a heavy bombardment presaged the enemy's intentions. Two hours later, the Germans stormed the battered British line, including the PPCLI's position on Bellewaarde Ridge. It was repulsed, at terrible cost, but the enemy kept coming, mounting three more major attacks during the day. The Patricias stood firm, but the line to the left gave way under enemy pressure. While British reinforcements rushed up to block the breakthrough at Frezenberg, the PPCLI calmly drew back its left flank to face the threat on that side. The regiment was now under attack from two directions, and losses were so heavy that Major Gault ordered every spare man – signallers, pioneers, even stretcher-bearers – into the firing line.

The battle lasted all day. The weather was warm and sunny, but the dwindling numbers of Patricias did not take much notice. Lieut. Hugh Niven, who was a sales representative for an Edmonton-based mining company before the war, recalled the bitter fighting and the special skills that these veterans brought to it:

> We had four machine-guns. They were buried three or four times during the day with the shell fire. But they were always dug out. At the end of the day we had two left of the four. But we had really been trained in the fifteen rounds' rapid fire. We were getting off the fifteen rounds a minute, and the Germans thought they were machine-guns, and they were rifles.[13]

Fortunately, the Patricias were equipped with the British-made Lee-Enfield rather than the Ross rifle, which had let down the other Canadians in the salient. Cpl. H.G. Hetherington remembered, "I fired rifle after rifle until they were actually too hot to hold," and he had to pick up weapons from the wounded and dead lying all around. "There was always a target to aim at," said Hetherington. "They were coming in masses because I was aiming at Germans for hours."[14]

The fighting ended with the onset of darkness, and British troops relieved the Patricias shortly before midnight. The defence of Bellewaarde Ridge on 8 May cost the regiment 392 men, killed, wounded, or missing. The toll included Major Gault, who was twice-wounded. The PPCLI came out of the line under the command of Lieutenant Niven, who found himself in charge of three officers and 150 other ranks.

Bellewaarde Ridge was the graveyard of the original members of Princess Patricia's Canadian Light Infantry. When it entered the Ypres salient in early April, the PPCLI was probably the most experienced unit in the entire BEF. By the time it left the salient in late May, it had suffered 658 casualties.[15] But it had won the respect and admiration of the entire British army. As it moved to the rear, the rest of the 80th Brigade lined the road and cheered wildly. "No regiment could have fought with greater determination or endurance," wrote the 27th Division's commander, General Snow, who added that "many would have failed where they succeeded."[16]

Desultory fighting continued in the salient until the end of May. On the twenty-fourth the Germans launched a final gas attack, the biggest yet attempted, on a four-and-a-half-mile front. The British, though, were now equipped with primitive gas masks, and the enemy's chlorine clouds had little effect on the outcome. The PPCLI's Bellewaarde Ridge and Mouse Trap Farm, the bullet-riddled headquarters of General Turner while his Third Canadian Infantry Brigade fought it out, were among the landmarks to fall to the Germans. But few other gains were made, and both sides turned their attention elsewhere.

For the next two years, the opposing lines around the Ypres salient remained virtually unchanged.

CHAPTER FOURTEEN

"The Dominion Will Be Justly Proud"

The Second Battle of Ypres was a relatively minor affair so far as the Great War was concerned. It certainly was not, as some historians have suggested and as Allied wartime propaganda proclaimed, a "decisive" struggle. While the British had staved off a disaster of considerable proportions in the salient, the fact remains that the Germans were never in a position to exploit properly the victory gained over the French on 22 April. The attack was strictly limited to enable the Germans to test chlorine gas as a weapon and to mask the movement of troops from the Western Front to Russia.

The casualties were staggering, in terms of the troops employed in the fighting. The British lost 59,275 men killed, wounded, and missing, while the Germans admitted to 34,873. The actual losses on both sides were probably quite similar; German casualties throughout the war tended to be lower than the British losses because of differences in "book-keeping," not the least of which was the German refusal to consider lightly wounded men casualties.[1]

One casualty was the hitherto fairly cordial relationship between the French and British. The conduct of the Frenchman, Ferdinand Foch, was nothing short of reprehensible; at one point he confessed to his commander-in-chief, General Joseph Joffre, that in his reports to Field-Marshal French "I have painted the picture . . . blacker than [it] appear[s] to me," a ploy to win British co-operation for French counter-attacks that often failed to materialize.[2] The pitiful performance of the French army confirmed in the minds of many British generals the suspicion that their allies were not so militarily brilliant as popularly believed. One of these was Gen. Sir Douglas Haig, the dour Scot who commanded the First Army and who would succeed Sir John French as commander-in-chief of the BEF before the end of 1915. Haig, writing in his diary on 24 April, observed of the Ypres battle:

This surprise of the French should never have happened. It seems to have been a distinctly bad performance, and the possibility of its happening was never realised by Foch and Co.

These French leaders are a queer mixture of fair ability (not more than fair) and ignorance of the practical side of war. They are not built for it by nature. They are too excitable, and they never seem to think of what the enemy may do. And they will not see a nasty situation as it really is, and take steps to meet it.

However, the enemy in this case is probably as much surprised at the magnitude of his success as are the French, and he does not seem to have sufficient troops on the spot to follow up his first success – luckily for the Allies![3]

After Ypres, gas attacks became commonplace. Both sides used increasingly lethal gases for the balance of the war, delivered by artillery shells or by the demonstrably unreliable system of wind-assisted clouds. (With the prevailing winds blowing into their faces, the Germans usually emerged as the losers.) While the Germans were able to mount twenty-four gas-cloud attacks during the next three years, the French countered with twenty and the British with no fewer than 150.[4] Steady improvements in protection and detection equipment, however, limited the effects of these various poison gases.

Poison gas never became a decisive weapon, thanks to the Canadian stand at Ypres. With only improvised protection, they stood firm in the face of the chlorine cloud that had earlier routed the French forces on their left. As the Canadian official history notes, "the paralyzing surprise of its first appearance on the battlefield had passed, and it was henceforth only another of the known horrors of war."[5] Although gas remained a gruesome weapon, its psychological impact had been minimized.

The Canadian soldiers, however, refused to take undue credit for their heroic fight. "All I can remember," stated one survivor, "was that I was in a [dugout] for about three days and three nights and now I am told I am a hero. Isn't that fine?"[6]

Others, in later years, would argue that naïveté was a bigger factor than bravery. The gunner with the promising future, Andy McNaughton, recalled:

Somehow we felt it was the normal course of war. It was unpleasant, it's true, but nobody got very excited about it. Now, later on, when we'd learned a little bit about war, I honestly think we wouldn't have been there at all; we'd have been off within the next couple of hours, but nobody thought of that at Ypres.[7]

"We mustn't boast too much," declared Maj. Victor Odlum, the Vancouver *Daily Star*'s publisher, "because it wasn't heroism that made us stay there and fight through that battle. We just did not know how to get out. . . . The only thing to do as far as we could see was just stay where we were. And we did." An artillery lieutenant, Elliot Greene, suggested of the Canadians "that if they were better troops they would have withdrawn immediately, and if they'd have been worse troops, they wouldn't have been there at all – they'd have panicked." Added Pte. George Patrick of the 2nd (Eastern Ontario) Battalion: "No one had any idea of getting out. We didn't know enough about it to know that we were licked. We went in there and we were going to stay there, and that was that."[8]

Modesty aside, the Canadians gained a reputation for themselves in this battle. As the Second Brigade's General Currie – not an unbiased observer, of course – later commented, "the untried amateur soldiers suddenly became transformed into a skilful body of veterans." Through "the devotion and self sacrifice of every man," he believed, the Canadians at Ypres had set "the future standard for Canada's fighting forces."[9] Ahead lay the blood-lettings at Festubert, Mount Sorrel, the Somme, Vimy Ridge, Hill 70, Passchendaele, and the remarkable victories during the war's last hundred days: Amiens, the Drocourt–Quéant line, and the Canal du Nord. In the course of these battles great and small, the Canadians established themselves as storm troops par excellence. But the foundation of their reputation had been laid in their trial by fire at Ypres.

Friend and foe alike paid tribute to the Canadians in the wake of the April 1915 battle. Even the Germans, who had been so quick to dismiss the Canadians as a colonial rabble of no consequence, admitted that the newcomers had acquitted themselves admirably. The German official account, published after the war, recognized the "obstinate resistance" and "tenacious determination" of the Canadians.[10]

On the Allied side, the accolades were many. King George cabled congratulations "on the splendid and gallant way in which the Canadian Division fought . . . north of Ypres. . . . The Dominion will be justly proud."[11] The French commander-in-chief, General Joffre, expressed his thanks for "la promptitude du concours apporté aux nôtres par la division canadienne,"[12] and his British counterpart, Field-Marshal French, declared that "the Canadians held their ground with a magnificent display of tenacity and courage; and it is not too much to say that the bearing and conduct of these splendid troops averted a disaster which might have been attended with the most serious consequences."[13] The Second Army's General Smith-Dorrien (while he still held the post) was "convinced that with less gallant and determined troops, the disaster which occurred outside the line they were holding might have been converted into a serious defeat of our troops."[14] He elaborated his feelings in a conversation with General Currie:

> Currie, when I first heard of the attack by poison gas and of the retirement of the troops on your left, I threw up my hands and foresaw the greatest disaster that ever overtook the British army. If every man in the salient had tried to get out that night, I should not have blamed them; and when I thought of all the troops that were there, all the transports and guns trying to get across those four bridges over the canal . . . I shuddered with horror.
>
> Then I got a message that the Canadians were holding on. I would not believe it; I could not believe it. I sent out one of my staff, and he brought back the message that it was perfectly true.[15]

The response from Canada was equally effusive. "Canada saved the day," trumpeted the Montreal *Daily Star*. "Our Canadian boys, unused to war and summoned to arms only at the close of last summer, have taken their place by the side of European veterans, and heroically bore the brunt of a savage German attempt to break the allied line." Said the Toronto *Star*: "The last has been heard, we hope, from those poor sports among us who declared that our men would be unequal to valors and sacrifices of war because they lacked a certain docility and deference of demeanor which has been supposed to be a requisite of discipline in army." The Winnipeg *Telegram* contended that the Canadians had "acquitted themselves gloriously. They have worthily fulfilled the highest expectations of a nation that never for a moment has doubted their courage and their ability to hold their own with the best troops on the continent." The Calgary *Daily Herald* followed a similar line: "We are proud of our soldier boys as we knew we should have reason to be. . . . The casualty list is a heavy one and there is mourning and sorrow in many a Canadian home today, but the bereaved at least have the satisfaction of knowing that their loved ones were lost bravely facing the foe and in a righteous cause."[16]

Government leaders were just as pleased as the newspapermen. "Report of splendid gallantry and efficiency of Division under your command has thrilled all Canada with pride," Prime Minister Borden cabled General Alderson. Militia Minister Hughes added his congratulations to the commander of the Canadian Division: "We rejoice in their gallantry but while mourning the loss of many brave comrades our one great desire is to avenge the loss. The hearts of all Canadians are with them."[17]

No one was happier than Alderson. Addressing the infantry brigades by turn, along with engineers and artillery, the little Englishman was hard pressed to control his emotions:

> I would first of all tell you that I have never been so proud of anything in my life as I am of this Armlet with "1 Canada" on it that I wear on my right arm. . . .
> You will remember the last time I spoke to you, just before you went into the trenches at Sailly, now over two months ago, I told you about my old Regiment – the R[oyal] W[est] Kents – having gained a reputation for not budging from their trenches, no matter how they were attacked. I said then that I was quite sure that in a short time, the Army out here would be saying the same of you.
> I little thought – we none of us thought – how soon those words would come true. But now to-day, not only the Army out here but all Canada, All England, and all the Empire, are saying it of you.[18]

If the individual Canadian soldier had distinguished himself, the same cannot be said of his senior officers. On the whole, the leadership qualities displayed at the battalion, brigade, and divisional levels left a lot to be desired.

Surprisingly, only one Canadian officer lost his job as a direct consequence of the Second Battle of Ypres. The Toronto MP, John Currie of the 15th Battalion, was sent home soon afterwards. Of the eleven other battalion commanders in the Canadian Division, three were killed before they had a chance to prove themselves: the 4th Battalion's A.P. Birchall, William Hart-McHarg of the 7th, and the Alberta rancher, the 10th's Russell Boyle. Only one of the remaining eight colonels was outstanding – the 8th Battalion's Louis Lipsett, the British regular – but all were eventually promoted. Two others, besides Lipsett, became major-generals commanding divisions, and both were former militiamen from Quebec: the 2nd Battalion's David Watson and Fred Loomis of the 13th. The rest became brigadier-generals,* as did two acting battalion commanders, the 7th's Victor Odlum and Dan Ormond of the 10th. Again, only Lipsett proved himself to be a commander of unusual capabilities; tragically, he was killed in action less than a month before the end of the war. Most of the others were competent, but not otherwise notable.

---

*Frank Meighen, the Montreal milling-company executive who commanded the 14th Battalion, was promoted in 1916 and sent to the main Canadian training centre at Bramshott, England. In 1918, however, he reverted to the rank of lieutenant-colonel so he could return to combat, leading the 87th (Canadian Grenadier Guards) Battalion.

On the other hand, several gunners showed promise. Throughout the battle, the artillery had lived up to its motto, *Quo Fas et Gloria Ducunt* – Where Duty and Glory Lead – and that service would continue to make an outstanding contribution until the end of the war. "Dinky" Morrison, the former editor of the Ottawa *Citizen*, would go on to command the Canadian Corps artillery. Two others, Andy McNaughton and Harry Crerar, rose to prominence, McNaughton as commander of the Corps heavy artillery, Crerar as the Corps counter-battery officer, and both would command the First Canadian Army during the next war.

Generalship was another matter. Overall it was mediocre, although certainly no worse than that exhibited by the British, French, or Germans. Nevertheless, as one staff officer acerbically commented, "Had we been a British Division and under the War Office, I am quite certain that either General Alderson or General Turner, or both of them, would have lost their commands."[19] This is probably true, but there were mitigating circumstances. Both were responsible for forces that were far too big for their respective staffs to handle – Alderson at one point commanded thirty-three Canadian and British battalions, the equivalent of nearly three divisions – due to the dubious policy of v Corps and the Second Army of committing fresh formations piecemeal, without regard for unit boundaries. And both Alderson, back at Château des Trois Tours, and Turner, brushing debris off his maps in Mouse Trap Farm, were victimized by the poor communications that plagued everyone.

It seems plain, however, that neither Alderson nor Turner was able to grasp the situation. Rather than initiating action, they were usually to be found reacting, often belatedly, to enemy moves. Alderson was repeatedly misled by inaccurate information from Turner, but much of the problem arose from the fact that the divisional headquarters, at Château des Trois Tour, west of the Canal de l'Yser, were too far removed from the scene to allow Alderson to exert effective control of the Canadian Division. (General Snow, the antagonistic commander of the 27th Division, established his headquarters in a flimsy dugout east of the canal, in the heart of the salient.) By contrast, Turner's location at Mouse Trap Farm was virtually in the front lines within a few hours of the first gas attack, and the Third Brigade's courageous commander was under shell and small-arms fire for the best part of seventy hours, during which he had insufficient sleep, another factor in his weak performance. To make matters even worse, Turner was poorly served by his staff, especially the brigade-major, Garnet Hughes. Excuses notwithstanding, Turner's preoccupation with the GHQ line on 24 April nearly proved fatal – not once, but twice – for the neighbouring Second Brigade.

Neither the First Brigade's Malcolm Mercer nor Harry Burstall, the division's chief gunner, can be fairly assessed on the basis of Second Ypres. General Mercer, the former Toronto lawyer, was given little opportunity to prove himself, a circumstance which would describe his brief war-time career. Of his four Ontario battalions, he was left with only two, the 1st and 4th, after the 2nd and 3rd were attached to Turner's brigade for most of the battle. This effectively reduced him to the status of glorified onlooker, and it must have rankled to see a brigade being improvised under a lower-ranking British officer, Colonel Geddes, while Mercer and his staff at First Brigade headquarters had so little to do throughout the fighting. Similarly, General Burstall had no chance to exercise real command of the Canadian artillery, which fought by brigades and batteries over a wide area, on both sides of the canal, often under British jurisdiction. Burstall, however, would later demonstrate his competence as a divisional commander in the last two years of the war.

The sole bright spot was Arthur Currie. The big brigadier, a militiaman who had never before been in combat, proved himself to be a natural leader who could delegate authority to reliable subordinates. In sharp contrast to the other four generals in the Canadian Division, Currie won rave reviews for his performance at Second Ypres. "I was struck at once," recalled Col. Cecil Romer, a British professional who served at divisional headquarters, "both during my telephone conversations and visits to the General, by his calmness in a crisis; and what pleased me most of all was that he never lost a certain dry humor, which was rather characteristic of him."[20] Lt.-Col. C.H. Mitchell called Currie the "one outstanding figure in the 2nd Battle of Ypres,"[21] and Maj. Andy McNaughton was left with the "very favourable impression of a cool and collected commanding officer who knew what he was about."[22] Maj. T.C. Irving, an engineer who surveyed the Second Brigade's positions before and during the battle, later wrote that if there was one man "who should be given credit for holding back the Germans at Ypres, it is Currie."[23]

Official recognition of Currie's deeds soon followed. King George appointed him a Companion in the Order of the Bath, the first in a long string of such honours, and the French government named him a commander in the Legion d'Honneur.

Still, with this battle controversy crept into Currie's record. He was later criticized for leaving his command post on 24 April to seek the reinforcements to save the Second Brigade. The worst offender was Sir Sam Hughes – he was knighted in August 1915 – who repeatedly slandered Currie in the House of Commons after the war. Currie might have owed Sam and Garnet Hughes for his initial appointment as a brigadier in 1914, but Currie did not allow that debt to alter his belief that the younger

Hughes was incompetent. It was an opinion that dated back to their days together in the militia in Victoria, and Second Ypres only confirmed it. Consequently, Currie vigorously opposed Garnet's promotions, eventually derailing his bid to command a combat division. When his son ended the war in an obscure administrative post in London, Sir Sam took Currie to task publicly. The recurring theme was Currie's alleged disregard for the lives of his troops – a slanderous charge that Hughes dared not repeat outside the sanctity of Parliament. In the process, Hughes raised the spectre of 24 April 1915. "I am not questioning Arthur Currie's motive in going back," Hughes stated in 1919, "I merely say it was unmilitary for him as a brigadier to leave his position."[24] In another attack, Hughes claimed: "Had I remained in office six weeks longer not only General Currie but several other officers would have been asked to hand in their resignations."[25]

Currie's actions can, however, be easily justified. By staying where he was, the brigadier was making no real contribution to the brigade's life-and-death struggle; as one historian notes, "at least he displayed boldness in going back for more reinforcements when other means had failed."[26] And any hint of cowardice on his part can be dismissed with equal ease. "Throughout the entire attack he frequently shared exposed positions with his soldiers,"[27] and on 25 April he moved his report centre to Gravenstafel, close behind the front line, for the entire day.

By the end of 1915 all but Burstall had been promoted. In September, Alderson was placed in command of the newly formed Canadian Army Corps. Currie was given the veteran First Division; the new Second Division went to Turner. On Christmas Day the Third Division was formed, under Mercer.

Only Currie prospered. In the wake of Ypres, his capabilities were noted by his British superiors. Sir John French remarked that Currie was the "most suitable of the three brigadiers" in the Canadian Division.[28] "Currie," concluded Alderson, "is the one who I have no hesitation in saying would, with a good staff, command a Divn well."[29] Indeed, he distinguished himself as a divisional commander and went on, in the summer of 1917, to command the Canadian Corps, the first nonregular officer to reach that level of responsibility in the entire BEF. He was so highly regarded that British prime minister David Lloyd George planned to install Currie as commander-in-chief of the BEF if the war lasted into 1919. It ended in November 1918, and Currie returned to Canada with an impressive array of honours and awards, including a knighthood, and was eventually promoted to full general, the first Canadian to achieve that rank.

He accomplished all of this under the threat of scandal. Luckily, he was still on amiable terms with Sam Hughes in 1915, and the militia minister proved that he could be as good an ally as he was a fearsome enemy. After learning of Currie's impropriety, Hughes dispatched an emissary to France in May, shortly after Second Ypres. Harold Daly survived the *Lusitania* tragedy – which caused so much heartbreak for Toronto's Ryerson family, among many others – and reached the battle-front to assure Currie that, as Daly later put it, "his personal interests were being looked after and that he was not on any account to worry."[30] This enabled Currie to repay other debts, amounting to thousands of dollars, from his failing business in Victoria, but the skeleton finally fell out of his closet in mid-1917, when he was taking over the Canadian Corps. Informed that the matter had come to the attention of the federal cabinet, Currie borrowed money from two wealthy subordinates, David Watson and Victor Odlum, and repaid the regimental fund. Although rumours about Currie's financial difficulties were widespread, they were not publicized until after his death in 1933.

Mercer was not as fortunate as Currie. He was killed in action on 2 June 1916 during his division's first battle, at Mount Sorrel in the Ypres salient.

Turner ended the war at a desk job in England. Alderson actively opposed his promotion to divisional command and lamented his lack of success: "I am sorry to say that I do not consider Turner really fit to command a Division and his name was not put forward by Sir John French, but Canadian politics have been too strong for all of us and so he has got it."[31] The "Canadian politics" that thus assisted the Quebec City businessman may have prevented his being sacked in early 1916, when he bungled the Second Division's first battle, at Saint-Eloi, also in the Ypres salient. But in November he was transferred to an administrative posting at Canadian Military Headquarters in London. The gunner, General Bur-stall, succeeded Turner in command of the Second Division, which he led for the balance of the war.

Alderson's days were numbered, too. Knighted in early 1916, he acted as Canadian Corps commander until May, when he was replaced by another British officer, Sir Julian Byng, who later served as governor-general of Canada. The wonder is that Alderson lasted as long as he did, because in the weeks and months after Ypres, he acquired a formidable enemy, Sam Hughes. Bitterly critical of the British command for its con-duct of the Ypres battle – "It is more congenial," he snorted, "to bury the dead of the enemy than to have the enemy bury ours" – Hughes concluded that Alderson was "unfit" to command the Canadian Division and recom-mended his replacement – by none other than Turner.[32]

The Ross rifle was the real reason behind Hughes's enmity. At Ypres the Ross had shown itself to be tragically unreliable in combat conditions. When it jammed during the battle, Canadian infantryman pronounced their judgement in no uncertain terms: of five thousand survivors, 1452 had thrown away their Ross rifles and picked up Lee-Enfields from British casualties.[33] Canadian commanders were sharply divided on the Ross rifle. General Currie contended that this "rifle is not as satisfactory as it should be," and the 13th Battalion's Colonel Loomis agreed: "The men have lost confidence in the Ross rifle as a service arm." An unnamed officer was much more vehement, informing Alderson that "it is nothing short of murder to send our men against the enemy with such a weapon." There were, however, opposing views. "I consider the Ross Rifle a satisfactory weapon," declared General Mercer, who was never near the action, while one of his battalion commanders, the 2nd's Colonel Watson, who was under fire, declared: "Majority of opinion strongly in favour of Ross rifle."[34]

Alderson quickly made up his mind: the Ross would have to go. "Canada will no doubt be extremely annoyed if fault is found with the rifle," he advised GHQ. "This, however, cannot be allowed to stand in the way when the question may be of life or death, and of victory and defeat."[35]

Hughes angrily rejected Alderson's contention. Claiming that the divisional commander did not "know the butt from the muzzle," he explained to Prime Minister Borden that "with good ammunition, that is proper brass," the Ross had not given "the slightest trouble."[36] A Hughes-appointed committee, which included the rifle's inventor, Sir Charles Ross, investigated the many complaints and concluded that the rifle's problems could be attributed to poor British ammunition, the Flanders mud, and unskilled soldiers.

By then, it was too late. In June 1915 Sir John French decided that something had to be done, and he did it. When Militia Minister Hughes refused the field-marshal's request to issue "an authoritative statement which will carry conviction to the men that their apprehensions are unfounded,"[37] French issued instructions "to re-arm the Canadian Division with the Lee-Enfield rifle."[38]

Hughes was a powerful adversary, however, and he fought a skilful rearguard battle against the growing numbers of military men who were becoming disenchanted with his beloved Ross Rifle. He saw to it that the next three divisions raised by Canada went overseas defiantly equipped with the Ross.* It was not until September 1916 that, at the insistence of

*Among the regiments of the Third Canadian Division was Princess Patricia's Canadian Light Infantry. When the Patricias transferred from the British 27th Division, they brought their Lee-Enfield rifles, while the rest of the new division used Ross rifles.

GHQ, the entire Canadian Corps was refitted with the Lee-Enfield, except for snipers, who continued to use the Ross effectively.

In March 1917 the Canadian government expropriated the Ross Rifle Factory in Quebec City, renaming it the Dominion Rifle Factory. Sir Charles Ross, who received a fair price for the factory, but lost his honorary colonelcy, never apologized for his rifle's shortcomings, maintaining to the bitter end that they were caused by "official blunders before the war."[39]

By then, Sam Hughes was gone as well. Prime Minister Borden, finding it impossible any longer to overlook his eccentricities and inefficiency – of which the Ross rifle fiasco was but one example – finally fired Hughes in November 1916. It was an ignominious end for the colorful, controversial man who had done so much to guide Canada's efforts early in the war.

Canada had changed, too. With the Second Battle of Ypres, the horror of the war had been brought home with cruel clarity, touching every community, large and small, across the country. No city lost more than Toronto, which had raised two battalions, the 3rd and 15th, and also had placed substantial numbers of men in three others, the 1st, 2nd, and 4th. Casualties among the Highlanders in the 15th Battalion exceeded the combined losses of the 13th and 14th battalions, which had been raised in Montreal, Canada's biggest city. But Montreal lost in other ways. So many prominent young men from "the Square Mile" died during that grim April in 1915 that Montreal never recovered. Helen Henderson, the Drummond family historian, believes that Montreal's decline as Canada's leading city can be traced not just to the war, but to the Second Battle of Ypres, which she describes as "a terrible blow to the city."[40]

The 1915 battle at Ypres gave Canadians a new perspective on war. Sadder and wiser, the country no longer exhibited the schoolboyish enthusiasm – in retrospect, so naïve – of Sam Hughes and many others, who, in the first weeks and months of the war, sought glory where none existed. Hundreds of thousands of young Canadian men would wear khaki before it was all over, but there was no need for brass bands to see them off, and the once-fervent crowds of well-wishers were sombre and subdued. After Ypres, there was no more bravado about an early victory over the Hun, no more fears of missing out on "the fun." The horrifyingly long casualty list from Flanders had come as a slap in the face – and they would be far, far exceeded by the ones to come out of the Somme in 1916, Vimy Ridge and Passchendaele in 1917, and the sustained fighting of the war's last hundred days in 1918.

Ultimately, there would be the reward of full nationhood. But in the spring of 1915 that was something that few foresaw. The immediate task was to win the war, and it was a grimly determined Canada that set about making its contribution to victory. The price in bloodshed and heartbreak would be considerable, perhaps exorbitant. Of that there could be no doubt whatever, after the Second Battle of Ypres.

"In Flanders Fields"

Although he had been a doctor for years and had served in the South African War, it was impossible to get used to the suffering, the screams, and the blood here, and Maj. John McCrae had seen and heard enough in his dressing station to last him a lifetime. As a surgeon attached to the 1st Field Artillery Brigade, Major McCrae, who had joined the McGill faculty in 1900 after graduating from the University of Toronto, had spent seventeen days treating injured men – Canadians, British, Indians, French, and Germans – in the Ypres salient.

It had been an ordeal that he had hardly thought possible. McCrae later wrote of it:

I wish I could embody on paper some of the varied sensations of that seventeen days. . . . Seventeen days of Hades! At the end of the first day if anyone had told us we had to spend seventeen days there, we would have folded our hands and said it could not have been done.[1]

One death particularly affected McCrae. A young friend and former student, Lieut. Alexis Helmer of Ottawa, had been killed by a shell burst on 2 May. Lieutenant Helmer was buried later that day in the little cemetery outside McCrae's dressing station, and McCrae had performed the funeral ceremony in the absence of the chaplain.

The next day, sitting on the back of an ambulance parked near the dressing station beside the Canal de l'Yser, just a few hundred yards north of Ypres, McCrae vented his anguish by composing a poem. The major was no stranger to writing, having authored several medical texts besides dabbling in poetry. In the nearby cemetery, McCrae could see the wild poppies that sprang up in the ditches in that part of Europe, and he spent twenty minutes of precious rest time scribbling fifteen lines of verse in a notebook.[2]

A young soldier watched him write it. Cyril Allinson, a twenty-two-year-old sergeant-major, was delivering mail that day when he spotted

McCrae. The major looked up as Allinson approached, then went on writing while the sergeant-major stood there quietly. "His face was very tired but calm as he wrote," Allinson recalled. "He looked around from time to time, his eyes straying to Helmer's grave." When he finished five minutes later, he took his mail from Allinson and, without saying a word, handed his pad to the young NCO. Allinson was moved by what he read:

> The poem was almost an exact description of the scene in front of us both.
>
> The word blow was not used in the first line though it was used later when the poem appeared in Punch. But it was used in the second last line. He used the word blow in that line because the poppies actually were being blown that morning by a gentle east wind.
>
> It never occurred to me at the time that it would ever be published. It seemed to me to be just an exact description of the scene.[3]

In fact, it was very nearly not published. Dissatisfied with it, McCrae tossed the poem away, but a fellow officer – either Lt.-Col. Edward Morrison, the former Ottawa newspaper editor who commanded the 1st Brigade of artillery,[4] or Lt.-Col. J.M. Elder,[5] depending on which source is consulted – retrieved it and sent it to newspapers in England. *The Spectator*, in London, rejected it, but *Punch* published it on 8 December 1915.

McCrae's "In Flanders Fields" remains to this day one of the most memorable war poems ever written. It is a lasting legacy of the terrible battle in the Ypres salient in the spring of 1915.

In Flanders fields the poppies blow
Between the crosses, row on row,
That mark our place; and in the sky
The larks, still bravely singing, fly
Scarce heard amid the guns below.
We are the dead. Short days ago
We lived, felt dawn, saw sunset glow,
Loved, and were loved, and now we lie
    In Flanders fields.

Take up your quarrel with the foe:
To you from failing hands we throw
The torch; be yours to hold it high.
If ye break faith with us who die
We shall not sleep, though poppies grow
    In Flanders fields.

252

Order of Battle, First Canadian Division

General Officer Commanding: Lt.-Gen. E.A.H. Alderson

First Brigade: Brig.-Gen. M.S. Mercer
1st (Western Ontario) Battalion (Lt.-Col. F.W. Hill)
2nd (Eastern Ontario) Battalion (Lt.-Col. D. Watson)
3rd (Toronto) Battalion (Lt.-Col. R. Rennie)
4th (Central Ontario) Battalion (Lt.-Col. A.P. Birchall)

Second Brigade: Brig.-Gen. A.W. Currie
5th (Western Cavalry) Battalion (Lt.-Col. G.S. Tuxford)
7th (British Columbia) Battalion (Lt.-Col. W.F.R. Hart-McHarg)
8th (90th Winnipeg Rifles) Battalion (Lt.-Col. L.J. Lipsett)
10th (Calgary-Winnipeg) Batttalion (Lt.-Col. R.L. Boyle)

Third Brigade: Brig.-Gen. R.E.W. Turner
13th (Royal Highlanders of Canada) Battalion (Lt.-Col. F.O.W. Loomis)
14th (Royal Montreal Regiment) Battalion (Lt.-Col. F.S. Meighen)
15th (48th Highlanders of Canada) Battalion (Lt.-Col. J.A. Currie)
16th (Canadian Scottish) Battalion (Lt.-Col. R.G.E. Leckie)

Divisional Artillery: Brig.-Gen. H.E. Burstall
1st Brigade, CFA (Lt.-Col. E.W.B. Morrison)
2nd Brigade, CFA (Lt.-Col. J.J. Creelman)
3rd Brigade, CFA (Lt.-Col. J.H. Mitchell)

1st, 2nd, 3rd Field Companies, Canadian Engineers
Special Service Squadron, 19th Alberta Dragoons
First Canadian Divisional Cyclist Company

Acknowledgements

If authors were left to their own devices, most books would be considerably less impressive, including this one. Fortunately, I had a lot of help with it, most notably from my publisher, Doug Gibson, whose interest, encouragement, and active participation in this project have made me a better writer. Thanks must also go to his assistant, Lynn Schellenberg, who so graciously tolerates my long-distance whining and snivelling, and to the copy editor, Shaun Oakey, whose polishing made the manuscript that much better. Any errors or omissions that remain are mine alone.

Welcome to Flanders Fields was written with the assistance of a grant from the Alberta Foundation for the Literary Arts. Others who contributed to the book include Colonel John Fletcher, whose military analysis added to my understanding of the Second Battle of Ypres; Wally Bennett, believed to be the sole surviving member of the 10th Battalion; Barry Agnew, military archivist at the Glenbow Museum; Tim Travers, history professor at the University of Calgary, who kindly lent me his superb manuscript on the Second Battle of Ypres: Don MacKay, author of *The Square Mile*, whose generous advice to Doug Gibson was so helpful; and Helen Henderson, whose charm, spirit, and intelligence are undiminished at eighty-six years of age.

As always, my parents and other family members have been most supportive. So, too, has Cindy Delisle, who will never let success, such as it is, go to my head!

Daniel G. Dancocks
Calgary, May 1988

Notes

Published sources are identified by author and, if necessary, by a shortened title, followed by the page number. A roman numeral preceding the page number indicates volume number. For full details, refer to the Bibliography.

Unpublished sources involve, of necessity, longer entries. The following abbreviations, in alphabetical order, are used for the institutions housing the collections that were consulted:

AO	Archives of Ontario (Toronto)
CBC	Canadian Broadcasting Corporation, Program Archives (Toronto)
CEA	City of Edmonton Archives
GM	Glenbow Museum (Calgary)
MUA	McGill University Archives (Montreal)
PAA	Provincial Archives of Alberta (Edmonton)
PABC	Provincial Archives of British Columbia (Victoria)
PAC	Public Archives Canada (Ottawa), now the National Archives of Canada
PAM	Provincial Archives of Manitoba (Winnipeg)
PANB	Provincial Archives of New Brunswick (Fredericton)

Prologue

1 Duguid, Appendix 111.
2 Phillips, 27.
3 Duguid, Appendix 111.
4 *Ibid.*
5 *Ibid.*
6 *Ibid.*
7 *Ibid.*
8 Phillips, 31, 31n.
9 Duguid, Appendix 111.
10 *Ibid.*
11 *Ibid.*
12 *Ibid.*
13 Phillips, 79.
14 Duguid, Appendix 111.
15 *Ibid.*

Chapter One

1 Churchill, 112.
2 Tuchman, 90.
3 *Ibid.*, 109.
4 *Ibid.*, 118.
5 *Ibid.*, 133.
6 *Ibid.*, 122.

Chapter Two

1 Nicholson CEF 5.
2 English, 26.
3 Brown, 395.
4 *Times History* II/243–44.
5 *World War* I/185.
6 Terraine *Haig* 108.
7 PAC, RG24 C5, volume 1854, file 58.
8 *Ibid.*
9 *Canadian Annual Review, 1914* (Toronto, 1915) 135.
10 Nicholson CEF 12–13.
11 *Canadian Annual Review, 1914* 134, 212.
12 CBC, "Flanders Fields," program 2.
13 Allen, 69.
14 Borden, I/209.
15 Duguid, I/209.
16 Borden, I/210–11.
17 Toronto *Globe* 3, 4/8/14.
18 Duguid, Appendix 6.
19 Haycock, 144–45.
20 Allen, 45.
21 Haycock, 98.
22 PAC, MG27 II D7, diary, 7/7/17.
23 Haycock, 154, 183, 209.
24 Borden, II/467.
25 PAC, MG26H, volume 451, diary, 6/8/14.
26 Borden, I/215, 219–20.
27 Allen, 70–71.
28 Duguid, I/9.
29 Borden, I/214.
30 *Canadian Annual Review, 1914* 143.
31 John Craig, 50.
32 Calgary *Daily Herald* 5/8/14.
33 English, 108.
34 *Times History* II/245.
35 Urquhart *16th* 368–69.
36 John Craig, 50.

37 Toronto *Globe* 1/8/14.
38 *Canadian Annual Review, 1914* 180.
39 Duguid, 1/8.
40 CBC, "Flanders Fields," program 2, Jack McLaren, C.E. Longstaff.
41 *Canada in the Great World War* III/32.
42 CBC, "Flanders Fields," program 2.
43 Urquhart *16th* 11.
44 Mathieson, 12.
45 CBC interview, 4/1/64.
46 *Letters* II/213-14.
47 *Times History* II/247.
48 Grace Craig, 25-27.
49 Dancocks, 26-27.
50 Mathieson, 12, 13.
51 Interview with author, 6/12/84.
52 CBC, "Flanders Fields," program 2.
53 *Ibid.*
54 Peat, 1-2.
55 Berton, 32.
56 *Times History* II/246-47.
57 Duguid, Appendix 40.
58 *Ibid.*, 42.
59 *Ibid.*, 43.
60 *Ibid.*, 42.
61 Haycock, 127.
62 Nichloson *CEF* 18.
63 Duguid, Appendix 44.
64 *Canadian Annual Review, 1916* (Toronto, 1917) 256.
65 *Debates, House of Commons* 2/1/16.
66 CBC interview, n.d.
67 *Debates, House of Commons* 23/1/16.
68 Haycock, 171.
69 Wallace, 176.
70 Duguid, Appendix 104.
71 Wallace, 177-78.
72 Haycock, 228.
73 Borden, 1/225-26.
74 Duguid, 1/114.
75 *Canada in the Great World War* III/137-38.
76 *Times History* II/240-41.
77 *Ibid.*, 242.
78 Duguid, 1/41.
79 *Canada in the Great World War* III/28.
80 *Ibid.*, 30-31.

Chapter Three

1 Nicholson *CEF* 20.
2 CBC, "Flanders Fields," program 2.
3 *Ibid.*
4 *Ibid.*
5 *Ibid.*
6 *Ibid.*
7 John Craig, 50.
8 Gibson, 52–53.
9 Interview with author, 5/5/88.
10 Edmonton *Daily Bulletin* 28/8/14.
11 Peat, 6.
12 PAC, MG30 E432, volume 1, diary, 1/9/14.
13 CBC, "Flanders Fields," program 2.
14 *Ibid.*, program 2, G. Eyles; program 3, J.W. Ross.
15 Duguid, Appendix 85.
16 Haycock, 212.
17 Scott, 17.
18 CBC, "Flanders Fields," program 2.
19 Haycock, 230.
20 CBC, "Flanders Fields," program 2, D.H.C. Mason.
21 Urquhart *16th* 18.
22 Berton, 42.
23 PAC, MG30 E236, volume 4, scrapbook.
24 Borden, 1/219.
25 Allen, 72.
26 PAC, MG26H, volume 361, Currie to S. Matson, 29/9/14.
27 Macphail, 23.
28 *Ibid.*
29 *Debates, House of Commons* 5/4/15.
30 Peat, 29.
31 Currie, 65.
32 Duguid, Appendix 219.
33 Haycock, 234.
34 Nicholson *CEF* 26–27.
35 PAC, MG30 E100, Currie to O.F. Brothers, 18/7/19.
36 Walker, "Machine Guns – The Past, The Present: The Future." *Canadian Defence Quarterly* (January 1926) 190.
37 CBC interview, 27/1/64.
38 PAC, RG24 C5, volume 1811, GAQ 3-9, memorandum, 26/9/14.
39 Nicholson *CEF* 26.
40 *Ibid.*, 24.
41 Duguid, Appendix 116.
42 Phillips, 80.

43 Fetherstonhaugh *13th* 10.
44 Peat, 12.
45 PAC, MG30 E204, memoirs.
46 Fetherstonhaugh *RMR* 10.
47 CBC, "Flanders Fields," program 3.
48 *Ibid.*
49 *World War* II/1192.
50 PAC, MG30 E100, Currie to C. Swayne, 23/1/18.
51 Gaffen, 11, 15, 22.
52 *Ibid.*, 28.
53 PAC, MG26H, volume 361, Currie to S. Matson, 29/9/14.
54 PAC, MG30 E78, volume 3, "I Remember Currie," T.G. Roberts.
55 MUA, H.M. Urquhart papers, Burstall, Kemmis-Betty interviews.
56 PAC, MG26H, volume 268, part 2, file 82(2), "Memorandum Respecting the Late Sir Arthur Currie," 13/8/34.
57 Urquhart *Currie* 43.
58 Haycock, 183.
59 Borden, 1/218.
60 *Ibid.*, 227.
61 *Canada in the Great World War* III/56.
62 PAC, MG30 E57, volume 15, diary, 16/9/14.
63 PAC, MG26H, volume 451, diary, 20/9/14.
64 Tucker, 5.
65 Swettenham *McNaughton* 32–33.
66 PAC, RG24 C5, volume 1811, GAQ 3–9, memorandum, 26/9/14.
67 Duguid, Appendix 98.
68 Borden, 1/220.
69 Duguid, Appendix 131.
70 *Ibid.*, 130.
71 *Ibid.*
72 Nicholson *CEF* 30; Duguid, Appendix 133.
73 Duguid, Appendix 135.
74 *Ibid.*, 86.
75 PAC, MG26H, volume 361, Currie to Matson, 29/9/14.
76 *Ibid.*, Matson to Borden, 19/10/14.
77 *Ibid.*, "Watching and Waiting" to Borden, 1/2/15.
78 PAC, MG30 E432, volume 1, diary, 30/9/14.
79 Nicholson *Gunners* 201.
80 PAC, RG24 C5, volume 1871, file 8.
81 PAC, MG30 E432, volume 1, diary, 30/9/14.
82 Borden, 1/221.
83 Haycock, 186–87.
84 Nicholson *CEF* 31.
85 Duguid, Appendix 152.

Chapter Four

1 Duguid, Appendix 132.
2 *The Glen* (regimental journal of the Calgary Highlanders), Spring 1984, 4.
3 PAC, MG30 E432, volume I, diary, n.d.
4 Macphail, 26.
5 AO, William Douglas papers, letter to Jennie, 14/10/14.
6 PAC, MG30 E432, volume I, diary, n.d.
7 PAC, MG30 E69, diary, 7/10/14.
8 Swettenham *McNaughton* 15.
9 *Ibid.*, 35, 35n.
10 CBC, "Flanders Fields," program 3.
11 PAC, MG30 E100, diary (henceforth, Currie diary), 13/10/14.
12 PAC, MG30 E69, diary, 13/10/14.
13 Currie diary, 14, 16/10/14.
14 *Canadian Annual Review, 1914* 101.
15 Urquhart *16th* 35.
16 Macphail, 56.
17 Nicholson CEF 28.
18 Duguid, Appendix 57.
19 Nicholson CEF 28.
20 *Ibid.*, 29.
21 PAC, MG30 E69, diary, 3/11/14.
22 CEA, W.A. Griesbach collection, "Lieutenant-General Sir Edwin Alderson, K.C.B."
23 PAC, MG30 E8, diary, 18/10/14.
24 Borden, I/221.
25 Nicholson CEF 34.
26 Haycock, 192.
27 *Canadian Annual Review, 1914* 217.
28 *Ibid.*, 200.
29 Haycock, 188.
30 Farwell *Soldiers* 347.
31 Duguid, I/126–27.
32 *Ibid.*, Appendix 119.
33 Trythall, 33.
34 *World War* II/1192.
35 Cassar *Courage* 20.
36 PAC, MG30 E157, volume 15, diary, 5/12/14.
37 Currie diary, 16, 17/10/14.
38 Currie, 69.
39 Duguid, I/123.
40 PAC, MG30 E69, diary.
41 Scott, 31.
42 PAC, MG30 E8, diary, 1/11/14.

43 CBC, "Flanders Fields," program 3.
44 PAC, MG30 E8, diary, 13/12/14.
45 *With the First Canadian Contingent* 41.
46 CBC, "Flanders Fields," program 3.
47 Duguid, Appendix 195.
48 Borden, 1/231.
49 CBC, "Flanders Fields," program 3.
50 *Ibid.*
51 Urquhart *16th* 32.
52 Calgary *Daily Herald* 13/2/15.
53 Macphail, 257–58.
54 Goodspeed *Battle* 83.
55 Duguid, 1/141–42.
56 Macphail, 29.
57 PAC, RG24 C5, volume 1832, GAQ 8–15D.
58 Swettenham *McNaughton* 36–37.
59 Duguid, 1/134.
60 PAC, MG30 E157, volume 15, diary, 3, 4/11/14.
61 Currie, 79.
62 CBC, "Flanders Fields," program 3.
63 CBC interview, 4/2/64.
64 Bagnall, 20.
65 *Ibid.*, 26.
66 Fetherstonhaugh *13th* 22.
67 Duguid, Appendix 189.
68 *Canadian Annual Review, 1914* 207.
69 Duguid, 1/138.
70 PAC, MG30 E8, diary, 19/12/14.
71 PAC, MG30 E432, diary, 25/12/14.
72 Tucker, 11.
73 Duguid, 1/110.
74 *Ibid.*, Appendix 109.
75 Haycock, 206.
76 *Ibid.*, 233.
77 Duguid, Appendix 205.
78 *Ibid.*, 219.
79 *Ibid.*, 220.
80 PAC, MG30 E8, diary, 30/1/15.
81 Duguid, Appendix 222.
82 PAC, RG24 C5, volume 1847, GAQ 11–65, Hughes speech, 9/11/16.
83 Duguid, 1/127.
84 *Ibid.*, 1/128–29, Appendix 192.
85 *World War* II/1189.
86 Currie diary, 1/1/15.

87 PAC, MG30 E8, diary, 1/1/15.
88 PAC, MG30 E432, diary, 21/1/15.
89 Reid, 30–31.
90 Duguid, 1/131.
91 *Ibid*.
92 Nicholson *Gunners* 205.
93 CBC, "Flanders Fields," program 3.
94 PAC, MG30 E69, diary, 19/1/15.
95 Nicholson CEF 40.
96 CBC, "Flanders Fields," program 3, S. Frost.
97 PAC, MG30 E75, volume 2, Currie to Alderson, 16/1/15.
98 Urquhart *Currie* 50.
99 *Ibid*., 48–49
100 *Ibid*., 299.
101 PAC, MG30 E58, Currie to C.A. Forsythe, 25/6/17.
102 PAC, MG30 E69, diary, 12/1/15.
103 CBC, "Flanders Fields," program 3.
104 PAC, MG30 E69, diary, 4/2/15.
105 PAC, MG30 E8, diary, 5/2/15.
106 Beattie, 33.
107 Duguid, 1/151.
108 Fetherstonhaugh RMR 24.
109 Mathieson, 42.
110 Calgary *Daily Herald* 11/2/15.

Chapter Five

1 PAC, MG30 E69, diary, 10/2/15.
2 PAC, MG40 E432, diary, 15/2/15.
3 CBC, "Flanders Fields," program 4.
4 Currie diary, 10, 11, 12, 13, 14/2/15.
5 CBC, "Flanders Fields," program 4.
6 PAC, MG30 E432, diary, 15/2/15.
7 CBC interview, 25/9/63.
8 PAC, MG30 E69, diary, 11/2/15.
9 CBC, "Flanders Fields," program 4.
10 Currie, 112.
11 *With the First Canadian Contingent* 51–52.
12 PAC, MG30 E8, diary, 20/2/15.
13 PAC, MG30 E1, diary, 15/2/15.
14 PAC, MG30 E69, diary, 15/2/15.
15 Beattie, 40–41.
16 Cassar *Courage* 31.
17 Swettenham *Seize* 61.
18 Marshall, 41.

19 *Ibid.*, 42.
20 *Ibid.*, 43.
21 Swettenham *Seize* 67.
22 Edmonds, vi.
23 Fetherstonhaugh RMR 29.
24 CBC interview, 27/1/64.
25 *Ibid.*, 4/2/64.
26 Nicholson *Gunners* 208.
27 *Ibid.*, 209.
28 Dancocks, 42.
29 Tucker, 41.
30 *Ibid.*, 46.
31 *Letters* 1/9.
32 Tascona, 75.
33 Gaffen, 20–28.
34 Tucker, 56.
35 *Ibid.*, 54.
36 PAC, MG30 E157, volume 15, diary, 22/2/15.
37 Tucker, 67.
38 *Ibid.*, 55.
39 CBC, "Flanders Fields," program 4.
40 *Ibid.*
41 *Ibid.*
42 Bassett, 39; Beattie, 44.
43 CBC, "Flanders Fields," program 4.
44 Peat, 95–97.
45 Calgary *Daily Herald* 26/3/15.
46 *Ibid.*, 19/3/15.
47 Tucker, 67.
48 *Ibid.*, 50.
49 CBC interview, 25/9/63.
50 Tucker, 45.
51 CBC, "Flanders Fields," program 4.
52 *Letters* 1/8.
53 CBC, "Flanders Fields," program 4.
54 *Ibid.*
55 *Ibid.*
56 Tucker, 49.
57 Duguid, Appendix 263.
58 *Ibid.*, 267.

Chapter Six
1 Swettenham *McNaughton* 13n.
2 Duguid, Appendix 270.

3 Tucker, 66.

4 *Letters* II/355.

5 Tucker, 73.

6 Nicholson *CEF* 53.

7 Currie diary, 10/3/15.

8 CBC, "Flanders Fields," program 4.

9 Nicholson *Gunners* 212.

10 CBC, "Flanders Fields," program 4.

11 PAC, MG30 E75, volume 2, file 3.

12 Currie diary, 24/3/15.

13 *With the First Canadian Contingent* 55.

14 PAC, MG30 E8, diary, 25/3/15.

15 Goodspeed *Battle* 78.

16 *The Mail & Empire* 12/4/15.

17 *Times History* V/213.

18 Maurice, 126.

19 Duguid, Appendix 299.

20 Tucker, 68–69.

21 *Ibid.*, 70.

22 *Ibid.*, 72–73.

23 *Ibid.*

24 *Ibid.*, 73.

25 PAC, MG30 EI, diary, 11/4/15.

26 Urquhart *16th* 52.

27 Tucker 83.

28 AO, MU2060, letter to Inspector, n.d.

29 PABC, R. MacIlree papers, letter to parents, 21/4/15.

30 *Letters* I/12.

31 Duguid, Appendix 317.

32 PABC, R. MacIlree papers, letter to parents, 21/4/15.

33 PAC, RG9 III C3, volume 4919, war diary, 10th Battalion (henceforth, 10th Battalion war diary), 16/5/15.

34 CBC interview, n.d.

35 PAC, MG14 C2, diary, 15/4/15.

36 PABC, R. MacIlree papers, letter to parents, 21/4/15.

37 CBC interview, n.d.

38 PAC, MG30 E8, diary, 20/4/15.

39 PAC, MG30 E204, memoirs.

40 PABC, R. MacIlree papers, letter to parents, 21/4/15.

41 PAC, MG30 E300, volume 16, W. Hart-McHarg to F. Buscombe, 21/4/15.

42 PAM, MG14 C2, diary, 20/4/15.

43 PAC, RG9 III C3, volume 4011, file 7, Currie to Alderson, 18/4/15.

44 PAC, MG30 E75, volume I, war diary, Second Brigade, 15/4/15.

45 Tascona, 77.

46 PAC, RG24 C5, volume 1820, GAQ 5–10.
47 PAM, MG14 C2, diary, 19/4/15.
48 Scott, 57.
49 Currie diary, 15/4/15.
50 CBC, "Flanders Fields," program 4.
51 PAC, MG30 E300, volume 24, narrative, n.d.
52 Swettenham *McNaughton* 45.
53 McWilliams, 23.
54 Edmonds, 193.
55 Blake, 87.
56 Duguid, Appendix 701.
57 McWilliams, 22.
58 Duguid, Appendix 706.
59 Edmonds, 192.
60 *Ibid.*, 189.
61 Duguid, Appendix 706d.
62 Edmonds, 164n.
63 Duguid, Appendix 320.
64 *Ibid.*, 318.
65 Edmonds, 164.
66 Duguid, Appendices 321, 323, 327.
67 Edmonds, 164n.
68 Duguid, Appendix 320.
69 *Ibid.*, 320, 321.
70 *Ibid.*, 706.

Chapter Seven
1 Nasmith, 178.
2 Duguid, Appendix 339.
3 *Ibid.*, 1/228.
4 *Ibid.*, 227.
5 *Ibid.*, Appendix 340.
6 PAC, RG9 III C3, volume 4011, folder 15, file 1, Alderson report, 13/5/15. (henceforth, Alderson report).
7 PAC, RG24 C5, volume 1822, GAQ 5–29, J. Currie to R.E.W. Turner, 6/5/15.
8 PAC, MG30 E300, volume 24, narrative, n.d.; *ibid.*, volume 16, narrative, n.d.; Peat, 143.
9 McWilliams, 45, 56.
10 Duguid, Appendix 706.
11 PAC, MG30 E75, volume 1, Second Brigade narrative of events, n.d. (henceforth, Second Brigade report).
12 PAC, RG24 C5, volume 1832, GAQ 8–15D (henceforth, Morrison account).
13 Cassar *Courage* 69–70.
14 Macphail, 300.

15 CBC, "Flanders Fields," program 5, J. Sproston.
16 PAC, MG30 E236, volume 4, scrapbook, 22/4/15.
17 Morrison account.
18 PAC, MG30 E75, volume 1, 7th Battalion narrative of events, 1/5/15 (henceforth, 7th Battalion report).
19 Currie, 216–17.
20 CBC, "Flanders Fields," program 5.
21 *Ibid.*
22 Morrison account.
23 *Ibid.*
24 *With the First Canadian Contingent* 79.
25 PAC, RG24 C5, volume 1822, GAQ 5–29, Currie to R.E.W. Turner, 6/5/15.
26 Duguid, 1/238.
27 PAC, MG30 E236, volume 4, scrapbook, 22/4/15.
28 Fetherstonhaugh *RMR* 50.
29 Duguid, Appendices 347, 351, 357, 370.
30 *Ibid.*, 364.
31 Tucker, 115.
32 *Canada in the Great World War* III/110.
33 Duguid, 1/235.
34 *Canada in Khaki* 12.
35 *Canada in the Great World War* III/110.
36 Fetherstonhaugh *RMR* 40–41.
37 CBC, "Flanders Fields," program 5.
38 Edmonds, 160n.
39 Duguid, Appendix 392.
40 7th Battalion report, op. cit.
41 PAC, MG30 E300, volume 24, narrative, n.d.
42 Alderson report.
43 CBC interview, n.d.
44 GM, Helen and Eric Adams papers, undated newspaper clipping.
45 Duguid, Appendix 372.
46 Interview with the author, 13/12/84.
47 PAC, MG30 E46, volume 4, file 7, "Account of the Charge of the Canadian Scottish," n.d. (henceforth, 16th Battalion report).
48 CBC, "Flanders Fields," program 5.
49 "The Canadian Scottish . . . ," 138.
50 Duguid, Appendix 388.
51 PAC, MG30 E46, volume 1, file 4, "Diary of Operations, 3rd Canadian Infantry Brigade," n.d. (henceforth, Third Brigade report).
52 10th Battalion war diary, 23/4/15.
53 GM, Helen and Eric Adams papers, undated newspaper clipping.
54 Scott, 62.
55 Fetherstonhaugh *RMR* 49.

56 PAC, MG30 E75, volume 1, Ormond report 28/4/15 (henceforth, 10th Battalion report).

57 10th Battalion war diary, 22/4/15.

58 *Letters* 1/10.

59 Tucker, 92.

60 10th Battalion war diary, 22/4/15.

61 16th Battalion report.

62 CBC interview, n.d.

63 10th Battalion report.

64 GM, Helen and Eric Adams papers, undated newspaper clipping.

65 *Letters* 1/10.

66 *Ibid.*, 15.

67 *With the First Canadian Contingent* 87.

68 Tucker 93.

69 *Ibid.*, 95.

70 *Ibid.*, 92.

71 "The Canadian Scottish . . . ," 139.

72 *With the First Canadian Contingent* 87.

73 GM, Helen and Eric Adams papers, undated newspaper clipping.

74 *Letters* 1/17.

75 16th Battalion report.

76 Tucker 99–100.

77 16th Battalion report.

78 CBC interview, 25/10/63.

79 16th Battalion report.

80 10th Battalion war diary, 23/4/15.

81 Third Brigade report.

82 CBC interview, 25/10/63.

83 *Ibid.*, 25/9/63.

84 Urquhart *16th* 59.

85 10th Battalion war diary, 23/4/15.

86 Duguid, Appendix 394.

87 CBC, "Flanders Fields," program 5.

88 10th Battalion report.

89 PAC, MG30 E69, diary, 23/4/15.

90 10th Battalion war diary, 23/4/15.

91 Tucker, 93.

92 Urquhart *16th* 62.

93 GM, Helen and Eric Adams papers, undated newspaper clipping.

94 10th Battalion war diary, 23/4/15.

95 Tucker, 76.

96 Urquhart *16th* 72.

97 *Canadian Daily Record* 25/7/19.

98 GM, Helen and Eric Adams papers, undated newspaper clipping.

99 Calgary *Daily Herald* 23/4/15.
100 Gibson, 55.
101 Calgary *Daily Herald* 22/4/15.

Chapter Eight
1 Edmonds, 190.
2 Nicholson CEF 70.
3 Nasmith, 183.
4 PAC, RG9 III C3, volume 4011, folder 13, file 3, report of ADMS, n.d.
5 PAM, Bert Goose papers, diary, 22,27/4/15.
6 Beattie, 62.
7 Alderson report.
8 McWilliams, 73-74.
9 Second Brigade report.
10 PAC, RG24 C5, volume 1820, GAQ 5-10, "An Account of the Second Battle of Ypres," n.d. (henceforth, Mathews account).
11 Second Brigade report.
12 PAC, RG24 C5, volume 1829, GAQ 7-30, 2 Company report, n.d.
13 Peat, 159, 161.
14 Duguid, Appendix 425.
15 Morrison account.
16 Duguid, 1/269.
17 Tucker, 103.
18 Wackett, 46.
19 Mathieson, 105.
20 Peat, 164.
21 *Canadian Annual Review, 1915* (Toronto, 1916) 390.
22 *Canada in the Great World War* IV/102.
23 *Letters* II/298.
24 *Canada in the Great World War* IV/105.
25 *Letters* II/363-64.
26 CBC, "Flanders Fields," program 5, G.W. Twigg.
27 Keegan, 264-65.
28 16th Battalion report.
29 10th Battalion report.
30 *Letters* I/10.
31 *Ibid.*, 15.
32 "The Canadian Scottish . . . ," 139-40.
33 CBC interview, 25/10/63.
34 *Ibid.*
35 *Canada in Khaki* 17-18.
36 *Letters* I/16.
37 Duguid, Appendix 453.
38 *Ibid.*, 462.

39 *Ibid.*, 472.
40 PAC, MG30 E46, volume 1, file 4, report of 3 Company, 15th Battalion, n.d. (henceforth, McLaren account).
41 PAC, RG24 C5, volume 1822, GAQ 5-29, Currie to Turner, 6/5/15.
42 Mathews account.
43 Tucker, 135.
44 PAC, MG30 E100, volume 11, "A Brave Soldier and a Gallant Gentleman," March 1929.
45 Second Brigade report.
46 7th Battalion report.
47 PAC, MG30 E300, volume 16, Odlum to Mrs. Hart-McHarg, 26/4/15.
48 Second Brigade report.
49 PAC, MG30 E100, volume 11, "A Brave Soldier and a Gallant Gentleman," March 1929.
50 PAC, MG30 E300, volume 16, Odlum to Mrs. Hart-McHarg, 26/4/15.
51 Tucker, 139-40.
52 Arthur, 233.
53 *Ibid.*, 101.
54 Liddell Hart, 161.
55 Duguid, Appendix 705.
56 *Ibid.*, 476.
57 *Ibid.*, 486.
58 Edmonds, 211.
59 Duguid, Appendices 489, 493.
60 *Ibid.*, 484.
61 Mathieson, 106.
62 Urquhart *16th* 62.
63 CBC, "Flanders Fields," program 5.
64 *Ibid.*
65 Nicholson *CEF* 70.
66 Grace Craig, 27-28.
67 *Canadian Annual Review, 1915* 392.
68 Edmonds, 207.
69 Duguid, 1/284.
70 Edmonds, 207.
71 McWilliams, 97-98.
72 Nicholson *CEF* 70.
73 Edmonds, 213.
74 "The Canadian Scottish . . . ," 140.
75 Duguid, 1/287-88.
76 Mathews account.
77 *Ibid.*
78 Duguid, Appendix 522.
79 *Ibid.*, 474.

80 McLaren account.
81 PAC, RG24 C5, volume 1822, GAQ 5–10, Currie to R.E.W. Turner, 6/5/15.
82 Currie, 235.

Chapter Nine
1 Mathews account.
2 McLaren account.
3 Duguid, 1/293.
4 Mathews account.
5 PAM, F.E. Chalmers papers, undated newspaper clipping.
6 Mathews account.
7 PAC, MG30 E75, volume 1, 8th Battalion narrative, 30/4/15 (henceforth, 8th Battalion report).
8 PAC, RG24 C5, volume 1825, GAQ 5–61, "Narrative of Brigadier-General G.S. Tuxford," 10/3/16 (henceforth, Tuxford account).
9 PAC, MG30 E300, volume 16, "Report of Narrative of Events, Ypres, April 22nd/26th, 1915, No. 1 Company, 7th Battalion," n.d. (henceforth, Warden account).
10 Urquhart Currie 72.
11 Tucker, 128–29.
12 PAM, MG14 C2, newspaper clipping, 16/11/15.
13 Mathews account.
14 PAM, MG14 C2, newspaper clipping, 1/11/15.
15 Mathews account.
16 AO, MU2060, letter to Inspector, n.d.
17 McLaren account.
18 Reid, 80–81.
19 AO, MU2060, letter to Inspector, n.d.
20 Duguid, 1/293.
21 Beattie, 71.
22 Letters II/167.
23 McWilliams, 106.
24 McLaren account.
25 Warden account.
26 PAC, RG24 C5, volume 1831, GAQ 7–45, "A Detailed Account of the Part of No. 3 Company, 90th Rifles (8th Battalion), Played in the Battle of Langemarck-St. Julien-Ypres," n.d. (henceforth, Morley account).
27 Duguid, Appendix 529.
28 CBC interview, 27/1/64.
29 Ibid., n.d.
30 Urquhart Currie 38.
31 PAC, MG30 E100, Currie report to Hughes, n.d.
32 Second Brigade report.
33 8th Battalion report.

34 McWilliams, 119.
35 PAC, RG24 C5, volume 1822, GAQ 5–29, Currie to R.E.W. Turner, 6/5/15.
36 CBC interview, 27/1/64.
37 *Ibid.*, n.d.
38 *Ibid.*
39 *Ibid.*, 25/9/63.
40 Warden account.
41 Morley account.
42 7th Battalion report.
43 Reid, 81–82.
44 PAA, Peter Anderson papers, memoirs (henceforth, Anderson account).
45 Murray, 51.
46 PAC, RG24 C5, volume 1829, GAQ 7–30, report of 2 Company, 2nd Battalion, n.d. (henceforth, Richardson account).
47 Goodspeed *Battle* 108.
48 Warden account.
49 CBC interview, n.d.
50 PAC, RG24 C5, volume 1822, GAQ 5–29, 14th Battalion report, n.d. (henceforth, 14th Battalion report).
51 Cassar *Courage* 122.
52 PAC, MG30 E300, volume 16, Odlum to Currie, 24/4/15.
53 Second Brigade report.
54 PAC, MG30 E300, volume 24, Odlum to Currie, 24/4/15.
55 Duguid, Appendix 535.
56 *Ibid.*, 532.
57 Second Brigade report.
58 Duguid, Appendix 529.
59 *Ibid.*, 539.
60 *Ibid.*, 540.
61 *Ibid.*, 541.
62 *Ibid.*, 543.
63 Beattie, 79.
64 Duguid, Appendix 545.
65 *Ibid.*, 544.
66 *Ibid.*, 544a.
67 Gorman, 21.
68 8th Battalion report.
69 McWilliams, 104.
70 Swettenham *McNaughton* 45.
71 PAC, MG30 E8, file 2, Creelman to H.C. Thacker, 16/6/16.
72 10th Battalion report.
73 Warden account.
74 *Ibid.*
75 7th Battalion report.

76 McWilliams, 118.
77 *Ibid.*, 119.
78 Scudamore *Episodes* 6.
79 CBC, "Flanders Fields," program 5, L.C. Scott.
80 PAC, MG30 E300, volume 24, narrative, n.d.
81 *Ibid.*
82 7th Battalion report.
83 *Ibid.*
84 PAC, MG30 E300, volume 16, Odlum to Turner, 24/4/15.
85 Scudamore *Episodes* 9.
86 PAC, MG30 E46, volume 1, file 4, G.M. Alexander report, n.d.
87 McWilliams, 122.
88 Duguid, Appendix 560.
89 7th Battalion report.
90 PAC, MG30 E300, volume 16, Odlum to Currie, 24/4/15.
91 Anderson account.
92 Richardson account.
93 A.W. Bennett, "An Account of Second Battle of Ypres," manuscript lent to author.
94 Interview with author, 13/12/84.
95 Duguid, Appendix 564.
96 Richardson account.
97 *Canada in the Great World War* III/113.
98 Duguid, Appendix 630.
99 *Canadian Annual Review, 1915* 391.
100 Goodspeed *Battle* 109.

Chapter Ten
1 Duguid, Appendix 554.
2 *Ibid.*, 557.
3 *Ibid.*, 551.
4 *Ibid.*, 556.
5 *Ibid.*, 580.
6 *Ibid.*, 586.
7 PAC, RG24 C5, volume 1822, GAQ 5-29, Watson to R.E.W. Turner, 27/4/15.
8 *Letters* 1/37.
9 Interview with author, 13/12/84.
10 *Ibid.*
11 Gibson, 55.
12 CBC, "Flanders Fields," program 5.
13 *Ibid.*
14 Cassar *Courage* 134.
15 Gibson, 55.
16 Goodspeed *Battle* 110.

17 Anderson account.
18 *Ibid.*
19 Reid, 83.

Chapter Eleven

1 Second Brigade report, op. cit.
2 Duguid, Appendices 545a, 545b.
3 PAC, MG30 E8, diary, 17/4/15.
4 Second Brigade report.
5 Urquhart *Currie* 82.
6 Second Brigade report.
7 Duguid, Appendix 565.
8 *Ibid.*, 560a.
9 Morley account.
10 Second Brigade report.
11 PAC, MG30 E100, volume 41, "Comments on 2nd Draft, British Official History," n.d. (henceforth, Currie comments).
12 Urquhart *Currie* 79.
13 Duguid, Appendix 565b.
14 *Ibid.*, 570.
15 Second Brigade report.
16 Currie comments.
17 Duguid, Appendix 587a.
18 Currie comments.
19 Bovey, 6.
20 Currie comments.
21 *Ibid.*
22 Second Brigade report.
23 Currie comments.
24 PAC, MG30 E75, volume 2, file 3, E.F. Lynn to H.M. Urquhart, 22/6/35.
25 Currie comments.
26 Travers, 8.
27 *Ibid.*, 1.
28 PAC, MG30 E75, volume 2, file 3, E.F. Lynn to H.M. Urquhart, 22/6/35.
29 Travers, 8-9.
30 Duguid, Appendix 600.
31 *Ibid.*, 645.
32 PAC, MG30 E246, volume 4, file 7, Villiers to A.F. Duguid, 31/12/35.
33 *Ibid.*
34 Currie comments.
35 PAC, RG24 C5, volume 1826, Lynn to T.C. Irving, 11/5/15.
36 PAC, MG26H, volume 361, Currie to S. Matson, 29/9/14.
37 8th Battalion report.
38 PAC, MG30 E8, file 2, J.J. Creelman to H.C. Thacker, 16/6/16.

39 Duguid, 1/135.
40 PAC, MG30 E8, file 2, Creelman to H.C. Thacker, 16/6/16.
41 Duguid, 1/325.
42 *Ibid.*
43 Third Brigade report.
44 Duguid, Appendix 616.
45 Cassar *Courage* 128–29.
46 Duguid, Appendix 330a.
47 *Ibid.*, 634.
48 Duguid, 1/335.
49 Keegan, 265–66.
50 Currie, 235.
51 Third Brigade report.
52 Duguid, Appendix 630.
53 Tuxford account.
54 Swettenham *McNaughton* 46.
55 PAC, MG30 E8, notes by A.F. Duguid.
56 *Ibid.*, diary, 13/5/15.
57 *Ibid.*, 2,4/5/15.
58 Warden account.
59 Duguid, 1/337.
60 Edmonds, 238.
61 Duguid, Appendices 596, 597.
62 Calgary *Daily Herald* 24/4/15.
63 *Ibid.*
64 *Ibid.*

Chapter Twelve
 1 Edmonds, 233.
 2 Duguid, Appendix 611.
 3 Edmonds, 234.
 4 Duguid, 1/330–31.
 5 *Ibid.*, Appendix 555.
 6 *Ibid.*, 619.
 7 *Ibid.*, 1/347.
 8 CBC interview, 27/1/64.
 9 Edmonds, 243.
10 Duguid, 1/350.
11 *Ibid.*
12 Second Brigade report.
13 Dancocks *Currie* 143.
14 Urquhart *Currie* 97.
15 CBC interview, 25/10/63.
16 Currie comments.

17 CBC, "Flanders Fields," program 5, F.B. Bagshaw.
18 Currie comments.
19 Second Brigade report.
20 PAC, MG30 E246, volume 4, file 7, Villiers to A.F. Duguid, 31/12/35.
21 PAC, MG30 E75, volume 2, file 3, Lynn to H.M. Urquhart, 22/6/35.
22 7th Battalion report.
23 *Ibid.*
24 PAM, F.E. Chalmers papers, undated newspaper clipping.
25 Tucker, 131.
26 PAC, MG30 E300, volume 16, Currie to Odlum, 12:45 P.M., Odlum to Currie, 2 P.M., 24/4/15.
27 Duguid, Appendix 659.
28 Second Brigade report.
29 Duguid, Appendix 665.
30 *Ibid.*, 666.
31 Currie comments.
32 PABC, R. MacIlree papers, letter, 29/4/15.
33 Mathews account.
34 PAM, MG14 C2, newspaper clipping, 13/12/15.
35 Mathews account.
36 7th Battalion report.
37 Second Brigade report.
38 *Ibid.*
39 Gorman, 25.
40 Second Brigade report.
41 Currie comments.
42 7th Battalion report.
43 Tuxford account.
44 Currie comments.
45 Tuxford account.
46 *Ibid.*
47 CBC, "Flanders Fields," program 5.
48 Tuxford account.
49 Tuxford account.
50 Mathews account.
51 PAC, MG30 E69, diary, 25/4/15.
52 PAC, MG30 E100, N.R. Robertson to R.H. Parmenter, 18/4/29.
53 Duguid, Appendix 677.
54 Currie, 261.
55 Duguid, Appendix 673.
56 Tuxford account.
57 Second Brigade report.
58 Duguid, Appendix 674.
59 Mathews account.

60 *Ibid.*
61 Tuxford account.
62 PABC, R. MacIlree papers, letter to parents, 29/4/15.
63 CBC interview, 25/10/63.
64 Currie comments.
65 *Ibid.*
66 Mathews account.
67 Second Brigade report.
68 Mathews account.
69 *Ibid.*
70 Second Brigade report.
71 *Ibid.*
72 A.W. Bennett, "An Account of the Second Battle of Ypres," manuscript lent
    to the author.
73 PAC, MG30 E100, volume 41, file 185, James Shotwell diary, 21/4/19.
74 Nicholson *CEF* 88n.
75 Second Brigade report.
76 CBC interview, 4/2/64.
77 *Ibid.*, 27/1/64.
78 Interview with author, 13/12/84.
79 Fetherstonhaugh *RMR* 46–47.
80 "The Canadian Scottish . . . ," 143.
81 Tucker, 141.
82 PAM, Bert Goose papers, diary, 1/5/15.
83 Morrison account.
84 Nicholson *Gunners* 231.
85 PANB, MC346, letter from Art to Neta, 29/4/15.
86 Nicholson *CEF* 92.
87 Duguid, Appendix 851.
88 Harker, 82.
89 Holland, 13.
90 8th Battalion report.
91 Goodspeed *Battle* 113.
92 8th Battalion report.
93 McWilliams, 154.
94 Duguid, 1/421, Appendix 851.
95 Morrison account.
96 PAC, MG30 E8, file 2, J.J. Creelman to H.C. Thacker, 16/6/16.
97 *Letters* 1/16.
98 AO, MU2060, letter to Inspector, n.d.
99 Tascona, 113–14.
100 AO, MU2060, letter to Inspector, n.d.
101 *Letters* 1/11.
102 Tucker, 113–14.

103 *Ibid.*, 104.
104 Calgary *Daily Herald* 26/4/15.

Chapter Thirteen

1. Duguid, 1/372-75.
2 Edmonds, 273.
3 Cassar *Tragedy* 225.
4 McWilliams, 178.
5 Edmonds, 401.
6 *Ibid.*, 402.
7 Cassar *Tragedy* 224.
8 McWilliams, 210.
9 Edmonds, 403.
10 Duguid, Appendix 691.
11 *Ibid.*, 696.
12 *Ibid.*, 1/397.
13 CBC, "Flanders Fields," program 5.
14 *Ibid.*
15 Duguid, 1/421.
16 *Ibid.*, 405.

Chapter Fourteen

1 Duguid, Appendix 703a.
2 *Ibid.*, 692.
3 Blake, 91.
4 McWilliams, 220-21.
5 Duguid, 1/407.
6 Scott, 72.
7 Swettenham *McNaughton* 45.
8 CBC, "Flanders Fields," program 5.
9 *World War* II/1193.
10 Duguid, Appendix 706.
11 *Ibid.*, 1/411.
12 *Ibid.*, Appendix 704.
13 *Ibid.*, 705.
14 *Ibid.*, 683.
15 PAC, MG30 E100, speech to Canadian Club, Ottawa, 19/8/19.
16 All quoted newspapers, 26/4/15.
17 Duguid, Appendix 699a.
18 PAC, RG24 C5, volume 1813, file 5-15K, "Words Spoken to the First Canadian Division," n.d.
19 Cassar *Courage* 129.
20 Dancocks *Currie* 55.
21 *Canadian Annual Review, 1919* (Toronto, 1920) 45.

22 PAC, MG26H, volume 358, interview transcript.
23 Strathroy *Age* 11/11/15.
24 *Debates, House of Commons* 29/9/19.
25 *Ibid.*, 16/6/20.
26 Cassar *Courage* 189.
27 PAC, MG30 E42, volume 4, memoirs.
28 Swettenham *Seize* 96.
29 PAC, MG30 E100, Alderson to Currie, 11/7/17.
30 Dancocks, 202.
31 Cassar *Courage* 208.
32 Borden, 1/229.
33 Duguid, Appendix 111.
34 *Ibid.*
35 *Ibid.*
36 Haycock, 249–50.
37 *Ibid.*
38 Duguid, Appendix 111.
39 Phillips, 81.
40 Interview with author, 5/5/88.

Epilogue
1 Bassett, 44.
2 PAC, MG30 E209, biographical note by Gertrude Hickmore.
3 Mathieson, 264.
4 PAC, MG30 E133, volume 4, "Origin of 'In Flanders Fields.'"
5 *Canadian Daily Record* 5/3/19.

Bibliography

Aitken, Sir Max. *Canada in Flanders* Volume I. London: Hodder & Stoughton, 1916.

Allen, Ralph. *Ordeal by Fire*. New York: Popular Library, 1961.

Arthur, Sir George. *Life of Lord Kitchener*. Volume III. London: Macmillan, 1920.

Bagnall, F.W. *Not Mentioned in Despatches*. North Vancouver: North Shore Press, 1933.

Bassett, John. *John McCrae*. Markham: Fitzhenry & Whiteside, 1984.

Beattie, Kim. *48th Highlanders of Canada, 1891–1928*. Toronto: 48th Highlanders of Canada, 1932.

Bell, F. McKelvey. *The First Canadians in France*. Toronto: McClelland, Goodchild & Stewart, 1917.

Bernhardi, Friedrich von. *On War of Today*. Volumes I, II. 1912. Reprint. New York: Garland, 1972.

Berton, Pierre. *Vimy*. Toronto: McClelland & Stewart, 1986.

Blake, Robert, ed. *The Private Papers of Douglas Haig, 1914–1919*. London: Eyre & Spottiswoode, 1952.

Borden, Henry, ed. *Robert Laird Borden: His Memoirs*. Volumes I, II. Toronto: McClelland & Stewart, 1969.

Bovey, W. "Sir Arthur Currie: The Corps Commander." *The Legionary* (July 1934).

Brown, Craig, ed. *The Illustrated History of Canada*. Toronto: Lester & Orpen Dennys, 1987.

———, and Desmond Morton. "The Embarrassing Apotheosis of a 'Great Canadian': Sir Arthur Currie's Personal Crisis of 1917." *The Canadian Historical Review* (March 1979): 41–63.

Canada in Khaki. Calgary: The Calgary Herald, 1917.

Canada in the Great World War. Volumes III, IV. Toronto: United, 1919.

Cassar, George. *Beyond Courage*. Ottawa: Oberon Press, 1985.

———. *The Tragedy of Sir John French*. Newark: University of Delaware, 1985.

Churchill, Winston S. *The World Crisis, 1914–1915*. London: Thornton, Butterworth, 1931.

Craig, Grace Morris. *But This is Our War*. Toronto: University of Toronto Press, 1981.

Craig, John. *The Years of Agony*. Toronto: Canada's Illustrated Heritage, 1977.

Currie, J.A. *"The Red Watch": With the First Canadian Division in Flanders*. Toronto: McClelland, Goodchild & Stewart, 1916.

Curry, Frederick C. *From the St. Lawrence to the Yser*. Toronto: McClelland, Goodchild & Stewart, 1916.

Dancocks, Daniel G. *Sir Arthur Currie*. Toronto: Methuen, 1985.

Duguid, A. Fortescue. *Official History of the Canadian Forces in the Great War, 1914-1919*. Volume I and Appendices. Ottawa: King's Printer, 1938.

Edmonds, J.E. *Military Operations, France and Belgium, 1915*. Volume I. London: Macmillan, 1927.

English, John. *Borden*. Toronto: McGraw-Hill Ryerson, 1977.

Farwell, Byron. *Mr Kipling's Army*. New York: W.W. Norton, 1981.

————. *Eminent Victorian Soldiers*. New York: W.W. Norton, 1985.

Fetherstonhaugh, R.G. *The 13th Battalion, Royal Highlanders of Canada, 1914-1919*. Montreal: 13th Battalion, Royal Highlanders of Canada, 1925.

————. *The Royal Montreal Regiment*. Montreal: Gazette, 1927.

Gaffen, Fred. *Forgotten Soldiers*. Penticton: Theytus, 1985.

Galbraith, John Kenneth. *The Scotch*. Toronto: Macmillan of Canada, 1964, 1985.

Gibson, Sally. *More Than an Island: A History of Toronto Island*. Toronto: Irwin, 1984.

Goodspeed, D.J. *The Armed Forces of Canada, 1867-1967* Ottawa: Queen's Printer, 1967.

————. *The Road Past Vimy*. Toronto: Macmillan, 1969.

————. *Battle Royal*. Brampton: Royal Regiment of Canada Association, 1979.

Gorman, G.W. "With the 'Little Black Devils'." *The Thunder Bay Historical Society: Ninth Annual Report*. Fort William: Times-Journal, 1918.

Harker, Douglas E. *The Dukes*. The British Columbia Regiment, 1974.

Haycock, Ronald G. *Sam Hughes*. Wilfrid Laurier University/National Museums of Canada, 1986.

Hodder-Williams, Ralph. *Princess Patricia's Canadian Light Infantry, 1914-1919*. Volumes I, II. London, Toronto: Hodder & Stoughton, 1923.

Holland, J.A. *The Story of the Tenth Battalion, 1914-1917*. London: Canadian War Records Office, 1918.

Holmes, Richard. *The Little Field-Marshal*. London: Jonathon Cape, 1981.

Jackson, H.M. *The Royal Regiment of Artillery, Ottawa, 1855-1952*. n.p., 1952.

Keegan, John. *The Face of Battle*. New York: Viking, 1976.

Keene, Louis. *"Crumps."* Boston, New York: Houghton Mifflin, 1917.

Letters from the Front. Volumes I, II. Toronto: Canadian Bank of Commerce, 1920.

Liddell Hart, B.H. *Reputations Ten Years Later*. Boston: Little, Brown, 1928.

Macphail, Sir Andrew. *Official History of the Canadian Forces in the Great War, 1914-1919: The Medical Services*. Ottawa: King's Printer, 1925.

Marshall, S.L.A. *World War I*. New York: American Heritage, 1964.

Mathieson, William D. *My Grandfather's War*. Toronto: Macmillan, 1981.

Maurice, Sir Frederick. *Lord Rawlinson*. London: Cassell, 1928.

McWilliams, J., and R.J. Steel. *Gas!* St. Catharines: Vanwell, 1985.

Morton, Desmond. *Ministers and Generals*. Toronto: University of Toronto Press, 1970.

————. *A Peculiar Kind of Politics*. Toronto: University of Toronto Press, 1982.

Murray, W.W. *The History of the 2nd Canadian Battalion*. Ottawa: The Historical Committee, 2nd Battalion, CEF, 1947.

Nasmith, George C. *Canada's Sons and Great Britain in the World War*. Toronto: John C. Winston, 1919.

Nicholson, G.W.L. *Canadian Expeditionary Force, 1914-19*. Ottawa: Queen's Printer, 1964.

————. *The Gunners of Canada*. Volume I. Toronto: McClelland & Stewart, 1967.

Peat, Harold R. *Private Peat*. New York: Grosset & Dunlap, 1917.

Phillips, R., F. Dupuis and J. Chadwick. *The Ross Rifle Story*. Sydney: Casket, 1984.

Prairie Sod and Goldenrod. Crossfield: Crossfield Historical Committee, 1977.

Read, Daphne, ed. *The Great War and Canadian Society*. Toronto: New Hogtown Press, 1978.

Reid, Gordon, ed. *Poor Bloody Murder*. Oakville: Mosaic, 1980.

Scott, Canon F.G. *The Great War as I Saw It*. Vancouver: Clarke & Stuart, 1934.

Scudamore, T.B. *A Short History of the 7th Battalion CEF*. Vancouver: Anderson & Odlum, 1930.

————. *Lighter Episodes in the Life of a Prisoner of War*. Aldershot: Gale & Polden, 1933.

Summers, Jack, and René Chartrand. *Military Uniforms in Canada, 1665-1970*. Ottawa: National Museums of Canada, 1981.

Swettenham, John. *To Seize the Victory*. Toronto: Ryerson, 1965.

————. *McNaughton*. Volume I. Toronto: Ryerson, 1968.

Tascona, Bruce, and Eric Wells. *Little Black Devils*. Winnipeg: Royal Winnipeg Rifles, 1983.

Terraine, John. *Douglas Haig, The Educated Soldier*. London: Hutchinson, 1963.

————. *To Win a War*. New York: Doubleday, 1981.

"The Canadian Scottish at the Second Battle of Ypres, April, 1915." *Canadian Defence Quarterly* (January 1925).

Times History of the War, The. Volumes II, V. London: The Times, 1915.

Travers, T.H.E. "Archival sources, the British and Canadian Official Historians, and the problem of Brigadier General Currie at Second Ypres, April 1915." Manuscript.

Trythall, A.J. *"Boney" Fuller*. London: Cassell, 1977.

Tuchman, Barbara W. *The Guns of August*. New York: Macmillan, 1962.

Tucker, A.B. *The Battle Glory of Canada*. London: Cassell, 1915.

Urquhart, Hugh M. *The History of the 16th Battalion (The Canadian Scottish)*. Toronto: Macmillan, 1932.

————. *Arthur Currie: The Biography of a Great Canadian*. Toronto: J.M. Dent, 1950.

Wackett, E. "Experiences with the First Western Ontario Regiment, Canadian Expeditionary Force." *Waterloo Historical Society: Fifth Annual Report*. Kitchener: Waterloo Historical Society, 1917.

Wallace, W. *The Memoirs of the Rt. Hon. Sir George Foster*. Toronto: Macmillan, 1933.

Williams, Jeffrey. *Princess Patricia's Canadian Light Infantry*. London: Leo Cooper, 1983.

Wilson, Barbara M., ed. *Ontario and the First World War, 1914-1918*. Toronto: The Champlain Society, 1977.

Winter, C.F. *The Hon. Sir Sam Hughes*. Toronto: Macmillan, 1931.

With the First Canadian Contingent. Toronto: Hodder & Stoughton/ Musson, 1915.

World War, The. Volumes I, II. New York: Grolier, 1920.

Worthington, Larry. *Amid the Guns Below*. Toronto: McClelland & Stewart, 1965.

Index

NEW BOOKS FROM
⟦A DOUGLAS GIBSON BOOK⟧
PUBLISHED BY McCLELLAND AND STEWART

ON THE SKY Zen and the Art of International Freeloading *by* Robert Hunter

"*On The Sky* is the funniest travel book written here or anywhere else in a long time."
Vancouver Sun   *Travel/Humour, 6 x 9, 256 pages, hardcover*

ALL IN THE SAME BOAT Family Cruising Around the Atlantic
by Fiona McCall and Paul Howard

Sailing from Toronto to Panama (via Africa) in a boat built in the back-yard –
with Penny, 6, and Peter, 4!
                Travel/Adventure, 6 x 9, 256 pages, 40 photos, maps, hardcover

WELCOME TO FLANDERS FIELDS The First Canadian Battle of the Great War:
Ypres, 1915 *by* Daniel G. Dancocks

They wanted to "get in on the fun" – and now we wear poppies because of what they
found at Ypres.   *Military/History, 6 x 9, 304 pages, photos, maps, hardcover*

NEXT-YEAR COUNTRY Voices of Prairie People *by* Barry Broadfoot

"Oh yes, I grew up in a cave ... " begins one of the many stories told to the author of
Ten Lost Years.   *Oral History, 6 x 9, 400 pages, hardcover*

UNDERCOVER AGENT How One Honest Man Took on the Drug Mob ... And Then the
Mounties *by* Leonard Mitchell and Peter Rehak

How the drug mob chose an honest man for their Canadian pipeline – and lost
$238,000,000.00 when he stayed honest.
                    Non-fiction/Criminology, 6 x 9, 176 pages, hardcover

THE PRIVATE VOICE A Journal of Reflections *by* Peter Gzowski

The man behind the voice on the radio is revealed in this personal, touching, and very
funny combined journal and life story.
                    Autobiography, 6 x 9, 320 pages, photos, hardcover

LADYBUG, LADYBUG ... *by* W.O. Mitchell

W.O. Mitchell brilliantly leads us from laughing at his humour to silent shock when a
child is kidnapped.   *Fiction, 6 x 9, 288 pages, hardcover*

OTHER TITLES FROM

⟦A DOUGLAS GIBSON BOOK⟧

PUBLISHED BY McCLELLAND AND STEWART

THE PROGRESS OF LOVE by Alice Munro

"Probably the best collection of stories – the most confident and, at the same time, the most adventurous – ever written by a Canadian." *Saturday Night*

Fiction, 6 x 9, 320 pages, hardcover

FOUR DAYS OF COURAGE The Untold Story of the Fall of Marcos by Bryan Johnson

"What may well be the best book on the Marcos-Aquino election campaign and on the 'People Power' that toppled a tyrant ... ." *New York Times*

Politics/Journalism, 6 x 9, 288 pages, map and photographs, hardcover

THE RADIANT WAY by Margaret Drabble

"*The Radiant Way* does for Thatcher's England what *Middlemarch* did for Victorian England ... Essential reading!" Margaret Atwood   *Fiction, 6 x 9, 400 pages, hardcover*

DANCING ON THE SHORE A Celebration of Life at Annapolis Basin by Harold Horwood, *Foreword by* Farley Mowat

"A Canadian *Walden*" (*Windsor Star*) that "will reward, provoke, challenge and enchant its readers." (*Books in Canada*)

Nature/Ecology, 5 1/2 x 8 1/2, 224 pages, 16 wood engravings, hardcover

NO KIDDING Inside the World of Teenage Girls by Myrna Kostash

This frank, informative look at teenage girls today "should join Dr. Spock on every parent's bookshelf." *Maclean's*   *Women/Journalism, 6 x 9, 320 pages, notes, hardcover*

THE HONORARY PATRON   A Novel by Jack Hodgins

The Governor General's Award-winner's thoughtful and satisfying third novel mixes comedy and wisdom, "and it's magic". *Ottawa Citizen*

Fiction, 6 x 9, 336 pages, hardcover

RITTER IN RESIDENCE A Comic Collection by Erika Ritter

This collection by the noted playwright, broadcaster, and humorist reveals "a wonderfully funny view of our world". *Globe and Mail*

Humour, 5 1/2 x 8 1/2, 200 pages, hardcover

THE LIFE OF A RIVER by Andy Russell

This yarning history of the Oldman river area shows "a sensitivity towards the earth ... that is universally applicable." *Kingston Whig-Standard*

History/Ecology, 6 x 9, 184 pages, hardcover

THE INSIDERS Government, Business, and the Lobbyists by John Sawatsky

Investigative journalism at its best, this Ottawa exposé is "packed with insider information about the political process". *Globe and Mail*

Politics/Business, 6 x 9, 368 pages, photos, hardcover

PADDLE TO THE AMAZON The Ultimate 12,000-Mile Canoe Adventure by Don Starkell, *edited by* Charles Wilkins

"This real-life adventure book ... must be ranked among the classics of the literature of survival." *Montreal Gazette*   *Adventure, 6 x 9, 320 pages, maps, photos, hardcover*

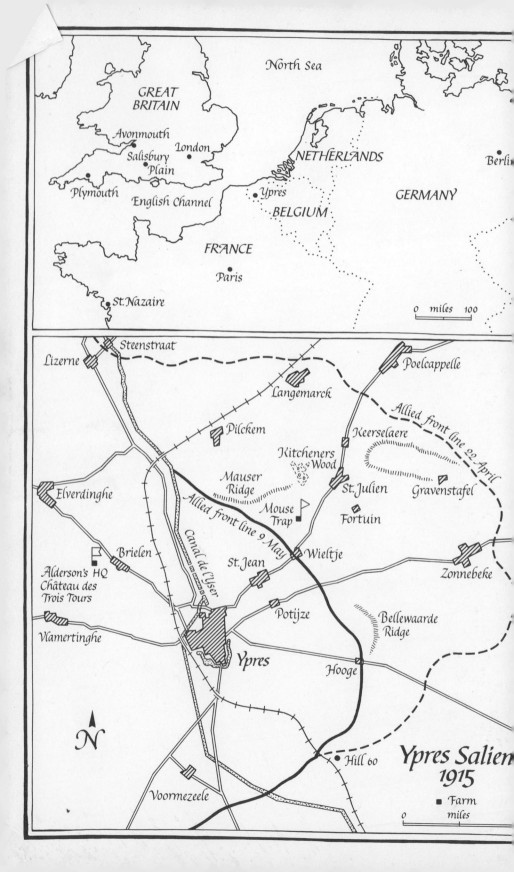

Top map:

North Sea

GREAT
BRITAIN

Avonmouth
London
Salisbury
Plain
Plymouth
English Channel

NETHERLANDS

Berli

GERMANY

Ypres

BELGIUM

FRANCE

Paris

St. Nazaire

0 miles 100

Bottom map:

Steenstraat

Lizerne

Poelcappelle

Langemarck

Allied front line 22 April

Pilckem

Keerselaere

Kitcheners
Wood

Mauser
Ridge

St. Julien

Gravenstafel

Elverdinghe

Allied front line 9 May

Mouse
Trap

Fortuin

Canal de l'Yser

Brielen

St. Jean

Wieltje

Zonnebeke

Alderson's HQ
Château des
Trois Tours

Potijze

Bellewaarde
Ridge

Vlamertinghe

Ypres

Hooge

N

Hill 60

Ypres Salien
1915

■ Farm
miles

Voormezeele

0